third edition

The Basic Guide to SuperVision and Instructional Leadership

Carl D. Glickman
Professor Emeritus of Education
University of Georgia

Stephen P. Gordon
Texas State University

Jovita M. Ross-Gordon
Texas State University

PEARSON

Boston Columbus Indianapolis New York San Francisco Upper Saddle River
Amsterdam Cape Town Dubai London Madrid Milan Munich Paris Montreal Toronto
Delhi Mexico City São Paulo Sydney Hong Kong Seoul Singapore Taipei Tokyo

Vice President and Editorial Director: *Jeffery W. Johnston*
Senior Acquisitions Editor: *Meredith Fossel*
Associate Editor: *Anne Whittaker*
Editorial Assistant: *Andrea Hall*
Vice President, Director of Marketing: *Margaret Waples*
Marketing Manager: *Christopher Barry*
Senior Managing Editor: *Pamela D. Bennett*
Production Editor: *Kerry Rubadue*
Production Manager: *Susan EW Hannahs*
Senior Art Director: *Jayne Conte*
Cover Designer: *Karen Noferi*
Permissions Administrator: *Rebecca Savage*
Cover Art: *Fotolia*
Full-Service Project Management: *Nitin Agarwal/Aptara®, Inc.*
Composition: *Aptara®, Inc.*
Cover and Text Printer/Bindery: *Courier/Westford*
Text Font: *Sabon LT Std*

Credits and acknowledgments for materials borrowed from other sources and reproduced, with permission, in this textbook appear on the appropriate page within the text.

Every effort has been made to provide accurate and current Internet information in this book. However, the Internet and information posted on it are constantly changing, so it is inevitable that some of the Internet addresses listed in this textbook will change.

Library of Congress Cataloging-in-Publication Data
Glickman, Carl D.
The basic guide to supervision and instructional leadership / Carl D. Glickman, Stephen P. Gordon, Jovita M. Ross-Gordon.—3rd ed.
p. cm.
ISBN-13: 978-0-13-261373-6
ISBN-10: 0-13-261373-5
1. School supervision. I. Gordon, Stephen P. II. Ross-Gordon, Jovita M. III. Title.
LB2806.4.G557 2013
371.2'03—dc23 2011042242

10 9 8 7 6 5 4 3 2 1

PEARSON

ISBN 10: 0-13-261373-5
ISBN 13: 978-0-13-261373-6

Preface

The first edition of the longer version of this text, *SuperVision of Instruction: A Developmental Approach*, urged readers to take a wider view of instructional supervision, to expand its knowledge base to include areas of study such as the school environment and adult studies and to broaden its skill base to include a wide repertoire of technical and interpersonal skills. The book agreed with the field that clinical supervision was a powerful vehicle for helping teachers to improve instruction, but it also called for extending the scope of supervision to include the tasks of group development, professional development, curriculum development, and action research and to integrate those tasks in schoolwide efforts to improve teaching and learning.

The initial response of traditionalists to the first edition's call for rethinking supervision was, shall we say, reserved. Soon, however, the book was embraced by professors, graduate students, and practitioners, and over the years, its popularity in both university classrooms and PK–12 schools has been more than was ever anticipated. With this third edition of *The Basic Guide to SuperVision and Instructional Leadership*, we once again ask educators to broaden their view of instructional supervision to include what we call the *cultural tasks* of supervision: facilitating change, addressing diversity, and building community. We believe that changing demographics, the achievement gaps between various groups of students, and an increasingly complex and diverse yet interdependent world mean that supervisors and teachers really have no choice but to address cultural tasks (as discussed in Part 6 of the book) if schools are to be viable institutions for preparing students to be fulfilled and contributing members of a democratic society.

New to This Edition

New features of the book include the following:

- An updated discussion of adult learning and implications for instructional supervision (Chapter 4)
- Role Play chapter feature that provides structured scenarios that allow for practice of the four interpersonal approaches of developmental supervision: directive control, directive informational, collaborative, and nondirective (Chapters 7, 8, 9, and 10)
- New Chapter, *Facilitating Change*, describes and evaluates theories of educational change, change at the individual level, the changing conditions of teaching, norms of continuous school improvement, and other concepts associated with successful school change (Chapter 20)

- New Chapter, *Addressing Diversity*, examines economic, racial, and ethnic achievement gaps and the "cultural clashes" largely responsible for those gaps (Chapter 21)
- Discussions of the characteristics of culturally responsive schools and teachers as well as strategies for promoting and encouraging the development of culturally responsive schools and teachers (Chapter 21)
- New Chapter, *Building Community*, presents the concepts of the democratic community, moral community, professional learning community, and inquiring community (Chapter 22)
- Strategies and suggestions for engaging the school with the larger community it serves (Chapter 22)

In addition to providing three new chapters on the cultural tasks of supervision, this edition continues to address topics such as the following:

- Collegial supervision that is the province of teachers as well as supervisors and is characterized by collegiality, reflective inquiry, and professional dialogue
- Supervision as a process, rather than a position, characterized by democratic governance and collective action toward a cause beyond oneself
- The need to examine and articulate beliefs about the purpose of education, curriculum, student learning, teaching, and supervision
- The integration of adult learning and adult development theories with instructional supervision
- Alternative approaches to supervision, all focused on teachers' development of higher levels of thought, expertise, and commitment
- A variety of tools for assessing, planning, observing, and evaluating

We invite readers of the third edition to use this book as a basis for reflection, dialogue, and critique concerning the present state of teaching and learning in our schools, as well as for envisioning how they can apply the ideas in this text to individually and collectively work to improve our classrooms, schools, and communities.

MyEdLeadershipLab™

Help your students bridge the gap between theory and practice with MyEdLeadershipLab™. MyEdLeadershipLab™ connects your course content to video- and case-based real world scenarios, and provides:

- ***Assignments & Activities*** assess candidates' understanding of key concepts and skill development. Hints and feedback provide scaffolding and reinforce key concepts.

- ***Building Ed Leadership Skills*** exercises that offer opportunities for candidates to develop and practice skills critical to their success as school leaders. Suggested responses are available to instructors, making grading easy.
- ***Multiple-Choice Quizzes*** help candidates gauge their understanding of important topics and prepare for success on licensure examinations.

Access to MyEdLeadershipLab™ can be packaged with this textbook or purchased standalone. To find out how to package student access to this website and gain access as an Instructor, go to www.myedleadershiplab.com, email us at edleadership@pearson.com, or contact your Pearson sales representative.

Acknowledgments

It is impossible to acknowledge all those who have contributed to the development of this book. We would like to acknowledge the contribution of our colleague Edward Pajak, who developed with Glickman the directive informational supervisory approach in the early 1980s; he continues to provide a guiding influence on the field of supervision. A host of colleagues—school practitioners, graduate students, and university faculty members—have provided us with settings, collaborations, and discussion for field-testing developmental and democratic propositions about supervision. We are grateful to the reviewers of this edition: Don Benton, Henderson State University; Judith L. Irvin, Florida State University; Robert Mendoza, Argosy University; Shirley J. Mills, University of Texas Pan American; and Keith Myatt, California State University, Dominguez Hills.

Contents

part 1

Introduction

chapter 1

SuperVision for Successful Schools

outline

- SuperVision: A New Name for a New Paradigm
- Supervisory Glue as a Metaphor for Success
- Organization of This Book
- Supervision and Moral Purpose

Visit the **MyEdLeadershipLab™** site for *The Basic Guide to SuperVision and Instructional Leadership*, Third Edition to enhance your understanding of chapter concepts. You'll have the opportunity to practice your skills through video and case based Assignments and Activities as well as Building Leadership Skills units, and prepare for your certification exam with Practice for Certification quizzes.

Take a walk with us. First, let's step into Finnie Tyler High School, with a student body of 1,200, in a lower- to middle-class urban neighborhood. A sign by the entrance tells all visitors to report to the office. In the halls, we see students milling around, boys and girls talking in groups, couples holding hands, one couple intertwined romantically in a corner. The bell rings and students scurry to the next class. We find the school office and introduce ourselves to the secretary and school principal, who are expecting our visit. They welcome us and assure us that we may move around the school and talk to students, teachers, and other staff. The school population has been notified of our visit and understands that we have come to see how Tyler High School operates. The principal tells us we will find Tyler a pleasant place. Equipped with a floor plan of classrooms and other facilities, we continue on our way.

The principal's description is accurate: Students seem happy and uninhibited, socializing easily with each other even during instruction time. Teachers joke with students. In the faculty lounge, we hear laughter that rises, falls, and then rises again. Several teachers have told us about the traditional Friday after-school gatherings at the local pizza parlor, where teachers and administrators socialize over a drink.

Classrooms vary considerably from each other; teachers tell us they can teach however they wish. Most teachers stand at the front of the room, lecturing, asking questions, and assigning seatwork. Some, however, take a less structured approach, allowing students to work alone or in small groups. There is an unhurried atmosphere. Students move at a leisurely pace, and classes seldom start on time. Teachers of the same subjects use the same textbooks but otherwise seem to have discretion to function as they please. As one seven-year veteran teacher at this school sums it up: "We have an ideal situation. We like each other, and the administration leaves us alone. I am observed once a year. I have one faculty meeting a month to attend. I love the other teachers and we have a great time together. The kids are fine, not as academic as they should be, but this school is a nice place for them. I wouldn't want to teach anyplace else."

Now let's drive across town to Germando Elementary School, with 600 students, located in a wealthy, suburban part of the city. Again, we follow the sign to the office. A few students are standing with their noses against the wall by their classroom doors. Otherwise, the halls are vacant and still; all classroom doors are shut. In the principal's office sit two students with tears in their eyes, obviously fearful of their impending conference with the principal. The principal welcomes us and hands us a preplanned schedule of times to visit particular teachers. She tells us not to visit any classroom during instructional time. "I think you will find that I run a tight ship," she says. "Teachers and students know exactly what is expected of them and what the consequences are for ignoring those expectations. Teachers are here to teach, and I see to it that it happens."

Moving down the halls, we are struck by the similarity of the classrooms. The desks are in rows; the teacher is in front; the school rules are posted on the right of the chalkboard. At the first recess time, the students seem to erupt onto the playground. Expecting to find a group of teachers in the faculty lounge, we are surprised to find only two people. One is knitting and the other is preparing a cup of coffee. All the other teachers have remained in the classrooms, either alone or with one other teacher.

Continuing our observation after recess, we find that teachers at each grade level not only work with the same textbooks but are on the same pages as well. When we ask about this, one teacher tells us that the principal has standardized the entire curriculum and knows what is being taught in every classroom at each moment of the day. At the first faculty meeting in August, the principal lays out materials, schedules, and time lines developed by the central office. We ask how the principal can enforce such procedures, and the teacher replies, "She asks for weekly lesson plans, visits my room at least once every two weeks, and has other central office personnel visit and report back to her."

In the classrooms we visit, students are generally quiet but restless. They appear attentive; those who are not are disciplined. Teachers are mostly businesslike; some show warmth toward their students, others do not. We conclude our visit with three separate interviews of teachers. It seems that teaching in Germando is perceived as a job to do. Whether one likes them or not, the principal's rules and regulations are to be followed. Teachers mention that when they have attempted to make modest changes in their instruction, they have been told to drop the changes and return to the school plan. All three mention the teacher who last year refused to follow the reading textbook and was subsequently forced to resign.

Finnie Tyler High School and Germando Elementary School are examples of real schools. Which is the successful school? Which has better attendance, attitudes, and achievement? *Neither does!* Both are ineffective, mediocre schools. The successful schools in the same system are quite different from either. Our first conclusion might be that these schools are very different. Tyler High School appears to have little supervision of instruction, whereas Germando has too much. According to the definition of instructional supervision presented in this book, however, *neither* school has effective instructional supervision. It also might appear that Tyler meets teachers' individual needs, whereas Germando meets organizational goals set by the principal. In successful schools, however, individual needs are fulfilled through organizational goals. In these two schools, *neither* need is being met. Finally, the working environments in these two schools only appear to be dissimilar; soon we will see how similar they really are.

The last school on our tour is Progress Middle School. Our first stop at Progress is the school office, where we are informed by the school secretary that the principal will meet with us at the end of the period. The principal is teaching Mr. Simmons's class while Simmons observes another teacher as part of a peer coaching program involving a number of teachers. The secretary invites us to wait for the principal in the teachers' lounge, where several teachers are spending their preparation period. As we relax with a soda, we listen to an animated discussion among the teachers concerning an interdisciplinary unit of instruction they are planning. The teachers are brainstorming alternative teaching and assessment strategies for the unit and discussing how these strategies could be connected to the unit's theme.

Soon the principal joins us and invites us on a tour of the school. During the tour, we note that classroom environments are work oriented, as well as warm and supportive. In some classrooms, students are involved in hands-on inquiry. In other classrooms, cooperative learning is taking place. In still others, teachers are challenging students to reflect on lesson content by using higher-level questioning and inviting student opinions on the lesson topic. A commonality across all classrooms is students engaged in active learning. Teachers give students feedback on their performance and provide alternative learning opportunities and special attention to those experiencing difficulties.

After school, we attend a meeting of the school leadership council, made up primarily of teachers. The council is considering action research proposals submitted by faculty liaison groups. Each proposal is focused on improvement of curriculum and instruction. Much of the debate among council members is concerned with whether the proposed research will assist in meeting the school's vision, mission, and goals agreed on two years earlier by the entire faculty. At times the debate becomes heated. Clearly the council is taking its decision making seriously. The principal is a voting member of the council but does not have veto power over council decisions, which are made by majority rule.

Germando Elementary is an example of a *conventional school*—characterized by dependency, hierarchy, and professional isolation. Finnie Tyler is an example of a *congenial school*—characterized by friendly social interactions and professional isolation. A successful school like Progress Middle School is a *collegial school*—characterized by purposeful adult interactions about improving schoolwide teaching and learning. Professional respect is a byproduct of discussing issues with candor, accepting disagreements as integral to change, and respecting the wisdom and care of all for arriving at educational decisions for students.

Collegial schools establish learning goals for all students consistent with the responsibility of education in a democratic society. These schools are always studying teaching and learning, setting common priorities, making decisions about internal changes and resource allocations, and assessing effects on student learning. These schools are driven by (1) a covenant of learning—mission, vision, and goals; (2) a charter for schoolwide, democratic decision making; and (3) a critical study process for informing decisions and conducting action research (Glickman, 1993, 2003). In effect, successful schools create a *SuperVision* of instruction, democratically derived and studied, that gives purpose and direction to the common world of adults.

SuperVision: A New Name for a New Paradigm

Like schools, supervision can be conventional, congenial, or collegial. Throughout most of its history, supervision has operated from within a conventional paradigm (worldview), attempting to control teachers' instructional behaviors. Based on what we know about successful schools, the time has come to move from conventional schools (still dominant in the United States) and congenial schools (less prevalent but still present throughout the nation) toward collegial schools (growing in number and success). *A paradigm shift toward the collegial model, if it is to succeed, must include a shift away from conventional or congenial supervision toward collegial supervision.* This view of supervision includes all of the following:

1. A collegial rather than a hierarchical relationship between teachers and formally designated supervisors
2. Supervision as the province of teachers as well as formally designated supervisors
3. A focus on teacher growth rather than teacher compliance
4. Facilitation of teachers collaborating with each other in instructional improvement efforts
5. Teacher involvement in ongoing reflective inquiry (Gordon, 1997, p. 116)

Jo Blase captures the spirit of this new, collegial approach to supervision in the following description:

> Leadership is shared with teachers, and it is cast in coaching, reflection, collegial investigation, study teams, explorations into the uncertain, and problem solving. It is position-free supervision wherein the underlying spirit is one of expansion, not traditional supervision. Alternatives, not directives or criticism, are the focus, and the community of learners perform professional—indeed, moral—service to students. (cited in Gordon, 1995)

Collegial supervision, then, stands in sharp contrast to traditional approaches to supervision (Keedy and Simpson, 2002).

Given the fact that the historic role of supervision has been inspection and control, it is not surprising that most teachers do not equate supervision with collegiality. When teachers have been asked to make word associations with the term *instructional supervision,* most of the associations have been negative, as indicated by the following list (Gordon, 1997, p. 118):

Control	Directive
Step-by-step	Irrelevant
Lack of creativity	Waste of time
Lack of free choice	Restricting
Evaluation	Rules
Negative	Dog and pony show
Nonexistent	Big brother
Jumping through hoops	Intimidating
Boring	Constantly under watch
Paperwork	Anxiety
Bureaucrat	Boss
Monitoring instruction	Stress
Guidelines for testing	Need for detailed lesson plans
Authority	Administrative micromanagement
Unrealistic	Yuck!

The traditional definition of *supervision* is to "watch over," "direct," "oversee," "superintend." The history of instructional supervision is viewed most often as an instrument for controlling teachers. It seems that a new term for describing the collegial model of instructional leadership espoused in this book is in order. Therefore, the first word in the title of this book is *SuperVision,* a term that denotes a common vision of what teaching and learning can and should be, developed collaboratively by formally designated supervisors, teachers, and other members of the school community. The word also implies that these same persons will work together to make their vision a reality—to build a democratic community of learning based on moral principles calling for all students to be educated in a manner enabling them to lead fulfilling lives and be contributing members of a democratic society.*

Supervisory Glue as a Metaphor for Success

We can think of supervision as the *glue* of a successful school. Supervision is the function in schools that draws together the discrete elements of instructional effectiveness into whole-school action. Research shows that those schools that link their instruction and classroom management with professional development, direct assistance to teachers, curriculum development, group development, and action research under a common purpose *achieve their objectives* (MacKenzie, 1983; Bernauer, 2002; Calhoun, 2002). In other words, when teachers accept common goals for students and therefore, complement each other's teaching and when supervisors work with teachers in a manner consistent with the way teachers are expected to work with students, then—and only then—does the school reach its goals. Regardless of a school's grade span, socioeconomic setting, or physical characteristics, successful schools have a common glue that keeps a faculty together and creates consistency among a school's various elements.

Effective supervision requires knowledge, interpersonal skills, and technical skills. These are applied through the technical supervisory tasks of direct assistance to teachers, curriculum development, professional development, group development, and action research, and the cultural tasks of facilitating change, addressing diversity, and building community. This adhesive pulls together organizational goals and teacher needs and provides for improved learning.

Organization of This Book

Figure 1.1 demonstrates the scope and organization of this book. For those in supervisory roles, the challenge to improving student learning is to apply certain knowledge, interpersonal skills, and technical skills to the technical tasks of direct

*To avoid awkwardness of writing, from this point we use the spelling *SuperVision* only in particular headings. But the point is that SuperVision and instructional leadership are integrated and interchangeable concepts.

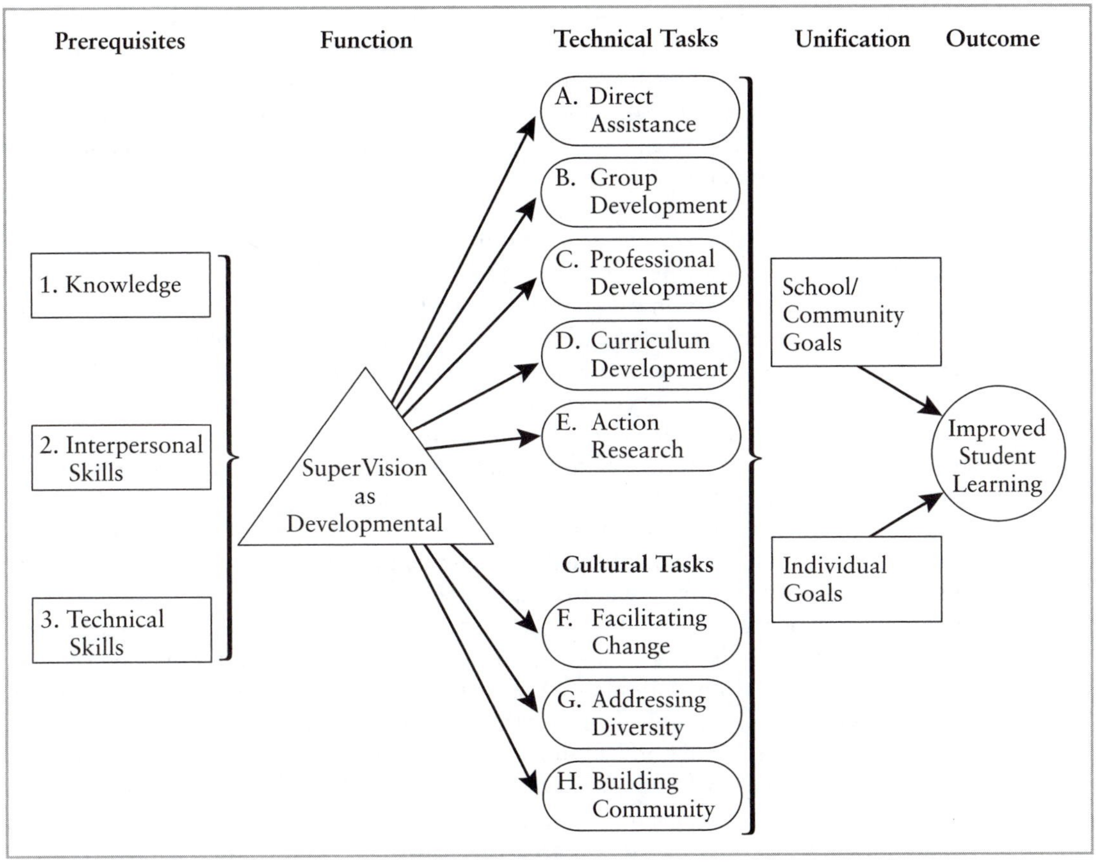

figure **1.1** **SuperVision and Successful Schools**

assistance, group development, curriculum development, professional development, and action research, as well as the cultural tasks of facilitating change, addressing diversity, and building community to enable teachers to teach in a collective, purposeful manner, uniting organizational goals and teacher needs. As the supervisor allows teachers to take greater control over their own professional lives, a school becomes a dynamic setting for learning.

To facilitate such collective instructional improvement, those responsible for supervision must have certain prerequisites. The first is a *knowledge* base. Supervisors must understand the exception—what teachers and schools can be—in contrast to the norm—what teachers and schools typically are. They must to understand how knowledge of adult and teacher development and alternative supervisory practices can help break the norm of mediocrity found in typical schools. Second, there is an *interpersonal skills* base. Supervisors must know how their own interpersonal behaviors affect individuals as well as groups of teachers, and then study ranges of interpersonal behaviors that might be used to promote more positive and change-oriented relationships. Third, the supervisor must have *technical skills* in observing, planning, assessing, and evaluating instructional improvement. Knowledge, interpersonal skills, and technical competence are three complementary aspects of supervision as a developmental function.

Supervisors have certain educational tasks at their disposal that enable teachers to evaluate and modify their instruction. In planning each task, the supervisor must plan specific ways of giving teachers a greater sense of professional power to teach students successfully. Technical supervisory tasks that have such potential to affect teacher development are direct assistance, group development, professional development, curriculum development, and action research. *Direct assistance* (A) is the provision of personal and ongoing contact with the individual teacher to observe and assist in classroom instruction. *Group development* (B) is the gathering together of teachers to make decisions on mutual instructional concerns. *Professional development* (C) includes the learning opportunities for faculty provided or supported by the school and school system. *Curriculum development* (D) is the revision and modification of the content, plans, and materials of classroom instruction. *Action research* (E) is the systematic study by a faculty of what is happening in the classroom and school with the aim of improving learning. Cultural tasks that can assist both school and teacher development include facilitating change, addressing diversity, and building community. *Facilitating change* (F) includes both assisting innovation and developing the capacity of the school and teachers to change with a changing environment. *Addressing diversity* (G) means developing both culturally responsive teachers and culturally responsive schools to ensure equity for all. *Building community* (H) involves fostering democracy, moral action, professional learning, and inquiry in the school, as well as engaging the larger community in collaborative efforts to improve the school and community.

By understanding how teachers grow optimally in a supportive and challenging environment, the supervisor can plan the tasks of supervision to bring together the school community's goals and teacher needs into a single fluid entity. The unification of individual teacher needs with organizational goals in "a cause beyond oneself" has been demonstrated to promote powerful instruction and improved student learning.

Figure 1.1, therefore, presents the organization of this textbook in a nutshell. Part II is devoted to essential knowledge. Part III deals with interpersonal skills. Part IV explains technical skills the supervisor needs, and Part V discusses the application of such knowledge and skills to the technical tasks of supervision. Finally, Part VI introduces the cultural tasks of supervision and show how supervision can integrate individual needs with school community goals to improve schools, teaching, and learning.

Supervision and Moral Purpose

Supervision based on moral purpose begins with the school community asking two broad questions:

1. What type of society do we desire?
2. What type of educational environment should supervision promote in order to move toward the society we desire?

If even part of the answer to the first question involves a democratic society in which all members are considered equal, then the answer to the second question must involve creating an educational environment that prepares students to be members of that democratic society. We can take this one step further and say that the answer involves creating a school that mirrors the democratic society that we desire.

We ground this book in a SuperVision of schools that deliver on the promise of education that promotes a better democracy for all (see Gordon, 2001; Glickman, 2003). To do so, we cannot think of ourselves as first-grade teachers, high school mathematics teachers, middle school counselors, central office specialists, high school principals, or superintendents. These positions are reflections of where we locate our bodies to go to work, but the names don't reflect where we must locate our minds and our hearts. Educators are the primary stewards of the democratic spirit. The total of our efforts is far greater than the particulars of our job (Glickman, 1998b).

The democratic impulse for renewing education continues to resonate in the thoughts of many local teachers, parents, administrators, and citizens in schools throughout this country—perhaps among more people than ever before. However, schools blessed with such far-sighted people are still in the margin. The challenge to bring an inclusive definition of democracy as the guiding principle into public education is enormous (Glickman, 1998a, 1999; Scheurich, 1998). We have been here before, and we might fall short once again. But whether we succeed or simply keep the spirit alive, we will have let other generations of educators and citizens know that this is the most important fight in which to engage—the democratic education of our students for a just and democratic society.

MyEdLeadershipLab™

Go to Topic 1, Supervision: Roles and Responsibilities, in the MyEdLeadershipLab™ site at www.myedleadershiplab.com for *The Basic Guide to SuperVision and Instructional Leadership*, Third Edition, where you can:

- Find learning outcomes for Supervision: Roles and Responsibilities along with the national standards that connect to these outcomes.
- Complete Assignments and Activities that can help you more deeply understand the chapter content.
- Apply and practice your understanding of the core skills identified in the chapter with the Building Leadership Skills unit.
- Prepare yourself for professional certification with a Practice for Certification quiz.

REFERENCES

Bernauer, J. 2002. Five keys to unlock continuous school improvement. *Kappa Delta Phi Record, 38*(2), 89–92.

Calhoun, E. F. 2002. Action research for school improvement. *Educational Leadership, 59*(6), 18–24.

Glickman, C. D. 1993. *Renewing America's schools: A guide for school-based action.* San Francisco: Jossey-Bass.

Glickman, C. D. 1998a. Educational leadership for democratic purpose: What do we mean? *The International Journal of Leadership in Education, 1*(1), 45–53.

Glickman, C. D. 1998b. *Revolutionizing America's schools.* San Francisco: Jossey-Bass.

Glickman, C. D. 1999. A response to the discourse on democracy: The dangerous retreat. *The International Journal of Leadership in Education, 2*(1), 43–46.

Glickman C. D. 2003. *Holding sacred ground: Courageous leadership for democratic schools.* San Francisco: Jossey-Bass.

Gordon, S. P. (Ed.). 1995, April. *Newsletter of the Instructional Supervision Special Interest Group of the American Educational Research Association.*

Gordon, S. P. 1997. Has the field of supervision evolved to a point that it should be called something else? *Yes.* In J. Glanz and R. F. Neville (Eds.), *Educational supervision: Perspectives, issues, and controversies* (pp. 114–123). Norwood, MA: Christopher-Gordon Publishers.

Gordon, S. P. 2001. The good school. *Florida Journal of Educational Leadership, 1*(2), 13–15.

Keedy, J. L., and Simpson, D. S. 2002. Principal priorities, school norms, and teacher influence: A study of sociocultural leadership in the high school. *Journal of Educational Administration and Foundations, 16*(1), 10–41.

MacKenzie, D. E. 1983. Research for school improvement: An appraisal of some recent trends. *Educational Researcher, 12*(4), 8.

Scheurich, J. J. 1998. The grave dangers in the discourse on democracy. *The International Journal of Leadership in Education, 1*(1), 55–60.

part 2

Knowledge

Part 2 examines the prerequisite knowledge for supervision. Chapter 2 considers the pessimistic news—why schools are typically ineffective. The causes of ineffectiveness are traced to the teaching career and the school environment. Chapter 3 explains the optimistic news found in school research on characteristics of successful schools, with particular attention to those work environment factors within the province of supervision. Chapter 4 explains how optimal adult development contrasts with the teaching career. Chapter 5 looks at how beliefs about education and supervision provide the foundation for supervisory practice. While moving from pessimism to optimism to realism, we will be riding through highly explosive grounds. Reactions of delight, anger, chagrin, hope, and disagreement are to be expected as current research challenges us to rethink current supervisory practices.

chapter 2

The Norm
WHY SCHOOLS ARE AS THEY ARE

outline

- The Work Environment or Culture of Schools
- The Legacy of the One-Room Schoolhouse
- Blaming the Victim and Structural Strain
- Viewing School Culture in the Context of the Larger Culture

Visit the **MyEdLeadershipLab™** site for *The Basic Guide to SuperVision and Instructional Leadership*, Third Edition to enhance your understanding of chapter concepts. You'll have the opportunity to practice your skills through video and case based Assignments and Activities as well as Building Leadership Skills units, and prepare for your certification exam with Practice for Certification quizzes.

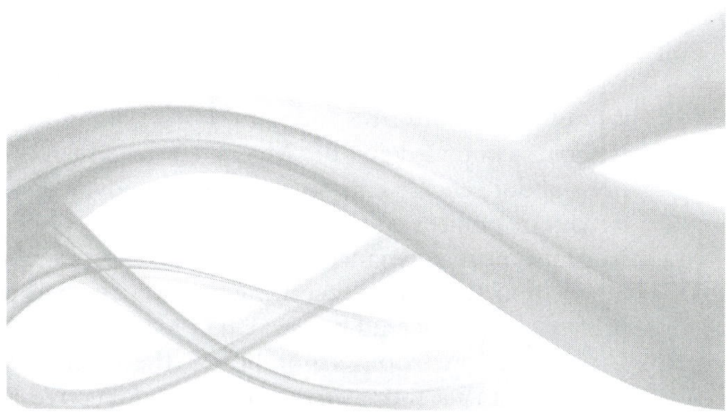

Our eyes must be wide open as we examine historical aspects of schools, teachers, and leadership. We must acknowledge that schools cannot be left alone to do business as usual, if we are serious about lasting instructional improvement.

The Work Environment or Culture of Schools

How does it happen that in the same school district, teachers in two schools view their work so differently from each other? In Meadow Valley Middle School, teachers come to school within 15 minutes of the required arrival time and leave school 15 minutes after the last bell. If a teacher arrives earlier or stays later, other teachers' questions and glances make that teacher feel as if he or she shouldn't be working more than the required time. To do so is to violate an unspoken norm that teachers have come to accept about the proper amount of time to spend in school. Yet one and a half miles across town, at the other middle school in the same district, the norms about proper time are different. At Mountain View Middle School, teachers are in their classrooms 45 minutes ahead of time, sharing coffee with each other, organizing materials, and conferring with individual students. One hour after school each day, the majority of staff are still there, working industriously in their own rooms, conducting tutorials, calling parents, and checking on tomorrow's plans. If a teacher arrives later or leaves earlier, the questions and glances of other teachers make him or her feel that a taboo is being violated.

Teachers in both schools work under the same district regulations, yet their expectations about work in their particular school are quite different. Why is this so? How does this come about? What have been the enduring norms of schools, and how have they been established? The answers to these questions are quite important if we are to know how to intervene in our own schools so as to minimize resistance and capitalize on school beliefs that give impetus to student learning.

The Legacy of the One-Room Schoolhouse

Discussing the present work environment of schools without discussing the one-room schoolhouse would be comparable to talking about issues in Western democracies without acknowledging the Magna Carta. Much of what exists in beliefs and expectations about schools can be traced to the idyllic-looking, clapboard, one-room schoolhouses of pioneer times. The teacher was responsible for the total instruction of all students, the maintenance of the building, keeping the stove filled with wood, and cleaning the floors. Our first schoolteachers were seen as working in an honorable but menial profession, poorly paid but second only to the preacher in prestige (Lortie, 1975).

In the one-room schoolhouse, the teacher was responsible for all that transpired within its four walls; therefore, collective action in a school was automatic.

What the teacher wanted to do about curriculum and instruction was what the school did! This legacy of independence, isolation, and privatization of teaching remains alive and well in many schools today. Instead of having physically separated one-room schoolhouses, we often see the one-room schoolhouses repeated every few yards down a school corridor. Each teacher sees his or her students, within the four walls, as his or her own school. Although the old one-room school is physically gone, it still holds a pervasive grip on the minds and actions of many teachers and schools.

The sense of classrooms as being private places is in direct contrast to the research on norms of improving schools:

> Research suggests that the schools with the greatest student learning going on are those which do not isolate teachers, but instead encourage professional dialogue and collaboration. Teaching in effective schools is a collective, rather than individual enterprise. (Freiberg and Knight, 1987, p. 3)

The one-room schoolhouse of pioneer times has spawned a deep-seated institutional belief among educators that is characterized by isolation, psychological dilemmas, routine, inadequate induction of beginning teachers, inequity, lack of career stages, lack of professional dialogue, lack of involvement in school decisions, lack of a shared technical culture, and conservatism. Many educators accept that these characteristics are simply part of a school culture, and there is little doubt that they pervade the minds and beliefs of most teachers and administrators. However, instructional leaders question whether beliefs and practices acceptable in the past are appropriate for the present, when we must initiate a new culture based on purposeful and collective beliefs about school, students, and teaching. Let's look at the characteristics of today's education that are derived from the one-room schoolhouse of bygone days.

Isolation

The isolation and individualism of teachers has been observed in all major studies of their work environment. As an example of this isolation, Dreeben (1973) noted:

> Perhaps the most important single property of classrooms, viewed from a school-wide perspective, is their spatial scattering and isolation throughout school buildings; and because teachers work in different places at the same time, they do not observe each other working . . . the implications of this spatial isolation are far reaching. (p. 468)

As Dreeben pointed out, classrooms are set up structurally in such a way that teachers are difficult to supervise, do not receive feedback from others, and cannot work collaboratively. During a typical workday, a teacher will talk to only a few other adults—on the way to the classroom in the morning, for 20 minutes or so at lunch and recess, and at the end of the day on the way out of the building. While teaching, teachers in most schools are invisible to each other and lack any concrete knowledge of what other teachers are doing in their classrooms.

Sarason (1996) points out that *physical* teacher isolation can lead to *psychological* isolation:

> What does it mean to go through a work day with no sustained personal contact with another adult? Being and talking with children is not psychologically the same as being and talking with peers. . . . When one is almost exclusively with children—responsible for them, being vigilant in regard to them, "giving" to them—it must have important consequences. *One of the consequences is that teachers are psychologically alone even though they are in a densely populated setting.* It is not only that they are alone, but they adapt to being alone. (p. 133; emphasis in original)

Teachers who have experienced long-term psychological isolation tend to view their work environment as limited to *their* classroom, *their* students, and *their* teaching. Although their isolation was initially involuntary, over time they have adapted to and accepted the tradition of isolation (Sarason, 1996; Brooks, Hughes, and Brooks, 2008); they now resist opportunities for professional dialogue and collaboration with other teachers that might arise.

Psychological Dilemma and Frustration

The teacher's work environment is marked by incessant psychological encounters. In just a few minutes of observation, one might see a teacher ask a question, reply with a smile to a student's answer, frown at an inattentive student, ask a student to be quiet, put a hand on a student's shoulder, and begin to lecture. Teachers have thousands of such psychological encounters in a normal schoolday (Jackson, 1968). A look, a shrug, and a word all have intended meanings between teacher and students.

Each day an elementary teacher meets with 25 to 35 students for six and one-half hours. A secondary teacher meets with 100 to 150 students for five to seven 50-minute periods. All this human interaction takes place in a 900 square-foot room, where a teacher must instruct, manage, discipline, reinforce, socialize, and attend to multiple occurrences. This crowded professional life makes teachers wish for smaller classes to reduce the psychological demand of constant decision making. Sarason (1996) described this incessant demand as a psychological dilemma:

> The teacher feels, and is made to feel, that one's worth as a teacher will be judged by how much a class learns in a given period of time. The strong feeling that teachers have about the complexity of their tasks stems from the awareness that they are expected to bring their children (if not all, most) to a certain academic level by a time criterion in regard to which they have no say. Faced with numbers and diversity of children and the pressure to adhere to a time schedule presents the teacher not with a difficult task but an impossible one. *I say impossible because I have never met a teacher who was not aware of and disturbed by the fact that he or she had not the time to give to some children in the class the kind of help they needed.* (p. 187; emphasis in original)

To maintain their own sanity in the face of an overload of psychological encounters and an inability to attend to the psychological needs of each student in a confined and regulated workplace, teachers often cope by routinizing classroom activity. The classroom routine for students becomes similar to the outside routine for teachers. For example, a science teacher might have students listen to a 20-minute presentation, followed by a 10-minute question-and-answer period and then by 20 minutes of seatwork. An elementary teacher might have three reading groups who rotate to him or her for 15 minutes each; each group reads aloud, responds to teacher questions, and then does worksheets. By routinizing what happens within the classroom, a teacher avoids making hundreds of decisions. The routinization of teaching allows the teacher to avoid the inherent conflict between being overwhelmed psychologically by the responsibility for teaching a large number of students and being aware of neglecting the personal needs of individual students.

Routine of the Teaching Day

The routine of the teaching day is imposed by administrative fiat, school board policy, and state guidelines. Every classroom teacher is required to be at school before students enter and to remain until they have departed. In primary or elementary schools, a teacher has specific times for recess and lunch, as well as approximate time allocations for teaching a given subject (for example, 45 minutes for reading, 30 minutes for mathematics, 30 minutes twice a week for social studies). The teacher is assigned a certain number of students and has responsibility for them for the entire day and school year. He or she is expected to remain physically in the assigned classroom for the entire schoolday, with the exception of recess, lunch, or special classes. Outside the classroom, teachers also have scheduled responsibilities for lunch, recess, and dismissal. In middle schools, junior high schools, and senior high schools, the schoolday is different from that of elementary schools but still has a set routine. A secondary teacher has four to seven different classes of students meeting at specific times each day for an extended period (11, 18, or 36 weeks). Again, the teacher begins and dismisses each class at a prescribed time and has regular duties outside the classroom (for example, monitoring the lunchroom, halls, or bathrooms).

Sarason (1996) raises a critical question concerning the effects of routine on teachers and students:

> *If teaching becomes neither terribly interesting nor exciting to many teachers, can one expect them to make learning interesting or exciting to children?* If teaching becomes a routine, predictable experience, does this not have inevitable consequences for life in the classroom? The model classroom does not allow me other than to conclude that children and teachers show most of the effects of routinized thinking and living. (p. 200; emphasis in original)

Inadequate Induction of Beginning Teachers*

Teaching has been a career in which the greatest challenge and most difficult responsibilities are faced by those with the least experience—a strange state of affairs indeed! Beginning teachers in many schools are faced with a number of environmental difficulties: inadequate resources, difficult work assignments, unclear expectations, a sink-or-swim mentality, and reality shock (Gordon, 1991; Gordon and Maxey, 2000; Colley, 2002; Johnson and Kardos, 2002; McCann and Johannesen, 2004). As we describe these difficulties, we invite you to reflect on your own first year of teaching and to recall if they were part of your entrance to the profession.

Inadequate Resources. If a teacher makes known that he or she will not be returning in the fall, then after the last day of school other teachers often descend on the vacant classroom and remove materials that will be useful to them. Not only are instructional materials removed but also desks, tables, and chairs! In their place are put those discarded items and furniture that no one else wants. Additionally, teachers may jockey around for the more spacious, better-lighted classrooms. Thus, for the incoming year, the neophyte teacher with the least amount of experience often steps into the physically least desirable classroom in the school, with discards for furniture and equipment and few instructional materials.

Difficult Work Assignments. Experienced staff and administration often arrange for the so-called problem children and/or lowest-achieving groups of students to be assigned to the newest teacher. In addition, the least interesting and most difficult courses usually are assigned to beginners (Kurtz, 1983; Johnson, 2001; Stansbury, 2001). New teachers are often given larger classes and more duties than experienced teachers (Romatowski, Dorminey, and Van Voorhees, 1989; Birkeland and Johnson, 2002).

Unclear Expectations. A common complaint among first-year teachers is that they are never sure what is expected of them as professionals (Kurtz, 1983; Johnson and Kardos, 2002). Administrators, other teachers, parents, and students express conflicting expectations of the beginner, leaving the neophyte in a quandary about whose expectations he or she should try to meet. A failure to socialize novice teachers into a professional community leads to what Corcoran (1981) has called the "condition of not knowing" (p. 20).

Sink-or-Swim Mentality. For a variety of reasons, beginning teachers are left on their own to "sink or swim." Administrators and experienced teachers tend to view the first year of teaching as a necessary "trial by fire" through which all neophytes

*Parts of this section are adapted from Stephen P. Gordon, *How to Help Beginning Teachers Succeed,* pp. 1–6. Reprinted by permission of the Association for Supervision and Curriculum Development, Alexandria, VA.

must pass. Many experienced colleagues are reluctant to provide assistance to beginning teachers. Some veterans think it is only fair that new teachers should pass through the same trials and tribulations that they navigated when they were beginners. Some see it as a process that "weeds out" weak teachers, allowing only the strong to survive. Other experienced teachers are reluctant to assist beginners because of the norms of individualism and privacy that pervade the school culture.

Beginners often are reluctant to ask the principal or colleagues for help when they are experiencing management or instructional problems. This is due to the fact that teaching is the only profession in which a novice is expected to assume the same (or more) responsibilities at the same level of competence as experienced colleagues. Novice teachers often do not ask for help because they fear that a request for assistance will call into question their professional competence. In fact, neophytes often go to great lengths to conceal their classroom problems (Newberry, 1978).

Reality Shock. Veenman defined *reality shock* as "the collapse of the missionary ideals formed during teacher training by the harsh and rude reality of classroom life" (1984, p. 143). Individuals tend to enter teaching with idealized visions of what it will be like. Classroom management problems, student learning difficulties, and the environmental difficulties already discussed tend to destroy those ideals rather quickly. Moreover, neophytes are faced with the numbing realization that they are unprepared to deal with the harsh realities of teaching. This realization can lead to disillusionment and professional paralysis (Corcoran, 1981; Chubbuck, Clift, and Alland, 2001).

Effects of Environmental Difficulties. The environmental problems just discussed can cause tremendous stress and eventually lead to physical and emotional problems. Novice teachers tend to have more negative attitudes about themselves, their teaching, their profession, and students at the end than at the beginning of their first year of teaching (Gordon, 1991). Between one-third and one-half of teachers drop out of the profession within their first seven years of teaching (Metropolitan Life, 1985; Ingersoll and Smith, 2003), with up to 15 percent leaving each of the first two years (Schlechty and Vance, 1981). Many of the most promising teachers are the ones who leave the profession early in their careers (Harris and Collay, 1990; Feiman-Nemser, 2003). America's schools must hire millions of teachers over the next several years to replace those leaving the teaching profession. Finally, as a result of their initial negative experiences, many teachers who stay in the profession develop a survival mentality, a narrow set of teaching methods, and resistance to experimentation and change that may last throughout their teaching careers (Huling-Austin, 1986; Romatowski, Dorminey, and Van Voorhees, 1989; Gordon and Maxey, 2000).

Inequity

The inequity between experienced and beginning teachers is not the only type of disparity often found in conventional districts and schools. Schools located in lower-income communities often are not provided the same resources as other schools in the same district. The physical facilities in low-income schools may be in ill repair and even present health and safety hazards. Class sizes often are larger than those in middle- or upper-class schools. Textbooks and instructional materials may be woefully out of date or nonexistent. Low-income schools may be short-changed on human resources as well. Many teachers in low-income schools are teaching outside of their field (Ingersoll, 2002; Achinstein, Ogawa, and Speiglman, 2004). New teachers often stay at low-income schools only until they are eligible to transfer to other schools, creating problems with faculty and school stability. The personnel problems in low-income schools often are blamed on the difficulty and frustration of teaching low-achieving students, but the major cause of the problem is that districts often provide neither sufficient resources and incentives to attract the most qualified teachers nor sufficient support to retain them.

Inequity for low-income and racial/ethnic minority students and students in at-risk situations also can be a problem within schools that include a diverse student body. Large percentages of low-income groups often are placed in remedial tracks where they miss out on the richer, higher-level curriculum taught to other students. In many schools, there is little or no attempt to consider the culture or learning styles of racial/ethnic minority students when designing curriculum, selecting instructional materials, or preparing lessons. Worse still, both unconscious and overt racism go unchallenged by supervisors and teachers in some schools. It may not be easy or comfortable for educators in conventional schools to examine inequity critically, but admitting the presence of inequity is the first step toward removing it from our schools.

Unstaged Career

More prestigious professions avoid such an abrupt transition from student to full professional. Physicians, lawyers, engineers, and scientists all experience several transition years of apprenticeship, internship, and junior membership on the job before they qualify for full rights and responsibilities in the profession.

This set of circumstances leads to the negative characteristic of the teaching profession that perhaps most significantly differentiates it from others—an unstaged career. More prestigious occupations have rigorous screening and requirements. Furthermore, they have a transitional or proving-ground stage; only when an aspirant has been judged competent by senior members does the junior member step into the next stage of the career, which provides high visibility, greater challenge, a substantial increase in salary, and responsibility for monitoring and judging the next wave of junior members. For example, a law school graduate must pass the bar exam and then serve as a clerk, as a legal aide, or as a junior member of a law firm. He or she works behind the scenes on writing and research that are credited to his or her superior. After proving competence over time, however, the lawyer then becomes a partner in a firm, a public prosecutor or defender, or an independent attorney. This movement brings visibility and stature in the profession and the right to have one's own apprentices to do the less challenging, less exciting work.

Teaching, however, has been unstaged from entry to exit. Education majors take courses, spend time in schools, perform as student teachers, and then graduate from college into their own classrooms as teachers. After that, no matter how many years they continue to teach, they do not move into another stage. The 20-year veteran teacher has the same classroom space, number of students, and requirements as the first-year teacher.

Lack of Dialogue about Instruction

Generally, people in schools do not talk about their work—teaching—with each other. DeSanctis and Blumberg (1979) found that the length of instruction-related discussion among teachers in a typical schoolday in a high school in New York was two minutes. Little's (1982) study of schools, Rosenholtz's (1985) review of effective schools, and Pajak and Glickman's (1987) study of 15 exemplary elementary and secondary schools in three improving districts pointed to one essential dimension of successful schools: Professionals constantly talk with each other, in a problem-solving, action-oriented way, about teaching. This talk is generated through faculty and committee meetings, in-service workshops, observations and conferences, faculty lounge contacts, and other informal occasions. This talk is of a specific nature: the teaching of and learning by students. Of course, teachers talk with each other in all schools, but the talk is typically of a more social nature—telling stories about students, parents, administrators, community, and school events.

For teachers to talk often and seriously with each other about the core of their job—instruction and curriculum—is a rarity in many schools. Time is not planned for it to occur. Faculty meetings are information giving, and when school concerns are raised, they are often deflected to noninstructional matters such as schedules, district policies, extracurricular responsibilities, and building maintenance.

Lack of Involvement in Schoolwide Curriculum and Instructional Decisions

If teachers don't see each other at work, don't talk with each other about their work, and see teaching as what goes on within their own four walls, it is not surprising that they are not given the opportunity, time, or expectations to be involved in decisions about curriculum and instruction beyond their four walls. Goodlad's (1984) study of schooling found that teachers' involvement in decisions about curriculum and instruction was virtually nil. Blumberg (1987) refers to one of the basic problems with public schools as "situations premised on having mature, competent adults as employees, yet treating these same adults as children when it comes to deciding and operationalizing their work." Boyer (1983) is even more adamant, referring to schools as impoverished intellectual climates for adults. The norm in most schools is that teachers are not expected to contribute experience, knowledge, and wisdom to decisions about the common good of educating students.

Lack of a Shared Technical Culture

Colleagues within a shared technical culture possess common purpose, expertise, and methods for analyzing and solving problems. They have developed sophisticated performance standards and communicate through a shared technical language. Imagine that a team of surgeons is about to perform a heart transplant operation. Each member of the team shares extensive knowledge of the cardiovascular system as well as state-of-the-art surgical procedures that will be used during the operation. The purpose of the surgery, as well as the technical means for achieving that purpose, are clear to each team member. Both in planning and performing the operation, the surgeons communicate in a complex technical language, much of which would be difficult for a layperson to understand. During the operation, the surgeons receive precise feedback from advanced technology and each other on the patient's condition. Should complications arise during the operation, the surgeons rely on their expertise and each other to analyze the problem and take corrective action. The patient's survival is never assured, but the shared technical culture of the surgical team greatly enhances the patient's chances for recovery.

Unlike advanced professional communities, most schools are not characterized by shared technical cultures. Isolation, lack of dialogue, inadequate induction, and lack of involvement in schoolwide decisions all inhibit the development of such cultures among teachers. Based on his classic sociological study of schools and teachers, Lortie's (1975) description of school culture is in sharp contrast to the shared technical culture we have been discussing.

> There is little "state of the art". . . . The image projected is more individualistic, teachers are portrayed as an aggregate of persons each assembling practices consistent with his experience and peculiar personality. It is not what "we the colleagues" know and share which is paramount, but rather what I have learned from experience. (p. 79)

Conservatism

The lack of a shared technical culture and the resulting ambiguity and uncertainty foster teacher conservatism. One aspect of this conservatism is a set of restricted, teacher-centered instructional methods. After reviewing data from observations of more than 1,000 classrooms, John Goodlad (1984) concludes the following:

> The domination of the teacher is obvious in the conduct of instruction. Most of the time the teacher is engaged in either frontal teaching, monitoring, students' seat work, or conducting quizzes. Relatively rarely are students actively engaged in learning directly from one another or in initiating processes of interaction with teachers.

When students work in smaller groups, they usually are doing the same thing side by side, and these things tend to be determined by the teacher. (pp. 123–124)

Beyond reliance on traditional teaching methods, less obvious aspects of conservatism can be observed in most schools, including the following:

- An emphasis on short-range rather than long-range instructional goals
- Satisfaction with successes with individual lessons, students, and projects rather than with the continuous growth of all students
- Reliance on personal experience rather than educational research
- Narrow limits on the types and degree of collegiality and collaboration in which teachers are willing to engage
- A reflexive resistance to curricular or instructional innovations

Such conservatism is not surprising considering the isolation and psychological dilemma found in the traditional school environment. The irony is that conservatism, which results largely from the other environmental problems we have described, tends to hinder efforts to solve those very same problems!

Blaming the Victim and Structural Strain

Researchers on school reform and student learning are telling us loud and clear that we cannot improve education by simply legislating higher standards and higher stakes. To this point, policy makers do not appear to be listening. Moreover, none of the popular legislated reforms are aimed at improving the school as a culture or workplace. Thus, the problems described earlier in this chapter remain largely unaddressed. In fact, these problems are aggravated by the external control brought about by legislated reform and the diminishing ability of teachers to engage in professional decision making.

Either the work environment of schools must be altered or we must accept that, regardless of extrinsic rewards, schools are not the place for our best teachers and thinkers. Supervision of instruction can play a strong role in reshaping the work environment to promote norms of collegiality and collective action, or supervision can remain another control apparatus "to keep teachers in their place." We cannot continue to blame the victims for not shaking the institutional chains that shackle every attempt to work together in the instructional interest of all students.

Viewing School Culture in the Context of the Larger Culture

Our discussion of legislated learning opens the door to consideration of how other forces in the larger culture affect schools and how educators should respond to these forces. In one sense, of course, we want our public schools to serve our culture, inculcating students with democratic values, preparing them to be contributing members of society, and so forth. We would be naive, however, if we did not realize that there are factors in our culture than can have negative effects on teachers and their students. Donald Thomas and William Bainbridge (2002), for example, argue that there are a variety of public policies that harm children's education:

- Millions of children in the United States live in poverty and without proper health care, which prevents them from developing their full cognitive potential.
- Most U.S. schools are underfunded. Schools in low-wealth states and districts are especially hard hit, with inadequate instructional materials, little technology, unsafe buildings, and less-qualified teachers.
- Poorly regulated child-care centers across the nation damage children's creativity and development.
- The federal government, although requiring special accommodations for students with disabilities, provides inadequate funding for such assistance.

Beyond harmful public policies, we must not forget that many of the social evils that have long victimized so many of our citizens, including racism, classism, sexism, homophobia, and religious prejudice, are still present and still harming our nation's children. We would be foolish to ignore the fact that these evils exist not only in the larger culture but also inside our schools (Weiner, 2003; Kao, 2004).

MyEdLeadershipLab™

Go to Topic 1, Supervision: Roles and Responsibilities, in the MyEdLeadershipLab™ site at www.myedleadershiplab.com for *The Basic Guide to SuperVision and Instructional Leadership*, Third Edition, where you can:

- Find learning outcomes for Supervision: Roles and Responsibilities along with the national standards that connect to these outcomes.
- Complete Assignments and Activities that can help you more deeply understand the chapter content.
- Apply and practice your understanding of the core skills identified in the chapter with the Building Leadership Skills unit.
- Prepare yourself for professional certification with a Practice for Certification quiz.

REFERENCES

Achinstein, B., Ogawa, R., and Speiglman, A. 2004. Are we creating separate and unequal tracks of teachers? The effects of state policy, local conditions, and teacher characteristics on new teacher socialization. *American Educational Research Journal, 41*(3), 557–603.

Birkeland, S., and Johnson, S. M. 2002. What keeps new teachers in the swim? *Journal of Staff Development, 23*(4), 18–21.

Blumberg, A. 1987. *A discussion on the effects of local, state, and federal mandates on supervisory practices.* Annual conference of the Council of Professors of Instructional Supervision, Philadelphia, November.

Boyer, E. L. 1983. *High school: A report on secondary education in America.* New York: Harper & Row.

Brooks, J., Hughes, R., and Brooks, M. 2008. Fear and trembling in the American high school: Educational reform and teacher alienation. *Educational Policy, 22*(1), 45–62.

Chubbuck, S. M., Clift, R. T., and Alland, J. 2001. Playing it safe as a novice teacher: Implications for programs for new teachers. *Journal of Teacher Education, 52*(5), 365–376.

Colley, A. C. 2002. What can principals do about new teacher attrition? *Principal, 81*(4), 22–24.

Corcoran, E. 1981. Transition shock: The beginning teacher's paradox. *Journal of Teacher Education, 32*(3), 19–23.

DeSanctis, M., and Blumberg, A. 1979. *An exploratory study into the nature of teacher interactions with other adults in the schools.* Paper presented at the annual meeting of the American Educational Research Association, San Francisco, April.

Dreeben, R. 1973. The school as a workplace. In R. M. Travers (Ed.), *Second handbook of research on teaching* (pp. 450–473). Chicago: Rand McNally.

Feiman-Nemser, S. 2003. What new teachers need to learn. *Educational Leadership, 60*(8), 25–29.

Freiberg, H. J., and Knight, S. 1987. *External influences of school climate.* Paper presented at the annual meeting of the American Educational Research Association, Washington, DC, April.

Goodlad, J. I. 1984. *A place called school.* New York: McGraw-Hill.

Gordon, S. P. 1991. *How to help beginning teachers succeed.* Alexandria, VA: Association for Supervision and Curriculum Development.

Gordon, S. P., and Maxey, S. 2000. *How to help beginning teachers succeed.* Alexandria, VA: Association for Supervision and Curriculum Development.

Harris, M. M., and Collay, M. P. 1990. Teacher induction in rural schools. *Journal of Staff Development, 11*(4), 44–48.

Huling-Austin, L. 1986. What can and cannot reasonably be expected from teacher induction programs. *Journal of Teacher Education, 37*(1), 2–5.

Ingersoll, R. M. 2002. Deprofessionalizing the teaching profession: The problem of out-of-field teaching. *Educational Horizons, 80*(1), 28–31.

Ingersoll, R., and Smith, T. 2003. The wrong solution to the teacher shortage. *Educational Leadership, 60*(8), 30–33.

Jackson, P. W. 1968. *Life in classrooms.* New York: Holt, Rinehart & Winston.

Johnson, H. R. 2001. Administrators and mentors: Keys in the success of beginning teachers. *Journal of Instructional Psychology, 28*(1), 44–49.

Johnson, S. M., and Kardos, S. M. 2002. Keeping new teachers in mind. *Educational Leadership, 59*(6), 12–16.

Kao, G. 2004. Social capital and its relevance to minority and immigrant populations. *Sociology of Education, 77*(2), 172–175.

Kurtz, W. H. 1983. Identifying their needs: How the principal can help beginning teachers. *NASSP Bulletin, 67*(459), 42–45.

Little, J. W. 1982. Norms of collegiality and experimentation: Workplace conditions of school success. *American Educational Research Journal, 19*(3), 325–340.

Lortie, D. C. 1975. *School teacher: A sociological study.* Chicago: University of Chicago Press.

Lortie, D. C. 1986. Teacher status in Dade County: A case of structural strain. *Kappan, 67*(8), 568–575.

McCann, T. M., and Johannesen, L. 2004. Why do teachers cry? *Clearing House, 77*(4), 138–145.

Metropolitan Life. 1985. *Former teachers in America.* New York: Author.

Newberry, J. 1978. The barrier between beginning and experienced teachers. *The Journal of Educational Administration, 16*(1), 46–56.

Pajak, E., and Glickman, C. 1987. *Dimensions of improving school districts.* Presentation to the annual conference of the Association for Supervision and Curriculum Development, New Orleans, March.

Romatowski, J. A., Dorminey, J. J., and Van Voorhees, B. 1989. *Teacher induction programs: A report.* (ERIC ED 316 525)

Rosenholtz, S. J. 1985. Effective schools: Interpreting the evidence. *American Journal of Education, 93*(3), 352–388.

Sarason, S. B. 1996. *Revisiting the culture of the school and the problem of change.* New York: Teachers College Press.

Schlechty, P. C., and Vance, V. S. 1981. Do academically able teachers leave education? The North Carolina case. *Kappan, 63*(2), 106–112.

Stansbury, K. 2001. What new teachers need. *Leadership, 30*(3), 18–21.

Thomas, M. D., and Bainbridge, W. L. 2002. No child left behind: Facts and fallacies. *Phi Delta Kappan, 83,* 781–782.

Veenman, S. 1984. Perceived problems of beginning teachers. *Review of Educational Research, 54*(2), 143–178.

Weiner, L. 2003. Why is classroom management so vexing to urban teachers? *Theory into Practice, 42*(4), 305–312.

chapter 3

The Exception

WHAT SCHOOLS CAN BE

outline

- Early Effective Schools Research
- The Second Wave of Effective Schools Research
- Context Studies in Effective Schools Research
- Has Effective Schools Research Outlived Its Usefulness?
- The Legacy of Effective Schools Research
- From Effective Schools to School Improvement
- A Cause beyond Oneself
- Connecting School Improvement to the Local Community and Larger Society

Visit the **MyEdLeadershipLab™** site for *The Basic Guide to SuperVision and Instructional Leadership*, Third Edition to enhance your understanding of chapter concepts. You'll have the opportunity to practice your skills through video and case based Assignments and Activities as well as Building Leadership Skills units, and prepare for your certification exam with Practice for Certification quizzes.

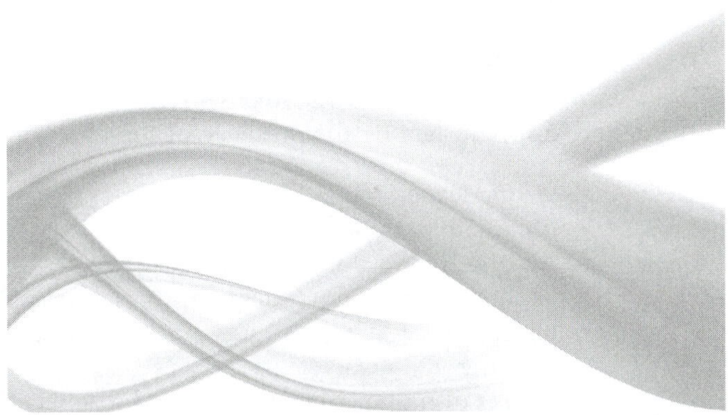

When we analyze the definitions of school success, we find great divergence in goals and practices. What do we mean by *school success*, and how do we measure it? Is the measure of school success short term—higher achievement scores on standardized basic-skills tests? Is school success measured by improved student attitudes toward learning, social behavior, displays of creative work, critical writing or thinking, attendance, grades, promotion, retention, or community or extracurricular participation? The instructional goals that a school sets and how these goals are measured reflect how the staff members collectively understand and prioritize their beliefs about education. A successful school is foremost an organization that defines good education for itself, through its goals and desired practices, and then engages in collective action to achieve that vision (Glickman, 1987).

Early Effective Schools Research

Beginning in the mid-1970s, research began to focus on individual schools that are exceptional, that consistently achieve results far superior to those of schools in general. In composition of student body, location, socioeconomic setting, and per-pupil expenditure, these schools do not differ from schools in general. Yet whether they are in poor urban areas or in wealthy suburbs, they succeed while others fail.

Ronald Edmonds (1979), after discovering that the results of his own research were consistent with those of other independent investigations, was confident enough to predict that *all schools could be effective:*

> It seems to me, therefore, that what is left of this discussion are three declarative statements: (a) We can, whenever and wherever we choose, successfully teach all children whose schooling is of interest to us; (b) We already know more than we need to do that; and (c) Whether or not we do it must finally depend on how we feel about the fact that we haven't so far. (p. 22)

Edmonds conducted three different studies. His first study was of 2 inner-city schools in Detroit; the second was of 55 effective schools in the Northeast; and the third included 20 schools in inner-city New York. Edmonds's findings were consistent with those of other early effective schools studies. He found that effective schools were distinguished by the presence of the following:

- Strong leadership
- A climate of expectation
- An orderly but not rigid atmosphere
- Communication to students of the school's priority of learning the basics
- Diversion of school energy and resources when necessary for maintaining priorities
- Means of monitoring student (and teacher) achievement

The Second Wave of Effective Schools Research

Beginning in the latter half of the 1980s, a new wave of effective schools research was carried out. These new studies, relying on more sophisticated research designs and new statistical analysis techniques (Creemers, 1996), tended to result in longer lists of correlates than the early effects research (Mortimore et al., 1988; Levine and Lezotte, 1990; Teddlie and Stringfield, 1993). After reviewing "second wave" effective schools research generated in a number of countries, Austin and Reynolds (1990, pp. 168–174) reported the following characteristics of effective schools:

- Site management
- Leadership
- Staff stability
- Curriculum and instructional articulation and organization
- Staff development
- Maximized learning time
- Widespread recognition of academic success
- Parental involvement and support
- Collaborative planning and collegial relationships
- Sense of community
- Clear goals and expectations commonly shared
- Order and discipline

Although agreeing with the early effective schools research on the need for such things as strong leadership, order, and agreed-on priorities, the second wave of research introduced new correlates, such as site-based management, professional development, parental involvement, and teacher collaboration and collegiality.

Context Studies in Effective Schools Research

Traditional effective schools research has been criticized for reporting characteristics common to effective schools while ignoring differences between schools from various contexts (Hannaway and Talbert, 1993). Examples of context include location (urban, suburban, rural), socioeconomic status (SES), students' ethnicity and race, and school level (elementary, middle, or high school).

Makedon (1992) has maintained that schools identified as effective have not closed the achievement *gap* between students of low and middle SES. Cook, Semmel, and Gerber (1995) reported that in schools seeking to apply effectiveness research, general student achievement increased, but special education student achievement decreased. Pierce (1991) concluded that implementation of factors identified in effective schools research failed to bring about significant achievement gains for language minority students. The fact that implementation of traditional effective schools correlates often fails to raise the achievement of low-income (Gustafson, 2002), racial/ethnic minority, and special needs students has led to effectiveness research aimed specifically at these groups. Context studies on schools with high-achieving low-income and racial/ethnic minority students (Stedman, 1987; Pierce, 1991; Scribner, 1999) identify a number of school characteristics:

- Respect for cultural pluralism
- A culture of caring
- Basic skills supplemented with rich academic programs
- Shared governance involving leaders, teachers, parents, and students
- Professional development to help teachers address cultural and special needs
- Teaching aimed at preventing academic problems

Has Effective Schools Research Outlived Its Usefulness?

Many educators have raised concerns about using the effective schools research as the basis of school reform. One concern is that effective schools have usually been identified by student scores on standardized literacy and mathematics tests, despite the fact researchers have warned against using such tests to judge a school's performance (Cuban, 1998). Another concern is that effective schools research is *correlational;* there is a significant positive correlation between the identified characteristics and the chosen measure of school effectiveness, but the research has not shown that these characteristics *cause* the effectiveness they have been associated with. Yet another problem with the effectiveness research is discussed by Hill (1998):

> School effectiveness research has not found a satisfactory way of dealing with the fact that schools and school education are essentially about growth, progress, and change. Researchers have been reduced to taking snapshots of phenomena, to focusing on achievement rather than rates of progress of students, and on measuring current status rather than charting change over time. (p. 428)

For these reasons, as well as continuing problems in research design and methodology, many experts believe that effective schools research has outlived its usefulness and that it is time to base school reform efforts on a new research paradigm.

The Legacy of Effective Schools Research

Despite criticism of effects research, it has left a positive legacy (Taylor, 2002). It disproves the earlier conclusions that socioeconomic status determines student achievement and that schools and teachers have little effect on student learning.

Larry Cuban (1998) points out that basic values of effective schools reformers of the early 1970s—that all children can learn, the importance of academic achievement, the need for accountability—have now been adopted by those who make and influence public policy.

Joseph Murphy (1992) suggests that since effective schools correlates tend to change in different studies and contexts, educators must move beyond a narrow interpretation of school effectiveness to a set of broad principles that underlie the various correlates. Murphy maintains that these principles constitute the real legacy of the effective schools research and include the following:

1. All students can learn.
2. Schools should focus on student outcomes and assess progress toward rigorously reaching those outcomes.
3. Schools should assume a fair share of the responsibility for student learning.
4. Schools should be structurally, symbolically, and culturally linked, providing for consistency and coordination throughout the school community (pp. 165–168).

Although the legacy of effective schools research is secure, the prevalent opinion of researchers is that this body of research, *by itself,* provides an insufficient basis for school reform. Additional research beyond the effects studies is necessary. This leads us to the topic of school improvement research.

From Effective Schools to School Improvement

Although effective schools research is still being carried out, over the last several years *school improvement research* has taken center stage. Before reviewing the research in this area, let's discuss differences between the two types of research. As noted by Bennett and Harris (1997), effects research asks the question, "What do effective schools look like?" and school improvement research asks, "How do schools improve over time?" Effects research examines inputs, throughputs, and outputs and emphasizes organizational structure, whereas school improvement research is focused on school culture and the change process (Bennett and Harris, 1997; Rust and Freidus, 2001; Bernauer, 2002; Fullan, 2002, 2005; Harris, 2002; Johnson, Johnson, and Gilhiam, 2005). Effects research takes statistical snapshots of performance measures and their correlates, whereas school improvement research is concerned with long-term growth, often examined through case studies (Bollen, 1996). In short, school improvement research is concerned with the *how* of successful schools. Although the specific characteristics of successful school improvement efforts vary somewhat across the research on school improvement (see Little, 1982; Rosenholtz, 1989; Levine, 1991; Teddlie and Stringfield, 1993; Hopkins, Ainscow, and West, 1994; Wasley, Hampel, and Clark, 1997; Joyce, Calhoun, and Hopkins, 1999), a consensus has emerged on the most important factors. Figure 3.1 provides a composite list of these characteristics.

- Varied sources of leadership, including teacher leadership
- Consideration of individual school context and culture
- Parental involvement
- Shared vision and continuous revisioning
- External and internal support, including time, moral, and technical support
- Focus on teaching and learning
- Ongoing professional development, including continuous analysis, reflection, and growth
- Instructional dialogue
- Teacher collaboration
- Democratic, collective inquiry, including action research
- Integration of improvement efforts into a coherent program
- Data-based feedback on improvement efforts using multiple measures

figure **3.1** **Characteristics of Improving Schools**

After reviewing both the effective schools and the school improvement research, it becomes clear that these are not entirely separate types of research. Rather, effects research has informed and provided a foundation for school improvement research. Together, the two types of studies provide us with a knowledge base for developing successful schools.

A Cause beyond Oneself

Later chapters on observation (Chapter 13), direct assistance (Chapter 15), professional development (Chapter 17), and curriculum development (Chapter 18) explain how a supervisor can use the research on effective classroom practice with teachers. For now, however, the outside-the-classroom but within-the-school factors that correlate with or predict school success provide the more significant issue. *Every major research study on successful schools has noted the organizational phenomenon of collective action, agreed-on purpose, and belief in attainment* (Pratzner, 1984). However, every major research study on ineffective schools has noted an absence of such purpose. Successful schools do not happen by accident; supervision is the force that shapes the organization into a productive unit.

Clearly, one characteristic of successful schools is that each teacher has "a cause beyond oneself." Teachers do not view their work as simply what they carry out within their own four walls. In successful schools, teachers see themselves as part of the larger enterprise of complementing and working with each other to educate students. For successful schools, education is a collective rather than an individual enterprise.

Connecting School Improvement to the Local Community and Larger Society

Successful school improvement efforts extend beyond school walls. School improvement must connect to the community in a number of ways. First, it is important that parents and other community members be involved in planning, implementing, and assessing school improvement efforts. The days of limiting parent and community involvement in schools to parent–teacher conferences, bake sales, and chaperoning field trips quickly is coming to an end. Parents and community members must be involved in decision making about the school's mission and goals and in helping educators and students reach improvement goals. This shared decision making can be accomplished in a number of ways, including parent and community representatives on school councils, open forums with parent and community members, and parent surveys on school needs and improvement efforts (McGaughy, 2000; Doyle, 2004; Sanders and Lewis, 2005; Muller and Thorn, 2007).

Successful schools do not treat parents and community members as outsiders. Rather, parents are welcome in successful schools and invited to participate in a variety of school and classroom activities. Many successful schools now include parent councils, as well as parent centers coordinated and staffed by parents and serving as hubs for parent and community involvement in the school. In addition to sharing school turf and decision making with parents, educators must interact with parents and families on a regular basis in community centers, neighborhoods, and homes. Many parents are unable to visit schools on a regular basis because of work schedules, transportation problems, or anxiety based on past negative experiences with schools. Educators must reach out to parents in such circumstances, to collaborate not only in the education of individual children but also in decisions about school improvement.

It is important to connect school improvement and community development. As Davies (2002) argued, "School success and community success are linked. Public schools are seldom able to be much better than neighborhoods and surrounding communities. Neighborhoods and communities are seldom able to stay healthy and attractive without good schools" (p. 392). Schools and community agencies can coordinate community services such as health care, social services, recreation programs, and community activities. Proponents of "full-service community schools" propose that schools become hubs of education *and* community services (Dryfoos, 2002).

The supervisor's role in connecting schools with their communities and the larger society should mirror the role of teachers in that same venture. The supervisor becomes a co-learner and facilitator as teachers, students, and communities explore ways to use partnership to improve student learning, develop communities, and, ultimately, improve society.

MyEdLeadershipLab™

Go to Topic 10, Facilitating Change, in the MyEdLeadershipLab™ site at www.myedleadershiplab.com for *The Basic Guide to SuperVision and Instructional Leadership*, Third Edition, where you can:

- Find learning outcomes for Facilitating Change along with the national standards that connect to these outcomes.
- Complete Assignments and Activities that can help you more deeply understand the chapter content.
- Apply and practice your understanding of the core skills identified in the chapter with the Building Leadership Skills unit.
- Prepare yourself for professional certification with a Practice for Certification quiz.

REFERENCES

Austin, G., and Reynolds, D. 1990. Managing for improved school effectiveness: An international survey. *School Organization, 10*(2), 167–178.

Bennett, N., and Harris, A. 1997. *Hearing truth from power? Organization theory, school effectiveness, and school improvement.* Paper presented at the annual meeting of the American Educational Research Association, Chicago, March.

Bernauer, J. 2002. Five keys to unlock continuous school improvement. *Kappa Delta Pi Record, 38*(2), 89–92.

Bollen, R. 1996. School effectiveness and school improvement: The intellectual and policy context. In D. Reynolds, R. Bollen, B. Creemers, D. Hopkins, L. Stoll, and N. Lagerweij (Eds.), *Making good schools: Linking school effectiveness and school improvement.* New York: Routledge.

Cook, B. G., Semmel, M. I., and Gerber, M. M. 1995. *Are recent reforms effective for all students?* Paper presented at the annual meeting of the American Educational Research Association, San Francisco, April. (ERIC ED 385 012)

Creemers, B. 1996. The school effectiveness knowledge base. In D. Reynolds, R. Bollen, B. Creemers, D. Hopkins, L. Stoll, and N. Lagerweij (Eds.), *Making good schools: Linking school effectiveness and school improvement* (pp. 36–58). New York: Routledge.

Cuban, L. 1998. How schools change reforms: Redefining reform success and failure. *Teachers College Record, 99*(3), 453–477.

Davies, D. 2002. The 10th school revisited: Are school/family/community partnerships on the reform agenda now? *Phi Delta Kappan, 83,* 388–392.

Doyle, L. H. 2004. Leadership for community building: Changing how we think and act. *The Clearing House, 77*(5), 196–199.

Dryfoos, J. 2002. Full-service community schools: Creating new institutions. *Phi Delta Kappan, 83,* 398–399.

Edmonds, R. 1979. Effective schools for the urban poor. *Educational Leadership, 37*(1), 15–24.

Fullan, M. 2002. The change leader. *Educational Leadership, 59*(8), 16–20.

Fullan, M. 2005. Turnaround leadership. *The Educational Forum, 69*(2), 174–181.

Glickman, C. D. 1987. Good and/or effective schools: What do we want? *Kappan, 68*(8), 622–624.

Gustafson, J. P. 2002. Missing the mark for low-SES students. *Kappa Delta Pi Record, 38*(2), 60–63.

Hannaway, J., and Talbert, J. 1993. Bringing context into effective schools research: Urban–suburban differences. *Educational Administration Quarterly, 29*(2), 164–186.

Harris, A. 2002. *School improvement: What's in it for schools?* New York: Routledge.

Hill, P. W. 1998. Shaking the foundations: Research driven school reform. *School Effectiveness and School Improvement, 9*(4), 419–436.

Hopkins, D., Ainscow, M., and West, M. 1994. *School improvement in an era of change.* New York: Teachers College Press.

Johnson, W. L., Johnson, A. M., and Gilhiam, B. 2005. A second- and third-order analysis of work culture. *Research in the Schools, 12*(2), 56–71.

Joyce, B., Calhoun, E., and Hopkins, D. 1999. *The new structure of school improvement: Inquiring schools and achieving students.* Philadelphia: Open University Press.

Levine, D. V. 1991. Creating effective schools: Findings and implications from research and practice. *Phi Delta Kappan, 72,* 389–393.

Levine, D. V., and Lezotte, W. 1990. *Unusually effective schools: A review and analysis of research and practice.* Madison, WI: National Center for Effective Schools Research and Development.

Little, J. W. 1982. Norms of collegiality and experimentation: Workplace conditions of school success. *American Educational Research Journal, 19*(3), 325–340.

Makedon, A. 1992. *Is Alice's world too middle class? Recommendations for effective schools research.* (ERIC ED 346 612)

McGaughy, C. 2000. Community development and education: A tripod approach to improving America. *Urban Review, 32*(4), 385–409.

Mortimore, P., Sammons, P., Stoll, L., Lewis, D., and Ecob, R. 1988. *School matters.* Berkeley: University of California Press.

Muller, L., and Thorn, J. 2007. Advancing toward shared decision making. *Principal Leadership, 7*(6), 45–48.

Murphy, J. 1992. Effective schools: Legacy and future directions. In D. Reynolds and P. Cuttance (Eds.), *School effectiveness: Research, policy, and practice* (pp. 164–170). London: Cassell.

Pierce, L. V. 1991. *Effective schools for national origin language minority students.* Washington, DC: The Mid-Atlantic Equity Center.

Pratzner, F. C. 1984. Quality of school life: Foundations for improvement. *Educational Researcher, 13*(3), 20–25.

Rosenholtz, S. J. 1989. *Teachers' workplace: The social organization of schools.* New York: Longman.

Rust, F. O., and Freidus, H. (Eds.). 2001. *Guiding school change: The role and work of change agents.* New York: Teachers College Press.

Sanders, M. G., and Lewis, K. C. 2005. Building bridges toward excellence: Community involvement in high schools. *The High School Journal, 88*(3), 1–9.

Scribner, A. P. 1999. High performing Hispanic schools: An introduction. In P. Reyes, J. D. Scribner, and A. P. Scribner (Eds.), *Lessons from high performing Hispanic schools: Creating learning communities.* New York: Teachers College Press.

Stedman, L. C. 1987. It's time we change the effective schools formula. *Kappan, 69*(3), 215–224.

Taylor, B. O. 2002. The effective schools process: Alive and well. *Phi Delta Kappan, 83*(5), 375–378.

Teddlie, C., and Stringfield, S. 1993. *Schools make a difference: Lessons learned from a 10-year study of school effects.* New York: Teachers College Press.

Wasley, P., Hampel, R., and Clark, R. 1997. The puzzle of whole-school change. *Phi Delta Kappan, 78,* 690–697.

chapter 4

Adult and Teacher Development within the Context of the School

CLUES FOR SUPERVISORY PRACTICE

outline

- Adults as Learners
- Adult and Teacher Development

Visit the **MyEdLeadershipLab™** site for *The Basic Guide to SuperVision and Instructional Leadership*, Third Edition to enhance your understanding of chapter concepts. You'll have the opportunity to practice your skills through video and case based Assignments and Activities as well as Building Leadership Skills units, and prepare for your certification exam with Practice for Certification quizzes.

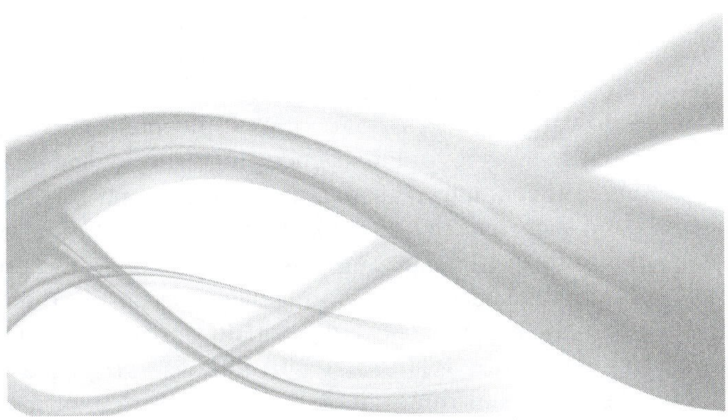

The research on adult learning and development has been prolific. We have attempted to distill the knowledge of adult and teacher development that has direct applications for supervision and supervisors. Readers who desire more detail should refer to the references at the end of the chapter. The use of such readily available and potentially rich knowledge about human growth can be extremely valuable to those who work with adults. If schools are to be successful, supervision must respond to teachers as changing adults.

Adults as Learners

Instructional improvement takes place when teachers improve their decision making about students, learning content, and teaching. The process of improving teacher decision making is largely a process of adult learning. Thus, research and theory on adult learning is an important component of the knowledge base for instructional supervision.

Intelligence and Wisdom

Two basic questions drove much of the early research on adult learning ability: Does ability to learn diminish with age? Are there differences between the learning process of adults and children? Thorndike and associates (1928) were among the first to suggest that adult learning did not peak in youth and diminish steadily thereafter (a common belief of their day).

Horn and Cattell (1967) identified two categories of intelligence: fluid and crystallized. *Fluid intelligence,* which depends heavily on physiological and neurological capacities, peaks early and explains why youth excel on tasks requiring quick insight, short-term memorization, and complex interactions (Merriam and Caffarella, 1999; Klauer and Phye, 2008). *Crystallized intelligence,* assessed by untimed measures calling for judgment, knowledge, and experience, is more heavily influenced by education and experience. Hence, older individuals show an advantage when it is measured.

Contemporary theories of intelligence have extended the notion that intelligence consists of multiple components or factors. Most readers of this text are familiar with Howard Gardner's theory of multiple intelligences (1983, 1999). Gardner initially posited seven types of intelligence (linguistic, logical–mathematical, musical, spatial, bodily kinesthetic, intrapersonal, and interpersonal). He later added naturalistic intelligence and suggested there are likely other forms of intelligence. Gardner's ideas are also relevant to supervision. Supervisors can identify and utilize the learning strengths of individual teachers when assisting them with instructional improvement efforts. Supervisors can also assist teachers in gradually expanding their repertoire of learning strategies.

Sternberg (1985, 1990) likewise proposed a theory of intelligence that may be helpful in thinking about the cognition of teachers called a *triarchic theory of intelligence*. It consists of three subtheories, the first of which is referred to as *componential;* it deals with cognitive processing and with what has traditionally been discussed in trying to understand intellectual ability. The second subtheory is *experiential,* which suggests that assessing intelligence requires consideration not only of the mental components but of the level of experience at which they are applied as well. Sternberg, intrigued by the differences between novices and experts suggests that experience promotes both the ability to respond automatically to routine situations and to deal effectively with novel situations. Thus, novice teachers can be expected to require different types of supervision than those who are more experienced.

Although the first two subtheories deal with processes said to be universal, Sternberg's third *contextual* subtheory deals with *socially influenced abilities.* Individuals are said to cope with life's challenges by adapting to the environment, shaping the environment, or selecting a different environment—all the while being influenced by what is considered appropriate and intelligent behavior within one's cultural milieu. This last contextual subtheory becomes important when one examines how teachers deal with challenging situations. Some obviously have greater capacities than others to adapt to or change the classroom and school environment. Through appropriate supervision, teachers can be assisted in broadening their array of adaptation and change strategies. It is this kind of practical intelligence that intrigues Sternberg and other theorists who propose that not enough attention has focused on the demonstration of adult intelligence through the identification and solution of real-world problems.

Theories of Adult Learning

As research increasingly put to rest the question of whether adults could continue to learn, attention focused on how their learning differed from that of children. The focus of the following overview of adult learning theories is on those theories that have received particular attention over recent decades. A chronological review of the literature on adult learning reveals in greater detail what this brief overview suggests—a shift from a psychological orientation (Tough, 1971; Knowles, 1980) toward a sociocultural orientation (Amstutz, 1999; Hayes and Flannery, 2000; Hansman, 2001).

Andragogy. The *theory of andragogy,* popularized in this country by Malcolm Knowles, has become one of the better-known theories of adult learning in recent years. Knowles (1980) proposed four basic assumptions of adult learning:

1. Adults have a psychological need to be self-directing.
2. Adults bring an expansive reservoir of experience that can and should be tapped in the learning situation.
3. Adults' readiness to learn is influenced by a need to solve real-life problems often related to adult developmental tasks.
4. Adults are performance centered in their orientation to learning—wanting to make immediate application of knowledge.

Later, Knowles added a fifth assumption—that adult learning is primarily intrinsically motivated (Knowles, 1984). The theory of andragogy no longer receives the uncritical acceptance that it once did, with questions increasingly raised about the extent to which these assumptions are exclusively true of adults (Tennant, 1986), the extent to which self-direction is an actual versus a desirable preference of adult learners (Brookfield, 1986), and the conditions under which andragogy may or may not apply (Pratt, 1988; Rachal, 2002). Knowles himself, before his death in 1997, came to acknowledge that differences between adults and children as learners may be a matter of degree and situation rather than a rigid dichotomy. Nevertheless, the theory of andragogy is still accepted by many as a broad guide to thinking about adults' learning (Merriam, 2001).

Self-Directed Learning. Even as self-direction in learning was emerging as one of the most challenged assumptions within andragogy, a distinct body of theory and research on adults' self-directed learning (SDL) was evolving. Allen Tough (1971) is generally credited with providing the first comprehensive description of self-directed learning—learning that adults engage in systematically as part of everyday life and without benefit of an instructor. A long-standing body of research on this topic has documented the ubiquitousness of adults' self-directed learning and led to the development of numerous models of self-directed learning as well as several instruments intended to measure it (Merriam, 2001; Eneau, 2008).

The implications of the concept of self-directed learning are numerous for those who seek to foster teachers' growth and development through developmental supervision. Supervision should foster rather than inhibit self-directed learning by matching supervisory behaviors with teachers' readiness for self-direction. It is important to recognize that not all adults appear to be equally ready for self-directed learning, nor is an individual equally prepared for self-directed learning in every situation. Variables like background knowledge and degree of confidence affect the level of support adults may need in their learning efforts (Pratt, 1988). Just as Grow (1991) recommended that instructors match their teaching style to the estimated stage of self-direction of adult learners, so too the effective supervisor will adapt his or her supervisory style in response to the degree of self-directed readiness exhibited by the teacher in a given context.

Transformational Learning. For some who question whether either andragogy or SDL theory represent a learning theory that is uniquely adult, transformative learning theory—proposed and revised most prominently by Jack Mezirow (2000)—offers an appealing alternative. Indeed, Taylor (2007) concludes from his critical review of recent research on transformational learning (TL) that TL has replaced andragogy as the iconic educational philosophy of the field of adult education. This theory grew out of Mezirow's research with reentry women in higher education. He offers the following definition of transformative learning:

> Transformative learning refers to the process by which we transform our taken-for-granted frames of reference (meaning perspectives, habits of mind, mind-sets)

> to make them more inclusive, discriminating, open, emotionally capable of change, and reflective so that they may generate beliefs and opinions that will prove more true or justified to guide action. (pp. 7–8)

Kegan (2000) contrasts transformative learning (changes in *how* we know) with informative learning (changes in *what* we know), adding that we all experience potentially important kinds of change that do not bring about a fundamental shift in our frames of reference. Merriam (2004) argues that a relatively high level of cognitive development is a prerequisite of the critical reflection on experience, which is key to transformational learning. Erickson (2007) however, suggests that transformative learning is possible for adult learners of differing developmental levels, although the nature of the process may be influenced by their developmental level.

Perspective transformation often is described as triggered by a significant life event, originally referred to by Mezirow (2000) as a disorienting dilemma. Perspective transformation also can occur in response to minor events that create an opportunity for reflection and redirection, or may occur when an accumulation of internal dilemmas creates a growing sense of disillusionment (Taylor, 2000; Erickson, 2007). A teacher's trigger for transformative learning may occur in a situation as obvious as experiencing failure for the first time when she accepts a new position in an urban setting, or as subtle as having a conversation with a gay student about the impact of other students' homophobic jokes on his learning.

Cranton (1994) recommended that the educator should reflect critically on his or her own perspective of being an educator. She also described the processes by which the educator might accomplish this:

> The educator, in order to develop the meaning perspective of being an educator would: increase self awareness through consciousness-raising activities, make his or her assumptions about beliefs about practice explicit, engage in critical reflection on those assumptions and beliefs, engage in dialogue with others, and develop an informed theory of practice. (p. 214)

The strategies Cranton suggested that may be useful in this process are varied, and include writing journals, visiting the classrooms of colleagues, conducting criteria analysis of incidents that epitomize their notions of success or failure in practice, experimenting with practice, eliciting feedback from learners, and consulting or engaging in dialogue with colleagues.

Experience and Learning: Situated Cognition, Informal and Incidental Learning

Many cite Brown, Collins, and Duguid (1989) as a seminal work in proposing a theory of *situated cognition*. Essentially, they propose that education is misconceived to the degree that it emphasizes the acquisition of decontextualized, and abstract knowledge. They insist that lasting knowledge emerges as learners engage in authentic activity embedded in specific situations. Linking situated cognition to Schön's (1983) work on acquisition of professional knowledge through "knowing-in-action," Wilson (1993) suggests that adults learn *in* experience as they act in situations and are acted on by situations, rather than the traditional assumption that adults learn *from* experience.

Extending the parallel with craft apprenticeships, Brown, Collins, and Duguid (1989) and others emphasize the cognitive *apprenticeship* as a means for learners to acquire knowledge as participants in a community of practice (Gonzales and Nelson, 2005; Tilley and Callison, 2007). Wilson (1993) makes an analogy between the cognitive apprenticeship and Schön's (1983) *reflective practicum* (Lea and Griggs, 2005). Lave and Wenger (1991) describe the role of *communities of practice,* or self-organized groups who share a common sense of purpose and a desire to learn from one another. Each of these strategies offers a valuable approach for fostering professional development of teachers, particularly those who are new to the field or to a particular school culture. In line with situated cognition theory, teachers would most effectively acquire knowledge useful in a new situation by being immersed directly in real practice situations, with support from experienced colleagues whose methods might include modeling and coaching.

More recently, interest in the ties between adult learning and experience have been explored in examinations of learning in the workplace that have found that much of the meaningful learning that occurs in that context is of the informal and incidental variety, rather than the highly structured learning traditionally associated with workplace training (Kerka, 1998). Marsick and Watkins (1990, 2001) offer a theory of informal and incidental learning. *Informal learning* is usually intentional but less structured than formal learning, and includes self-directed learning, networking, informal coaching, and mentoring. *Incidental learning,* however, is defined as a byproduct of some other activity and is most often tacit or unconscious at the time.

Marsick and Watkins (1990, 2001) suggest that those wishing to help adults improve their informal learning (i.e., supervisors) might assist adults in identifying conditions in the sociocultural context that help them learn more effectively or that stand in the way of learning. Once such factors are identified, supervisors can help the learner deal with or change them.

Holistic Adult Learning

In recent years, a number of authors, eschewing the tendency in Western culture to equate learning with *only* the cognitive and rational dimensions of learning, speak of the need to study adult learning in a *holistic* fashion, including noncognitive dimensions such as somatic or embedded knowing, narrative learning, and spiritual learning. Merriam, Caffarella, and Baumgartner (2007) dedicate an entire chapter to noncognitive dimensions of learning in the latest edition of *Learning in Adulthood,* including embodied, spiritual, and narrative learning. Clark (2001) attributes the growing attention to *somatic learning* (which includes an interest in kinesthetic learning and the role of emotions in learning) in part to the legitimization of the body as a source of knowledge through the women's movement.

Observing recent trends across several disciplines toward paying greater attention to spirituality, Tolliver and Tisdell (2006) similarly invite those involved in the education of adults to look for ways to bring their own spirituality into the learning environment and to engage the spirituality of adult learners by introducing activities that activate meaning making through imagery, symbol, metaphor, poetry, art, and music. Such activities, Tolliver and Tisdell maintain, can be used to promote transformative learning by engaging the whole person and assisting the learner in developing a more authentic identity without imposing a religious or spiritual agenda, even without any explicit discussion of spirituality.

Finally, Clark (2001), and more recently Rossiter and Clark (2007), examine the place of *narrative* in adult learning. They stress the power of storytelling and particularly the creation of one's personal narrative as an aid for learning and intentional change. Clark (2001) also discusses the benefits of teachers of adults producing their own educational biographies as a tool for understanding how their own learning has shaped who they are. She refers to the work of Dominice (2000), who has explicated a methodology for assisting adult learners in extended courses to develop an educational biography.

In a qualitative study of eight experienced educators, Beattie, Dobson, Thornton, and Hegge (2007) integrate all the forms of noncognitive learning discussed here. In describing their study, they say:

> The research is grounded in a narrative tradition of research on teacher development where teacher learning is viewed as a creative, holistic, relational endeavor in which the personal and professional are intimately connected. It makes connections between narrative inquiry, holistic education and teacher development, and has the potential to make a contribution to the body of knowledge in teachers' knowledge/learning by exploring and describing the aesthetic and spiritual dimensions of educators' ways of knowing and being. (p. 119)

The authors' description of findings is generously sprinkled with excerpts from the narratives of teachers discussing the aesthetic and spiritual dimensions of their growth as professionals.

Critical Perspectives on Adult Learning

In recent decades, a number of philosophical and theoretical orientations challenged dominant perspectives on adult learning, such as andragogy, self-directed learning, transformative learning, and experiential learning. These critical perspectives include feminism (Tisdell, 2005), critical theory (Habermas, 1992; Welton, 1995), critical race theory (Ianinski, Wright, and Rocco, 2003), critical multiculturalism (Ross-Gordon et al., 2005; Guy, 2005), and postmodernism (Foucault, 1977; Lyotard, 1984; Usher, Bryant, and Johnston, 1997).

Kilgore (2001) offers a brief synopsis of the critical and postmodern perspectives of adult learning, analyzing both their similarities and differences. As she notes, each of these perspectives challenges pillars of adult learning theory, such as andragogy and self-directed learning, as exclusionary and overly focused on the individual. Both critical and postmodern perspectives share assumptions that knowledge is socially constructed, along with an interest in power as a factor in learning. They differ, however, in other significant ways.

Critical theorists argue that *hegemony* (dominant influence or authority wielded by those in power) operates to preserve inequities linked to structures of privilege and oppression based on categories like race, ethnicity, gender, class, and age. In this view, learning involves two things: reflecting on the hegemonic assumptions that often guide our practices, and perhaps acting to change the practices as well as the assumptions. (An example given by Kilgore is that of use and misuse of standardized tests.) Social justice is viewed as a core value. Postmodern theorists, however (Foucault, 1977; Lyotard, 1984; Usher, Bryant, and Johnston, 1997), resist embracing *any* universal truth, emphasizing that knowledge is multifaceted and truths shift according to the experience and context of the knower. The same individual can even hold multiple perspectives on a topic based on situational variables or in their multifaceted identities (what Sheared, 1999, refers to as *polyrhythmic realities*).

Power is a consideration for each framework, but in different ways. For instance, critical theories are interested in how the status quo (e.g., an individualistic focus on learning that research suggests may be culturally biased toward certain groups) can be interrupted to create more emancipatory knowledge (e.g., a greater emphasis on group learning, which research suggests is more culturally relevant for some groups of learners). Power is seen as held by some over others; for instance, the traditional role of principals invests them with greater power than teachers. From the postmodern perspective, power is present in every relationship and can be exercised by anyone to one degree or another. We must analyze (or deconstruct) the situation to know how power is being used (whether for repressive or liberating purposes) and by whom. In this view, teacher and parent participation in site-based management or participatory action research projects become tools both for producing knowledge collaboratively and for negotiating and rearranging power relationships.

Teachers as Adult Learners

Sternberg's (1985, 1990) work on the experiential component of adult intelligence indicates that novice teachers must be supervised differently than experienced teachers. For example, many beginning teachers have more difficulty assessing and responding to novel teaching situations and problems than their experienced colleagues and thus are in need of more intensive support. Both Sternberg's (1985, 1990) and Gardner's (1983) research on multiple intelligences takes us beyond differences between novice and experienced teachers and points to the need for identifying and utilizing different learning strengths of teachers at all levels of experience.

The need to individualize teacher learning, indicated by the literature on adult learning, stands in sharp contrast to the actual treatment of teachers. Many supervisors treat teachers as if they were all the same, rather than individuals in various stages of adult growth. In most schools, teachers receive the same in-service workshops, the same observations, and the same assessments. It is as if teachers were stamped out of teacher training institutes as identical and thereafter have no further need to be viewed as individual learners. The research on adults shows the lack of wisdom of such assumptions (Mathis, 1987).

Sternberg's (1985, 1990) discussion of socially influenced abilities points to the need for teachers to engage in learning aimed at developing a variety of strategies for adapting to or changing their classroom and school environment. Mezirow (2000), Mezirow associates (1991), and Brookfield's (1986) work on adult learning indicates that in order to learn and grow, teachers must participate in a continuous cycle of collaborative activity and reflection on that activity, and must develop the powers of critical thinking. Finally, Knowles (1980, 1984), Mezirow (2000), Mezirow and associates (1991), and Brookfield (1986) support the notion of the supervisor facilitating teacher growth toward empowerment and self-direction. Figure 4.1 reviews the knowledge on adult learning and its implications for instructional supervision.

Unfortunately, many schools do not foster collaborative action, reflection, critical thinking, or teacher empowerment. Rather, the hierarchical structure of many school systems—as well as the environmental problems of isolation, psychological dilemma, and lack of a shared technical culture discussed in Chapter 2—tends to work against the type of growth described in the adult learning literature. To the contrary, Drago-Severson's (2004, 2007) qualitative study of principals as professional development leaders found that those who successfully exercised their leadership to promote adult learning consistently employed four strategies, which she refers to as *pillar practices*:

1. Encouraging various forms of teaming/partnering with colleagues within and outside school (e.g., teaching teams, curriculum teams, technology teams, diversity teams, developing partnerships with other organizations)
2. Providing opportunities for teachers to serve in leadership roles (e.g., mentoring graduate student interns, knowledge-based management, technology leaders, sharing decision making, leading accreditation teams)
3. Promoting collegial inquiry (e.g., reflection through writing and dialogue)
4. Mentoring

According to Drago-Severson (2008), these pillar practices, particularly when adapted to teachers' developmental stages, foster transformative rather than informative learning.

Knowledge about Adult Learning

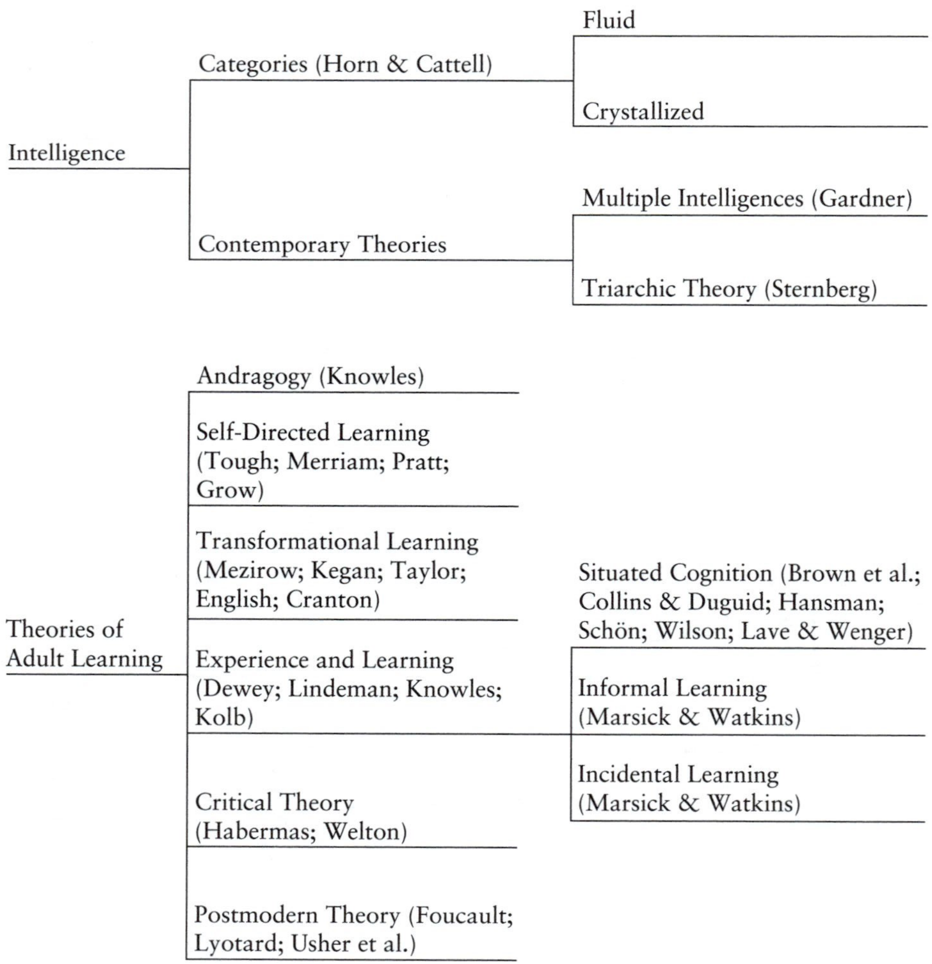

Implications for Instructional Supervision

1. Differentiate supervision based on teachers' experience, learning strengths, and readiness level for self-directed learning.
2. Assist teachers develop a variety of learning adaptations and change strategies.
3. Help teachers to identify, analyze, and solve classroom and school problems.
4. Link learning about instructional innovations to teachers' past learnings.
5. Allow ample time for teachers to integrate innovations into their teaching repertoires gradually.
6. Foster experiential learning, a continuous cycle of active experimentation and reflection on action.
7. Facilitate teacher empowerment and self-direction.
8. Support dialogue and collegial learning among teachers.
9. Help teachers take advantage of conditions supportive of learning and change nonsupportive conditions.
10. Foster teachers' critical thinking.
11. Help teachers consider multiple perspectives on issues and problems.

figure **4.1** **Adults as Learners**

Adult and Teacher Development

Literature on adult development can be seen as reflecting several distinct but related approaches. Just a few decades ago, the study of human development focused on children, and adulthood was either not a consideration or was thought to represent a period of stability. For several decades, theory and research concerning adult development emphasized development as an orderly progression. Because much of the work in this area was done by developmental psychologists, there was an emphasis on the change processes occurring in the individual with relatively little consideration to his or her interaction with the environment. Early approaches to adult development were rooted in such a tradition. Over time, alternative views of adult development evolved, with less concern for a universal progression and greater interest in the interaction between the individual and the social environment. Subsequent sections of this chapter discuss adult development according to these five subtopics: (1) stage development, (2) life cycle development, (3) transition events, (4) role development, and (5) sociocultural influences on adult development.

Stage Theories of Adult and Teacher Development

We begin discussion of adult development by focusing on developmental stage theories. Levine (1989) delineated the characteristics of stages:

> First and foremost is their structural nature. Each stage is a "structured whole," representing an underlying organization of thought or understanding. Stages are qualitatively different from one another. All emerge in sequence without variation; no stage can be skipped. Finally stages are "hierarchically integrated"; that is, progressive stages are increasingly complex and subsume earlier stages. Individuals always have access to the stages through which they have passed. Under ordinary circumstances or with proper supports, people will generally prefer to use the highest stages of which they are capable. (p. 86)

It may be helpful to look more closely at several specific stage theories.

Cognitive Development. Piaget described four stages of cognitive development: sensorimotor, preoperational, concrete operations, and formal operations (Ginsburg and Opper, 1979). The person at the formal operations stage has already progressed beyond reasoning only for the "here and now" and can project into and relate time and space. A person at the formal operations stage uses hypothetical reasoning, understands complex symbols, and formulates abstract concepts.

Some researchers have found that formal thought is not demonstrated by all adults. There has been considerable exploration of characteristic adult forms of thinking that go beyond Piaget's fourth stage to a postformal operations stage

Concrete Operations		Formal Operations		Postformal Operations
0	········➤········	0	········➤········	0

***figure* 4.2 Adult Cognitive Development Continuum**

Source: Adapted from Stephen P. Gordon (1990). *Assisting the Entry-Year Teacher: A Leadership Resource.* Columbus, OH: Ohio Department of Education. Used with permission.

(Riegel, 1973; Arlin, 1975; Merriam and Caffarella, 1999). Terms like *dialectical thought* (Riegel, 1973; Kramer, 1983), *integrative thought* (Kramer, 1987), and *epistemic cognition* (Taranto, 1987) have been used to describe the highest stage of cognition observed in adults. Figure 4.2 represents the adult cognitive developmental continuum.

Ammon (1984) explored teachers' cognitive development in a study of a two-year graduate teacher education program with an emphasis on Piagetian theory. This emphasis was intended to teach the adult preservice and in-service teachers about child development as well as to promote the teachers' own development. As the teachers studied Piagetian and related developmental theory, their concepts of students, learning, and teaching changed. They progressed from simplistic to more complex, and interactive explanations of student behaviors, development, and learning. These teachers also moved from a conception of teaching as "showing and telling" to creating a learning environment designed to foster the students' learning and development. The teachers' views on learning shifted from passive reception to active construction. They also came to think of their roles differently, as facilitating learning rather than imparting knowledge.

Conceptual Development. One developmental framework closely related to cognitive development that has been studied significantly with teachers is that of conceptual development. Hunt, Butler, Noy, and Rosser (1978) defined *conceptual level (CL)* "in terms of (1) increasing conceptual complexity, as indicated by discrimination, differentiation, and integration and (2) increasing interpersonal maturity, as indicated by self–definition and self-other relations." Hunt and coworkers placed individuals on a continuum from most concrete (lowest CL) to most abstract (highest CL).

Persons of *low CL* evaluate things in a simple, and concrete fashion. They tend to view issues in "black and white." Individuals of low CL have difficulty defining a problem they are experiencing and respond to the same problem in a habitual manner, despite the fact that the repeated response is not solving the problem. They must be shown how to solve the problem. Persons of *moderate CL* are becoming more abstract in their thinking. They can define the problem and generate a limited

0··········➤··········	0··········➤··········	0
Low Conceptual Level (Concrete Thinking)	Moderate Conceptual Levl (Moderately Abstract Thinking)	High Conceptual Level (Highly Abstract Thinking)

***figure* 4.3 Conceptual Development Continuum**

Source: Adapted from Stephen P. Gordon (1990). *Assisting the Entry-Year Teacher: A Leadership Resource.* Columbus, OH: Ohio Department of Education. Used with permission.

number of possible solutions, but have difficulty formulating a comprehensive plan. They still need some assistance in solving a complex problem. Persons of *high CL* are abstract thinkers. They are independent, self-actualizing, resourceful, and flexible, and possess a high capacity for integration. Figure 4.3 represents the conceptual development continuum.

High-concept teachers have been found to differ from low-concept teachers in terms of both teaching approach and teacher-generated classroom atmosphere. High-concept teachers rate higher on what are generally considered to be more positive characteristics (e.g., warmth, perceptiveness, empathy, flexibility, ingenuity, task effectiveness, smoothness, consistency), and low-concept teachers rate higher on more educationally negative characteristics (e.g., innovativeness, rule orientation, punitiveness, anxiety) (Harvey, White, Prather, Alter, and Hoffmeister, 1966; Heck and Davis, 1973; Reiman and Thies-Sprinthall, 1998).

Hunt and Joyce (1967) found correlations between teacher conceptual level and ability to use learners' needs as a basis for planning and evaluation. High-concept teachers used a greater range of learning environments and teaching methods. Similarly, Hopkins (1990) found that high-stage teachers used new methods of teaching at a rate four times greater than their counterparts at lower stages. Parkay (1979), in a study of inner-city high school teachers, found that high-concept teachers stimulated positive student attitudes and student achievement gains and were less susceptible to professional stress. A study of 52 teachers by Calhoun (1985) found that teachers with high conceptual thought provided more corrective feedback to students, gave more praise, and were less negative and punitive. These teachers were more varied in their instructional strategies and were able to elicit more higher-order conceptual responses from their students than teachers of moderate and lower levels of conceptual thought.

Moral Development. Kohlberg and Armon (1984) identified three broad categories of morality: the preconventional level, the conventional level, and the postconventional

0 ········➤········ 0 ········➤········ 0

Preconventional Level	Conventional Level	Postconventional Level

figure 4.4 **Moral Development Continuum**

Source: Adapted from Stephen P. Gordon (1990). *Assisting the Entry-Year Teacher: A Leadership Resource.* Columbus, OH: Ohio Department of Education. Used with permission.

level. They further delineated two stages of development within each of these levels, with the second stage more advanced and organized than the first. Across the three levels, reasoning shifts from a self-centered perspective to one that increasingly considers the perspectives and rights of others. The individual at Level I makes decisions from a self-centered orientation. At Level II, individuals "Do the right thing" because that is what is expected according to social norms. Finally, at Level III, moral decisions serve to recognize the social contract and to uphold individual rights. Although conflicts between these principles and legal mandates are recognized as problematic in the lower stage of Level III, moral principles come to take precedence by the time an individual reaches the highest stage of moral development. Kohlberg and Armon see the higher stages as superior, and see enhancing development as an appropriate aim for education. Figure 4.4 represents the moral development continuum.

It is important here to mention the work of Carol Gilligan (1979, 1982), who compared conclusions from Kohlberg's model of moral development with conclusions from her own research with women discussing personal decisions. People at the top of Kohlberg's stages worry about interfering with others' rights, whereas those at the top of Gilligan's stages worry about errors of omission, such as not helping others when you could. At Gilligan's highest stage, *morality* is conceived in terms of relationships, and *goodness* is equated with helping others. Gilligan proposed that a different conception of development emerges from the study of women's lives:

> The shift in women's judgment from an egocentric to a principled ethical understanding is articulated through their use of a distinct moral language, in which the terms "selfishness" and "responsibility" define the moral problem as one of care. Moral development then consists of the progressive reconstruction of this understanding toward a more adequate conception of care. (1979, p. 442)

Several small-scale studies investigate relationships between teachers' moral development and their understandings of teaching and learning. Johnston (1985) found that teachers scoring low on the same test of moral reasoning possessed a narrow conception of the on-task students (working quietly and individually on an assignment provided by the teacher). Teachers with the highest scores on moral reasoning considered students' perspectives and the complex, continuous nature of learning while resisting classifying students as on task or off task based solely on behavioral observation. Reiman and Parramore (1994) found first-year teachers at higher moral reasoning levels to exhibit greater concern for the instructional needs of their students.

Ego Development. Ego is both a process of striving for coherence and meaning in one's life and a structure with its own internal logic (Levine, 1989). This is one of the few developmental theories derived from the study of women, but it has been applied subsequently to numerous samples of women and men. Loevinger (1976) has identified 10 stages of ego development that individuals can pass through. Orientations toward symbiotic, impulsive, and self-protective behaviors are manifest in the early stages. In these lower stages, a person depends on others for solutions to problems. In the middle stages of ego development, the individual exhibits conventional behaviors. At the higher stages, the adult becomes individualistic, autonomous, and integrated. The person at the highest stage of ego development is able to synthesize what seem to be unrelated or opposing concepts to individuals at lower stages (Witherell and Erickson, 1978). Adults at the beginning point on the continuum might be classified as *fearful*; those at the midpoint on the continuum can be called *conforming*; and adults at the end of the continuum (those with the most mature egos) are referred to as *autonomous*. Figure 4.5 represents the ego development continuum.

Cummings and Murray (1989) found that teachers at different levels described different roles of a teacher, with those at lower levels of ego development focusing on the role of the teacher as information disseminator and caregiver, and those at higher levels emphasizing the role of the teacher in helping students learn to learn. Based on their findings, they conclude that lower-level teachers may not have the resources to cope with the intricacies of the student–teacher relationships or deal with the complexity of the learning process.

Levels of Consciousness. Robert Kegan (1994, 2000), a self-acknowledged neo-Piagetian, is a more recent entrant on the scene of adult developmental psychology with his theory of levels of consciousness. As with the Piagetian shift from concrete to formal operations, the development of abstract thinking is a key characteristic of

0 ··········► ··········0 ··········► ··········0

Fearful — Conforming — Autonomous

figure **4.5** **Ego Development Continuum**

Source: Adapted from Stephen P. Gordon (1990). *Assisting the Entry-Year Teacher: A Leadership Resource.* Columbus, OH: Ohio Department of Education. Used with permission.

movement from Kegan's adolescent stage of *durable category* level to a more mature *cross-categorical* (or *third-order*) *consciousness*. The person functioning at the cross-categorical level is capable of thinking abstractly, reflecting on his or her own emotions, and being guided by beliefs and values that ensure loyalty to the larger community. At this stage, the adult experiences a new construction of reality, with the needs, wants, and desires of others figuring as prominently as his or her own (Taylor and Marienau, 1995). Only with the transition from cross-categorical to *systems* (or *fourth-order*) *consciousness*, however, does the individual move beyond defining himself or herself in terms of those duties, devotions, and values to become a truly independent and autonomous person. At this level, we can look objectively at our own perspective, compare it with those of others, and work to reconcile differences, a process associated with transformational learning (Kegan, 2000). It is the systems level of consciousness that is said to be necessary to meet the various demands of modern adult life (parenting, partnering, working, continued learning), but Kegan contends many do not reach this stage until their 30s or 40s, if at all. Finally, as is common with stage theories, Kegan posits a level rarely achieved, *trans-systems* (or *fifth-order*) *consciousness*.

Kegan's model suggests our expectations may be high, both for ourselves and others. In the preface to his book *In Over Our Heads: The Mental Demands of Modern Life* (1994), he especially appealed to those who provide education, training, and supervision for other adults to be mindful of the mental demands we place on others, such as our expectation that teachers, even those recently graduated as traditional-age students, exhibit high levels of critical thinking and metacognitive skills, although he speculates these skills may not be fully evolved for many until their 30s and 40s. Kegan's model is compatible with Drago-Severson's (2004, 2007) learning-oriented model of school leadership, and also provides a framework that is consistent with the principles of developmental supervision. Figure 4.6 depicts the continuum of adult consciousness.

Stages of Concern. In the 1960s and early 1970s, Frances Fuller (1969) conducted pioneer studies of teacher concerns. In analyzing both her own studies and six others, she found that the responses by hundreds of teachers at various stages of experience showed different concerns.

0 ········➤········	0 ········➤········	0
Durable Category (Concrete)	Cross-Categorical (Abstract)	System/Trans-Systems (Complex)

figure **4.6 Adult Consciousness Continuum**

Source: Adapted from Stephen P. Gordon (1990). *Assisting the Entry-Year Teacher: A Leadership Resource.* Columbus, OH: Ohio Department of Education. Used with permission.

Teachers at the *self-adequacy* stage are focused on survival. They are concerned with doing well when a supervisor is present, getting favorable evaluations, and being accepted and respected by students and other teachers (Adams and Martray, 1981). Their primary concern is making it through the schoolday.

With survival and security assured, teachers think less of their own survival needs and begin to focus on *teaching tasks*. At this stage, teachers become more concerned with issues related to instructional and student discipline. They begin to think about altering or enriching the classroom schedule, the teaching materials, and their instructional methodology. Instructional concerns include the pressures of teaching, routinization and inflexibility of the teaching environment, student load, workload, and lack of academic freedom. Discipline concerns include class control, conflict between student and adult values and attitudes, and disruptive students (Adams and Martray, 1981). Concerns at this stage can be characterized as focused on the teaching environment and teaching responsibilities.

Superior teachers are at the highest stage of concern, referred to as the *teaching impact* stage. At this stage, teachers are most concerned with the impact on students' learning and students' well-being, even if it means departing from rules and norms. Academic concerns at this stage include diagnosing and meeting individual needs, sparking unmotivated students, and facilitating the intellectual and emotional development of students. The teacher with mature concerns also tends to be interested in the whole child, including interest in student health and nutrition, use of drugs by students, dropout prevention, and so on (Adams and Martray, 1981). The unfolding of teachers' concerns evolves on a continuum reflecting a shifting perspective, from "I" concerns to concerns for "my group" to concerns for "all students." Figure 4.7 represents the continuum of teacher concerns.

Integrating Stage Development Theories. Investigators of adult and teacher development postulate that the various developmental characteristics are related (Sullivan, McCullough, and Stager, 1970; Oja and Pine, 1984). These findings suggest that many teachers at a given level (low, moderate, or high) in one developmental characteristic may operate at the same general level in another developmental characteristic. The probable relationship of various developmental characteristics allows one to make tentative composite descriptions of teachers of generally low, moderate, and high levels of stage development. Figure 4.8 reviews the six adult/teacher development continuums.

0 ·······················➤······················· 0 ·······················➤······················· 0

Self-Adequacy | Teaching Tasks | Teaching Impact

figure **4.7** **Teacher Concerns Continuum**

Low Developmental Stages	Moderate Developmental Stages	High Developmental Stages
	COGNITIVE	
Concrete	Formal	Postformal
	CONCEPTUAL	
Low (Concrete)	Moderate (Moderately Abstract)	High (Highly Abstract)
	MORAL	
Preconventional	Conventional	Postconventional
	EGO	
Fearful	Conforming	Autonomous
	LEVELS OF CONSCIOUSNESS	
Durable Category (Concrete)	Cross-Categorical (Abstract)	System//Trans-Systems (Complex)
	TEACHER CONCERNS	
Self-Adequacy	Teaching Tasks	Teaching Impact

figure **4.8** **Teacher and Adult Stage Development**

Source: Adapted from Stephen P. Gordon (1990). *Assisting the Entry-Year Teacher: A Leadership Resource.* Columbus, OH: Ohio Department of Education. Used with permission.

The majority of teachers appear to be in relatively moderate to low stages of cognitive, conceptual, moral, and ego development—probably no different from the adult population at large (Wilkins, 1980; Oja and Pine, 1981; Rest, 1986). So what? What difference does it make that many teachers are not complex thinkers or autonomous? A teacher daily faces as many as 150 students of various backgrounds, abilities, and interests, some of whom succeed while others fail. Concrete, rigid thinking on the part of the teacher cannot possibly improve instruction. As Madeline Hunter (1986) noted, "Teaching ... is a relativistic situational profession where *there are no absolutes*" (italics in original).

Teacher improvement can only come from abstract, multi-informational thought that can generate new responses toward new situations. Glassberg's (1979) review of research on teachers' stage development as related to instructional improvement concluded that teachers at higher stages of development appear to be more effective in the classroom.

Research on effective instruction (Berman and McLaughlin, 1978; Rutter et al., 1979; Porter and Brophy, 1988; O'Keefe and Johnston, 1989; Glatthorn, 2000; Hargreaves and Moore, 2000; Tieso, 2001) indicates that effective instruction is based on adaptation of curriculum and materials to local settings and particular learning goals. In other words, effective teachers think about what they are currently doing, assess the results of their practice, explore with each other new possibilities for teaching students, and consider students' perspectives. Effective teaching has been misunderstood and misapplied as a set and sequence of certain teaching behaviors (review previous day's objectives, present objectives, explain, demonstrate, guided practice, check for understanding, etc.). This explanation of effectiveness is simply untrue. Rather, successful teachers are thoughtful teachers (Porter and Brophy, 1988; Ferraro, 2000; Elliott and Schiff, 2001).

Evidence of the relationship between high-stage attainment of teacher development and effective instructional practice can be found in several research studies. The works of Thies-Sprinthall and Sprinthall (1987), Phillips and Glickman (1991), Oja and Pine (1981), and Parker (1983) are particularly important because they suggest that teachers, when provided with a stimulating and supportive environment, can reach higher stages of development. Yet, other research indicates that most teachers do not reach those higher stages.

Life Cycle Development, Teachers' Life Cycles, and the Teaching Career

The next area of adult development to be discussed is research on age-linked life cycle development. These theorists too have sought to define sequential and normative patterns of development. The pioneering theorists in this tradition tended to look at very broad age periods and the patterns or issues for resolution associated with them (Erikson, 1950; Buhler, 1956), whereas later theorists have tended to posit a greater number of specific age periods (Gould, 1978; Levinson et al., 1978).

The study by Daniel Levinson and his colleagues (1978) of 40 men ranging in age from mid-30s to mid-40s is among the most frequently cited studies of life cycle development. This research described how individuals alternate through periods of stability and transition in a life structure whose critical components typically revolve around work and family. A number of subsequent studies of women have substantiated the model in part, but differences have been found in the timing and quality of transitions and the ages associated with transitional periods among women (Roberts and Newton, 1987; Levinson and Levinson, 1996). Some of the variability among women is related to whether they have followed a more traditionally female orientation to family versus a more typically masculine orientation to career during early adulthood (Lieblich, 1986; Roberts and Newton, 1987).

Occupational development of teachers appears to run counter to the needs of teachers as they progress through the adult life cycle. Works by Levinson (1978) and Neugarten (1977) point to early adulthood as a period of bravado, romance, and the pursuit of dreams. The young adult ages 20 to 35 is on an exciting search for status, comfort, and happiness in work, family, and friends. The middle years, ages 35 to 55, provide some disillusionment, reflection, and reordering of priorities according to a reassessment of one's capabilities and opportunities. In teaching, however, the young adulthood period, which should be one of romance, quickly becomes one of disillusionment.

Let's ask the next question: What happens when the natural inclination of the middle-age teacher to reflect and reorder his or her teaching priorities confronts the same six periods of 30 students that he or she has faced for the previous 20 years? One might expect a further despair of any impulse to change and improve. Finally, what about the older teacher who is perceived by many as an anomaly, a relic who has remained in teaching because of inability to advance into administration or supervision. The acquisition of 30 years of experience coincides with the natural time for consolidating achievements and identifying one's remaining career objectives. Instead, there is only the same job—the same job as that of the new teacher down the hall, who might be the age of the older teacher's grandchild. Where is the sense of responsibility, generativity, and accomplishment in seniority? Old and new teachers are treated the same, accorded the same status, and expected to conform to the same routines.

Teaching appears to be a topsy-turvy occupation, running against the natural adult life cycle. Those who continue to make lasting improvement and enhance their students' educational lives should have our utmost respect. If not fortunate enough to be in a school that responds to and supports phases of the adult life cycle, the effective teacher truly transcends the system and educates in spite of, not because of, the school.

Gehrke (1991) argues that we should more fully incorporate our understanding of adult development in developing programs for new teachers. This means both fostering the generative motivations of mature teachers and being sensitive to the fact that many young teachers are dealing with needs for intimacy. Levine (1987) argues that profitable activities that capitalize on young teachers' enthusiasm might include opportunities to work on new teaching methods, to develop curricula, and to initiate projects. The key is nurturing their need for innovation and adventure and helping them establish and cultivate close collegial relationships that meet their needs for intimacy.

Levine (1987) encourages placing midlife teachers in situations permitting "a combination of teaching and administrative responsibilities that expands an adult's authority and mobility without sacrificing his or her expertise with children" (p. 16). Work on decision-making committees and mentorship of younger colleagues can provide such an outlet. Krupp (1982) argues that lack of career centrality and on-the-job retirement can be countered by bringing the older teachers' interests into the school. For instance, older teachers' interests in computers, photography, and gardening can be brought into the curriculum or extracurricular programs for students.

Transition Events

A third approach to adult development focuses more explicitly on the kinds of events associated with life transitions. Some theorists resist accepting the study of what are variably called *life events, critical events,* or *marker events* as part of the rubric of adult development because such a focus does not attempt to describe a universal, orderly sequence of development. However, Fiske and Chiriboga (1990) note that more recent models of adult development emphasize the role of transition events in our lives.

Life events have been typologized in a variety of ways. One typology, offered by Willis and Baltes (1980), seems to relate directly to the salience of the event for the individual. Events can be positive or negative, anticipated or unanticipated. Although events associated with expected transitions in adult lives are often the impetus for adult growth (Aslanian and Brickell, 1981), it appears to be the unanticipated event, even if negative, that may provide the greatest opportunity for change and growth (Krupp, 1982; Fiske and Chiriboga, 1990).

Neugarten (1977) and Neugarten and Neugarten (1987) studied the timing of events such as childbearing, occupational advancement and peaking, children leaving home, retirement, personal illness, and death of a spouse or close friend. Many of these events are common to all or most adults; the time of their occurrence, according to Neugarten and Neugarten (1987), influences how the person responds and continues with life. For example, the Blum and Meyer (1981) study of the recovery of adult men from severe heart attacks highlighted the difference in timing of critical events. Young men were bitter and hostile toward their heart attack and couldn't wait to resume their previous lives. Middle-age men were reflective about the heart attack and seriously weighed whether they wanted to continue to live as they had before. They contemplated changes in family relations, job, and living environments. Older men were accepting and grateful that the heart attack had left them alive with the opportunity to finish some of their desired retirement plans. As one can see, the same event—a heart attack—resulted in quite different reactions, depending on the time and age of the adult.

Both personal transition events (e.g., marriage, birth of a child, divorce, death of a loved one) and professional transition events (e.g., entry into the profession, tenure, transferring schools, becoming a lead teacher or department chairperson) can have a significant impact on a teacher's career and teaching. Traditionally, personal and transitional events have been ignored and professional transitions have been given pro forma recognition by the school organization. Krupp (1987) suggests that staff development programs providing an environment of trust and collegiality, as well as adult transition support networks within schools, can be an important means of assisting teachers as they prepare for anticipated change events, such as retirement, or cope with unanticipated changes, such as the sudden dependency of a parent. The support networks and professional development recommended by Krupp to assist teachers have been largely nonexistent in schools.

One exception in recent years has been the emergence of beginning teacher assistance programs, including the assignment of support teams and mentors to novice teachers. Hopefully, beginners' assistance programs will become the foundation on which career-long support for personal and professional transitions becomes available. Beyond formal support programs, schools must become the type of collegial, caring, growth-oriented communities that sustain teachers in times of transition.

Role Development

One recent direction in work on adult development emphasizes adult social roles, generally examining how adult lives are characterized by interacting roles related to work or career, family life, and personal development. Juhasz (1989) developed a model of adult roles that incorporates each of three major roles: family, work, and self. These roles are depicted as intertwining, sometimes in synchrony, sometimes with different momentum and force. This model emphasizes the active involvement of adults who take roles and choose which roles they will place emphasis on at given points in their lives, with self-esteem as the driving force "directing energies toward roles that will best enhance feelings of worth" (p. 307).

School systems and supervisors traditionally have been concerned only with teachers' professional roles, ignoring their personal and family roles. The few efforts intended to address the relationship of the three domains have been criticized as being beyond the scope of supervision, an inappropriate use of school resources, and superfluous to the improvement of teaching and learning. Yet, the literature on adult role development tells us that we cannot compartmentalize the personal, family, and professional aspects of a teacher's life. Put succinctly, teachers' other adult roles have direct effects on their instruction. Supervision, however, largely fails to provide teachers with support to help them understand the interaction of their various adult roles, cope with role conflict and resulting stress, and develop the proper balance and synergy among alternative roles.

Beyond Universal Conceptions of Development: The Sociocultural Context of Adult Development

From the 1980s and through the present, a significant body of research emerged examining the impact of social structural variables (e.g., race, class, gender, disability, sexual orientation) on adult development (Clark and Caffarella, 1999), with greatest emphasis on the effects of gender and race/ethnicity. The intent of some researchers has been to develop more robust and inclusive theories, describing a broader range of people than earlier theories. In other cases, especially for researchers informed by the postmodern resistance to "grand" theories, there has been no such attempt at "umbrella" theories of adult development (Kilgore, 2001). The latter researchers have been interested in offering previously unavailable pictures of adult development for individuals from groups marginalized in the construction of knowledge about adult development, as well as in illustrating how structural variables like gender, race, and class intersect in the construction of our identities (Sheared, 1999; Tisdell, 2000; Graue, 2005).

The Role of Gender in Adult Development. Much of the literature examining the relationship of gender and adult development has looked specifically at women, in response to the initial claim that their lives and experiences were not accounted for in the early development of adult development theory. Emerging theory and research have taken two forms, in some cases extending or adapting earlier work based primarily on men and in other cases starting afresh with female or mixed gender samples.

In the first strand is the work of Gilligan (1982), challenging Kohlberg's model of moral development (Kohlberg and Turiel, 1971). Her work suggests men and women base their moral decisions on different criteria, with women using an ethic of caring and men an ethic of justice. Similarly, Josselson (1987) reexamines Erikson's stage theory of psychosocial development, postulating four potential outcomes of Erikson's identity stage for women. Primary among her findings is that maintaining a sense of connectedness and affiliation with others was crucial for women.

The second strand of research consists of studies based specifically on the lives of women. One of the most cited sources in this strand is *Women's Ways of Knowing,* by Belenky, Clinchy, Goldberger, and Tarule (1986). Resisting the notion of hierarchical stages, Belenky and colleagues point to the development of *voice* as central to women's development and delineated five positions or categories in the development of women's knowledge: silence, received knowledge, subjective knowledge, procedural knowledge, and constructed knowledge. The developmental ideal is the integration of all five categories. Also representing this strand of research is the work of Peck (1986), who theorizes that women's lives consist of three contiguous layers, including an outermost core of sociohistorical context; a flexible, bidirectional "sphere of influence" consisting of the sum of multiple relationships; and, finally, a center core of self-definition. These spheres are presumed to be constantly interacting as women move through their lives. Caffarella and Olson (1993) summarize the research on women's development in terms of four themes: the centrality of relationships, the importance and interplay of social roles, the dominance of role discontinuities and change as the norm for women, and the diversity of experience across age cohorts. Given the predominance of women in the teaching workforce, it seems important that supervisors become familiar with those models of adult development that reveal the distinctive developmental concerns women may bring.

The Role of Race and Ethnicity in Adult Development. Chavez and Guido-DiBrito (1999) provide an excellent overview of models of racial and ethnic identity, two prominent stands of work contributing to an understanding of the impact of race and ethnicity on adult learners. Cross (1971, 1995) develops one of the earliest of these models, focusing on the development of racial identity among African Americans. According to this model, Blacks move from a stage of limited awareness of race (a stage Chavez and Guido-DiBrito question) to later stages of embracing first an Afrocentric identity and finally a multicultural identity. Similarly, Parham (1989) focuses on how experiences with negative differential treatment by others become the trigger for formation of racial identity among Blacks. Chavez and Guido-DiBrito (1999), however, posit that immersion in one's own racial group acts as the primary trigger for such identity development. Similarly, they take issue with the focus on perceptions of other groups inherent in the most prominent model of White racial identity development, that of Helms (1993, 1995), who stresses interracial exposure as a powerful trigger for the development of a White racial identity that moves beyond a dominant group assumption of White superiority toward a nonracist frame. Chavez and Guido-DiBrito argue that Helms's model places inordinate emphasis on the intersection of racial perceptions of others and racial perception of self. They are more intrigued by models of ethnic identity development.

Phinney (1990), however, developed a model describing an ethnic identity process that can be applied to all groups. She emphasizes two issues faced by members of nondominant group members: (1) dealing with stereotyping and prejudicial treatment by the dominant group, and (2) resolving the clash between the value systems of their own ethnic culture and that of the dominant culture by negotiating a bicultural value system.

Several implications for adult learning can be drawn from these models. The models generally suggest that although most individuals from White ethnic groups typically experience learning that is grounded in their own cultural norms, they may struggle with or resist learning in less familiar multicultural environments. This has implications for efforts in the area of diversity training. However, those from nondominant cultural groups often must learn to be at least bicultural in their learning if they are to succeed in mainstream learning environments. For instance, Alfred (2001) points to the development of bicultural competence as a factor in the career development of successful (tenured) African American women faculty. She also points to the assistive role that White male mentors play in some cases. Similarly, teachers from nondominant groups are likely to find that they must learn to navigate two or more cultures successfully; their mentors must remain sensitive to the challenges this presents.

table 4.1 **Conceptual Models of Adult Development**

Universal, Orderly, Sequential		Interactive, Socially Contexted		
Hierarchical Stages	**Life Cycle Phases**	**Transition Events**	**Role Development**	**Sociocultural Variables**
Cognitive Piaget, Perry	*Goal Phases* Buhler	*Critical Events* Brim and Ryff	*Family, Work, and Self* Juhasz	*Spheres of Influence* Peck
Moral Gilligan, Kohlberg	*Critical Issues* Erikson	*Stressful Events* Fiske et al.	*Love, Work, and Learning* Merriam and Clark	*Women's Ways of Knowing* Belenky et al.
Conceptual Hunt	*Stability vs. Transition* Levinson	*On Time/Off Time* Neugarten		*Ethnic Identity Development* Phinney
Ego Loevinger				
Levels of Consciousness Kegan				
Concern Fuller				

Recent research on women's development and research on the place of race and ethnicity in identity development have challenged our thinking about the degree to which any single theory of adult development can adequately describe all adult lives. For those who seek to provide assistance to teachers, familiarity with this literature serves as a reminder of the tremendous degree of difference that exists among the adult learners who constitute the teaching force.

Review of Adult/Teacher Development Models

Table 4.1 presents a schematic review of the five conceptual frameworks for adult development. One thing all five approaches have in common is the supposition that adult lives are characterized by change and adaptation. For teachers, as with all adult learners, the one thing we can be certain of is that things will not remain the same; thus, individuals must learn to cope with changes as they arise. Supervision provides the opportunity for ascertaining the levels, stages, and issues of adult development in schools and assisting the teacher's professional development in the context of these realities.

MyEdLeadershipLab™

Go to Topic 8, Professional Development, in the MyEdLeadershipLab™ site at www.myedleadershiplab.com for *The Basic Guide to SuperVision and Instructional Leadership*, Third Edition, where you can:

- Find learning outcomes for Professional Development along with the national standards that connect to these outcomes.
- Complete Assignments and Activities that can help you more deeply understand the chapter content.
- Apply and practice your understanding of the core skills identified in the chapter with the Building Leadership Skills unit.
- Prepare yourself for professional certification with a Practice for Certification quiz.

REFERENCES

Adams, R. D., and Martray, C. 1981. *Teacher development: A study of factors related to teacher concerns for pre, beginning, and experienced teachers.* Paper presented at the annual meeting of the American Educational Research Association, Los Angeles, April.

Alfred, M. V. 2001. Expanding theories of career development: Adding the voices of African American women in the White academy. *Adult Education Quarterly, 51,* 108–127.

Ammon, P. 1984. Human development, teaching and teacher education. *Teacher Education Quarterly, 11*(4), 95–108.

Amstutz, D. 1999. Adult learning: Moving toward more inclusive theories and practices. In T. C. Guy (Ed.), *Providing culturally relevant adult education: A challenge for the twenty-first century* (*New Directions for Adult and Continuing Education,* no. 82). San Francisco: Jossey-Bass.

Arlin, P. K. 1975. Cognitive development in adulthood: A fifth stage. *Developmental Psychology, 11,* 602–606.

Aslanian, C. B., and Brickell, H. M. 1981. *Americans in transition.* New York: College Entrance Examination Board.

Beattie, M., Dobson, D., Thorton, G., and Hegge, L. 2007. Interacting narratives: Creating and recreating the self. *International Journal of Life-long Education, 26*(2), 119–141.

Belenky, M. F., Clinchy, B. M., Goldberger, N. R., and Tarule, J. M. 1986. *Women's ways of knowing: The development of self, voice, and mind.* New York: Basic Books.

Berman, P., and McLaughlin, M. W. 1978. *Federal programs supporting educational change, Vol. 8. Implementing and sustaining innovations.* Santa Monica, CA: Rand Corporation. (ERIC ED 159 289)

Blum, L. S., and Meyer, R. 1981. *Developmental implications of myocardial infarction for mid-life adults.* Paper presented at the annual meeting of the American Educational Research Association, Los Angeles, April.

Brookfield, S. 1986. *Understanding and facilitating adult learning.* San Francisco: Jossey-Bass.

Brown, J. S., Collins, A., and Duguid, P. 1989. Situated cognition and the culture of learning. *Educational Researcher, 18*(1), 32–42.

Buhler, C. 1956. *From childhood to maturity.* London: Routledge and Kegan Paul.

Caffarella, R. S., and Olson, S. K. 1993. Psychosocial development of women: A critical review of the literature. *Adult Education Quarterly, 43*(3), 125–151.

Calhoun, E. F. 1985. *Relationship of teachers' conceptual level to the utilization of supervisory services and to a description of the classroom instructional improvement.* Paper presented at the annual meeting of the American Educational Research Association, Chicago, April.

Chavez, A. F., and Guido-DiBrito, F. 1999. Racial and ethnic identity and development. In M. C. Clark and R. S. Caffarella (Eds.), *An update on adult development theory: New ways of thinking about the life course (New Directions for Adult and Continuing Education,* no. 84). San Francisco: Jossey-Bass.

Clark, M. C. 2001. Off the beaten path: Some creative approaches to adult learning. In S. Merriam (Ed.), *An update on adult learning (New Directions for Adult and Continuing Education,* no. 89) (pp. 83–91). San Francisco: Jossey-Bass.

Clark, M. C., and Caffarella, R. S. 1999. *An update on adult development theory: New ways of thinking about the life course (New Directions for Adult and Continuing Education,* no. 84). San Francisco: Jossey-Bass.

Cranton, P. 1994. *Understanding and promoting transformative learning.* San Francisco: Jossey-Bass.

Cross, W. E., 1995. The psychology of Nigrescence: Revising the Cross model. In J. G. Ponterott, J. M Casa, L. A. Suzuki, and C. M. Alexander (Eds.), *Handbook of multicultural counseling.* Thousand Oaks, CA: Sage.

Cross, W. E., Jr. 1971. Toward a psychology of Black liberation: The Negro-to-Black convergence experience. *Black World, 20*(9), 13–27.

Cummings, A. L., and Murray, H. G. 1989. Ego development and its relation to teacher education. *Teaching and Teacher Education, 5*(1), 21–32.

Dewey, J. 1938. *Experience and education.* New York: Collier.

Dominice, P. 2000. *Learning from our lives: Using educational biographies with adults.* San Francisco, CA: Jossey-Bass.

Drago-Severson, E. 2004. *Helping teachers learn: Principal leadership for adult growth and development.* Thousand Oaks, CA: Corwin Press.

Drago-Severson, E. 2007. Helping adults learn: Principals as professional development leaders. *Teachers College Record, 109*(1), 70–125.

Drago-Severson, E. 2008. Four practices that serve as pillars for adult learning. *Journal of Staff Development, 29*(4), 60–63.

Elliott, V., and Schiff, S. 2001. A look within. *Journal of Staff Development, 22*(2), 39–42.

Eneau, J. 2008. From autonomy to reciprocity, or vice versa? French personalism's contribution to a new perspective on self-directed learning. *Adult Education Quarterly, 59*(3), 229–248.

English, L. M. 2005. Historical and contemporary explorations of the social change and spiritual directions of adult education. Teachers College Record, 107 (6), 1169–1192.

Erickson, D. M. 2007. A developmental re-forming of the phases of meaning in transformational learning. *Adult Education Quarterly, 58*(1), 61–80.

Erikson, E. H. 1950. *Childhood and society.* New York: Norton.

Erikson, E. H. 1963. *Childhood and society* (2nd ed.). New York: Norton.

Ferraro, J. M. 2000. *Reflective practice and professional development.* Washington, DC: ERIC Clearinghouse on Teaching and Teacher Education. (ERIC ED 449 120)

Fiske, M., and Chiriboga, D. A. 1990. *Change and continuity in adult life.* San Francisco: Jossey-Bass.

Foucault, M. 1977. *Power/Knowledge.* New York: Pantheon Books.

Fuller, F. F. 1969. Concerns of teachers: A developmental conceptualization. *American Educational Research Journal,* 6(2), 207–266.

Gardner, H. 1983. *Frames of mind: The theory of multiple intelligences.* New York: Basic Books.

Gardner, H. 1999. *Intelligence reframed: Multiple intelligences for the 21st century.* New York: Basic Books.

Gehrke, N. J. 1991. Seeing our way to better helping of beginning teachers. *Educational Forum, 55*(3), 233–242.

Gilligan, C. 1979. Woman's place in man's life cycle. *Harvard Educational Review, 49*(4), 431–446.

Gilligan, C. 1982. *In a different voice.* Cambridge, MA: Harvard University Press.

Ginsburg, H., and Opper, S. 1979. *Piaget's theory of intellectual development* (2nd ed.). Englewood Cliffs, NJ: Prentice Hall.

Glassberg, S. 1979. *Developing models of teacher development.* (ERIC ED 171 685)

Glatthorn, A. A. 2000. *The principal as curriculum leader: Shaping what is taught and tested* (2nd ed.). Thousand Oaks, CA: Corwin Press.

Gonzales, A. H., and Nelson, L. M. 2005. Learner-centered instruction promotes student success. *T.H.E. Journal, 32*(6), 10, 12, 14–15.

Gould, R. L. 1978. *Transformations.* New York: Touchstone Books.

Graue, E. 2005. Theorizing and describing preservice teachers' images of families and schooling. *Teachers College Record, 107*(1), 157–185.

Grow, G. 1991. Teaching learners to be self-directed: A stage approach. *Adult Education Quarterly, 41*(3), 125–149.

Guy, T. G. 2005. Culturally relevant adult education. In L. M. English (Ed.), *International encyclopedia of adult education* (pp. 180–184). London: Palgrave Macmillan.

Habermas, J. 1992. *Moral consciousness and communicative action.* Cambridge: Polity.

Hansman, C. A. 2001. Context-based adult learning. In S. Merriam (Ed.), *The new update on adult learning theory (New Directions for Adult and Continuing Education, no. 89).* San Francisco: Jossey-Bass.

Hargreaves, A., and Moore, S. 2000. Curriculum integration and classroom relevance: A study of teachers' practice. *Journal of Curriculum and Supervision, 15*(2), 89–112.

Harvey, O. J., White, B. J., Prather M., Alter, R., and Hoffmeister, J. 1966. Teachers' belief systems and preschool atmospheres. *Journal of Educational Psychology, 57,* 373–381.

Hayes, E., and Flannery, D. D. 2000. *Women as learners: The significance of gender in adult learning.* San Francisco: Jossey-Bass.

Heck, E. J., and Davis, C. S. 1973. Differential expression of empathy in a counseling analog. *Journal of Counseling Psychology, 20,* 101–104.

Helms, J. E. 1993. Introduction: Review of racial identity terminology. In J. E. Helms (Ed.), *Black and White racial identity: Theory, research and practice.* Westport, CT: Praeger.

Helms, J. E. 1995. An update of Helms' White and people of color racial identity models. In J. G. Ponterott, J. M. Casas, L. A. Suzuki, and C. M. Alexander (Eds.), *Handbook of multicultural counseling.* Thousand Oaks, CA: Sage.

Hopkins, D. 1990. Integrating staff development and school improvement: A study of personality and school climate. In B. Joyce (Ed.), *ASCD Yearbook: Changing school culture through staff development.* Alexandria, VA: Association for Supervision and Curriculum Development.

Horn, J. L., and Cattell, R. B. 1967. Age differences in fluid and crystallized intelligence. *Acta Psychological, 26,* 107–129.

Hunt, D. E., Butler, L. F., Noy, J. E., and Rosser, M. E. 1978. *Assessing conceptual level by the paragraph completion method.* Toronto: Ontario Institute for Studies in Education.

Hunt, D. E., and Joyce, B. R. 1967. Teacher trainee personality and initial teaching style. *American Educational Research Journal, 4*(3), 253–255.

Hunter, M. 1986. To be or not to be—Hunterized. *Tennessee Educational Leadership, 12,* 70.

Ianinski, S. D., Wright, U., and Rocco, T. S. 2003. Critical race theory and adult education: Critique of the literature in *Adult Education Quarterly.* In D. Flowers, M. Lee, A. Jalipa, E. Lopez, A. Scelstate, and V. Sheared (Eds.), *Proceedings of the 44th Annual Adult Education Research Conference* (pp. 175–180). San Francisco: San Francisco State University.

Johnston, M. 1985. How elementary teachers understand the concept of "on-task": A developmental critique. *The Journal of Classroom Interaction, 21,* 15–24.

Josselson, R. 1987. *Finding herself: Pathways to identity development in women.* San Francisco: Jossey-Bass.

Juhasz, A. M. 1989. A role-based approach to adult development: The triple helix model. *International Journal of Aging and Human Development, 29*(4), 301–315.

Kegan, R. 1994. *In over our heads: The mental demands of modern life.* Cambridge, MA: Harvard University Press.

Kegan, R. 2000. What "form" transforms?: A constructive-developmental perspective on transformational learning. In J. Mezirow and Associates (Eds.), *Learning as transformation: Critical perspectives on a theory in progress.* San Francisco: Jossey-Bass.

Kerka, S. 1998. *New perspectives on mentoring.* ERIC Digest No. 194. (ERIC ED 418 249)

Kilgore, D. W. 2001. Critical and postmodern perspectives on adult learning. In S. B. Merriam (Ed.), *The new update on adult learning theory (New Directions for Adult and Continuing Education,* no. 89). San Francisco: Jossey-Bass.

Klauer, K. J., and Phye, G. D. 2008. Inductive reasoning: A training approach. *Review of Educational Research, 78*(1), 85–123.

Knowles, M. S. 1980. *The modern practice of adult education: From pedagogy to andragogy* (2nd ed.). Chicago: Association/Follett.

Knowles, M. S. 1984. *Andragogy in action: Applying modern principles of adult learning.* San Francisco: Jossey-Bass.

Kolb, D. A. 1984. Experiential learning. Englewood Cliffs, NJ: Prentice Hall.

Kohlberg, L., and Armon, C. 1984. Three types of stage models used in the study of adult development. In M. Commons, F. A. Richards, and C. A. Armon (Eds.), *Beyond formal operations: Late adolescent and adult cognitive development.* New York: Praeger.

Kohlberg, L., and Turiel, E. 1971. Moral development and moral education. In G. Lessor (Ed.), *Psychology and educational practice.* Chicago: Scott, Foresman.

Kramer, D. A. 1983. Post-formal operations? A need for further conceptualization. *Human Development, 26*(2), 91–105.

Kramer, D. A. 1987. *Improved learning in aging: Implications for education.* Paper presented at Information and Aging: Coalitions for the Future, New Brunswick, NJ, April. (ERIC ED 283 098)

Krupp, J. 1982. *The adult learner: A unique entity.* Manchester, CT: Adult Development and Learning.

Lave, J., and Wenger, E. 1991. *Situated learning: Legitimate peripheral participation.* New York: Cambridge University Press.

Lea, V., and Griggs, T. 2005. Behind the mask and beneath the story: Enabling students-teachers' to reflect critically on the socially-constructed nature of their "normal" practice. *Teacher Education Quarterly, 32*(1), 93–114.

Levine, S. L. 1987. Understanding life cycle issues: A resource for school leaders. *Journal of Education, 169*(1), 7–19.

Levine, S. L. 1989. *Promoting adult growth in schools.* Boston: Allyn and Bacon.

Levinson, D. J., Darrow, C. N., Klein, E. B., Levinson, M. H. and Mckee, B. 1978. *The seasons in a man's life.* New York: Knopf.

Levinson, D. J., and Levinson, J. D. 1996. *The seasons of a woman's life.* New York: Knopf.

Lieblich, A. 1986. Successful career women at midlife: Crises and transitions. *International Journal of Aging and Human Development, 23*(4), 301–312.

Lindeman, E. 1926. *The meaning of adult education.* New York: New Republic.

Loevinger, J. 1976. *Ego development.* San Francisco: Jossey-Bass.

Lyotard, J. F. 1984. *The postmodern condition: A report on knowledge.* Minneapolis: University of Minnesota Press.

Marsick, V. J., and Watkins, K. 1990. *Informal and incidental learning in the workplace.* New York: Routledge.

Marsick, V. J., and Watkins, K. E. 2001. Informal and incidental learning. In S. Merriam (Ed.), *The new update on adult learning theory (New Directions for Adult and Continuing Education,* no. 89). San Francisco: Jossey-Bass.

Mathis, C. 1987. Educational reform, the aging society and the teaching profession. *Journal of Education, 169*(1), 80–88.

Merriam, S. B. 2001. Something old, something new: Adult learning theory for the twenty-first century. In S. Merriam (Ed.), *The new update on adult learning theory (New Directions for Adult and Continuing Education,* no. 89) (pp. 93–96). San Francisco: Jossey-Bass.

Merriam, S. B. 2004. The role of cognitive development in Mezirow's transformational learning theory. *Adult Education Quarterly, 55*(1), 60–68.

Merriam, S., and Caffarella, R. 1999. *Learning in adulthood* (2nd ed.). San Francisco: Jossey-Bass.

Merriam, S., Caffarella, R., and Baumgartner, L. 2007. *Learning in adulthood: A comprehensive guide* (3rd ed.). San Francisco: Jossey-Bass.

Mezirow, J. D., and associates. 1991. Fostering critical reflection in adulthood. *A guide to transformative and emancipatory learning.* San Francisco: Jossey-Bass.

Mezirow, J. M. 2000. Learning to think like an adult: Core concepts of transformation theory. In J. M. Mezirow & Associates (Eds.), *Learning as transformation: Critical perspectives on a theory in progress.* San Francisco: Jossey-Bass.

Neugarten, B. L. 1977. Personality and aging. In J. E. Birren and K. W. Schaie (Eds.), *Handbook of the psychology of aging.* New York: Van Nostrand Reinhold.

Neugarten, B., and Neugarten, D. 1987. The changing meaning of age. *Psychology Today, 21*(5), 29–33.

Oja, S. N., and Pine, G. J. 1981. *Toward a theory of staff development.* Paper presented at the annual meeting of the American Educational Research Association, Los Angeles, April.

Oja, S. N., and Pine, G. J. 1984. *Collaborative action research: A two-year study of teachers' stages of development and school contexts.* Durham, NH: University of New Hampshire.

O'Keefe, P., and Johnston, M. 1989. Perspective taking and teacher effectiveness: A connecting thread through three developmental literatures. *Journal of Teacher Education, 40*(3), 20–26.

Parham, T. 1989. Cycles of psychological Nigrescence. *The Counseling Psychologist, 17*(2), 187–226.

Parkay, F. W. 1979. *Inner-city high school teachers: The relationship of personality traits and teaching style to environmental stress.* Paper presented to the Southwest Educational Research Association, Houston.

Parker, W. C. 1983. *The effect of guided reflection and role-taking on the interactive decision making of teachers.* Paper presented at the annual meeting of the American Educational Research Association, Montreal, April.

Peck, T. A. 1986. Woman's self-definition in adulthood: From a different model? *Psychology of Women Quarterly, 10*(3), 274–284.

Phillips, M. D., and Glickman, C. D. 1991. Peer coaching: Developmental approach to enhance teacher thinking. *Journal of Staff Development, 12*(2), 20–25.

Phinney, J. S. 1990. Ethnic identity in adolescents and adults: Review of the research. *Psychological Bulletin, 108,* 499–514.

Porter, A. C., and Brophy, J. 1988. Synthesis of research on good teaching: Insights from the work of the Institute for Research on Teaching. *Educational Leadership, 45*(7), 78–85.

Pratt, D. D. 1988. Andragogy as a relational construct. *Adult Education Quarterly, 38,* 160–181.

Rachal, J. R. 2002. Andragogy's detectives: A critique of the present and a proposal for the future. *Adult Education Quarterly, 52*(3), 210–227.

Reiman, A. J., and Parramore, B. 1994. The first year of teaching: Assignment, expectations, and development. In S. Odell and M. O'Hair (Eds.), *Diversity and teaching.* Orlando, FL: Harcourt Brace Jovanovich.

Reiman, A. J., and Thies-Sprinthall, L. 1998. *Mentoring and supervision for teacher development.* New York: Longman.

Rest, J. 1986. *Moral development: Advances in research and theory.* New York: Praeger.

Riegel, K. 1973. Dialectical operations: The final period of cognitive development. *Human Development, 16,* 346–370.

Roberts, P., and Newton, P. M. 1987. Levinsonian studies of women's adult development. *Psychology and Aging, 2,* 154–163.

Ross-Gordon, J., Brooks, A. K., Clunis, T., Parsells, R., and Parker, U. 2005. An analysis of work-related literature focusing on race and ethnicity. In R. J. Hill and R. Kiely (Eds.), *Proceedings of the 46th Annual Adult Education Research Conference* (pp. 375–380). Athens: University of Georgia.

Rossiter, M., and Clark, M. C. 2007. *Narrative and the practice of adult education.* Malabar, FL: Krieger.

Rutter, M., Maughan, B., Martimore, P., Ouston, J., and Smith, A. 1979. Fifteen thousand nouns. Secondary schools and their effects on children, Cambridge, MA: Harvard University Press.

Schön, D. A. 1983. *The reflective practitioner: How professionals think in action.* New York: Basic Books.

Sheared, V. 1999. Giving voice: Inclusion of African American students' polyrhythmic realities in adult basic education. In T. C. Guy (Ed.), *Providing culturally relevant adult education: A challenge for the twenty-first century* (*New Directions for Adult and Continuing Education,* no. 82). San Francisco: Jossey-Bass.

Sternberg, R. J. 1985. *Beyond IQ: A triarchic theory of human intelligence.* New York: Cambridge.

Sternberg, R. J. 1990. *Metaphors of mind: Conceptions of the nature of intelligence.* New York: Cambridge.

Sternberg, R. J. 2001. Why schools should teach for wisdom: The balance theory of wisdom in educational settings. *Educational Psychologies, 36*(4), 227–245.

Sullivan, E. V., McCullough, G., and Stager, M. A. 1970. Developmental study of the relationship between conceptual, ego, and moral development. *Child Development, 41,* 399–411.

Taranto, M. A. 1989. Facets of wisdom: A theoretical synthesis. *The International Journal of Aging and Human Development*, *29*(1), 1–21.

Taylor, E. 2007. An update on transformative learning theory: A critical review of the empirical research (1999–2005). *International Journal of Lifelong Education, 26*(2), 173–191.

Taylor, K. 2000. Teaching with developmental intention. In J. Mezirow and Associates (Eds.), *Learning as transformation: Critical perspectives on a theory in progress.* San Francisco: Jossey-Bass.

Taylor, K., and Marienau, C. 1995. Bridging practice and theory for women's adult development. In K. Taylor and C. Marienau (Eds.), *Learning environments for women's adult development: Building toward change* (*New Directions for Adult and Continuing Education,* no. 65). San Francisco: Jossey-Bass.

Tennant, M. 1986. An evaluation of Knowles' theory of adult learning. *International Journal of Lifelong Education, 5*(2), 113–122.

Thies-Sprinthall, L., and Sprinthall, N. A. 1987. Experienced teachers: Agents for revitalization and renewal as mentors and teacher educators. *Journal of Education, 169*(1), 65–79.

Thorndike, E. L., Bregman, E. O., Tilton, J. W., and Woodyard, E. 1928. *Adult learning.* New York: Macmillan.

Tieso, C. 2001. Curriculum: Broad brushstrokes or paint-by-the-numbers? *The Teacher Educator, 36*(3), 199–213.

Tilley, C. L., and Callison, D. 2007. New mentors for new media: Harnessing the instructional potential of cognitive apprenticeships. *Knowledge Quest, 35*(5), 26–31.

Tisdell, E. 2000. Feminist pedagogies. In E. Hayes and D. Flannery (Eds.), *Women as learners: The significance of gender in adult learning.* San Francisco: Jossey-Bass.

Tisdell, E. J. 2005. Feminism. In L. M. English (Ed.). *International encyclopedia of adult education* (pp. 254–257). London: Palgrave Macmillan.

Tolliver, D. E., and Tisdell, E. J. 2006. Engaging spirituality in the transformative higher education classroom. In E. Taylor (Ed.), *Teaching for change: Fostering transformational learning* (*New Directions for Adult and Continuing Education,* no. 109) (pp. 37–47). San Francisco: Jossey-Bass.

Tough, A. 1971. *The adult's learning projects: A fresh approach to theory and practice in adult learning.* Toronto: Ontario Institute for Studies in Education.

Usher, R., Bryant, I., and Johnston, R. 1997. *Adult education and the postmodern challenge.* London: Routledge.

Welton, M. R. 1995. The critical turn in adult education theory. In M. R. Welton (Ed.). *In defense of the lifeworld* (pp. 11–38). Albany: State University of New York Press.

Wilkins, R. A. 1980. If the moral reasoning of teachers is deficient, what hope for pupils. *Kappan, 61*(8), 548–549.

Willis, S. L., and Baltes, P. B. 1980. Intelligence in adulthood and aging: Contemporary issues. In L. W. Poon (Ed.), *Aging in the 1980s: Psychological issues.* Washington DC: American Psychological Association.

Wilson, A. L. 1993. The promise of situated cognition. In S. Merriam (Ed.), *An update on adult learning theory* (*New directions for adult and continuing education,* no. 57). San Francisco: Jossey-Bass.

Witherell, C. S., and Erickson, V. L. 1978. Teacher education as adult development. *Theory and Practice, 17,* 229–238.

chapter 5

Reflections on Schools, Teaching, and SuperVision

outline

- Effective and Good Schools: The Same?
- Instructional Improvement and Effective Teaching
- Beliefs about Education
- Supervisory Beliefs
- Supervisory Platform as Related to Educational Philosophy
- Checking Your Own Supervisory Beliefs
- What Does Your Belief Mean in Terms of Supervisor and Teacher Responsibility?

Visit the **MyEdLeadershipLab™** site for *The Basic Guide to SuperVision and Instructional Leadership*, Third Edition to enhance your understanding of chapter concepts. You'll have the opportunity to practice your skills through video and case based Assignments and Activities as well as Building Leadership Skills units, and prepare for your certification exam with Practice for Certification quizzes.

As we seek ways to improve school and classroom instruction, we must understand how present thinking, beliefs, and practices in the field of supervision interact with instruction and the assumptions about students and teachers as learners. This chapter shows how issues of school and teaching effectiveness must be resolved by human judgments about goals and purposes. Next, we look at how one's supervisory beliefs are related to a particular educational philosophy or platform. An instrument is then provided to help clarify each person's own supervisory belief, and we examine how one's own supervisory belief fits along a control continuum. Finally, some propositions about supervisory belief and consequences for teacher development are presented.

How do we reconcile the uncertainties of supervision, teaching, and instructional improvement? How do we know whether we are progressing in the desired direction? Unless we reflect on our own beliefs, there is little to steer us.

Sergiovanni and Starratt (1983) note the importance of understanding one's own supervisory beliefs:

> What is needed is some firm footing in principle. Some have called our often unexpressed constellation of principles a platform. Just as a political party is supposed to base its decisions and actions on a party platform upon which it seeks election, so, too, supervisory personnel need a platform upon which, and in the light of which, they can carry on their work. With a clearly defined platform, they can begin to take a position relative to educational practices, looking beyond the surface behavior to probe for the real consequences of a variety of school practices. (pp. 226–227)

Knowing oneself as a supervisor is necessary before considering alternative practices and procedures. To move from a platform, we must first know where we are standing. Let's look at the human decisions that a supervisor must make about school improvement, teaching effectiveness, and one's purpose in working with teachers.

Effective and Good Schools: The Same?

In discussing questions about supervision, teaching, and school improvement, there is no certainty about how to arrive at an answer. The issue of effective schools highlights the human values that drive school decisions and actions (Glickman, 1987).

Many of the clarion calls for school reform cite the findings from research on effective teaching and effective schools as examples of how schools and classrooms should change. The reformers tell us that the goal of all schools should be *effectiveness*—as measured by such factors as students' scores on high-stakes achievement tests. Furthermore, we should narrow the academic focus of the curriculum; test students more frequently; raise standards for promotion; and have teachers state specific and measurable objectives and follow a prescribed instructional approach that involves reviewing, explaining, demonstrating, guiding practice, checking for understanding, and summarizing. The findings of the recent research on effective teaching and effective schools are treated as scientific laws that apply to *all* teachers and *all* schools.

The findings of the research on effective teaching and effective schools are too often equated with what is desirable or good. By failing to distinguish between *effectiveness* and *goodness,* we avoid two central questions in education. The first question with which schools and school systems must deal is: What is good? Only after that question has been answered should we deal with the second question: How do we become effective? The current fascination with findings from the research on effectiveness has blinded schools and school systems to the more basic question of goodness.

Do higher test scores justify labeling a school "good" if the price for those higher scores has been an increase in the dropout rate? Are higher scores in reading and mathematics "good" if students gain them at the expense of time spent in studying science, social studies, art, or music? Is an average gain of eight points on reading test scores worth the increased allocation of time and resources to direct instruction in reading? Is that gain more desirable than maintaining current achievement levels in reading but devoting a greater proportion of class time to a whole-language approach that emphasizes creative writing or critical thinking?

The research on effective schools and effective teaching does not answer these questions for us. The research is neutral: It does not choose our goals but simply tells us how to accomplish certain things (which may or may not be among our goals). Educators who care about the fate of all children must define *goodness* before they worry about *effectiveness;* as supervisors, we must first clarify our own definitions.

Instructional Improvement and Effective Teaching

Let's continue this reflection on practice by taking an innocuous statement about supervision that virtually no one would take issue with: The goal of supervision is to improve instruction. It sounds nice, until we ask for a definition of what type of instruction we wish to improve. Effective teaching, to a large extent, depends on what you are trying to teach. Consider the following examples:

- If the goal is for students to master basic skills, then effective teaching might involve explanation, demonstration, practice, feedback, and more practice.
- If the goal is for students to learn classical culture, then effective teaching might consist of reading the great works, lecture, and Socratic discussion.
- If the goal is for students to become problem solvers, then effective teaching might call for exposing students to real-world problems and active student involvement in testing possible solutions and reaching resolutions.

- If the goal is social development, then effective teaching might consist of structuring cooperative learning and community building activities.
- If the goal is personal development, then effective teaching might mean facilitation of students' self-directed learning and self-assessment.
- If the goal is critical inquiry, then effective teaching might require the teacher to challenge students' current values and assumptions and to ask students to critique dominant belief systems, social structures, and power relationships.

In the final analysis, what constitutes instructional improvement and successful teaching can be defined only within the context of particular instructional goals, local learning environments, and individual students. This means that the search for a single instructional model—effective for all learning content, students, and situations—is futile.

A more productive course of action is to identify various instructional strategies that are effective in relation to identified instructional goals and individual students. If this proposition is accepted, the supervisor's role becomes one of assisting teachers to clarify school and classroom instructional goals, develop a variety of instructional strategies (direct instruction, constructivist teaching, cooperative learning, classroom dialogue, service learning, and so on), "mix and match" instructional strategies to learning goals and students, and assess the effects of instruction for the purpose of continuous improvement. With such a supervision emphasis, effective instruction is seen as the teacher's ability to use various ways of teaching according to a variety of learning goals and student learning styles.

To the mix of multiple learning goals and multiple instructional models, Ornstein (1990) adds the concept of *teaching style:*

> Teaching style is a truncated version of a personality and philosophical type. Everyone must develop his or her own style of teaching and feel comfortable in the classroom. In short, teachers must develop their own repertoire, relative to their own physical and mental characteristics and their students. Thus, there is no one ideal type but a multiple set of teacher types or styles. Teacher style is a matter of choice and comfort, and what works for one teacher with one set of students may not work for another. (p. 84)

Teaching style, of course, can change and broaden over time, allowing for the expansion of a teacher's repertoire of instructional strategies. However, attempting to force a teacher to immediately adopt strategies that strongly conflict with his or her current teaching style is inconsistent with both the principles of adult learning and the concept of the teacher as a professional. It is better initially to invite teachers to learn and try out new strategies that are consistent with their current style and then facilitate teachers' continued development of teaching style and repertoire over time.

Instructional improvement can be defined as helping teachers acquire teaching strategies consistent with their instructional goals and compatible with their general teaching styles that increase the capabilities of students to make wise decisions in varying contexts (with regard to peers, adults, academics, and life). Effective teaching consists therefore of those teaching decisions about actions, routines, and techniques that increase the decision-making capabilities of students.

Beliefs about Education

We discussed earlier in this chapter how the definition of effective instruction depends on school and teacher instructional goals. Instructional goals, in turn, are ultimately based on beliefs concerning such things as the purpose of education, what should be taught, the nature of the learner, and the learning process. Whether or not they are conscious of it, teachers' and supervisors' educational philosophies have a significant impact on instruction and instructional improvement efforts. The following are summaries of educational platforms of three teachers with different beliefs about education:

> Joan Simpson believes that the purpose of education should be to transmit a prescribed body of basic knowledge, skills, and cultural values to students. To do this effectively, the teacher must exercise control over the classroom, lesson content, and students. Content should be broken first into discrete academic areas and then into small elements, and learning should take place in a series of small, sequential steps. All students should be expected to master the same content. Grades and other types of external motivation are necessary to assure student learning.
>
> Bill Washington believes that the purpose of education should be student growth, especially in inquiry and problem-solving skills. To promote such growth, the teacher conveys existing knowledge, but also encourages students to experiment in order to test old ideas and find solutions to new problems. Bill believes that because inquiry is most successful in a democratic environment, the teacher should share control of the learning environment with students. Because problem solving often takes place within a social context, students should learn social skills as well as academic content.
>
> Pat Rogers believes that each child is unique and that the primary purpose of education should be to meet students' individual needs. The teacher should foster the development of each student toward his or her fullest potential. This means addressing students as whole persons by fostering their physical, emotional, cognitive, moral, and social development. Such holistic education includes facilitating student self-inquiry. Pat believes that students should have as much control over their own learning environment as their maturity level permits. Teachers should base lessons on students' experience, concerns, and interests. Students should be allowed to participate in assessing their own learning.

The three educational platforms just described do indeed represent contrasting beliefs. Based on their educational beliefs, Joan Simpson, Bill Washington, and Pat Rogers, no doubt, have quite different definitions of instructional improvement and effective teaching! You may view one of these educational platforms as quite similar to your own, you may agree with parts of each, or you may have an entirely different set of beliefs. In any case, it is important for you to clarify your own educational beliefs. By reflecting on the following questions, you can begin to build your educational platform:

1. What should be the purpose of education?
2. What should be the content of the school curriculum?
3. Who should control the learning environment?
4. What should be the relationship of teacher and students?
5. Under what conditions is student learning most successful?
6. What motivates students to do their best in school?
7. What is your definition of *effective teaching?*
8. What personal characteristics are possessed by a successful teacher?
9. How should the teacher assess student learning?
10. What is your definition of a *good school?*

Supervisory Beliefs

Most supervisors, of course, are former teachers. As a result, their views about learning, the nature of the learner, knowledge, and the role of the teacher in the classroom influence their view of supervision. After all, supervision is in many respects analogous to teaching. Teachers wish to improve students' behavior, achievement, and attitudes. Supervisors similarly wish to improve teachers' behavior, achievement, and attitudes.

The supervisory platforms of three supervisors are described next. As you read these platforms, note the relationship between the beliefs they contain and the teacher beliefs present in the three educational platforms discussed earlier in this chapter.

> Bob Reynolds believes that the purpose of supervision is to monitor teachers to determine if their instruction includes the elements of effective instruction. If those elements are observed, the supervisor should provide positive reinforcement to assure that they continue to be included in the teacher's lessons. Bob believes that if a teacher is not using or is incorrectly using the elements of effective instruction, the supervisor has a responsibility to provide remedial assistance by explaining and demonstrating correct instructional behaviors, setting standards of improvement, and monitoring and reinforcing the teacher's improvement efforts. In short, the supervisor

should have primary responsibility for instructional improvement decisions.

Jan White believes that the purpose of supervision is to engage teachers in mutual inquiry aimed at the improvement of instruction. The supervisor and teacher should share perceptions of instructional problems, exchange suggestions for solving those problems, and negotiate an improvement plan. The improvement plan becomes a hypothesis to be tested by the teacher with the supervisor's assistance. Thus, Jan believes that supervisors and teachers should share the responsibility for instructional improvement.

Shawn Moore believes that the purpose of supervision should be to foster teacher reflection and autonomy and to facilitate teacher-driven instructional improvement. The supervisor should be concerned with the teacher's self-concept and personal development as well as the teacher's instructional performance. It is critical for the supervisor to establish a relationship with the teacher characterized by openness, trust, and acceptance. Shawn believes that the supervisor should allow the teacher to identify instructional problems, improvement plans, and criteria for success. The supervisor can assist the teacher's self-directed improvement through active listening, clarifying, encouraging, and reflecting. Thus, the teacher should have primary responsibility for instructional improvement decisions, with the supervisor serving as an active facilitator.

These descriptions show that supervisory platforms can be as varied as educational platforms. When we compare the educational platforms of Joan Simpson, Bill Washington, and Pat Rogers with the supervisory platforms of Bob Reynolds, Jan White, and Shawn Moore, we can see that both types of platforms reveal basic beliefs about knowledge, human nature, and control.

By answering the following questions, you can begin the process of clarifying your own beliefs about instructional supervision. We suggest that you write responses to the questions, save your responses, and reassess your supervisory platform after you have finished reading this text.

1. What is your definition of *instructional supervision*?
2. What should be the ultimate purpose of supervision?
3. Who should supervise? Who should be supervised?
4. What knowledge, skills, attitudes, and values are possessed by successful supervisors?
5. What are the most important needs of teachers?
6. What makes for positive relationships between supervisors and teachers?
7. What types of activities should be part of instructional supervision?
8. What should be changed regarding the current practice of instructional supervision?

Supervisory Platform as Related to Educational Philosophy

Many educators view discussions of educational philosophy as overly abstract and irrelevant to the real world of supervisors and teachers. Yet, a supervisor's actions in working with teachers are based on supervisory beliefs, which in turn reflect a broader educational philosophy. There are many different philosophies. Some, such as idealism and realism, date back to ancient times. Others, such as pragmatism and behaviorism, have been developed within the past century. Even more recent has been the emergence of progressivism, reconstructionism, and existentialism. Philosophies are numerous and overlapping, and many have historical roots in each other.

To unravel the major philosophical trends in education, one must decipher how philosophies differ from each other and then build overriding conceptual categories. Each conceptual category or superphilosophy is created by grouping various philosophies that have central agreement on the type and scope of education. In other words, there may be disagreement on the specific nature of knowledge, truth, and reality, yet they hang together as a general educational philosophy because they are in agreement on the purpose and treatment of education.*

With educational application in mind, divergent philosophies can be simplified and classified. Three major educational superphilosophies have direct relevance to supervision: essentialism, progressivism, and existentialism (Johnson, Collins, Dupuis, and Johansen, 1973). However, we prefer the more general term *experimentalism,* as described by Morris (1961), to *progressivism.*

Essentialism

Essentialism as a philosophy is derived from idealism and realism. *Idealism,* which dates back to Plato, espouses a belief in absolutes: The world we live in is merely a reflection of reality. Reality, truth, and standards of morality exist beyond our common ways of knowing. Only by training the mind do we glimpse the ultimates. Yet training the mind is not sufficient in itself; it only brings the mind nearer to grasping reality. Divine revelation, insight, and faith are the necessary elements for ultimate knowledge of what exists. Therefore, idealism emphasizes truth and reality existing outside of people. It is absolute and unchanging.

Realism, developed at the onset of the Industrial Age, places a similar emphasis on truth and reality being outside of people. Instead of humankind and the outer environment being separated from each other, realism maintains that humanity is part and parcel of that environment. The world is a preordained, mechanistic reality. All of existence operates according to scientific, cause-and-effect relations. It is as if

*The descriptions of philosophy are taken from C. D. Glickman and J. P. Esposito, *Leadership Guide for Elementary School Improvement: Procedures for Assessment and Change* (Boston: Allyn & Bacon, 1979), p. 20.

existence is a clock that always runs according to mechanical principles governing levers, gauges, and gears. Humans have no existence apart from this clock; they are a part of the predetermined machine. Knowledge is learning how the machine works; truths are the scientific laws of regulation. Nothing exists outside the principles of nature. The purpose of education is to condition the mind to think in a natural and logical way. The mind should be trained to become consciously aware of the predetermined nature of the world.

Essentialism, created by William L. Bagley in 1938, encompassed the educational philosophies of idealism and realism. He took the ideas of knowledge being eternal and outside of humankind (idealism—absolutes; realism—natural laws) to form pedagogy. Essentialists emphasize that there is a body of timeless knowledge, both historical and contemporary, that is of value to the living.

Essentialism in terms of supervision emphasizes the supervisor as the person who teaches truths about teaching to teachers. Supervisors are those most knowledgeable about those absolute standards. Teachers are then handled mechanistically to systematize and feed content to students. As teachers digest these teaching truths, they move closer to being good teachers.

Experimentalism

As Western society became more industrialized, optimism and confidence in human ability to control nature emerged. The philosophy of *pragmatism,* developed by Charles S. Peirce and William James, emphasized what people can do to nature rather than what nature does to humankind. John Dewey, circa 1920, further expanded on the writings of James by putting the individual squarely in the context of society. Humans can both reform and be reformed by society. Dewey's philosophy is, of course, the well-known school of progressive thought. *Reconstructionism* is a further offshoot of both pragmatism and progressivism. Richard Pratte (1971) cites the pamphlet *Dare the School Build a New Social Order?,* written by George S. Counts in 1932, as a guiding document for the then-radical notion that schools and students were the reformers of society.

Experimentalism emerges from the philosophies of pragmatism, progressivism, and reconstructionism. They hold in common a historical break from the more traditional philosophies of realism and idealism. The essentialist idea that knowledge, truth, and morality exist as absolute and outside humans was rejected. The emerging faith in the scientific method, the ability of humans to create their own laws, principles, and machines, and the fact that such humanmade inventions would work for them demanded an accompanying philosophy. Experimentalism provided that philosophy.

Reality was what worked. If a person could form a hypothesis, test it, and find it to work, then it was regarded as tentatively true. On repeated experimentation with the same results, it became real. Yet experimentalists would never claim an absolute truth. The human environment was believed to be constantly changing, so that what one can do and prove today may not be probable tomorrow. A new situation and a different approach may alter yesterday's reality. Experimentalists point to the historical evidence of Newton's law of gravity as a past truth that has given way to Einstein's theory of relativity; they believe that in time, a new theory will replace Einstein's. The use of trial and error in a laboratory setting is the key to evaluating the outcome of action. Therefore, experimentalists do not view knowledge as absolute or external to human capabilities. Rather, knowledge is a result of the interaction between the scientific person and the environment.

The educational application of experimentalist thinking to supervision is well documented in Dewey's writings. Supervisors view schools as laboratories for working with teachers to test old hypotheses and to try new ones. Supervisors work democratically with teachers to achieve collective ends that will help everyone. Supervisors are not solely conveyors of age-old wisdom; they are both the conveyors of the rudimentary knowledge of the time and the guiders of trial-and-error, exploratory learning.

Existentialism

Existentialism as a school of thought is derived from the rejection of the other philosophies encompassed in essentialism and experimentalism. As such, it is a large category for many diverse philosophers. They have in common a scorn for rational, empirical, and systematic thinking as the way of knowing reality. As previously mentioned, the essentialists believe in rational thinking to help elevate the mind to uncover the absolutes of the universe. Experimentalists believe in rational, scientific thinking to explore and frame the relevant knowledge of the times. However, the existentialists believe that this same rational thinking restricts humans from discovering existence and therefore keeps them ignorant.

This philosophy has roots in the writings of Sören Kierkegaard in the mid-nineteenth century. It has been popularized in drama and literature by such proponents as Albert Camus and Jean-Paul Sartre. The basic tenet of the philosophy is that the individual is the source of all reality. All that exists in the world is the meaning the individual puts on his or her own experiences. There is no absolute knowledge, no mechanical working of the universe, and no preordained logic. To believe in such inventions is merely the narrow, incorrect way humans interpret their own experiences.

Beyond the individual there is only chaos. The only reality that exists is one's own existence. Only by looking within oneself can one discern the truth of the outside disorder. Humanity is paramount. Human dignity and worth are of greatest importance; they are the source and dispenser of all truth. With this realization, one acquires a profound respect for all human beings and their uniqueness. Human relations become very important, affirming individual worth and protecting the individual's right to discover his or her own truth. Humans are totally free, not shaped by others or restricted by the flux of the times. They hold within themselves the capacity to form their own destiny.

This philosophy of education, applied to supervision, means a full commitment to individual teacher choice. The supervisor provides an environment that enables the

table **5.1** **Comparing Three Superphilosophies**

	Essentialism	Experimentalism	Existentialism
View of Reality (knowledge, truth, morality)	Exists outside humans, absolute, unchanging	Reality is what works; it is tentative, constantly changing	Individual is source of all reality; individual defines reality
How to Learn about Reality	Train the mind to think rationally	Interact with environment; experiment	Engage in self-discovery; create meaning
Application to Supervision	Supervisor is expert; mechanistically transmits instructional knowledge to teacher	Supervisor works democratically with teachers to test old hypotheses and try new ones	Supervisor facilitates teacher exploration and autonomous decision making

teacher to explore his or her own physical and mental capabilities. Teachers must learn for themselves. The supervisor does not dispense information and shies away from intrusively guiding a teacher. Supervisors help when needed, protect the rights of others to self-discovery, and encounter the teacher as a person of full importance. Table 5.1 compares the three superphilosophies.

Checking Your Own Supervisory Beliefs

Let's step back and watch ourselves at work. First, we consider how we act with individual teachers, and then with groups. Read Box 5.1, the Supervisory Interpersonal Behaviors Questionnaire for Working with Individuals, and select the approach you most often take.

Next, take a look at the interpersonal behaviors you typically use when meeting with groups of teachers (Box 5.2). Please respond to the Supervisory Interpersonal Behaviors Questionnaire for Working with Groups.

The supervisory approaches in the Supervisory Interpersonal Behaviors Questionnaires correspond to the philosophies of essentialism, experimentalism, and existentialism and are labeled *directive* supervision, *collaborative* supervision, and *nondirective* supervision. Glickman and Tamashiro (1980, p. 76) wrote:

> Directive Supervision is an approach based on the belief that teaching consists of technical skills with known standards and competencies for all teachers to be effective. The supervisor's role is to inform, direct, model, and assess those competencies.
>
> Collaborative Supervision is based on the belief that teaching is primarily problem solving, whereby two or more persons jointly pose hypotheses to a problem, experiment, and implement those teaching strategies that appear to be most relevant

box 5.1

Supervisory Interpersonal Behaviors Questionnaire for Working with Individuals: A Scenario

The schoolday has just ended for students at Whichway School. Just as the teacher sits down at the desk, you (the supervisor) appear at the door and the teacher invites you in. "How is everything going?" you ask. Looking at the large stack of papers to correct, the teacher predicts a number of them will reflect that the students did not understand the work. "It's very frustrating working with this class. They have such a wide range of ability!" Then the teacher mentions another source of frustration: "Some of the students are discipline problems and their behavior results in class disruption."

After further discussion, the teacher and you agree that you will come into the classroom to observe what is going on, followed by a conference to discuss the classroom visit.

A few days later, after you have observed in the classroom and carefully analyzed the collected information, you begin to plan for the conference. You consider a number of approaches to use in the conference to help the teacher.

Approach A. Present what you saw in the classroom and ask for the teacher's perceptions. Listen to each other's responses. After clarifying the problem, each of you can propose ideas. Finally, you agree on what is to be done in the classroom. You mutually identify an objective and agree to an action plan that both of you work together to carry out. The plan is for both of you to make.

Approach B. Listen to the teacher discuss what is going on in the classroom. If asked, you offer your perceptions regarding what you observed. Encourage the teacher to analyze the problem further, and ask questions to make sure the teacher is clear about his or her view of the problem. If the teacher requests your views on how to proceed, respond, but only if asked. Finally, ask the teacher to determine and detail the actions he or she will take and find out if you might be of further help. The plan is the teacher's to make.

Approach C. Share your observations with the teacher and tell the teacher what you believe to be the major focus for improvement. Ask the teacher for input into your observations and interpretations. Based on your own experience and knowledge, carefully delineate what you believe are alternative actions to improve the classroom and ask the teacher to consider and select from the options. The plan to follow is chosen by the teacher from the supervisor's suggestions.

Approach D. Present your beliefs about the situation and ask the teacher to confirm or revise the interpretation. After identifying the problem, offer directions to the teacher on what should be done and how to proceed. You can go into the classroom to demonstrate what you are telling the teacher to do, or tell the teacher to observe another teacher who does well in this particular area. Praise and reward the teacher for following the given assignment.

Response. Most often, I use Approach ________.

Interpretation.

Approach A: A cluster of *collaborative behaviors* in which the supervisor and teacher share the decision making about future improvement.

Approach B: A cluster of *nondirective behaviors* in which the supervisor helps the teacher formulate his or her own decisions about future improvement.

Approach C: A cluster of *directive informational behaviors* in which the supervisor frames the teacher's choices about future improvement.

Approach D: A cluster of *directive control behaviors* in which the supervisor makes the decision for the teacher.

Source: Adapted from an instrument developed by Katherine C. Ginkel (1983). "An Overview of a Study Which Examined the Relationship between Elementary School Teachers' Preference for Supervisory Conferencing Approach and Conceptual Level of Development," a paper presented at the annual meeting of the American Educational Research Association, Montreal, April. Used with permission of Katherine C. Ginkel.

box 5.2

Supervisory Interpersonal Behaviors Questionnaire for Working with Groups: A Scenario

You (the supervisor) have just called on the science teachers to decide on a policy for allowing students to use laboratory equipment outside of regular class time. Many students have complained about not having enough class time for doing their experiments. The issue is how and when to free up more laboratory time (before school, at lunchtime, during study hall, after school) for students under the supervision of certified teachers. How would you work with the science teachers to make a decision?

Approach A. Meet with the staff and explain that they must decide what to do about this issue. Present the information you have about the problem and ask for clarification. Paraphrase what they say and, once the teachers verify your summary, ask them to decide among themselves what they are going to do. Remain in the meeting, helping to move the discussion along by calling on people, asking questions, and paraphrasing, but do not become involved in making your own position known or influencing the outcome in any conscious way.

Approach B. Meet with the staff by first explaining that you have to make a decision that will meet the needs of students, teachers, and supervisor. Either by consensus or, if not, then by majority vote, make a decision. You should listen, encourage, clarify, and reflect on each staff member's perception. Afterward, ask each member, including yourself, to suggest possible solutions. Discuss each solution; prioritize the list; and, if no consensus emerges, call for a vote. Argue for your own solution, but go along with the group's decision.

Approach C. Meet with the staff and explain to them that there are several permissible actions that you have thought about that could remedy this situation. You would like them to discuss and agree on which of these actions or combinations of actions they would like to implement. Lay out the alternatives, explain the advantages and disadvantages of each, and then allow the group to discuss and decide among your alternatives.

Approach D. Meet with the staff and tell them you want their feedback before you make a decision about the issue. Make it clear that the staff's involvement is to be advisory. Ask for their suggestions, listen, encourage, clarify, and paraphrase their ideas. After everyone has had a chance to speak, decide what changes should be made. Tell them what you are going to do, when the changes will be made, and that you expect them to carry out the plan.

Response. Most often, I would use Approach ________.

Interpretation.

Approach A: A cluster of *nondirective behaviors* in which the supervisor assists the group to make its own decision.

Approach B: A cluster of *collaborative behaviors* in which the supervisor works as part of the group in making a group decision.

Approach C: A cluster of *directive informational behaviors* in which the supervisor works as the framer of choices among which the group is to decide.

Approach D: A cluster of *directive control behaviors* in which the supervisor makes the decision for the group.

Source: Adapted from an instrument developed by Katherine C. Ginkel (1983). "An Overview of a Study Which Examined the Relationship between Elementary School Teachers' Preference for Supervisory Conferencing Approach and Conceptual Level of Development," a paper presented at the annual meeting of the American Educational Research Association, Montreal, April. Used with permission of Katherine C. Ginkel.

in their own surroundings. The supervisor's role is to guide the problem-solving process, be an active member of the interaction, and keep the teachers focused on their common problems.

Non-Directive Supervision has as its premise that learning is primarily a private experience in which individuals must come up with their own solutions to improving the classroom experience for students. The supervisor's role is to listen, be nonjudgmental, and provide self-awareness and clarification experiences for teachers.

What Does Your Belief Mean in Terms of Supervisor and Teacher Responsibility?

Beliefs about supervision and educational philosophy can be thought of in terms of decision-making responsibility (Table 5.2). An essentialist philosophy is premised on the supervisor being the expert on instruction and therefore having major decision-making responsibility. A situation of high supervisor responsibility and low teacher responsibility is labeled *directive supervision.* An experimentalist philosophy is premised on the supervisor and teachers being equal partners in instructional improvement; equal supervisor and teacher responsibility is labeled *collaborative supervision.* Existentialist philosophy is premised on teachers discovering their own capacities for instructional improvement. Low supervisor responsibility and high teacher responsibility is labeled *nondirective supervision.*

As we clarify our own educational philosophy and supervisory beliefs, we rarely find a pure ideological position. Therefore, Sergiovanni and Starratt's (1983) idea of a supervisory platform becomes helpful. What combination of various philosophies and beliefs do we consider important? Perhaps our beliefs are mainly essentialist and directive yet contain parts of experimentalism and collaboration; or perhaps we have another combination of beliefs. A particular platform is not right or wrong; rather, it is an assessment of the bits and pieces we use to create the floor we stand on.

Where You Stand Depends on Where You Sit: Effects of Culture on Beliefs

A person's cultural background is an important aspect of what he or she believes about education. There is a natural tendency for members of the dominant culture

table 5.2 Relationship of Philosophy, Control, and Supervisory Belief

Educational Philosophy	Decision-Making Responsibility	Supervisory Belief
Essentialism	Supervisor high, teacher low	Directive
Experimentalism	Supervisor equal, teacher equal	Collaborative
Existentialism	Supervisor low, teacher high	Nondirective

to support curriculum and instruction that transmit that culture to students. Students from minority cultures, however, may find it difficult to adapt to curriculum and instruction intended to convey the dominant culture and may resist (sometimes passively, sometimes actively) the transmission of that culture. This is not just a question of an unfortunate mismatch between dominant and minority cultures that eventually will be overcome as minority cultures are assimilated. Schools that marginalize the cultures of particular students marginalize those students as well. What is especially insidious about such marginalization is that educators may not realize they are partly responsible for its occurrence.

Educators' beliefs about education often are influenced by cultural assumptions they may not be aware of because the assumptions are so deeply ingrained and taken for granted. These assumptions can influence the curriculum that educators design, their relationships with students and parents, the lessons they plan, and so forth. Because of the influences of our cultural assumptions and beliefs on students, it is not sufficient for us simply to articulate our beliefs and then base educational goals and practices on those beliefs. Rather, we should attempt to identify and examine our cultural assumptions critically. Such critique, often done in dialogue with others, can cause us to change assumptions that have negative effects on colleagues and students.

Identifying and critiquing cultural assumptions is not easy for individuals and schools to do. It usually is necessary to begin with an examination of our actions, cultural artifacts, and espoused beliefs and then to begin to search below the surface of those actions, artifacts, and beliefs for underlying assumptions. At the individual level, this might mean reflecting on questions such as the following:

- Do I have more difficulty working with some cultural groups than others? If so, why?
- How congruent are my espoused beliefs and actions when working with cultural groups different from my own?
- How does my cultural background influence my expectations of and interactions with parents?
- How does my cultural background contribute to my perceptions of effective teaching?
- How does my cultural background affect my expectations of students in general? How does it affect my expectations of different student groups?

These questions provide entry points for critical reflection that can expand our understanding of cultural assumptions. Questions such as the following can assist groups in their critical examination of cultural effects on the school as an organization:

- How does the dominant culture inform our goals as a school? How do other cultures contribute to our goals?
- How is the dominant culture represented in our curriculum, including textbooks and curriculum materials? Are other cultures reflected positively in our curriculum?

- How do our cultural beliefs affect the way students are grouped and placed in various programs in our school?
- How do our cultural beliefs affect the school's disciplinary practices?
- How do our cultural beliefs affect the way we assess student learning?
- How do our cultural beliefs affect the way we interact with our students' families?

Another catalyst for changing beliefs is a better understanding of cultures different from our own. This can be done by reading literature about other cultures and about multicultural education, talking with students and colleagues from other cultures, interacting with parents and community members from different cultures in various community settings, and sharing educational and leadership roles within the school with representatives of various cultures. Better understanding of cultures, especially when achieved through interaction with those cultures, can overcome personal bias, change educational beliefs, and ultimately inform a different and more diverse educational practice.

MyEdLeadershipLab™

Go to Topic 3, Types of Supervision, in the MyEdLeadershipLab™ site at www.myedleadershiplab.com for *The Basic Guide to SuperVision and Instructional Leadership*, Third Edition, where you can:

- Find learning outcomes for Types of Supervision along with the national standards that connect to these outcomes.
- Complete Assignments and Activities that can help you more deeply understand the chapter content.
- Apply and practice your understanding of the core skills identified in the chapter with the Building Leadership Skills unit.
- Prepare yourself for professional certification with a Practice for Certification quiz.

REFERENCES

Glickman, C. D. 1987. Good and/or effective schools: What do we want? *Kappan, 68*(8), 622–624.

Glickman, C. D., and Tamashiro, R. T. 1980. Determining one's beliefs regarding teacher supervision. *Bulletin, 64*(440), 74–81.

Johnson, J. A., Collins, H. W., Dupuis, V. L., and Johansen, J. H. 1973. *Foundations of American education.* Boston: Allyn and Bacon.

Morris, V. C. 1961. *Philosophy and the American school.* Boston: Houghton Mifflin.

Ornstein, A. C. 1990. A look at teacher effectiveness research: Theory and practice. *NASSP Bulletin, 74*(528), 78–88.

Pratte, R. 1971. *Contemporary Theories of Education.* Scantron: Intext Educational Publishers, College Division

Sergiovanni, T. J., and Starratt, R. J. 1983. *Supervision: Human perspectives* (3rd ed.) (pp. 226–227). New York: McGraw-Hill.

part 3

Interpersonal Skills

The organization of this book is outlined in Figure 1.1 in Chapter 1. The prerequisites for supervision as a developmental function are knowledge, interpersonal skills, and technical skills. Part 2 examines the critical knowledge base. Part 3 describes interpersonal skills. Chapter 6 introduces the supervisory behavior continuum, Chapter 7 details the use of directive control behaviors, Chapter 8 details the use of directive informational behaviors, Chapter 9 details the use of collaborative behaviors, Chapter 10 details the use of nondirective behaviors, and Chapter 11 discusses in detail the theory and practice of developmental supervision.

Knowledge of what needs to be done for teacher growth and school success is the base of a triangle for supervisory action (Figure P3.1). Knowledge must be accompanied by interpersonal skills for communicating with teachers and technical skills for planning, assessing, observing, and evaluating instructional improvement. We next turn to the interpersonal skill dimension.

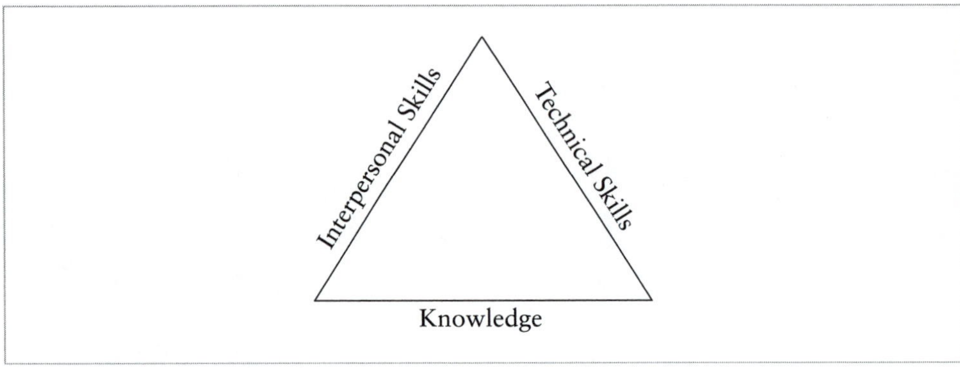

figure **P3.1** **Prerequisite Dimensions for a Supervisor**

chapter 6

Supervisory Behavior Continuum

KNOW THYSELF

outline

- Outcomes of Conference
- Valid Assessment of Self
- Johari Window
- Cognitive Dissonance
- Comparing Self-Perceptions with Others' Perceptions
- Comparing Self-Perceptions to Recorded Behaviors

Visit the **MyEdLeadershipLab™** site for *The Basic Guide to SuperVision and Instructional Leadership*, Third Edition to enhance your understanding of chapter concepts. You'll have the opportunity to practice your skills through video and case based Assignments and Activities as well as Building Leadership Skills units, and prepare for your certification exam with Practice for Certification quizzes.

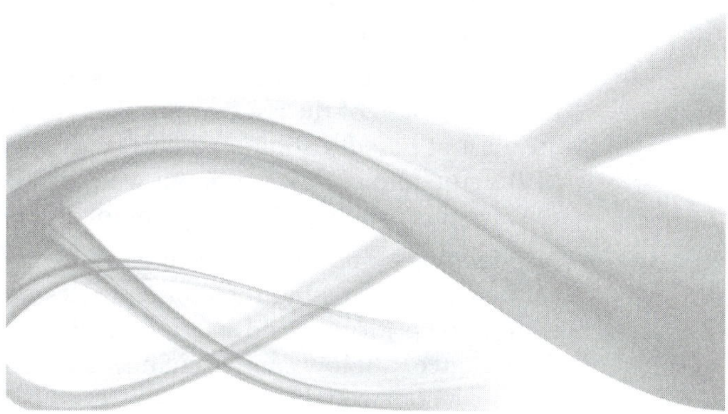

This chapter looks at the range of interpersonal behaviors available to a supervisor who is working with individuals and groups of teachers. It assesses how supervisors typically behave with staff in school settings and then determines other behaviors that might be used skillfully and effectively. Chapters 7 through 10 provide training in each of four clusters of interpersonal skills.

What are the categories of behaviors? Broad categories of supervisory behaviors have been derived from many years of collecting supervisors' observations in meetings with individuals and groups of teachers for purposes of making classroom or school decisions (Wolfgang and Glickman, 1980; Glickman, 1981, 2002). These categories encompass almost all observed supervisor behaviors that are deemed purposeful. A *purposeful* behavior is defined as one that contributes to the decision being made at the conference or meeting. The derived categories of supervisory behaviors are listening, clarifying, encouraging, reflecting, presenting, problem solving, negotiating, directing, standardizing, and reinforcing. Definitions of each category are as follows:

- *Listening.* The supervisor sits and looks at the speaker and nods his or her head to show understanding. Gutteral utterances ("uh-huh," "umm") also indicate listening.
- *Clarifying.* The supervisor asks questions and statements to clarify the speaker's point of view: "Do you mean that?" "Would you explain this further?" "I'm confused about this." "I lost you on . . ."
- *Encouraging.* The supervisor provides acknowledgment responses that help the speaker continue to explain his or her positions: "Yes, I'm following you." "Continue." "Ah, I see what you're saying; tell me more."
- *Reflecting.* The supervisor summarizes and paraphrases the speaker's message for verification of accuracy: "I understand that you mean . . .," "So, the issue is . . .," "I hear you saying . . ."
- *Presenting.* The supervisor gives his or her own ideas about the issue being discussed: "This is how I see it." "What can be done is . . .," "I'd like us to consider . . .," "I believe that . . ."
- *Problem solving.* The supervisor takes the initiative, usually after a preliminary discussion of the issue or problem, in pressing all those involved to generate a list of possible solutions. This is usually done through statements such as, "Let's stop and each write down what can be done." "What ideas do we have to solve this problem?" "Let's think of all possible actions we can take."
- *Negotiating.* The supervisor moves the discussion from possible to probable solutions by discussing the consequences of each proposed action, exploring conflict or priorities, and narrowing choices with questions such as, "Where do we agree?" "How can we change that action to be acceptable to all?" "Can we find a compromise that will give each of us part of what we want?"

- *Directing.* The supervisor tells the participant(s) either what the choices are: "As I see it, these are the alternatives: You could do A . . . , B . . . , or C . . . Which of these make the most sense to you, and which will you use?" *Or* the supervisor tells the participants what is to be done: "I've decided that we will do . . .," "I want you to do . . .," "The policy will be . . .," "This is how it is going to be." "We will then proceed as follows. . .."
- *Standardizing.* The supervisor sets the expected criteria and time for the decision to be implemented. Target objectives are set. Expectations are conveyed with words, such as: "By next Monday, we want to see . . .," "Report back to me on this change by . . .," "Have the first two activities carried out by . . .," "I want an improvement of 25 percent involvement by the next meeting." "We have agreed that all tasks will be done before the next observation."
- *Reinforcing.* The supervisor strengthens the directive and the criteria to be met by telling of possible consequences. Possible consequences can be positive, in the form of praise: "I know you can do it!" "I have confidence in your ability!" "I want to show others what you've done!" Consequences also can be negative: "If it's not done on time, we'll lose the support of . . .," "It must be understood that failure to get this done on time will result in . . ."

The foregoing categories of interpersonal supervisory behavior move participants toward a decision. Some supervisory behaviors place more responsibility on the teacher(s) to make the decision, others place more responsibility on the supervisor to make the decision, and still others indicate a shared responsibility for decision making. The categories of behaviors are listed in a sequence on the supervisory behavior continuum (Figure 6.1) to reflect the scale of control or power.

When a supervisor *listens* to the teacher, *clarifies* what the teacher says, *encourages* the teacher to speak more about the concern, and *reflects* by verifying the teacher's perceptions, then clearly it is the teacher who is in control. The supervisor's role is that of an active prober or sounding board for the teacher to make his or her own decision. The teacher has high control and the supervisor low control over the actual decision (big *T,* small *s*). This is seen as a *nondirective interpersonal approach.*

When a supervisor uses nondirective behaviors to understand the teacher's point of view but then participates in the discussion by *presenting* his or her own ideas, *problem solving* by asking all parties to propose possible actions, and then *negotiating* to find a common course of action satisfactory to teacher and supervisor, then the control over the decision is shared by all. This is viewed as a *collaborative interpersonal approach.*

When a supervisor *directs* the teacher in what the alternatives are from which the teacher might choose, and after the teacher selects, the supervisor *standardizes* the time and criteria of expected results, then the supervisor is the major source of information, providing the teacher with restricted choice (small *t,* big *S*). This is viewed as a *directive informational interpersonal approach.*

1 *Listening*	2 *Clarifying*	3 *Encouraging*	4 *Reflecting*	5 *Presenting*

T

s

Clusters of behaviors: Nondirective

Key: *T* = Maximum teacher responsibility *S* = Maximum supervisor responsibility
t = Minimum teacher responsibility *s* = Minimum supervisor responsibility

figure **6.1** **The Supervisory Behavior Continuum**

Finally, when a supervisor *directs* the teacher in what will be done, *standardizes* the time and criteria of expected results, and *reinforces* the consequences of action or inaction, then the supervisor has taken responsibility for the decision (small *t*, big *S*). The supervisor is clearly determining the actions for the teacher to follow. These behaviors are called a *directive control interpersonal approach.*

Outcomes of Conference

Another way of clarifying the distinctions among supervisory approaches is by looking at the outcomes of the conference and determining who controls the final decision for instructional improvement:

Approach	**Outcome**
Nondirective	Teacher self-plan
Collaborative	Mutual plan
Directive informational	Supervisor-suggested plan
Directive control	Supervisor-assigned plan

In the nondirective approach, the supervisor facilitates the teacher's thinking in developing a self-plan. In the collaborative approach, both supervisor and teacher share information and possible practices as equals in arriving at a mutual plan. In the directive informational approach, the supervisor provides the focus and the parameters of possible actions, and the teacher is asked to choose within the supervisor's suggestions. In the directive control approach, the supervisor tells the teacher what is to be done. Nondirective provides maximum teacher choice; collaborative, mutual choice; directive informational, selected choice; and directive control, no choice in the outcome of the conference.

6	7	8	9	10
Problem Solving	*Negotiating*	*Directing*	*Standardizing*	*Reinforcing*
				$\frac{t}{S}$
Collaborative			Directive Informational	Directive Control

Valid Assessment of Self

We must make sure that how we perceive ourselves is consistent with how others perceive us. As an example, let us give a personal instance of erroneous self-perception.

As a school principal in New Hampshire, one of the authors regarded himself as operating a successful school and being accessible to teachers. He could document success by external evidence—state and national recognition the school had received and complimentary letters from numerous visitors. He documented his accessibility through casual discussions with teachers in the lounge and by having an open-office policy for every staff member who wished to speak with him. In his third year as a principal at this particular school, the superintendent asked all principals in the school system to allow teachers to evaluate principal performance. One item on the evaluation form was "Ability to listen to others," followed by a numeric scale of responses from 1 ("rarely listens") to 7 ("almost always listens"). Before giving the form to teachers, the author filled out the same evaluation form according to his own perception of his performance. He confidently circled the number 7 on "ability to listen." Once the teachers' responses were collected and results were received, he was amazed to find that the lowest teacher rating on the entire survey was on that very item on which he had rated himself highest. To the author's chagrin, there was an obvious discrepancy between his own perception of performance and staff perceptions.

Johari Window

The Johari Window (Luft, 1970; Janas, 2001) provides a graphic way to look at what we know and do not know about our behavior (Figure 6.2). Visualize a window with four windowpanes. In this scheme, there are four windowpanes of the self

	Known to Supervisor	Not Known to Supervisor
Known to Teachers	1. Public self	2. Blind self
Not Known to Teachers	3. Private self	4. Unknown self

***Figure* 6.2 Adaptation of Johari Window**

Source: Adapted from Joseph Luft (1970). *Group Processes: An Introduction to Group Dynamics.* New York: National Press Books.

in which behaviors are either known or not known by self (the supervisor) and others (the teachers). In windowpane 1, there are behaviors that both supervisor and teachers know the supervisor uses. This is the *public self.* For example, the supervisor knows that when he or she is anxious, speech will become halting and hesitant; teachers are also aware of what such speech indicates.

In windowpane 2 is the *blind self*—behaviors the supervisor practices that are unknown to the self but are known to teachers. For example, as a school principal, one of the authors was displaying behaviors toward teachers that he thought were listening behaviors, but teachers saw the same behaviors as a failure to listen. Of course, once one becomes aware of teachers' perceptions of those behaviors, the blind self becomes the public self.

In windowpane 3 is the *private self*—behaviors the supervisor has knowledge about but that teachers do not know. For instance, in new situations a supervisor might mask his or her unsureness by being extroverted in greeting others. Only the supervisor knows that this behavior is covering up insecurity. Once the supervisor discloses this perception to others, the private self becomes public.

Finally, there is windowpane 4, the *unknown self.* There are actions a supervisor takes of which both supervisors and teachers are unaware. From time to time, the supervisor might rapidly shift his legs while speaking behind a table. Neither supervisor nor teachers are aware of this leg movement. Perhaps a supervisor becomes irritated while a certain teacher is speaking. The supervisor may not know why she is irritated or even that she feels this way, and the teacher may not know either. The unknown self is unconscious to all; it becomes private, blind, or public only by circumstances that create a new awareness.

What does the Johari Window have to do with supervision? We cannot become more effective as supervisors unless we know what we are doing. We may, at our discretion, decide to keep parts of ourselves private. (For example, we may not want teachers to know all the details of our life and personality.) Yet we must understand that by remaining largely private and not sharing the experiences that bind us as humans, we are creating a distance when we work with teachers. We may prefer formality and distance and may be able to document that such privateness accomplishes certain results. However, we must also accept that our privateness will be reciprocal and that staff may not easily discuss personal situations that may affect teaching performance. First, we must be aware of how private or public we are with our staff and determine if we desire teachers to be the same way with us. Second, as supervisors, we cannot afford to be blind to our own behaviors and the effect of those behaviors on others. We can improve only what we know; to believe only our own self-perceptions is to court disaster.

Cognitive Dissonance

Invalidity of perceptions creates *cognitive dissonance,* according to a model of motivation by psychologist Leon Festinger (1957). The model is based on the premise that a person cannot live with contradictory psychological evidence—that is, thinking of himself or herself in one way while other sources of information indicate that he or she is different. When the author's perception of his listening abilities were contradicted by teacher perceptions, mental turmoil or cognitive dissonance was created. For example, if you believe that you are a collaborative supervisor and then you receive feedback from teachers that you are a directive supervisor, this causes cognitive dissonance. We must wrestle with disparate perceptions and reconcile them. If not, the two differing sources of information will continue to bother us. This mental anguish strives to resolve the question of what is it that we really do. The resolution can come about in three alternative ways (Hyman, 1975).

First, we can dismiss the source of contrary evidence as biased and untrue. For example, the principal might rationalize, "Teachers simply don't understand what collaboration is." By dismissing the other source of information as erroneous, we can continue to believe that we are what we originally thought.

Second, we can change our own self-perception to conform to the other source of information and can then live with the new perception of ourselves. We accept that they are right and we are wrong; thus, our perception is now theirs—for example, "I really was wrong about my listening abilities, and I now reconcile myself to being a poor listener," or "The supervisor is really not collaborative but instead is, as the teachers say, directive." Accepting the other source of information makes dissonance vanish so that no further change is necessary.

Third, we can accept our original self-perception as how we wish to be perceived, use the other source of information as an indicator of how we are currently perceived, and then change our behaviors to be more similar to our wish. In other words, our perception was not accurate, but it still represents what we want to be. In our example, the author thought he was a good listener, but others said that he was not; so he attempted to change his listening behaviors in order to become a good listener. The supervisor thought he or she was collaborative but others said that he or she was directive; so he or she changed behavior to become more collaborative.

The third alternative to resolving cognitive dissonance creates behavioral change. Whenever we have an idea of how we desire to be matched against the reality of how others see us, there are conditions for individual change. The acknowledged gap between what is and what should be becomes a powerful stimulus to change. We change our behaviors and gather feedback from others to determine whether others are forming new perceptions of us and more positive results are forthcoming.

Comparing Self-Perceptions with Others' Perceptions

Box 6.1 provides an instrument that the supervisor uses to compare self-perceptions with teacher perceptions of supervisor performance. The Supervisor's Self-Assessment is divided into four sections—"Professional Characteristics," "Skills," "Individual Assistance," and "Schoolwide Assistance"—and yields a subscore for each section. The process of self-assessment begins with the supervisor completing and self-scoring the instrument. It is important for the supervisor to be totally open when completing the self-assessment, so as a general rule the supervisor should not be expected to share results with superiors or teachers. The supervisor next distributes the instrument to the teachers or a randomly selected sample of the teachers he or she supervises. It's important that the teachers complete and return the completed instruments anonymously. After calculating item, section, and overall means of teacher responses, the supervisor can compare self-perceptions with teacher perceptions. When comparing self-ratings to teacher ratings on any particular item, the supervisor can reach a variety of conclusions:

1. Supervisor and teacher satisfaction with the supervisor's performance
2. Supervisor satisfaction and teacher dissatisfaction with the supervisor's performance
3. Supervisor dissatisfaction and teacher satisfaction with the supervisor's performance
4. Supervisor and teacher dissatisfaction with the supervisor's performance

Any of the last three conclusions can be the basis for supervisor-defined improvement objectives and supervisor-designed action plans for the improvement of instructional assistance.

Comparing Self-Perceptions to Recorded Behaviors

Another way to create cognitive dissonance as a catalyst for improvement of supervisory practice is for the supervisor to compare his or her perceptions to data gathered on the supervisor's actual behaviors. One of the key processes a supervisor is

box 6.1

Supervisor's Self-Assessment

Directions for Completing: Place in the space before each item the number (1, 2, 3, or 4) of the response that most nearly indicates your level of agreement with the item:

1. Strongly disagree
2. Disagree
3. Agree
4. Strongly agree

Section A: Professional Characteristics

_____1. The supervisor is genuinely concerned with the growth and development of students.
_____2. The supervisor is genuinely concerned with the growth and development of teachers.
_____3. The supervisor is trustworthy.
_____4. The supervisor treats teachers fairly.
_____5. The supervisor is flexible.
_____6. The supervisor is ethical.

Section B: Skills

_____7. The supervisor displays communication skills.
_____8. The supervisor displays needs assessment skills.
_____9. The supervisor displays planning skills.
_____10. The supervisor displays group facilitation skills.
_____11. The supervisor displays problem-solving skills.
_____12. The supervisor displays change agency skills.
_____13. The supervisor displays observation skills.
_____14. The supervisor displays conflict resolution skills.

Section C: Individual Assistance

_____15. The supervisor effectively observes teaching and provides helpful feedback.
_____16. The supervisor provides useful instructional resources.
_____17. The supervisor fosters teacher reflection.
_____18. The supervisor demonstrates effective teaching.
_____19. The supervisor shares innovative instructional strategies.
_____20. The supervisor effectively assists beginning teachers.
_____21. The supervisor effectively assists teachers with instructional problems they are experiencing.
_____22. The supervisor effectively assists teachers to plan for instruction.
_____23. The supervisor effectively assists teachers to assess student learning.
_____24. The supervisor effectively assists teachers to individualize instruction.

Section D: Schoolwide Assistance

_____25. The supervisor effectively facilitates instructional dialogue among teachers.
_____26. The supervisor fosters a positive school culture.
_____27. The supervisor facilitates collective vision building.
_____28. The supervisor fosters teacher collaboration for schoolwide instructional improvement.
_____29. The supervisor fosters teacher empowerment.
_____30. The supervisor effectively facilitates teachers' professional development.
_____31. The supervisor effectively facilitates curriculum development.
_____32. The supervisor effectively facilitates program evaluation.

Directions for Scoring: For the instrument completed by the supervisor, add the ratings for the items in each section to find subtotals. The range of possible subtotals for each section follows:

Section A: Professional Characteristics, from 6 to 24.
Section B: Skills, from 8 to 32.
Section C: Individual Assistance, from 10 to 40.
Section D: Schoolwide Assistance, from 8 to 32.

The overall rating (the sum of the four subtotals) ranges from 32 to 128.

(*Continued*)

For the instrument completed by teachers, calculate the mean scores for each item, section, and the overall rating. For example, if five teachers responded to the same item with ratings of 2, 3, 3, 4, and 4, respectively, the teachers' mean rating for that item would be 3.2. For an example at the section level, if the subtotals on Section A from five teachers were 16, 18, 19, 21, and 22, the mean ratings for Section A would be 19.2. For the overall mean, if individual overall ratings by five teachers were 83, 92, 100, 112, and 118, the overall mean for teacher ratings would be 101.

responsible for is gathering data on classroom behaviors to assist teachers to improve their instruction. It makes sense, then, for the supervisor to analyze data on her or his own performance for the purpose of improved supervision. Data gathering on supervision often takes place while the supervisor is interacting with individual teachers or groups. The data can be gathered in a number of ways. Another supervisor can observe a conference or meeting that the observed supervisor is conducting and gather requested data. The supervisor can tape a supervisory conference or meeting and review the tape. The supervisor can analyze documents that reflect supervisory behaviors, such as e-mails, memos, and observation reports that she or he has prepared.

The purpose of analyzing these types of data is to compare the supervisor's perceptions to recorded supervisory behaviors. Comparison of perceptions to data can create the same types of cognitive dissonance as the comparison of supervisor and teacher perceptions discussed in the previous section. In fact, comparing supervisor perceptions to hard data may bring about cognitive dissonance more easily than comparison of supervisor and teacher perceptions. The cognitive dissonance caused by self-analysis of data on supervisory behaviors can lead to changes in supervisory behaviors.

MyEdLeadershipLab™

Go to Topic 4, Supervisory Skills, in the MyEdLeadershipLab™ site at www.myedleadershiplab.com for *The Basic Guide to SuperVision and Instructional Leadership*, Third Edition, where you can:

- Find learning outcomes for Supervisory Skills along with the national standards that connect to these outcomes.
- Complete Assignments and Activities that can help you more deeply understand the chapter content.
- Apply and practice your understanding of the core skills identified in the chapter with the Building Leadership Skills unit.
- Prepare yourself for professional certification with a Practice for Certification quiz.

REFERENCES

Festinger, L. 1957. *A theory of cognitive dissonance*. Stanford, CA: Stanford University Press.

Glickman, C. D. 1981. *Developmental supervision: Alternative practices for helping teachers improve instruction*. Alexandria, VA: Association for Supervision and Curriculum Development.

Glickman, C. D. 2002. *Leadership for learning: How to help teachers succeed*. Alexandria, VA: Association for Supervision and Curriculum Development.

Hyman, R. T. 1975. *School administrator's handbook of teacher supervision and evaluation methods* (pp. 46–47). Englewood Cliffs, NJ: Prentice Hall.

Janas, M. 2001. Getting a clear view. *Journal of Staff Development, 22*(2), 32–34.

Luft, J. 1970. *Group processes: An introduction to group dynamics*. New York: National Press Books.

Wolfgang, C. H., and Glickman, C. D. 1980. *Solving discipline problems: Alternative strategies for teachers*. Boston: Allyn & Bacon.

chapter 7

Directive Control Behaviors

outline

- Directive Control Continuum of Behaviors
- A History of Overreliance on Control
- When to Use Directive Control Behaviors
- Moving from Directive Control toward Directive Informational Behaviors
- Critical Reflection on Directive Control Supervision

Visit the **MyEdLeadershipLab™** site for *The Basic Guide to SuperVision and Instructional Leadership*, Third Edition to enhance your understanding of chapter concepts. You'll have the opportunity to practice your skills through video and case based Assignments and Activities as well as Building Leadership Skills units, and prepare for your certification exam with Practice for Certification quizzes.

Directive Control Continuum of Behaviors

The supervision using directive control behaviors takes over the teacher's problem. At first, the supervisor identifies the problem by gathering information from observations and discussing this information with the teacher. Next, the supervisor tells the teacher what to do and provides an explanation of why the suggestion will work. The supervisor concludes by reviewing the proposed action and reiterating expectations for the teacher. The teacher is left with a concrete understanding of what is expected.

As we look at a typical sequence of behaviors along the supervisory behavior continuum (Figure 7.1), keep in mind that the sequence and frequency of behaviors

1 Listening | *2 Clarifying* | *3 Encouraging* | *4 Reflecting* | *5 Presenting*

T

s

1. Identifying the problem
2. Asking the teacher for input into the problem
3. Understanding the teacher's perception of the problem
6. Asking the teacher for input into the solution

Key: *T* = Maximum teacher responsibility
t = Minimum teacher responsibility
S = Maximum supervisor responsibility
s = Minimum supervisor responsibility

***figure* 7.1** The Supervisory Behavior Continuum: Directive Control Behaviors

varies, especially in the beginning of the conference, but the directive control approach ends with the supervisor making the final decisions for the teacher. This chapter accentuates directive behaviors that control teacher actions:

1. Presenting: *Identifying the problem.* The supervisor begins with a general idea of what the needs and difficulties are. Having used observations and gathered information from other sources, the supervisor tells the teacher what seems to be the problem: "I understand that there is a problem with . . ."
2. Clarifying: *Asking the teacher for input into the problem.* The supervisor wants to gather direct information from the teacher about the problem prior to the

6 *Problem Solving*	7 *Negotiating*	8 *Directing*	9 *Standardizing*	10 *Reinforcing*
4. Mentally determining the best solution				
		5. Stating the solution		
			7. Modifying and detailing expectations	
				8. Summarizing and following up on expectations

t
S

solution stage. This is done by using the teacher in an advisory capacity, asking the teacher such questions as: "How do you see the problem?" "Why do you think these conditions exist?"

3. Listening: *Understanding the teacher's perception of the problem.* To gather maximum information in the shortest amount of time, the supervisor must attend carefully to what the teacher says. He or she listens both to the surface messages—"Computers are a waste of time"—and to underlying messages—"I don't know how to use the software"—in formulating a complete problem.
4. Problem solving: *Mentally determining the best solution.* The supervisor processes the information and thinks "What can be done?" After considering various possibilities, he or she selects the needed actions. The supervisor should be confident of indeed having a good, manageable solution to the problem before conveying it to the teacher.
5. Directing: *Stating the solution.* The supervisor tells the teacher in a matter-of-fact way what needs to be done: "I want to see you do the following . . ." The phrasing of the directive is important. Avoid timid, circular expectations: "Well, maybe you might consider doing . . .," or "Don't you think it would be a good idea to . . .?" The supervisor is not asking or pleading with the teacher, but *telling.* However, directing does not mean being vindictive, overbearing, condescending, or insulting. Avoid personal slights or paternalistic references: "I don't know why you can't figure out what needs to be done." "Why can't you get it right in the first place?" "Now listen, honey, I'm going to help you by . . ." A supervisor should state actions as *I* statements, not as what others think. Tell the teacher what *I* want to happen, not what parents, other teachers, or the superintendent would want to see. A statement such as this: "If the superintendent saw this, he would tell you to do . . ." is hiding behind someone else's authority. The supervisor must make statements based on his or her own position, credibility, and authority.
6. Clarifying: *Asking the teacher for input into the solution.* Possible difficulties with the supervisor's directive should be known before the teacher leaves the conference. For example, if circumstances exist that make teacher compliance with the directive impossible, it is better to adjust to those circumstances during the conference than to find out two weeks later why the plan failed. Therefore, after telling the teacher what is expected—"I want one-third of your students using the software program"—the supervisor must ask such questions as: "What do you need to carry out this plan?" "How can I help you carry out the plan?"
7. Standardizing: *Modifying and detailing expectations.* After considering the teacher's reactions to the directive, the supervisor solidifies the plan by building in the necessary assistance, resources, time lines, and criteria for expected success. The teacher is then told the revisions: "I can rearrange the visit time to . . ." "I will find those materials for you," "I will arrange for you to attend . . ." "I will change the time to three weeks."

8. Reinforcing: *Summarizing and following up on expectations.* The supervisor reviews the entire plan and establishes times for checking on progress. The supervisor closes the meeting by making sure the teacher clearly understands the plan: "Do you understand what you're to do?" "Tell me what it is you're now going to do."

A History of Overreliance on Control

Historically, control has been used by supervisors as a first rather than a last resort. The tradition has been to rely on controlling behaviors with all teachers in all situations (Gordon, 1992; Harpaz, 2005). At times, this has been done by tying supervision to summative evaluation systems requiring certain teaching behaviors. At other times, social pressure has been applied to force teachers to conform to generic research-based teaching methods. (The research cited during such efforts often has been misinterpreted and oversimplified.) Even worse, some supervisors wishing to reduce teacher resistance have combined control and manipulation, hoping to convince teachers that they have participated in a decision when in fact the supervisor knew all along what the decision would be.

We strongly disagree with supervisors using directive control behaviors with all teachers and in all situations. We also oppose using directive control behaviors indefinitely. Finally, in all cases, we oppose control through *manipulation.* Although we admit that directive control is necessary with some teachers and groups in some situations, we believe that it should be used only when no other supervisory approach is feasible. When using a directive control approach with a teacher or group, the supervisor should be ready to move away from directive control toward noncontrolling behaviors as soon as possible.

When to Use Directive Control Behaviors

Because directive behaviors raise issues of power, respect, expertise, and line and staff relationships, the following guidelines are given with caution. Directive control behaviors should be used in these instances:

1. When teachers are functioning at very low developmental levels.
2. When teachers do not have awareness, knowledge, or inclination to act on an issue that a supervisor, who has organizational authority, thinks to be of critical importance to the students, the teachers, or the community, then the directive control approach should most likely be used.
3. When teachers will have no involvement and the supervisor will be involved in carrying out the decision. If the supervisor will be held totally accountable and the teachers will not, then the directive control approach should probably be used.

4. When the supervisor is committed to resolving the issue and the teachers are not. When decisions do not concern teachers and they prefer the supervisor to make the decision, the directive control approach should most likely be used.
5. In an emergency, when the supervisor does not have time to meet with teachers, the directive control approach should be used.

Moving from Directive Control toward Directive Informational Behaviors

In long-term supervisory situations and relationships, the supervisor should begin to shift from a directive control to a directive informational approach as soon as possible. Stabilizing an unstable situation or giving a teacher or group intensive support tends to foster limited professional growth. Such growth is likely to continue only if the supervisor then begins to give the teacher or group limited opportunities to make decisions and assume some responsibility.

role play 7.1

Practicing Directive Control Behaviors

Directions: The class splits into groups of three. Using the teacher description and situation provided, one member of each group assumes the role of the teacher, one member assumes the role of supervisor, and one member becomes the observer. The "supervisor" and "teacher" role play a conference in which the supervisor uses a directive control approach to address the teacher's instructional problem. The observer takes notes on the supervisor's performance during the conference and shares those notes with the other two group members after the role play. Finally, all three participants engage in reflective discussion of the role play and the directive control approach. (To assist in the role plays in Chapters 7 through 10, see Appendix A, which reviews and compares all four supervisory approaches.)

Teacher Description and Situation: Middle school teacher Ben Crash has been overheard by the supervisor and other teachers yelling at his students as he tries to gain control of his class. Each time he yells at his students to "Quiet down" or "Go to your seats," they seem to get more out of control. Even to those in other classrooms or walking down the hall, it is apparent that Ben frequently loses control over his classes. As he loses control, he becomes louder and louder and begins to use abusive language with his students, telling them to "Shut up" or to "Quit acting like morons." Teachers and parents have complained about the way Ben yells at his students. Teachers on Ben's instructional team have told the supervisor that they believe the root of his problem is that he gives students contradictory and confusing directions when he is trying to start a new learning activity. During a recent classroom observation, the supervisor observed that Ben did indeed give contradictory directions that confused and frustrated students.

One way to do this is to begin to allow the teacher or the group *restricted choice*. For example, the supervisor might mandate an instructional improvement goal and then allow the teacher or group to choose from two or three clearly defined alternatives for meeting the goal. By doing this, the supervisor has begun movement toward directive informational supervision—an approach that is discussed in detail in Chapter 8.

Critical Reflection on Directive Control Supervision

The supervisor should reflect critically on directive control behaviors both during and after their use. Questions that might assist critical reflection include the following:

- Are teacher developmental levels low enough or the situation critical enough to require my use of directive control behaviors?
- What effects will my use of directive control behaviors have on my long-term professional relationship with the teacher or group?
- Are the decisions made through the use of directive control behaviors likely to be implemented?
- What is my plan for moving away from directive control behaviors as soon as possible?

MyEdLeadershipLab™

Go to Topic 3, Types of Supervision, in the MyEdLeadershipLab™ site at www.myedleadershiplab.com for *The Basic Guide to SuperVision and Instructional Leadership*, Third Edition, where you can:

- Find learning outcomes for Types of Supervision along with the national standards that connect to these outcomes.
- Complete Assignments and Activities that can help you more deeply understand the chapter content.
- Apply and practice your understanding of the core skills identified in the chapter with the Building Leadership Skills unit.
- Prepare yourself for professional certification with a Practice for Certification quiz.

REFERENCES

Gordon, S. P. 1992. Paradigms, transitions, and the new supervision. *Journal of Curriculum and Supervision, 8*(1), 62–76.

Harpaz, Y. 2005. Teaching and learning in a community of thinking. *Journal of Curriculum and Supervision, 20*(2), 136–157.

chapter 8

Directive Informational Behaviors

outline

- Directive Informational Continuum of Behaviors
- Comparing Directive Control and Directive Informational Statements
- When to Use Directive Informational Behaviors
- Moving from Directive Informational toward Collaborative Behaviors
- Critical Reflection on Directive Informational Supervision

Visit the **MyEdLeadershipLab™** site for *The Basic Guide to SuperVision and Instructional Leadership,* Third Edition to enhance your understanding of chapter concepts. You'll have the opportunity to practice your skills through video and case based Assignments and Activities as well as Building Leadership Skills units, and prepare for your certification exam with Practice for Certification quizzes.

Directive Informational Continuum of Behaviors

The supervisor who uses directive informational behaviors acts as the information source for the goal and activities of the improvement plan. The supervisor, through observation, determines a clear classroom goal for the teacher and directs the teacher to those activities that have a high degree of probability in achieving the goal. Through each step of the conference, the supervisor remains the information source

T / *s*	*1* *Listening*	*2* *Clarifying*	*3* *Encouraging*	*4* *Reflecting*	*5* *Presenting*
					1. Identifying the problem
		2. Asking the teacher for input into the problem			
	3. Understanding the teacher's perception of the problem				
	6. Asking the teacher for input on the alternatives				
		8. Asking the teacher to choose			

Key: *T* = Maximum teacher responsibility
t = Minimum teacher responsibility
S = Maximum supervisor responsibility
s = Minimum supervisor responsibility

***figure* 8.1** **The Supervisory Behavior Continuum: Directive Informational Behaviors**

but always asks and considers teacher feedback. Furthermore, the supervisor provides a range of alternatives from which the teacher is asked to choose. The conference concludes with teacher commitment to using several activities. The supervisor details the what, when, and how of implementing the activities, sets criteria for improvement, and reinforces the understanding of what is to be done.

As we look at a sequence of directive informational behaviors (see Figure 8.1), keep in mind that the supervisor is constantly framing the direction and choices for the teacher:

6	7	8	9	10
Problem Solving	*Negotiating*	*Directing*	*Standardizing*	*Reinforcing*

t
S

4. Mentally determining two or three alternative solutions

5. Stating alternatives for the teacher to consider

7. Framing the final choices

9. Stating the specific actions to be taken

10. Summarizing and following up on the plan

1. Presenting: *Identifying the problem.* Based on the observation and previous experience with the teacher, the supervisor begins by reviewing the summarized observations and concluding with an interpretation that seven students being nonparticipants throughout a class period is problematic. Therefore, the supervisor sees an important goal as "involving all students."
2. Clarifying: *Asking the teacher for input into the problem.* The supervisor is careful not to move too quickly into a planning phase until he or she checks to see what the teacher thinks of their interpretation of the problem. The teacher, although surprised, agrees and explains why these seven students have been neglected.
3. Listening: *Understanding the teacher's perception of the problem.* The supervisor listens to determine if the teacher accepts the problem and improvement goal as important, or if the teacher must provide further explanation.
4. Problem solving: *Mentally determining possible solutions.* The supervisor has given thought to some alternative solutions that might be considered by the teacher. When the teacher explains the reasons for students being uninvolved and what has been done, the supervisor mentally prepares to lay out the alternative solutions.
5. Directing: *Stating alternatives for the teacher to consider.* The supervisor carefully words the alternative solutions as possibilities, based on experience and knowledge, for the teacher to judge, consider, and respond.
6. Listening: *Asking the teacher for input on the alternatives.* The supervisor asks the teacher to react to the suggestions offered. The teacher has the opportunity now to give the supervisor information to modify, eliminate, and revise before finalizing the choices.
7. Directing: *Framing the final choices.* In a straightforward manner, the supervisor lays out what the teacher could do: "So, in the final analysis, these are the actions you could take . . ."
8. Clarifying: *Asking the teacher to choose.* The supervisor asks the teacher to decide and clarify which solutions or combinations will be used.
9. Standardizing: *Stating the specific actions to be taken.* At this juncture, the supervisor assists the teacher in developing specific activities (introduce cooperative learning, set up threesomes, identify one controversial topic, try for 15 minutes next Tuesday, etc.) and the criteria for success (e.g., "Let's see, when I come in next Thursday, whether four of these seven students can be called on and give prepared, on-target responses").
10. Reinforcing: *Summarizing and following up on the plan.* The supervisor concludes the conference by restating the goal, the activities to be taken, the criteria for success, and the follow-up time for the next observation or conference.

Comparing Directive Control and Directive Informational Statements

Students in supervision courses using this text often have difficulty distinguishing between directive control and directive informational behaviors, especially when practicing the different behaviors during role plays. This is not surprising, since there is often a thin line between controlling and informational language. And yet that thin line is a critical one.

The seminal work on this by Pajak and Seyfarth (1983), Glickman and Pajak (1986), and Pajak and Glickman (1989) underscores this point. The precise language used by a supervisor using a directive approach can be the difference between a successful and unsuccessful supervisory conference or group meeting. The following examples help you distinguish directive control from directive informational statements by a supervisor:

Directive Control (DC): It is essential that you improve your classroom management during your first-period math class.

Directive Informational (DI): I suggest the goal of improving your classroom management during your first-period math class.

DC: One of my expectations is that you attend the classroom management workshop being offered by the district.

DI: One alternative is for you to attend the classroom management workshop being offered by the district.

DC: You need to have a written lesson plan prepared for each class. Each plan must include the following elements . . .

DI: You could prepare more detailed lesson plans for this group. Each plan might include these additional elements . . .

DC: You must include a wider range of instructional strategies in your lessons.

DI: In my own teaching, I've found that using a wide range of instructional strategies improves student behavior and learning. You may wish to include a wider range of teaching strategies in your lessons.

DC: Do you have any questions concerning these new expectations?

DI: Do you have any questions concerning these possible actions?

DC: You will be required to make the changes we've discussed in accordance with this written time line.

DI: Which of the alternatives that we have discussed do you wish to try out?

DC: I will be observing your class again in four weeks, and I expect to see the following changes . . .

DI: I would be willing to visit your class again in four weeks to observe your progress in implementing the changes you have selected.

To summarize, the supervisor using directive control behaviors is analogous to a judge or police officer giving directives that must be followed (although the analogy eventually breaks down, because we know of no district where teachers go directly to jail for failing to follow a supervisor's suggestions for instructional improvement!). However, the supervisor using directive informational behaviors can be compared to a physician or attorney giving expert advice to a patient or client. The person receiving the advice does not have to follow it, but if he or she respects the expertise of the professional giving the advice, he or she will probably conclude that it is wise to act on the professional's suggestions. (If you begin to compare the salaries of physicians or attorneys with instructional supervisors, once again our analogy falls apart, but we've made our point!)

When to Use Directive Informational Behaviors

Directive informational behaviors revolve on expertise, confidence, credibility, and limiting choice (Grainer, 1967). Therefore, they should be used under the following circumstances:

1. When the teacher is functioning at fairly low developmental levels.
2. When the teacher does not possess the knowledge about an issue that the supervisor clearly possesses.
3. When the teacher feels confused, inexperienced, or is at a loss for what to do, and the supervisor knows of successful practices.
4. When the supervisor is willing to take responsibility for what the teacher chooses to try.
5. When the teacher believes that the supervisor is credible—a person who has the background and wisdom to know whereof he or she speaks.
6. When the time is short, the constraints are clear, and quick and concrete actions must be taken.

Moving from Directive Informational toward Collaborative Behaviors

In directive informational supervision, the teacher or group is given some choice but the supervisor still assumes *primary* decision-making responsibility. In the collaborative approach, the teacher and supervisor share decision-making responsibility equally. Movement from directive informational to collaborative is thus a matter of degree. The supervisor might begin that movement by suggesting an instructional improvement goal, asking the teacher or group to suggest one or two activities for moving toward the goal, and then suggesting a detailed action plan incorporating some of the teacher or group's proposed actions. Hopefully, the supervisor eventually will be able to enter a fully collaborative relationship with the teacher.

role play 8.1

Practicing Directive Informational Behaviors

Directions: The class splits into groups of three. Using the teacher description and situation provided here, one member of each group assumes the role of the teacher, one member assumes the role of the supervisor, and one member assumes the role of observer. The "supervisor" and "teacher" role play a conference in which the supervisor uses a directive informational approach to address the teacher's instructional problem. The observer takes notes on the supervisor's performance during the conference and shares those notes with the other two group members after the role play. Finally, all three participants engage in reflective discussion of the role play and the directive informational approach. (To assist in the role plays in Chapters 7 through 10, see Appendix A, which reviews and compares all four supervisory approaches.)

Teacher Description and Situation: High school teacher Norma Watson, who is White, has seen the demographics of her eleventh-grade social studies classes change dramatically over the last several years. The number of Latino students in the eleventh grade has gradually shifted from what used to be a small minority to 65 percent. Although Norma means well, she has found it difficult to relate to a number of her Latino students. The same lectures that used to captivate most of her students no longer capture students' attention. Many of Norma's Latino students have complained to other teachers and to the principal that Norma's lectures are boring and never include a Latino perspective. For the first time in her career, Norma has drawn complaints from both Latino and other parents about her lack of classroom management. Norma realizes she has a problem. She wishes to make the lessons more relevant to her Latino students and to recapture the classroom management that she once had, but she is at a loss as to how to do these things.

Critical Reflection on Directive Informational Supervision

Considering the following questions can assist the supervisor in reflecting critically on the use of directive informational behaviors:

- Is my interaction with the teacher or group truly informational rather than controlling, both in terms of technical language I use and the overall environment I create?
- Is the teacher or group provided alternative actions to consider that are clearly defined but also provide meaningful choice?
- Is the directive informational approach resulting in any unanticipated consequences?
- Is the directive informational approach working well with this teacher or group? Would another approach work better?

MyEdLeadershipLab™

Go to Topic 3, Types of Supervision, in the MyEdLeadershipLab™ site at www.myedleadershiplab.com for *The Basic Guide to SuperVision and Instructional Leadership*, Third Edition, where you can:

- Find learning outcomes for Types of Supervision along with the national standards that connect to these outcomes.
- Complete Assignments and Activities that can help you more deeply understand the chapter content.
- Apply and practice your understanding of the core skills identified in the chapter with the Building Leadership Skills unit.
- Prepare yourself for professional certification with a Practice for Certification quiz.

REFERENCES

Glickman, C. D., and Pajak, E. F. 1986. Supervisors' discrimination among three types of supervisory scripts. *Educational and Psychological Research, 6*(4), 279–289.

Grainer, L. E. 1967. Patterns of organizational change. *Harvard Business Review, 45,* 119–130. (See the "decisions from alternatives approach.")

Pajak, E. F., and Glickman, C. D. 1989. Informational and controlling language in simulated supervisory conferences. *American Educational Research Journal, 26*(1), 93–106.

Pajak, E. F., and Seyfarth, J. J. 1983. Authentic Supervision reconciles the irreconcilables. *Educational Leadership, 40*(8), 20–23.

chapter 9

Collaborative Behaviors

outline

- Collaborative Continuum of Behaviors
- Issues in Collaborative Supervision
- When to Use Collaborative Behaviors
- Moving from Collaborative toward Nondirective Behaviors
- Critical Reflection on Collaborative Supervision

Visit the **MyEdLeadershipLab™** site for The Basic Guide to SuperVision and Instructional Leadership, Third Edition to enhance your understanding of chapter concepts. You'll have the opportunity to practice your skills through video and case based Assignments and Activities as well as Building Leadership Skills units, and prepare for your certification exam with Practice for Certification quizzes.

Collaborative Continuum of Behaviors

The supervisor using collaborative behaviors wishes to resolve a problem that is shared equally with the teacher. The supervisor encourages the teacher to present his or her own perceptions and ideas, yet the supervisor also gives his or her own views in an honest and straightforward manner, with the result being a frank exchange of ideas. Both participants know they must agree on any course of action. In fact, when the disagree-

1 *Listening*	2 *Clarifying*	3 *Encouraging*	4 *Reflecting*	5 *Presenting*
	1. Identifying the problem as seen by the teacher			
2. Understanding the teacher's perception of the problem				
			3. Verifying the teacher's perception of the problem	
				4. Providing the supervisor's perception of the problem
	5. Seeking the teacher's understanding of the supervisor's perception of the problem			
		7. Accepting conflict		
			10. Summarizing the final plan	

T (left end) — s

Key: T = Maximum teacher responsibility; t = Minimum teacher responsibility; S = Maximum supervisor responsibility; s = Minimum supervisor responsibility

figure **9.1** **The Supervisory Behavior Continuum: Collaborative Behaviors**

ment becomes obvious, the supervisor restates the disagreement and reassures the teacher that he or she must find a mutual solution; disagreement is encouraged, not suppressed. As the conversation continues, some openings for possible agreements become apparent, and the supervisor steers the conversation toward those ends.

Figure 9.1 shows a prototype of collaborative behaviors according to the supervisory behavior continuum. A conference between supervisor and teacher begins with an understanding of each other's identification of the problem and

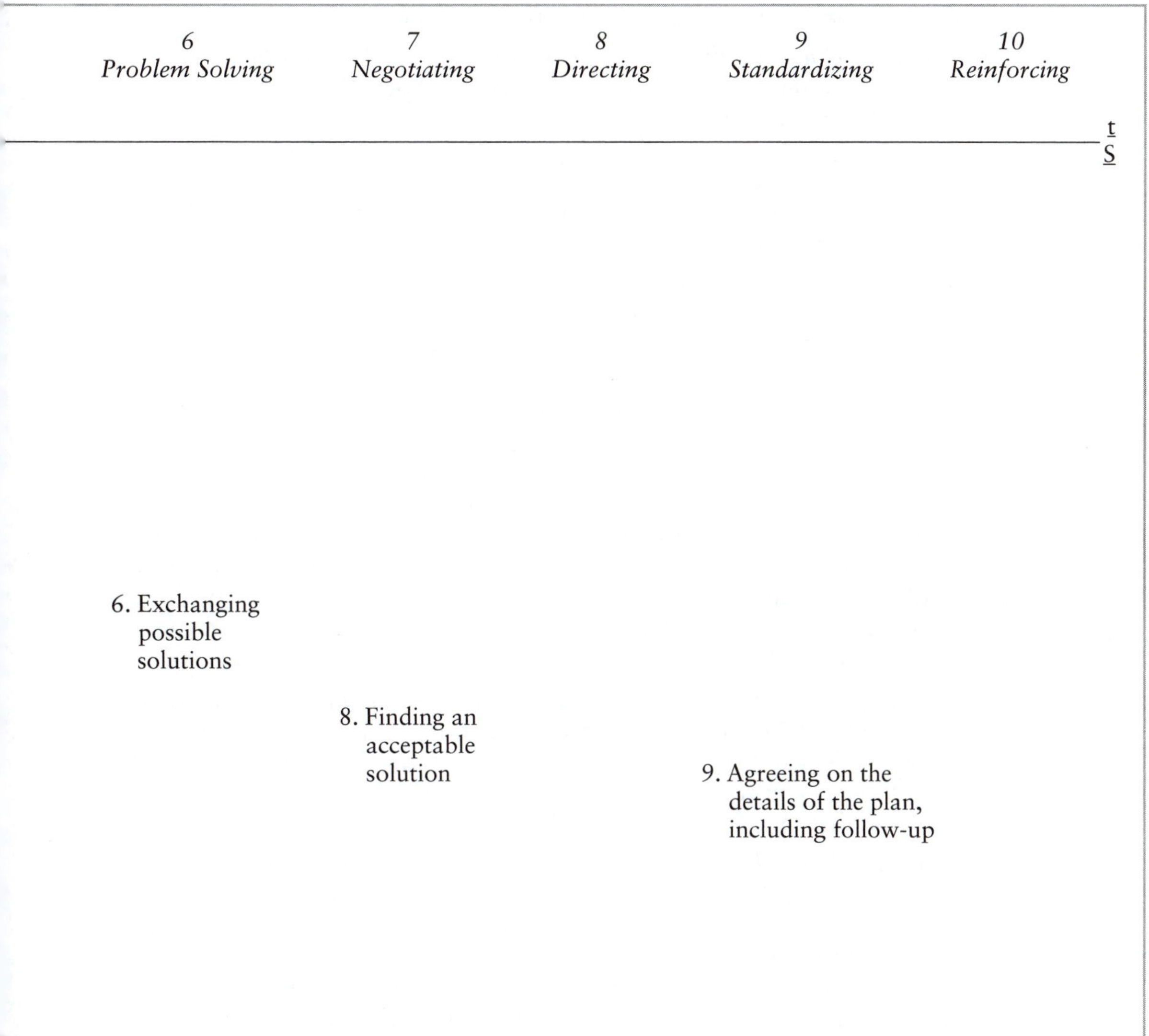

concludes with mutual agreement on the final plan. The reader should think of the supervisory behaviors as a piano keyboard, with the musician beginning by hitting the keys on the left, then playing the keys back and forth, and culminating by hitting the middle key—in other words—negotiating. The following list shows the 10 behaviors involved:

1. Clarifying: *Identifying the problem as seen by the teacher.* First, ask the teacher about the immediate problem or concern: "Please tell me what is bothering you." "Explain to me what you see as the greatest concern."
2. Listening: *Understanding the teacher's perception of the problem.* You (the supervisor) want to have as much information about the problem as possible before thinking about action. Therefore, when the teacher narrates his or her perceptions, the full range of nondirective behaviors should be used (eye contact, paraphrasing, asking probing questions, and being willing to allow the teacher to continue talking): "Tell me more." "Uh huh, I'm following you." "Do you mean . . .?"
3. Reflecting: *Verifying the teacher's perception of the problem.* When the teacher has completed his or her description of the problem, check for accuracy by summarizing the teacher's statements and asking if the summary is accurate: "I understand that you see the problem as . . . Is this accurate?"
4. Presenting: *Providing the supervisor's perception of the problem.* Until this point, we have seen an abbreviated nondirective conference. Instead of asking the teacher to begin thinking of his or her own possible actions, however, you now move in and become part of the decision-making process. Give your own point of view about the current difficulty and fill in any information about the situation of which the teacher might be unaware: "I see the situation in this way." "The problem, as I see it, is . . ." (To minimize influencing the teacher's position, it is better for you to give your perceptions only after the teacher has given his or hers.)
5. Clarifying: *Seeking the teacher's understanding of the supervisor's perception of the problem.* In the same way that you paraphrased the teacher's statement of the problem and asked for verification, you now ask the teacher to do likewise: "Could you repeat what you think I'm trying to say?" Once you feel confident that the teacher understands your views, problem solving can begin.
6. Problem solving: *Exchanging possible solutions.* If you and the teacher are familiar with each other and have worked collaboratively before, you can simply ask for a list of suggestions: "Let's both think about what might be done to improve this situation." Then listen to each other's ideas. If the teacher is not familiar with you or with the collaborative process, however, he or she may feel apprehensive about suggesting an idea that is different from the supervisor's. It might be better to stop the conference for a few minutes and

have both supervisor and teacher write down possible actions before speaking: "So that we don't influence each other on possible solutions, let's take the next few minutes and write down what actions might be taken and then read each other's list." Obviously, once actions are in writing, they cannot change according to what the other person has written. Therefore, you, as the supervisor, have promoted a spectrum of personal ideas ready to be shared and discussed.

7. Encouraging: *Accepting conflict.* To keep the conference from turning into a competitive struggle, you must reassure the teacher that disagreement is acceptable and that there are no winners or losers: "It appears that we have some different ideas on how to handle this situation. By disagreeing, we will find the best solution. Remember our agreement—we both have to agree with the solution before it will take place." You must genuinely believe that conflict between two caring professionals is productive for finding the best solution.
8. Negotiating: *Finding an acceptable solution.* After sharing and discussing, ask if there are suggestions common to both—"Where do we agree?"—and if there are suggestions markedly different—"Where do we differ?" If you find agreement, then the conference proceeds. However, if there is a vast difference in suggestions, then you can take four sequential actions. First, check to see whether the differences are as vast as they appear by having both participants (you and the teacher) explain thoroughly what is meant by your respective suggestions. Second, if the disagreement is still real, then find out how convinced each of you is that your suggestion be chosen: "How important is it to you that we do it your way?" If the importance of one person's suggestion is far greater than that of the other person's suggestion, then the question becomes whether one can give up his or her idea and live with the idea put forth by the other. Third, if grounds for agreement are not reached, you can consider a compromise: "How about if I give up this part of my suggestion and if you give up . . ." Or see if a totally new idea can be found: "Because we can't agree, let's drop our top choices for solutions and see if we can find another one."
9. Standardizing: *Agreeing on the details of the plan, including follow-up.* Once agreement on an acceptable action has been reached, the supervisor must attend to the details of time, place, and follow-up. When will the plan be implemented? Where will it take place? Who will help? What resources are needed? Who will follow up? When? These details must be discussed and agreed to so there is clarity and precision to the final plan.
10. Reflecting: *Summarizing the final plan.* The supervisor concludes the conference by checking that both parties agree to the action and details. The supervisor might do this verbally—"Could you repeat what you understand the plan to be and then I'll repeat my understanding"—or in writing—"Let's write this down together so that we are clear on what we've agreed to do."

Issues in Collaborative Supervision

One difficulty in working collaboratively occurs when the teacher or group believes a supervisor is manipulating the decision when in fact that is not the case. The teacher appears to concur with the supervisor's ideas and suggestions not because of their merit, but because the teacher believes the supervisor is really giving a directive. The underlying message the teacher perceives is, "This is my supervisor telling me what she thinks I should do. Even though she says we are making a joint decision, I know I had better do what she says." How does the supervisor know whether a teacher's agreement is sincere or mere compliance? The supervisor might confront the issue by asking the teacher whether he or she is agreeing or only pretending to agree with the supervisor's idea. Acknowledging that the supervisor suspects something is amiss brings the issue out into the open. A teacher who responds, "I don't believe you really are going to let me have equal say," can be dealt with more easily than is possible when a supervisor guesses at the teacher's hidden feelings.

Teachers who refuse to disclose their feelings probably have a history of being mistreated by supervisors. Until the supervisor can demonstrate consistently that he or she really means to be collaborative, no progress will be made. The teacher is not going to believe the supervisor is being collaborative until there is proof. True intent can be demonstrated by refusing to allow decisions to be made without teacher feedback. With nonresponsive and readily acquiescing teachers, a supervisor might say: "I don't know if you're agreeing with me because you like the idea or because of some power I hold over you. We won't carry out any action unless we both agree with that action. I want to be collaborative because I believe you have as much expertise on this matter as I do. Together we can make a better decision than separately. I'm uncertain why you are agreeing with me. Please tell me what you think."

A supervisor cannot find out what a teacher thinks without asking. As they continue to meet, the supervisor should begin by encouraging teachers to offer their own thoughts about the problem and suggestions for action. The supervisor initially should try to withhold any ideas of his or her own. Once the teacher's ideas are forthcoming, the supervisor then offers his or her ideas. When negotiating a final decision, the supervisor should let teachers take the lead.

When to Use Collaborative Behaviors

Collaboration should be used in these instances:

1. When teachers are functioning at moderate or mixed developmental levels.
2. When the teacher(s) and supervisor have approximately the same degree of expertise on the issue. If the supervisor knows part of the problem and teachers know the other part, the collaborative approach should be used.

role play 9.1

Practicing Collaborative Behaviors

Directions: The class splits into groups of three. Using the teacher description and situation provided below, one member of each group assumes the role of the teacher, one member assumes the role of the supervisor, and one member assumes the role of observer. The "supervisor" and "teacher" role play a conference in which the supervisor uses a collaborative approach to address the teacher's instructional problem. The observer takes notes on the supervisor's performance during the conference and shares those notes with the other two group members after the role play. Finally, all three participants engage in reflective discussion of the role play and the collaborative approach. (To assist in the role plays in Chapters 7 through 10, see Appendix A, which reviews and compares all four supervisory approaches.)

Teacher Description and Situation: Marcus Johnson is a third-grade teacher at Hopewell Elementary School. Recently, Marcus's school district eliminated art as a separate subject at the elementary level, but the district also adopted a policy calling for art to be integrated across the elementary curriculum. Marcus has been teaching at Hopewell for five years. Although he did not major in art education in college, he has taught art in his self-contained classroom since coming to Hopewell, and through self-directed professional development has become a fairly competent and creative art teacher. However, up to now he has focused his twice-a-week art periods purely on art; he has not been integrating the teaching of art with other content areas. In a recent hallway conversation with his supervisor, Marcus said that he has come up with some ideas for integrating art across the curriculum but could use some help in generating additional ideas.

3. When the teacher(s) and supervisor are both involved in carrying out the decision. If the teacher(s) and supervisor are held accountable for showing results to someone else (say, parents or the superintendent), then the collaborative approach should be used.
4. When the teacher(s) and supervisor are both committed to solving the problem. If teachers want to be involved and if leaving them out will lead to low morale and distrust, then the collaborative approach should be used.

Moving from Collaborative toward Nondirective Behaviors

The developmental supervisor attempts to move gradually from collaborative toward nondirective interpersonal behaviors. As the teacher or group increases expertise, problem-solving capacity, and motivation, the supervisor hands over more decision-making responsibility. An example of a transitional phase between the collaborative and nondirective approach is to use collaborative behaviors while assisting a teacher or group to decide on an instructional improvement goal, and then shift to nondirective behaviors as the teacher or group decides on actions to reach the goal. Nondirective behaviors are discussed in Chapter 10.

Critical Reflection on Collaborative Supervision

Questions to foster the supervisor's critical reflection on collaborative behaviors include the following:

- Beyond my mechanical use of collaborative behaviors, have I really given the individual or group equal decision-making power regarding the problem to be solved?
- Have I verified that the teacher or group perceives the decision-making process to be collaborative?
- Have I accepted conflict, and reassured the teacher or group that disagreement is part of the decision-making process?
- Have I continued the collaborative process toward a solution acceptable to both the teacher or group and me?

MyEdLeadershipLab™

Go to Topic 3, Types of Supervision, in the MyEdLeadershipLab™ site at www.myedleadershiplab.com for *The Basic Guide to SuperVision and Instructional Leadership*, Third Edition, where you can:

- Find learning outcomes for Types of Supervision along with the national standards that connect to these outcomes.
- Complete Assignments and Activities that can help you more deeply understand the chapter content.
- Apply and practice your understanding of the core skills identified in the chapter with the Building Leadership Skills unit.
- Prepare yourself for professional certification with a Practice for Certification quiz.

chapter 10

Nondirective Behaviors

outline

- Nondirective Continuum of Behaviors
- Initiating Nondirective Supervision
- Nondirective, Not *Laissez-Faire*, Supervision
- Issues with Nondirective Supervision
- When to Use Nondirective Behaviors
- Critical Reflection on Nondirective Supervision

Visit the **MyEdLeadershipLab™** site for *The Basic Guide to SuperVision and Instructional Leadership*, Third Edition to enhance your understanding of chapter concepts. You'll have the opportunity to practice your skills through video and case based Assignments and Activities as well as Building Leadership Skills units, and prepare for your certification exam with Practice for Certification quizzes.

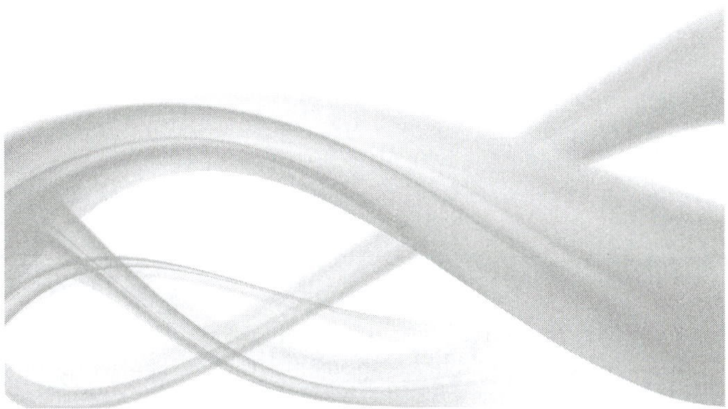

Nondirective Continuum of Behaviors

Nondirective supervision is based on the assumption that an individual teacher knows best what instructional changes must be made and has the ability to think and act on his or her own. The decision belongs to the teacher. The role of the supervisor is to assist the teacher in the process of thinking through his or her actions.

1 *Listening*	2 *Clarifying*	3 *Encouraging*	4 *Reflecting*	5 *Presenting*

T

s

1. Wait until the teacher's initial statement is made
2. Verbalize your understanding of the initial problem
3. Probe for the underlying problem or additional information
4. Show willingness to listen further
5. Constantly paraphrase understanding of the teacher's message

8. Ask the teacher for a commitment to a decision

10. Restate the teacher's plan

Key: T = Maximum teacher responsibility   S = Maximum supervisor responsibility
t = Minimum teacher responsibility   s = Minimum supervisor responsibility

figure **10.1** **The Supervisory Behavior Continuum: Nondirective Behaviors**

The supervisor behaves in ways that keep the teacher's thinking focused on observation, interpretation, problem identification, and problem solving. The supervisor does not interject his or her own ideas into the discussion unless specifically asked. All verbalizations by the supervisor are intended as feedback or to extend the teacher's thinking; they do not influence the actual design.

Figure 10.1 shows a typical pattern of supervisory interpersonal behaviors used in a nondirective conference. They begin with listening and end with asking the

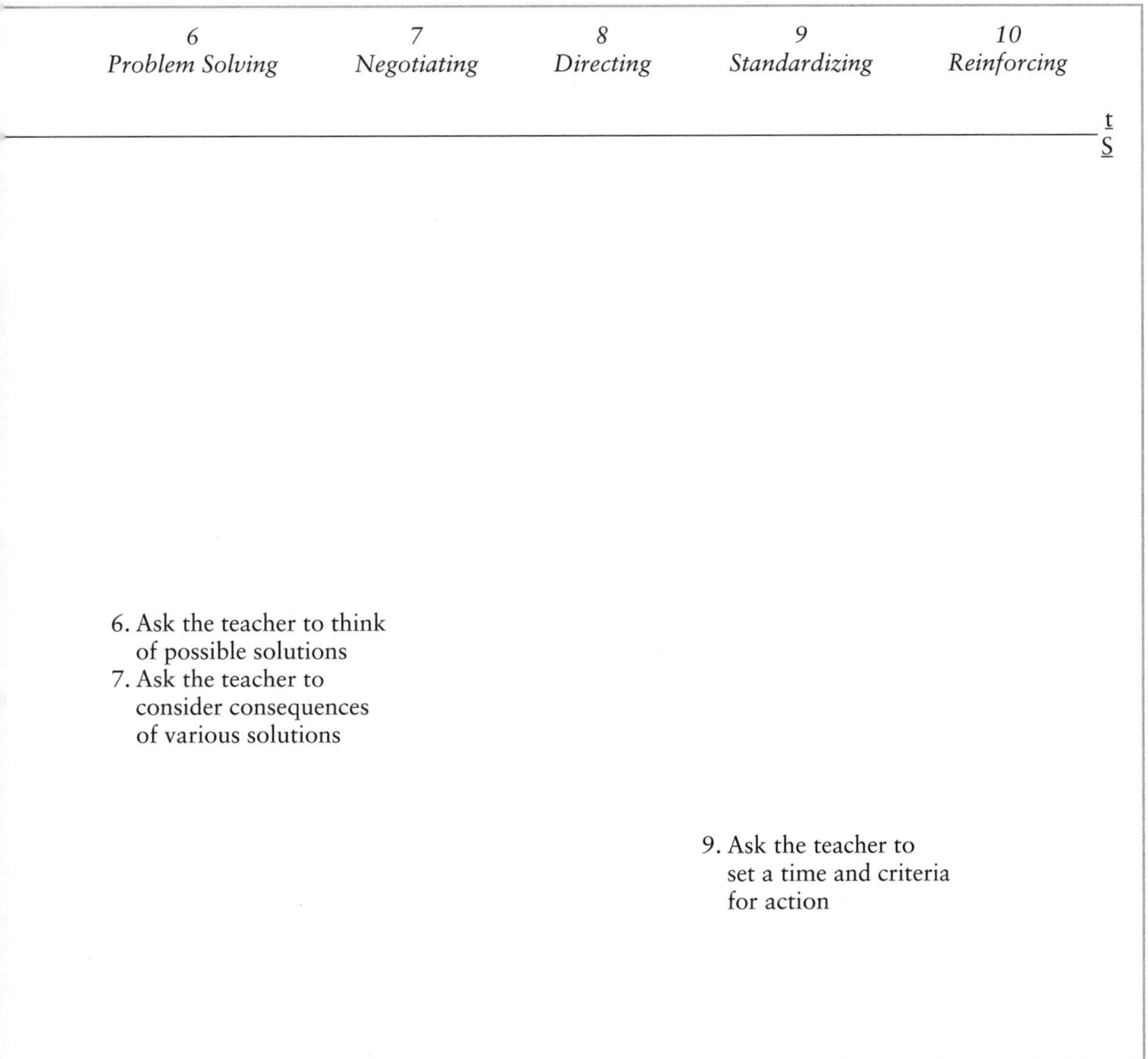

teacher to present his or her decision. The sequence of behaviors between start and finish can vary, but the end should be the same—a noninfluenced teacher decision. This sequence of behaviors is as follows:

1. Listening: *Wait until the teacher's initial statement is made.* Face and look at the teacher; concentrate on what is being said. Avoid thinking about how you see the problem or what you think should be done. It is not easy to restrain your mind from galloping ahead, but your job is to understand what the teacher initially has said.
2. Reflecting: *Verbalize your understanding of the initial problem.* Include in your statement the teacher's feelings and perceived situation: "You're angry because students don't pay attention." Wait for an acknowledgment of accuracy from the teacher: "Yes, I am, but . . ." Do not offer your own opinion; your job is to capture what the teacher is saying.
3. Clarifying: *Probe for the underlying problem or additional information.* You now ask the teacher to look at the problem in some different ways and to consider new information that might be contributing to the problem. Clarifying is done to help the teacher further identify, not solve, the problem. Questions such as: "Do you mean that you are really fed up with school?" "Is it a particular student who is getting to you?" and "When has this happened before?" are appropriate information-seeking questions. Avoid questions that are really solutions in disguise. Such questions as these: "Have you thought about taking up yoga to relax?" and "Maybe you could suspend that student for a few days—what do you think?" are inappropriate. Such leading or suggestive questions are attempts to influence the teacher's final decision.
4. Encouraging: *Show willingness to listen further as the teacher begins to identify the real problems.* Show that you will continue to assist and not leave the discussion incomplete. Statements such as these: "I'm following what you're saying; continue," "Run that by me again," and "I'm following you" are correct. Saying "I like that idea," "Yes, that will work," "Ah, I agree with that," are, even unintentionally, influencing behaviors. A teacher, like any other person, cannot help but be influenced by the judgments a supervisor is making on what he or she says. Encouraging keeps the teacher thinking; praise, however, influences the final decision.
5. Reflecting: *Constantly paraphrase understanding of the teacher's message.* Throughout the discussion, check on the accuracy of what you understand the teacher to be saying. When the teacher adds more information to the perceived problem or explains different sources of the problem, considers the possible actions, and finally makes a decision, the supervisor should paraphrase. First, whenever you are uncertain of what the teacher is saying, you should paraphrase with a statement such as: "I think you're saying . . ." or "I'm not sure, but do you mean . . ." Then you can sit back and allow the teacher to affirm or reject your understanding. Second, when the teacher has come to a halt in

thinking about the problem, the paraphrase should be used to jog the teacher's mind to reflect on what has already been said and what more must be done. For example, after a considerable pause in the teacher's talk, the supervisor might say, "Well, let me see if I can summarize what has been said so far . . ." or "So this is where you are—you're angry because . . ." Comprehensive summarizing allows the teacher to rest, mentally stand off from himself or herself, and think about what has been said. Usually, such paraphrasing stimulates the teacher to interject, add, and continue. Reflecting should not become mechanical or artificial, with the supervisor paraphrasing every teacher statement. Instead, it should be used judiciously when the supervisor is not completely clear about what has been said or when there is a long pause in the conversation. Incessant interjections of "I hear you saying . . . ," without aid or purpose, make teachers skeptical about the supervisor's concern.

6. Problem solving: *Ask the teacher to think of possible solutions.* After the teacher has finished identifying the problem and you are clear about his or her perception of the problem, your responsibility shifts to helping the teacher generate possible solutions. You can do this by asking such straightforward questions as: "What can you do about this?" "What else could be done?" "Think hard about actions that might help," or, "Let me see if you can come up with four to six possible solutions." It is helpful to allow the teacher to think for a minute or two about possible actions before verbalizing them. After solutions have been proposed, you should reflect on the proposals, check on their accuracy, and probe for others. Regardless of whether the teacher proposes only a few or many possibilities, if further probing is not successful, then you should move the conference on.
7. Problem solving: *Ask the teacher to consider consequences of various actions.*The moment of truth is almost at hand. Your emphasis is on having the teacher move from possible to probable solutions. Taking each solution in order, ask: "What would happen if you did . . . ?" "Would it work?" "What problems would be associated with it?" Finally, after having the teacher explore the advantages and disadvantages of each action, he or she should be asked to compare the various actions: "Which would work best?" "Why do you think so?" "How would that be better than the others?"
8. Presenting: *Ask the teacher for a commitment to a decision.* After you have explored possible actions and the teacher has compared their likelihood of success, you must emphasize that the teacher should select actions that are within his or her resources *(do-able),* can be implemented in a short period of time *(feasible),* and are concrete *(accountable).* A simple question—"Well, what will you do now that is likely to improve the situation?"—should cut quickly to the heart of the matter.
9. Standardizing: *Ask the teacher to set a time and criteria for action.* The teacher is assisted in monitoring his or her own decision about future improvement by specifying the time period during which the action will be implemented, when

various parts of the plan will be done, what resources are needed, and how the teacher will know the decision is working. A further series of supervisor questions to accomplish this purpose might be: "Now, tell me what you are going to do." "What will be done first, next, last?" "What do you need in order to do it?" "How will you know it's working?" "When will it be done?" When the teacher can answer these questions, the conference is near completion.

10. Reflecting: *Restate the teacher's plan.* Before leaving, repeat the teacher's entire plan with, "So you're going to do . . ." After the teacher verifies the restated plan, the session is over.

Initiating Nondirective Supervision

At a workshop facilitated by one of the authors, the author decided to illustrate the nondirective approach with an unstructured simulated conference, with the author taking the role of a supervisor and a volunteer participant assuming the role of a teacher. The focus of the conference was a real-world problem that the volunteer, a mentor-teacher, was experiencing. After a successful simulation in which the author used nondirective behaviors to facilitate the teacher's reflection on the problem, consideration of alternative solutions, and an action plan for solving the problem, the author congratulated the volunteer on a simulation well done. The teacher responded, "I don't feel as if I did a very good job. I didn't know what you were trying to get me to say. Was my solution the one you were looking for?" The author explained that there was no preconceived solution to the problem, that the "supervisor" in the role play was not trying to elicit any particular responses from the teacher. The teacher, who had been selected by his district as a mentor of other teachers because of his outstanding teaching and leadership, explained that he simply did not know how to respond to nondirective supervision because, in his many years of teaching, he had never been exposed to a nondirective approach.

This story illustrates the point that supervisors seldom use nondirective behaviors with teachers—indeed, the supervisory approach most often used is directive (Gordon, 1989). Moreover, supervisors sometimes create the illusion of using nondirective behaviors when, in fact, they are manipulating a supervisory conference or group meeting toward a predetermined decision. When this happens often enough, teachers realize that the supervisor is attempting to manipulate them. Without any experience with authentic nondirective supervision, it's no wonder that teachers are leery of the supervisor who is trying to use that approach with them for the first time.

What's the solution when a teacher is perfectly capable of solving his or her own instructional problems, but who, because of past experience, is likely to become confused or suspicious of the supervisor's first use of nondirective supervision? One technique is simply to explain to the teacher or group what nondirective supervision is, what specific behaviors are involved, and why the supervisor believes the teacher or group can benefit from the nondirective approach. Even when the supervisor has provided a rationale for nondirective supervision, some teachers may still be reluctant to identify problems, consider actions, commit to decisions, or establish criteria for success. When this happens, the supervisor should not automatically assume that the nondirective approach is inappropriate for the teacher or group. Rather, the supervisor should continue to build trust and rapport through active listening, probe for problems and related information, and encourage the teacher or group to describe situations and feelings. Eventually, the teacher or group should reach a stage of trust and self-confidence that enables them to consider alternatives and generate an improvement plan. Supervisor commitment to teacher self-direction, along with the use of appropriate interpersonal behaviors, ultimately leads to teacher-driven instructional improvement.

Nondirective, Not *Laissez-Faire*, Supervision

Some educators have criticized nondirective supervision by arguing that supervisors who use nondirective behaviors are abdicating their responsibility to assist teachers to improve their instructional performance. This is a valid argument against *laissez-faire* supervision, which advocates minimal supervisor involvement in the instructional improvement process. However, under our definition of *nondirective supervision*, the supervisor is actively involved in instructional improvement, clarifying, encouraging, reflecting, and facilitating teacher decision making at each stage of the improvement process.

Also, in developmental supervision, the nondirective approach is used only with those teachers who are operating at high levels of abstraction, motivation, and expertise. The developmental supervisor uses one of the other three supervisory approaches with teachers who are not ready to assume full decision-making responsibility.

Issues with Nondirective Supervision

Based on numerous skill-training sessions conducted with school leaders concerning using nondirective behaviors, two common issues and practical questions have arisen:

1. Can a supervisor really remain nonjudgmental and not influence the teacher's or group's decision?
2. What happens if the teacher or group desires the supervisor's input?

Whether a supervisor can really remain nonjudgmental is a legitimate concern. Even when one is consciously avoiding praise, not interjecting one's own ideas, and not offering solutions in the guise of questions, some influencing probably will take place. A study by Mears, Shannon, and Pepinsky (1979) analyzed the tapes of counseling sessions conducted by the most renowned expert on nondirectiveness, psychologist Carl Rogers, revealed a definite pattern to his interrupting the patient and to which statements he selected to paraphrase. It is apparent that any interaction between humans is bound to be influential. Frequency of eye contact, timing of questions, facial expressions, and ways of paraphrasing can always be interpreted by a teacher as approving or disapproving. There is no way to avoid influencing through unconscious supervisory responses. The best one can do is to minimize those behaviors that knowingly influence. One should not knowingly offer ideas, praise, or directions that influence the teacher's decision.

What if the teacher or group asks for the supervisor's suggestions? The answer to this question centers on timing. If the suggestions are asked for and given in the initial stages of a conference or meeting, before the teacher or group has been required to think through the issue, then such feedback structures the stream of subsequent thought and heavily influences the decision. If the suggestions are given after the teacher or group has already narrowed its own choices of actions, however, a supervisor's answer is not as influential. Ideally, it is better to refrain completely from giving one's own ideas. If asked, the supervisor might respond, "I'm sorry, but I don't want to answer that. Instead, I want you to think through what can be done. Only you know your own situation. Therefore, what *I* think is not as important as what *you* think."

When to Use Nondirective Behaviors

When and with whom should nondirective behaviors be used? A supervisor should consider using a nondirective approach in these situations:

1. When the teacher or group is functioning at high developmental levels.
2. When the teacher or group possesses most of the knowledge and expertise about the issue and the supervisor's knowledge and expertise are minimal: "If you don't know anything about it and they do, let them solve it."
3. When the teacher or group has full responsibility for carrying out the decision and the supervisor has little involvement: "If they are going to be accountable for it and you aren't, let them solve it."
4. When the teacher or group is committed to solving the problem but the problem doesn't matter to the supervisor: "If they want to act and you couldn't care less, let them decide."

There are special circumstances in which initial use of nondirective behaviors are appropriate even if the preceding criteria are not met. Regardless of teacher developmental level, expertise, responsibility, or commitment, when a teacher or group has become extremely emotional over a problem, rational problem solving using any of the four supervisory approaches may be unproductive. What may be more beneficial in such situations is the initial use of the nondirective behaviors of

role play 10.1

Practicing Nondirective Behaviors

Directions: The class splits into groups of three. Using the teacher description and situation provided below, one member of each group assumes the role of the teacher, one member assumes the role of the supervisor, and one member assumes the role of observer. The "supervisor" and "teacher" role play a conference in which the supervisor uses a nondirective approach to address the teacher's instructional problem. The observer takes notes on the supervisor's performance during the conference and shares those notes with the other two group members after the role play. Finally, all three participants engage in reflective discussion of the role play and the nondirective approach. (To assist in the role plays in Chapters 7 through 10, see Appendix A, which reviews and compares all four supervisory approaches.)

Teacher Description and Situation: Martha Martinez is a teacher at Nelson Middle School who has won numerous teaching awards. Martha has provided professional development in educational technology at district workshops, serves on the school's technology committee, and has provided expert peer coaching to many of the other teachers at Nelson on integrating technology across the curriculum. Martha recently has agreed to have her classroom serve as a demonstration classroom for using technology to improve the teaching of language arts. In two weeks, Martha will teach her first demonstration lesson. She will teach the lesson to her own seventh-grade language arts students, and five other language arts teachers from Nelson will be on hand to observe. Martha has requested a conference with her supervisor to discuss how she can make her demonstration lesson valuable both to her students and to the teachers who will be observing.

listening, clarifying, encouraging, and reflecting as the teacher or group describes the problem and expresses the anger, frustration, fear, resentment, or other feelings the problem has generated. Once the teacher or group has had the opportunity to vent emotions in the presence of an empathetic listener, the supervisor can then shift to a problem-solving mode, using the criteria of developmental level, expertise, responsibility, and commitment to select the appropriate supervisory approach for the problem-solving phase of the conference or meeting.

Critical Reflection on Nondirective Supervision

The supervisor should consider the following questions when reflecting on the use of nondirective behaviors:

- Is the teacher or group reluctant to assume decision-making responsibility? If so, what might be the reason for that reluctance?
- In addition to using overt nondirective behaviors such as clarifying, encouraging, and reflecting, do I avoid influencing the teacher or group through subtle comments or nonverbal behaviors?

- If the teacher or group asks for my input, do I respond appropriately?
- Am I actively facilitating the teacher or group's decision making, or do I sometimes slip into *laissez-faire* supervision?

MyEdLeadershipLab™

Go to Topic 3, Types of Supervision, in the MyEdLeadershipLab™ site at www.myedleadershiplab.com for *The Basic Guide to SuperVision and Instructional Leadership*, Third Edition, where you can:

- Find learning outcomes for Types of Supervision along with the national standards that connect to these outcomes.
- Complete Assignments and Activities that can help you more deeply understand the chapter content.
- Apply and practice your understanding of the core skills identified in the chapter with the Building Leadership Skills unit.
- Prepare yourself for professional certification with a Practice for Certification quiz.

REFERENCES

Gordon, S. P. 1989. *The theory of developmental supervision: An investigation of the critical aspects*. Unpublished Ed.D. dissertation, University of Georgia, Athens.

Mears, N. M., Shannon, J. W., and Pepinsky, H. B. 1979. Comparison of the stylistic complexity of the language of counselor and client across three theoretical orientations. *Journal of Counseling Psychology, 26*(3), 181–189.

chapter 11

Developmental SuperVision

THEORY AND PRACTICE

outline

- Rationale for Developmental Supervision
- Applying Developmental Supervision
- Not Algorithms, but Guideposts for Decisions
- Scenario and Discussion: Inappropriate Use of Interpersonal Behaviors?

Visit the **MyEdLeadershipLab™** site for *The Basic Guide to SuperVision and Instructional Leadership*, Third Edition to enhance your understanding of chapter concepts. You'll have the opportunity to practice your skills through video and case based Assignments and Activities as well as Building Leadership Skills units, and prepare for your certification exam with Practice for Certification quizzes.

Thus far in Part III, we have introduced developmental supervision and explained each of the four supervisory approaches (directive control, directive informational, collaborative, and nondirective). This chapter provides additional discussion of developmental supervision. The first part of the chapter presents the underlying rationale for developmental supervision. The second part explains how the model can be applied in practice.

Rationale for Developmental Supervision

One aspect of developmental supervision is the match of initial supervisory approach with the teacher's or group's developmental levels, expertise, and commitment. In Chapter 4, we described characteristics of teachers functioning at various stages of adult and career development. Teachers functioning at generally low developmental levels were described as performing at the concrete operations stage of cognitive development, low conceptual levels, the preconventional level of moral reasoning, the fearful stage of ego development, the durable category level of consciousness, and the self-adequacy stage of concern. Teachers or groups of low developmental levels, expertise, and commitment seem well matched to directive supervision. They have difficulty defining problems, have few ways of responding to problems, and are unlikely to accept decision-making responsibility. They clearly are in need of the structure and intensive assistance provided by directive supervision. For most teachers in need of direction, an informational directive approach is appropriate. For teachers functioning at extremely low levels of development, expertise, and commitment and with serious instructional problems, a controlling directive approach might be necessary.

Teachers of generally moderate developmental levels were described as functioning at the formal operations stage of cognitive development, moderate conceptual levels, the conventional level of moral reasoning, the conforming stage of ego development, the cross-categorical level of consciousness, and the teaching tasks stage of concern. Teachers or groups at moderate developmental levels, expertise, and commitment are usually best served by a collaborative supervisory approach. They can generate some possible solutions to an instructional problem but still need some assistance in examining all options and developing a comprehensive plan for instructional improvement. The brainstorming inherent in collaborative supervision allows the teacher or group to share perceptions and offer some possible alternatives for future action but also to receive the benefit of supervisor perceptions and proposals. Negotiated action plans made during collaborative supervision allow teachers to meet needs of emerging independence while receiving the moderate guidance needed to assure that the plan will lead to instructional improvement.

Teachers functioning at generally high developmental levels were described in Chapter 4 as being at the postformal operations stage of cognitive development, high conceptual levels, the postconventional level of moral reasoning, the autonomous stage of ego development, the systems or trans-systems level of consciousness, and the teaching impact stage of concern. Teachers or groups functioning at generally high developmental levels, expertise, and commitment are ready for the self-direction fostered by the nondirective supervisory approach. They are autonomous, explorative, and creative. They can think of a problem from many perspectives, generate a variety of alternative actions, think through each step of an action plan, and follow the plan through to completion.

The Problem of Variability

The fact that the criteria for selecting a supervisory approach may fluctuate means that choosing the best approach can become more complicated than the broad guidelines just discussed might suggest. The following possibilities must be kept in mind:

1. Individual or group levels of development, expertise, and commitment may vary. For example, a teacher might be functioning at high levels of consciousness as well as cognitive, conceptual, and moral development but at only moderate levels of ego development, concern, and commitment. In addition, a group might include teachers of low, moderate, and high developmental levels. Some general guidelines are to use a controlling directive approach if most characteristics of an individual or group indicate an extremely low decision-making capacity, informational directive supervision if most attributes point to a fairly low capacity, a collaborative approach if most characteristics indicate a moderate capacity, and nondirective supervision if most attributes point to a high capacity for decision making. When working with an individual or group with widely fluctuating characteristics, a collaborative approach would probably be most effective.
2. Characteristics of teachers and groups might change in certain situations. For example, a teacher who has successfully taught general science to middle school students for 10 years might regress to lower levels of development, expertise, or commitment after being transferred to a senior high school to teach chemistry and physics. Similarly, a faculty at a former junior high school might regress to lower levels of group development, expertise, or commitment after the campus has been converted to a middle school. In short, the developmental supervisor sometimes must change supervisory behaviors in order to adapt to a change in the teacher or group's situation.

Research on adult and teacher development can suggest guidelines for determining the best supervisory approach. The tremendous variability of teacher characteristics, however, means that the supervisor must choose his or her approach on a case-by-case basis, relying on the knowledge base on teacher characteristics, recent observations of and interactions with the teacher or group, and analysis of the current situation. One way to describe developmental supervision is to say that it provides teachers with as much initial choice as they are ready to assume and then fosters teachers' decision-making capacity and expanded choice over time.

Supervision for Teacher Development

The long-term goal of developmental supervision is teacher development toward a point at which teachers, facilitated by supervisors, can assume full responsibility for instructional improvement. There are several other reasons why we believe that teacher development should be a critical function of supervision.

- As described in Chapter 4, teachers functioning at higher developmental levels tend to use a wide variety of instructional behaviors associated with successful teaching.
- Teachers who have themselves reached high stages of cognitive, conceptual, moral, and ego development are more likely to foster their own students' growth in those areas. In a democratic society, it is vital that students learn to think reflectively, function at high stages of moral reasoning, and be autonomous decision makers.
- Teachers at higher levels of adult development, expertise, and commitment are more likely to embrace "a cause beyond oneself" and participate in collective action toward schoolwide instructional improvement—a critical element found in the effective schools research.

This section has focused on the *why* of developmental supervision. The remainder of the chapter is concerned with *how* developmental supervision can be applied in the real world of schools and teachers.

Applying Developmental Supervision

There are three phases of developmental supervision:

1. Choosing the best entry-level supervisory approach
2. Applying the chosen approach
3. Fostering teacher development while gradually increasing teacher choice and decision-making responsibility

Our discussion of applying developmental supervision addresses each of these three phases.

Phase 1: Choosing the Best Approach

There are two primary ways to assess a teacher's developmental levels, expertise, and commitment, all of which should be considered when choosing the supervisory approach to be used. One way is to observe the teacher teaching or working with other teachers. Another way is to discuss with the teacher his or her ideas about students, teaching, and instructional improvement.

The supervisor can use discussions with the teacher to find answers to the following questions:

1. Is the teacher aware of improvements that can be made in the classroom? Can the teacher identify those needs?
2. Has the teacher considered possible causes of the instructional needs? Does the teacher gather information from multiple sources about the instructional needs?
3. Can the teacher generate several possible solutions? How carefully does the teacher weigh the merits of each solution? Does the teacher consider what he or she can do to reach the goal without looking unrealistically for outside help?
4. Can the teacher be decisive in choosing a course of action? Does the teacher commit himself or herself to an implementation procedure?
5. Does the teacher do what he or she says?

Teacher responses to questions like these can provide clues to the appropriate supervisory approach.

Some cautions need to be made here concerning the organizational relation ship between the individual providing supervision and the teacher or group receiving supervision. Generally, directive control supervision should be used only by supervisors in line relationships with teachers (supervisors who have been given formal authority by the school district over teachers they are supervising). Informational directive supervision should be used only by those who are acknowledged by the organization to have special expertise. Examples of individuals with acknowledged expertise include supervisors in line or staff relationships with teachers, lead teachers, mentors of beginning teachers, and so on. Collaborative and nondirective behaviors can be used by supervisors in line or staff relationships, teachers designated as instructional leaders, and teachers in reciprocal helping relationships, such as peer coaches. Table 11.1 provides a review of supervisory approaches normally appropriate for use by those carrying out some common supervisory roles. The task of the person in a particular supervisory role is to choose the best approach from those appropriate for his or her role.

Phase 2: Applying the Chosen Approach

Can a supervisor shift from one approach to another when working with teachers and groups at different developmental levels? Stated differently, can the same supervisor effectively use directive informational, directive control, collaborative, and nondirective behaviors?

The question of *supervisor flexibility* was addressed by Gordon (1989, 1990) during a study in which he trained supervisors in developmental supervision and then asked each supervisor to work with separate teacher triads. The supervisors attempted informational directive supervision with one teacher, collaborative

table **11.1** **Supervisory Roles and Approaches**

	Approaches Appropriate for Particular Supervisory Roles			
Supervisory Roles	**Directive Control**	**Directive Informational**	**Collaborative**	**Nondirective**
Line Supervisor	X	X	X	X
Staff Supervisor		X	X	X
Lead Teacher		X	X	X
Designated Mentor		X	X	X
Peer Coach			X	X

supervision with a second teacher, and nondirective supervision with a third teacher. (Supervisors based their decisions on supervisory approach on earlier observations of and conferences with teachers.) When supervisors attempted the different approaches, their conferences with teachers were recorded. The conferences were analyzed to determine if attempted approaches were effectively used. The investigator found that 93 percent of the supervisors were able to implement informational directive supervision, 100 percent were able to engage in collaborative supervision, and 70 percent were able to use nondirective supervision. An implication of this study is that supervisors being trained to use developmental supervision must receive their most intensive training in nondirective supervision, which seems to be the most difficult approach for many to use.

What if a supervisor in the early stages of working with a teacher or group—even after preliminary observation and discussion—is not sure which supervisory approach to use? A good rule of thumb in such cases is to *prepare to use a collaborative approach, but be ready to shift to a nondirective or directive approach if necessary.* When preparing to use a collaborative approach a supervisor determines possible improvement goals, actions, and criteria to be considered and potentially integrated with goals, actions, and criteria suggested by the teacher or group. However, if during the early phases of the conference or meeting it becomes apparent that the teacher or group will be able to identify an appropriate goal and action plan on their own, then the supervisor can forget about his or her possible suggestions and shift to nondirective behaviors as a means of facilitating self-directed teacher planning. If, on the other hand, the teacher or group is unable to identify an obvious problem, any of its underlying causes, or any possible solutions, the supervisor can shift to a directive mode, mandating (directive control) or suggesting (directive informational) a goal, actions, and improvement criteria.

One type of supervisor flexibility is the ability to plan and implement different supervisory approaches with different teachers and groups. The ultimate supervisor flexibility, however, is the ability to "shift supervisory gears," so to speak, and effectively use an approach not originally planned because of new discoveries about teachers or the situation at hand. Like successful teachers, successful supervisors must be able to think on their feet and flex accordingly (Zellermayer and Margolin, 2005).

Phase 3: Fostering Teacher Development

Simply matching the best supervisory approach to the teacher or group's current developmental levels can promote some degree of teacher development. For example, Siens and Ebmeier (1996) found that teachers assisted by supervisors trained to tailor their conference approaches to teachers' levels of motivation, analytical skill, and knowledge experienced significantly more growth on a measure of reflective thinking than did a control group of teachers receiving only the regular supervision provided at their schools. Previous chapters in this text have discussed facilitating teacher development by gradually decreasing supervisor control and increasing teacher control over the decision-making process. There are additional strategies that supervisors can use to stimulate teacher development.

One method is to introduce teachers to new information about students and learning, innovative teaching strategies, and novel ways to frame and solve problems. Initially, new ways of thinking and acting that teachers are invited to explore should be linked to their existing knowledge, experience, and values. Gradually, teachers can be exposed to a broader spectrum of theory and practice.

Another method is to assign teachers to decision-making teams or learning groups in which most of the other members are functioning at slightly higher developmental levels. Significant, ongoing professional interaction with teachers of somewhat higher development will tend to pull the teacher of lower development toward the group's functioning level.

Lois Thies-Sprinthall (1984) has identified five conditions necessary to promote psychological/cognitive growth:

1. Role-taking experiences
2. Careful and continuous guided reflection
3. Balance . . . between real experience and discussion/reflection
4. Both personal support and challenge
5. Continuity (programs should be at least six months in length with meetings at regular intervals) (p. 54)

Phillips and Glickman (1991) studied a peer-coaching program that incorporated Thies-Sprinthall's five conditions for psychological/cognitive growth. The participants were 22 teachers who attended four professional development sessions in which they learned observation, problem solving, and collaborative and nondirective interpersonal skills. The workshops included lectures, demonstrations, practice observations, conference role playing, outside readings, and opportunities for discussion and reflection. A coaching cycle consisted of a preconference, classroom observation, postobservation conference, and follow-up session. Coaching partners engaged in four coaching cycles. Each teacher assumed the role of coach in two of the cycles and was coached by his or her partner in the other two cycles. The instructor and participants engaged in group debriefing sessions after each coaching cycle. Phillips and Glickman (1991) measured participants' conceptual levels before and after the program and found that a significant increase in teachers' conceptual levels had occurred by the end of the program. Exploratory research such as the study reported by Phillips and Glickman indicates that stimulation of teacher growth toward higher developmental levels is possible.

Not Algorithms, but Guideposts for Decisions

Eventually, we must discuss, question, and ask each other (in a supervisor–supervisee relationship) which supervisory approach has been most helpful in the past, which will be most helpful in the present, and which approach we should be striving for in the future. With the exception of emergency situations, this is the responsibility of both parties.

There are no algorithms to provide exactly correct responses to human behavior. Such formulas as "If individual X exhibits characteristics A, B, and C, then supervisor Y should do D, F, and G" do not and should not exist. Such algorithms are useful only in mechanically and technically controlled systems (such as computer operations, assembly production, or chemical alterations). Algorithms work in technical but not human endeavors, and it would be misleading to suggest that such supervision formulas are available. Instead, what is available is information about ourselves and others that can serve as guideposts to suggest what *might* be of use. Such developmental guideposts can help reduce some of the infinite complexity of the school world so that supervision can be a purposeful and thoughtful function for improving instruction.

Scenario and Discussion: Inappropriate Use of Interpersonal Behaviors?

Consider the following scenario:

> Megan Janson, a teacher at Lakeside High School, has come to instructional supervisor Jim Autry with a concern. Several female teachers have complained that Jim seems to be overly directive with them during conferences focused on instructional supervision. These same teachers have told Megan that they have heard from a number of male colleagues that Jim is nondirective when conferring with the male teachers.
>
> Megan, a close friend of Jim, tells him she wanted him to know this so he could reflect on the situation and decide what, if anything, to do about it. Jim has been using different supervisory approaches with different teachers and

groups lately, but has been trying to use collaborative supervision with most teachers and has been intentionally directive with only one female teacher and intentionally nondirective with only one male teacher. He is surprised and disturbed at the comments from female teachers reported by Megan.

What advice would you give Jim on each of the following issues?

1. How can Jim determine whether he is using directive behaviors with females better matched with a different approach, and/or being nondirective with males better matched with a different approach?
2. If Jim concludes that he really is using unintended interpersonal behaviors with some teachers, how can he explore possible reasons for such unintended behaviors?
3. If Jim eventually concludes that he has been engaging in unconscious gender bias in his supervisory conferences, what can he do to correct the situation? How can he verify improvement in this area?

> ## MyEdLeadershipLab™
>
> Go to Topic 3, Types of Supervision, in the **MyEdLeadershipLab™** site at www.myedleadershiplab.com for *The Basic Guide to SuperVision and Instructional Leadership*, Third Edition, where you can:
>
> - Find learning outcomes for Types of Supervision along with the national standards that connect to these outcomes.
> - Complete Assignments and Activities that can help you more deeply understand the chapter content.
> - Apply and practice your understanding of the core skills identified in the chapter with the Building Leadership Skills unit.
> - Prepare yourself for professional certification with a Practice for Certification quiz.

REFERENCES

Gordon, S. P. 1989. *The theory of developmental supervision: An investigation of the critical aspects.* Unpublished Ed.D. dissertation, University of Georgia.

Gordon, S. P. 1990. Developmental supervision: An exploratory study of a promising model. *Journal of Curriculum and Supervision, 5,* 293–307.

Phillips, M. D., and Glickman, C. D. 1991. Peer coaching: Developmental approach to enhancing teacher thinking. *Journal of Staff Development, 12*(2), 20–25.

Siens, C. M., and Ebmeier, H. 1996. Developmental supervision and the reflective thinking of teachers. *Journal of Curriculum and Supervision, 11*(4), 299–319.

Thies-Sprinthall, L. 1984. Promoting the developmental growth of supervising teachers: Theory, research programs, and implications. *Journal of Teacher Education, 35*(3), 53–60.

Zellermayer, M., and Margolin, I. 2005. Teacher educators' professional learning described through the lens of complexity theory. *Teachers College Record, 107*(6), 1275–1304.

part 4

Technical Skills

The supervisor who knows about characteristics of successful schools, the norms that mediate against success, and the ways teacher development contrasts with optimal adult development can begin to formulate a supervisory belief system that becomes a reality when interpersonal and technical skills of supervision are applied in practice.

Part 3 matches directive, collaborative, and nondirective interpersonal skills in working with developmental levels of individuals and groups of teachers. Part 4 deals with the technical supervisory skills needed in working with teachers to assess, plan, observe, and evaluate. Understanding schools and relating well to teachers are necessary components, but technical skills are equally important for accomplishing the tasks of supervision.

chapter 12

Assessing and Planning Skills

outline

- Assessing and Planning within the Organization
- Ways of Assessing Need
- Analyzing Organizational Needs
- Planning
- Cautions Concerning Planning

Visit the **MyEdLeadershipLab™** site for *The Basic Guide to SuperVision and Instructional Leadership*, Third Edition to enhance your understanding of chapter concepts. You'll have the opportunity to practice your skills through video and case based Assignments and Activities as well as Building Leadership Skills units, and prepare for your certification exam with Practice for Certification quizzes.

Assessing and planning are two sides of the same coin. *Assessing* involves determining where you and your staff have been and where you and your staff currently are. *Planning* includes deciding where you want to go and choosing the path you and your staff hope to traverse in order to reach that destination. Until you are certain of the origination and destination of your travel, a map is useless. Once you are certain, a route can be created.

Assessing and Planning within the Organization

We might think of assessing and planning as a recipe (Bruce and Grimsley, 1979). A plan for direct assistance, professional development, curriculum development, or group development has the same elements as a cooking recipe. *We decide our objective:* "to bake a sweet potato soufflé." (Thanks to Ms. Donna Bell for providing this culinary example.) Knowing our family's previous history of food preferences, we are confident that if we cook the soufflé correctly, they will enjoy it and we will be held in positive regard for at least 10 minutes. Next, *we determine the activities and when they will take place:*

Activity 1: Mash 6 cups of cooked sweet potatoes.

Activity 2: Beat into the mashed potatoes: 4 eggs, 1 cup butter, 2 cups sugar, 1 cup milk, 1 teaspoon vanilla.

Activity 3: Spread out in unbuttered pan.

Activity 4: Mix in a separate bowl: 1 cup brown sugar, ⅔ cup flour, 1 cup butter, 1 cup chopped pecans.

Activity 5: Spread this mix evenly over the potatoes.

Activity 6: Bake at 350° for 1 hour.

With the activities and times determined, *we must identify resources.* Equipment resources are an oven, measuring cups, measuring spoons, a large bowl, a pan, a mixing fork, and a spreading knife. Food resources are potatoes, eggs, butter, sugar, vanilla, brown sugar, flour, pecans, and milk.

Finally, *we evaluate the success* of our cooking endeavor by the following criteria: Everyone in our family will eat the sweet potato soufflé. At least two of the three members will ask for seconds. All of them will tell us we're wonderful cooks, and they will volunteer to wash the dishes.

If the supervisor tries acting as a gourmet of instructional cookery and planning recipes for success, all staff members will delight in the soufflé of instructional improvement. The food analogy has run its course (by now, you are probably heading for the refrigerator), and we can turn to assessing and planning within the school context. For purposes of illustration, let's take an example of an elementary reading supervisor who is responsible for developing revised curriculum guides in reading.

Ways of Assessing Need

The first question for the supervisor is: What do we hope to accomplish with a new curriculum guide? To answer this question, we must collect information about both the past and the present states of instruction. The supervisor can use multiple ways of assessing need: (1) eyes and ears, (2) systematic classroom and school observations, (3) official records, (4) review of teacher and student work products, (5) third-party review, (6) written open-ended survey, (7) check and ranking list surveys, (8) the Delphi technique, and (9) the nominal group technique.

Eyes and Ears

Talk to teachers, administrators, aides, and anyone else who works directly with the task under consideration. In this case, the supervisor should ask teachers and aides individually and in small groups what they believe are the strengths and weaknesses of the curriculum guide. How is it being used? Is it helpful, and in what ways? Where does it break down? When is it not useful?

Systematic Classroom and School Observations

This type of assessment goes beyond informal discussions and observation. It consists of the systematic gathering of quantitative or qualitative observation data. Chapter 13 provides a variety of classroom observation instruments. Such instruments can be used to assist the individual teacher, but also can be used to gather data from many classrooms and identify schoolwide instructional needs. For example, in a schoolwide needs assessment one of the authors coordinated, observers used the same observation instrument to gather data on instructional methods used in classrooms throughout the school. The observers found that most of the teachers in the school relied on lecture and independent seatwork as their primary instructional methods. It was concluded that there was a need for teachers to develop a wider variety of instructional methods. Observations also can be carried out in common areas of the school.

Official Records

Look at any documents that indicate the current use and effect of the task under consideration. In this case, what do achievement test scores show? How about diagnostic tests? Are students mastering skills, or are there certain areas that are consistently out of line with others? What about the curriculum guide itself? When was it last revised? What recent knowledge about writing curriculum guides, instructional approaches, and topics are not reflected in the current curriculum?

Review of Teacher and Student Work Products

Assessors can review teacher and student work products to assess need. Examples of teacher work products are unit and lesson plans, videos of teaching, and teacher portfolios. Examples of student work products include daily assignments, videos of student presentations, student projects, and student portfolios. Samples of work produced by several teachers or students can be reviewed to identify common instructional needs. In some schools, teachers build classroom and school portfolios that can be reviewed to analyze representative teacher and student work products.

Third-Party Review

Having a neutral outside person review the task area can be helpful. The supervisor might contact a university or central office consultant, a graduate doctoral student, or some other person with expertise to do an investigation and write a report. The third-party person should be given a clear description of the task (to look at the strengths and weaknesses of the curriculum guides), and care should be taken not to bias the third-party person's judgment. The report can then serve as an additional source of objective knowledge, not tied to any special interest in the forthcoming project.

Written Open-Ended Survey

To document and add to the information already received through eyes and ears and official records, a written survey can be administered. Send out a brief questionnaire that asks teachers, aides, administrators, and parents what they think about the current reading curriculum. Keep the survey brief, and word the questions simply, without education jargon. Figure 12.1 shows one example of such a survey.

Explanation: As you may know, this year we are determining changes to be made in our reading curriculum. Would you please take a few minutes to respond to the following questions? Please be frank! We will use the information to rewrite our curriculum guides.

Question 1. What do you think about the current reading curriculum?

Question 2. What are the strengths of the current reading curriculum?

Question 3. What are the weaknesses of the current reading curriculum?

Question 4. What changes do you believe would improve the reading curriculum?

figure 12.1 **Survey of Reading Curriculum**

Check and Ranking Lists

After gathering ideas of the strengths and weaknesses of the task at hand from many sources, the supervisor can ask staff to rank the ideas. The supervisor can then compile a group frequency and numerical priority for each idea previously mentioned. For example, if—through eyes and ears, official documents, and open-ended surveys—the supervisor has collected a list of ideas about perceived weaknesses of the current reading program, he or she then could disseminate the list (such as the list shown in Figure 12.2) back to teachers, aides, and others. The supervisor can meet with the staff and show the frequency of numbers assigned to each idea and the average score for each item. Those items receiving frequent low scores or with the lowest average scores are the first to focus on when discussing curriculum revisions. The ranking list can be further refined by having the participants do two separate rankings—first, to see how all the ideas rank, and second, to rerank a shortened list of prioritized ideas.

Delphi Technique

Another written way to prioritize needs is the Delphi technique, developed by the Rand Corporation (Weaver, 1971; Hostrop, 1975; Wilhelm, 2001). The technique, originally intended to forecast trends, is often used for needs assessment. It is a combination of open-ended survey and ranking. The supervisor sends around a problem statement to staff: "We are looking at revisions in the reading curriculum. Write down what you believe must be done." The supervisor retrieves the written comments, reproduces everyone's comments, and returns all the comments to the participants. Each participant reads the comments and then writes an individual synthesis

Directions: The following are the ideas for possible changes that you have suggested. Please prioritize this list by placing the number 1 next to the idea needing the greatest attention, number 2 next to the item needing the next most attention, and so on until all items are ranked.

____ Format of the guides.
____ Readability of the guides.
____ Activities to go with curriculum objectives.
____ Objectives and units dealing with reading newspapers.
____ Objectives and units dealing with reading in other subject areas.
____ More phonics and word recognition objectives.
____ Cross-reference units with materials in the classrooms.
____ Cross-reference objects with fourth-grade competency-based reading test.

figure 12.2 **Ranking Ideas for Improving Reading Curriculum**

of the various ideas. The supervisor then collects everyone's syntheses and makes a new list of all synthesized ideas. The new list goes back to the participants for ranking. The supervisor collects and computes average and frequency of ratings and then returns the tallies to participants to rerank. This procedure continues until clear priorities emerge.

Nominal Group Technique

The nominal group technique, made popular by Delbecq, Van de Ven, and Gustafson (1975), is an effective way to involve all individuals within large groups of stakeholders in needs assessment and goal setting. The process is outlined here in eight steps:

1. The large group is divided into small groups. Each small group is assigned a facilitator to explain and coordinate the process.
2. Each individual within a small group silently generates and writes perceived needs.
3. In round-robin manner, participants orally share with their small group one perceived need at a time. The facilitator records each idea on a flip chart. At this point, there is no discussion—only a listing of perceived needs.
4. Small-group discussions of each perceived need are led by the facilitators. The purpose of the discussion is clarification of the perceived needs, not debate on their validity.
5. Individuals within each small group rate all of the perceived needs listed in step 3. This step usually takes the form of participants assigning each perceived need a numerical value. For example, the facilitator might instruct group members to rate each need from 1 to 5, with an item assigned a value of 1 considered to be unimportant and an item rated a 5 perceived to be an extremely important need.
6. Each small-group facilitator collects all group members' ratings and calculates a mean for each perceived need. The facilitator rewrites the perceived needs in rank order by mean and shares the results with the small group.
7. Each small group submits its list of ranked needs (without the means) for large-group consideration. By preagreement, each small group might submit only its top-ranked needs (perhaps its top five needs) to the large group.
8. A lead facilitator then takes the large group through steps 4 through 6. In the large-group version of step 4, any participant can ask for clarification of any perceived need, with the appropriate small-group facilitator providing the requested clarification. In the whole-group version of step 5, each participant rates all perceived needs presented to the large group. The product of the large-group version of step 6 is a list of organizational needs in rank order.

Analyzing Organizational Needs

Some organizational needs are easily understood and addressed by supervisors and teachers, whereas others are more complicated and require analysis to determine their underlying causes before a plan can be formulated.

For decades, W. Edwards Deming (1986) argued for the use of data displays to examine factors that may contribute to organizational needs and problems. The words of Mary Walton (1986) should allay any anxiety concerning the use of such charts that the reader without expertise in complex data analysis might be experiencing:

> Some of the most useful statistical tools are neither difficult nor complicated to master. The level of mathematics necessary is no more than a seventh or eighth grader might learn. Several of the basic tools are merely ways of organizing and visually displaying data. In most cases, employees can collect the data and do much of the interpretation, and they are happy to do so because it gives them more responsibility. (p. 94)

Cause and Effect Diagrams

Figure 12.3 is an example of a cause and effect diagram, often referred to as a *fishbone diagram.* In our example, a newly formed staff-development committee has received feedback from teachers throughout the district that recent staff-development programs have been ineffective. Based on a series of interviews with representative groups of teachers, the committee constructed the cause and effect diagram in Figure 12.3.

Four general causes were identified for the ineffective professional development: (1) poor planning, (2) low-quality staff-development sessions, (3) inadequate support for the program, and (4) unsatisfactory program evaluation. Contributing causes within the poor planning category included failure to involve teachers in the planning process, the fact that the professional development plan was not based on teacher needs, and the absence of alternatives for staff from different grade levels, content areas, and specialty areas.

The poor quality of the staff-development sessions was attributed to several issues: too many teachers were present, each session was a one-shot workshop unrelated to the other workshops in the program, and the workshop presentations were of poor quality. The workshops were perceived to be substandard because the outside presenters did not have a good understanding of the school culture or the purposes of the program, and their presentations were too abstract to evoke teacher interest.

Problems with support included a lack of funds to purchase instructional materials necessary to implement ideas introduced in the workshops and a failure to provide support for teachers attempting to transfer workshop concepts to the

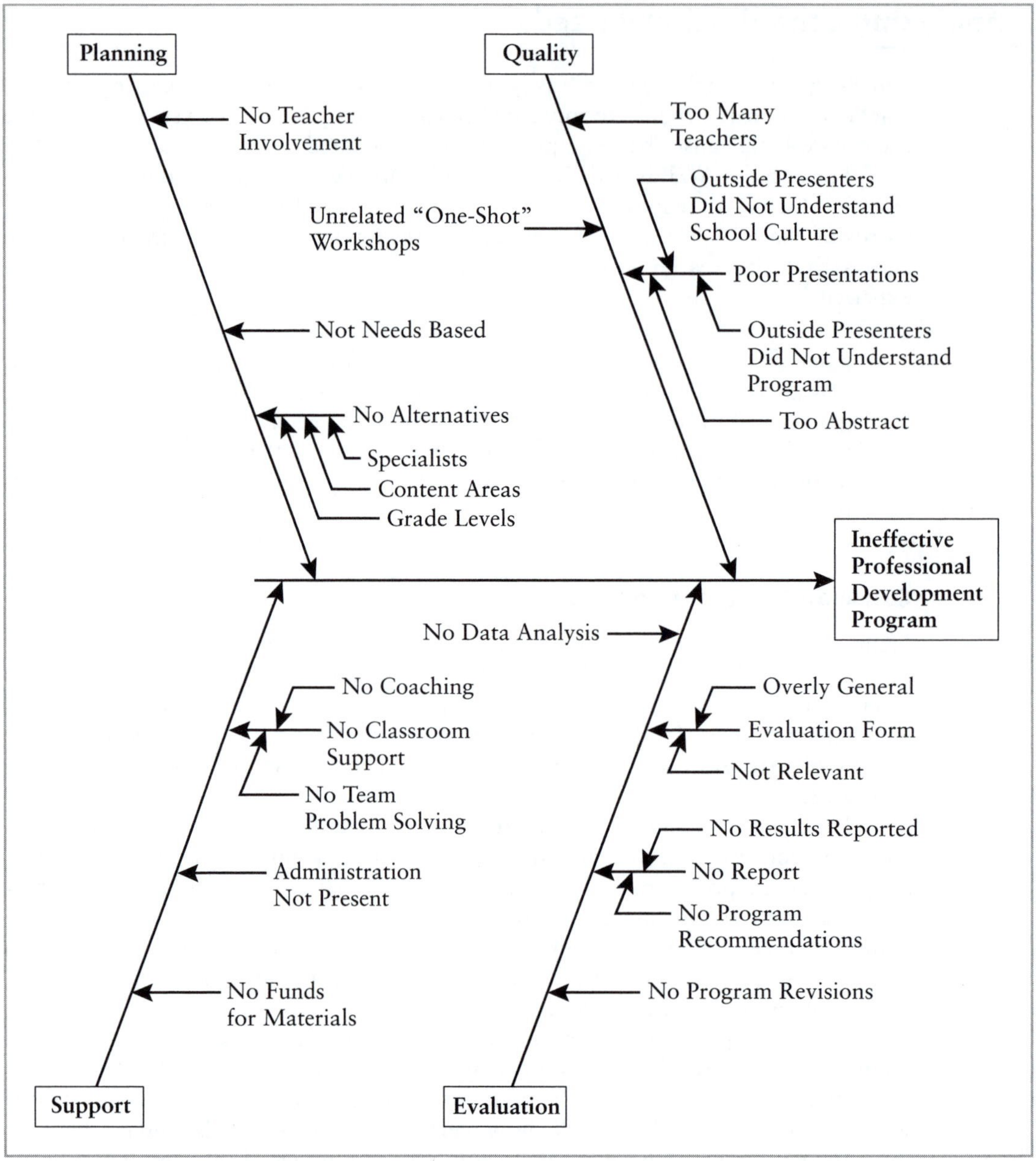

figure 12.3 **Cause and Effect Diagram**

classroom. Finally, the committee found that the district's evaluation of the program had been inadequate. The evaluation forms used by the district were the same ones used for all staff-development workshops; they were not relevant to the specific content of the workshops being assessed. In addition, the wording of the evaluation questions was so general that teachers were not sure what the questions were asking. Because no formal analysis of evaluation data took place, no information on program outcomes was available and no program revisions were made.

The "anatomy of a failure" depicted in Figure 12.3 is not the most pleasant project the planning committee could have undertaken, but the completed diagram was a valuable tool in planning future professional development programs.

Flowcharts

A flowchart can be used to review a process when either the process or conflicting perceptions of the process are resulting in unmet needs. When different parties involved in a process draw their own flowcharts, the charts often are dissimilar. Figure 12.4 shows a flowchart tracking what happens from the time a student is sent to the office for misbehavior until the student returns to class. This chart was drawn by the principal's secretary. Flowcharts of the same process drawn by the principal, the teacher, and the student might be very different from the secretary's and each other's!

Pareto Charts

A Pareto chart illustrates in descending frequency of size those factors that cause a need or problem. Displaying the relative impact of causal factors gives planners information to help them set priorities and allocate resources. Figure 12.5 illustrates a Pareto chart with bars showing the percentage of students dropping out of a senior high school for each of several reasons. Above the bars, a cumulative percentage line runs across the chart. This data would be valuable to a planning team designing a dropout prevention program.

Planning

After assessing and prioritizing needs and identifying causes, planning proceeds. Techniques of planning discussed in this section include affinity diagrams, impact analysis charts, Gantt charts, and force field analysis.

Affinity Diagrams

Let us assume that a needs assessment has identified a number of specific needs, with many of those needs appearing to be related to each other. An affinity diagram is a way of clustering needs and identifying broad goals that address a set of related

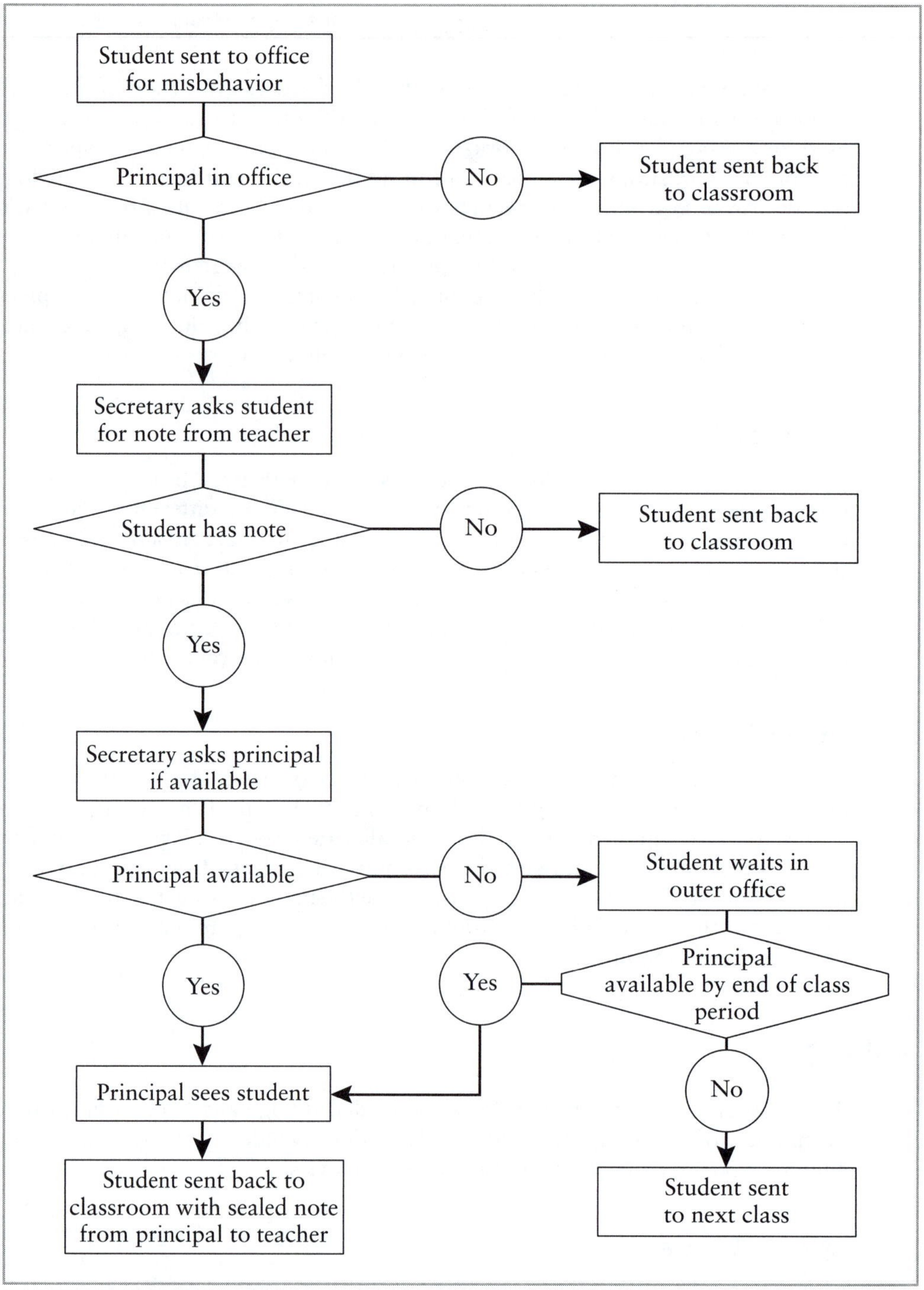

figure 12.4 **Flowchart**

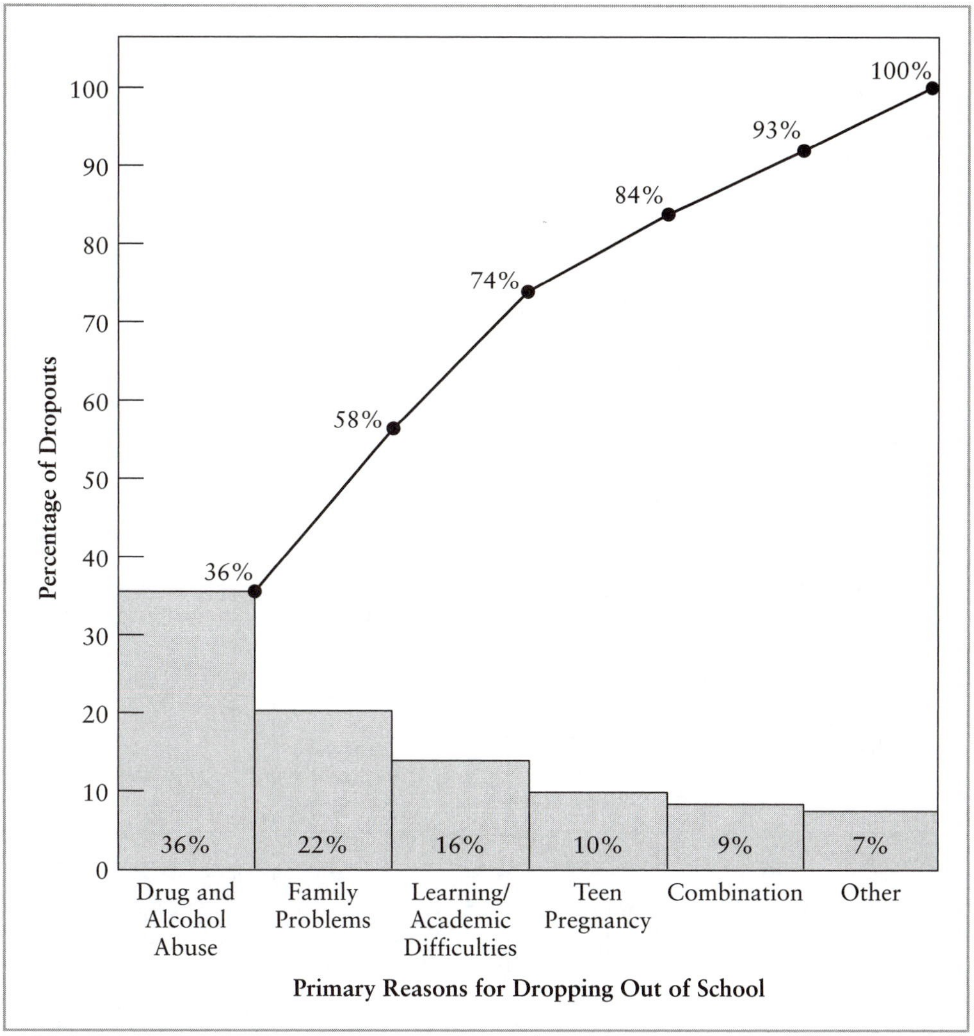

figure 12.5 **Pareto Chart**

needs. One way to begin the building of an affinity diagram is to list each identified need on a separate card or sticky note. Figure 12.6 displays results of a curriculum needs assessment. In the assessment, teachers, parents, and community members stated that students should attain each of the outcomes in Figure 12.6. The affinity diagram in Figure 12.7 clusters the curriculum needs and identifies a broad goal common to each cluster. Enfolding specific needs within larger categories enables the planning team to focus on a few broad goals while retaining information on specific needs.

Ethical Values	Math Skills	Commitment to Democratic Principles	Problem-Solving Skills
Commitment to Wellness	Acceptance of Others' Cultures	Understanding of History's Effects on the Present	Positive Self-Concept
Creative Expression	Health Awareness	Understanding of Basic Scientific Concepts	Commitment to Community Service
Collaborative Skills	Self-Monitoring Skills	Writing Skills	Physical Fitness
Reading Skills	Critical-Thinking Skills	Inquiry Skills	Persistence
Global Awareness	Work Ethic	Technological Literacy	Emotional Intelligence
Ability to Express Oneself Orally	Commitment to Social Justice	Interpersonal Skills	Geographic Literacy

figure **12.6** **Curriculum Needs, to Be Clustered in Affinity Diagram**

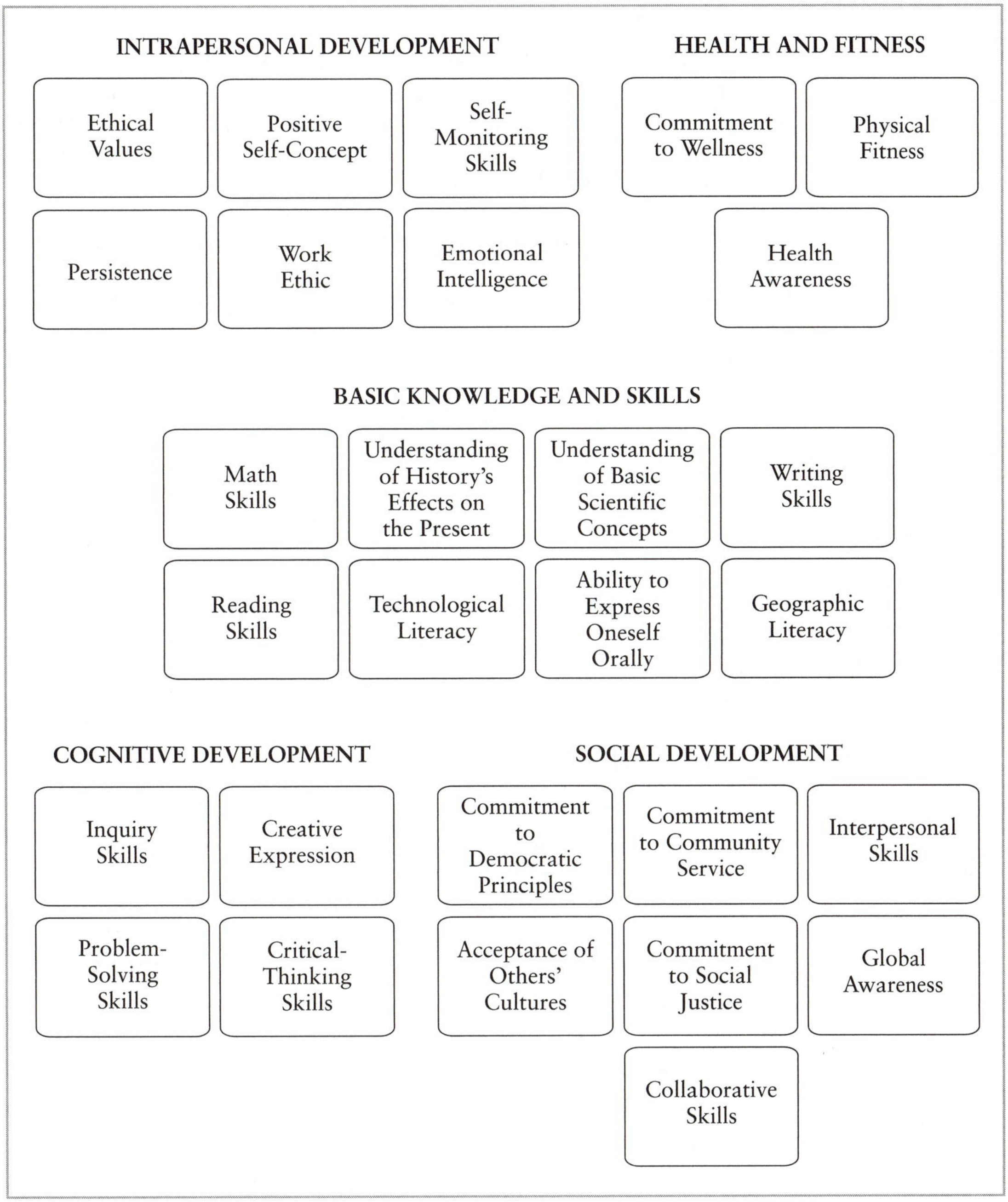

figure **12.7** **Affinity Diagram**

Impact Analysis Charts

An impact analysis chart is usually constructed early in the planning process. Its purpose is to assist planners in projecting whom and what a potential program or change will affect and what the effects might be. In Figure 12.8, triangles represent people and things on which a revised reading curriculum might have an impact. Predicted effects are symbolized by rectangles.

Impact analysis charts can become far more complex than the example in Figure 12.8. (The more ambitious the goals, the more extensive the chart.) Building and discussing impact analysis charts can help planners create a *conceptual map* of areas they want to address during the planning process. They can also help planners include objectives, activities, and evaluation procedures in their formal plan that they might otherwise neglect.

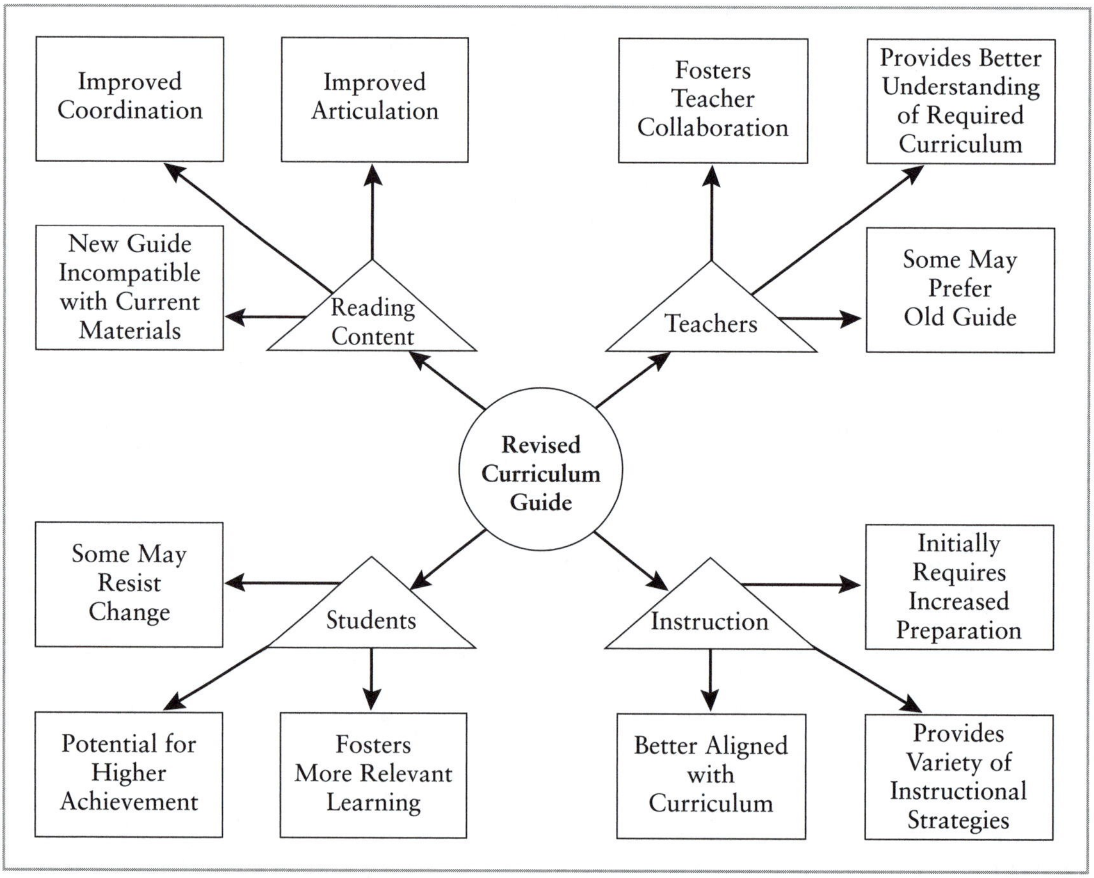

figure **12.8** **Impact Analysis Chart**

Gantt Charts

A Gantt chart is simply a graph that portrays the beginning and completion dates of each activity involved in completing the overall task (Bishop, 1976; Owen, 2002). As shown in Figure 12.9, the activities for revising the curriculum guides are placed on the left side of the chart. The beginning and ending time for each activity is shown by a white bar across the timeline. The supervisor can refer to the chart at any time to check on the progress of the project and be reminded of what groups and what subtasks should be receiving his or her attention.

Force Field Analysis

Force field analysis actually includes both assessment and planning, and can help educators define goals, analyze competing forces, and plan how to bring about needed change. A force field analysis consists of 10 phases:

1. Describe the desired state of affairs (what should be).
2. Describe the current state of affairs (what is).
3. Describe the gap between the desired and current state of affairs.
4. Describe the restraining forces: those forces that resist movement toward the desired state.
5. Describe the driving forces: those forces that can assist movement toward the desired state.
6. Select from the restraining forces those to be addressed during change efforts. Restraining forces that both are important and capable of being weakened are chosen.
7. Select from the driving forces those to be addressed during change efforts. Driving forces that both are important and capable of being strengthened are chosen.
8. For each restraining force chosen in phase 6, identify actions that weaken the restraining force.
9. For each driving force chosen in phase 7, identify actions that strengthen the driving force.
10. Integrate and sequence the actions chosen in phases 8 and 9 to create a comprehensive action plan for moving from the current state of affairs to the desired state of affairs. Include a plan for evaluating the effects of the action plan, and a timeline for implementing the action plan and evaluation.

A force field analysis is most effective if the descriptions of the desired and current state of affairs as well as restraining and driving forces are based on data gathered during the force field analysis, rather than the planners' perceptions alone.

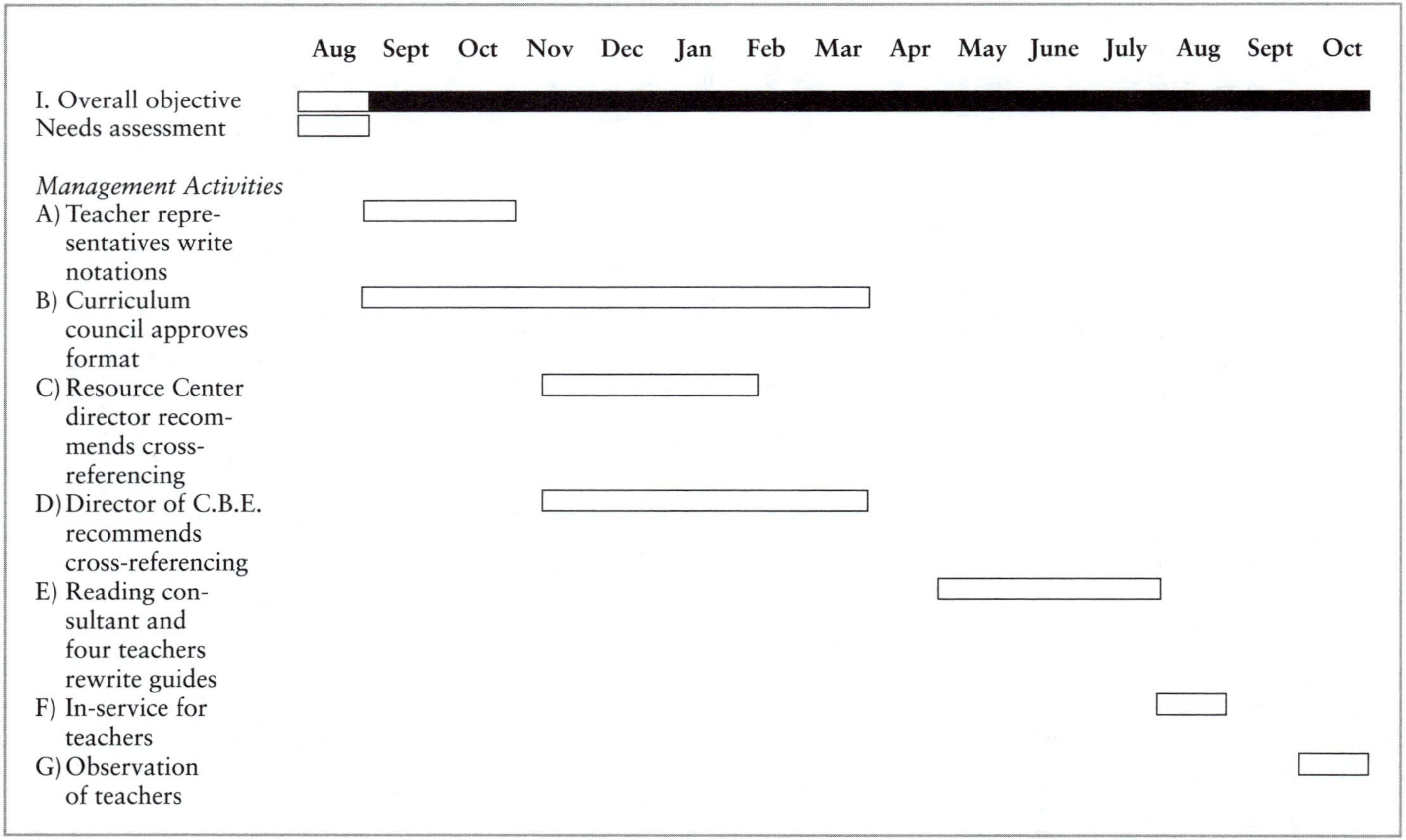

figure 12.9 **Gantt Chart Task: Revising Curriculum Guides**

Cautions Concerning Planning

Postmodern theory warns us that the rational analyses, predictions, controls, and measurements that make up conventional planning often are inconsistent with the multiplicity of realities and competing interests that make up the real world. Chaos theory reminds us that, unlike traditional plans, complex systems such as schools do not consist of simple cause-and-effect relationships, are affected by seemingly unrelated variables inside and outside the system, and are subject to unpredictable events and changes.

Do these cautions mean that we throw out the planning tools discussed in this chapter and simply "wing it" regarding instructional improvement? No, but they *do* mean that we change our traditional concept of planning to provide for the following:

- Planning centered on people—students, teachers, parents, and community members—not on planning tools and documents (the tools and documents should be used in the service of people)
- Decentralized planning, in which the supervisor becomes the coordinator of stakeholder teams actively involved in the planning process
- Diversity, in terms of both the groups represented and the ideas considered in the planning process
- Regular interaction among planners and between planners and those affected by the plan
- A recognition by planners of the complexity, multiplicity, and nonlinearity inherent in the school organization
- The consideration of alternative futures for the school community
- Improvement plans with built-in flexibility, allowing a fair degree of spontaneity and exploration during implementation
- Provisions for continuous and critical assessment of the plan during its implementation
- An understanding that the important thing is the goal the plan is intended to reach, not the plan itself, and a willingness to revise the plan when appropriate

MyEdLeadershipLab™

Go to Topic 4, Supervisory Skills, in the MyEdLeadershipLab™ site at www.myedleadershiplab.com for *The Basic Guide to SuperVision and Instructional Leadership*, Third Edition, where you can:

- Find learning outcomes for Supervisory Skills along with the national standards that connect to these outcomes.
- Complete Assignments and Activities that can help you more deeply understand the chapter content.
- Apply and practice your understanding of the core skills identified in the chapter with the Building Leadership Skills unit.
- Prepare yourself for professional certification with a Practice for Certification quiz.

REFERENCES

Bishop, L. J. 1976. *Staff development and instructional development: Plans and procedures.* Boston: Allyn & Bacon.

Bruce, R. E., and Grimsley, E. E. 1979. *Course supplementary reading—Introduction to supervision.* Unpublished manuscript, University of Georgia.

Delbecq, A. L., Van de Ven, A. H., and Gustafson, D. H. 1975. *Group techniques for program planning.* Glenview, IL: Scott Foresman.

Deming, W. E. 1986. *Out of the crisis.* Cambridge, MA: Massachusetts Institute of Technology.

Hostrop, R. W. 1975. *Managing education for results* (2nd ed.). Homewood, CA: ETC Publications.

Owen, J. 2002. *Making quality sense: A guide to quality, tools and techniques, awards and the thinking behind them.* London: Learning and Skills Development Agency.

Walton, M. 1986. *The Deming management method.* New York: Putnam.

Weaver, W. T. 1971. The Delphi forecasting method. *Kappan, 52,* 267.

Wilhelm, W. J. 2001. Alchemy of the oracle: The Delphi technique. *Delta Pi Epsilon Journal, 43*(1), 6–26.

chapter 13

Observing Skills

outline

- Formative Observation Instruments Are Not Summative Evaluation Instruments
- Ways of Describing
- Quantitative Observations
- Qualitative Observations
- Tailored Observation Systems
- Types and Purposes of Observation
- Cautions Concerning Observations

Visit the **MyEdLeadershipLab™** site for *The Basic Guide to SuperVision and Instructional Leadership,* Third Edition to enhance your understanding of chapter concepts. You'll have the opportunity to practice your skills through video and case based Assignments and Activities as well as Building Leadership Skills units, and prepare for your certification exam with Practice for Certification quizzes.

Observation is a two-part process—first *describing* what has been seen, and then *interpreting* what it means. The mind almost simultaneously processes a visual image, integrates that image with previously stored images related to satisfactory and unsatisfactory experiences, and ascribes a value or meaning to that image. If a student yawns, our mind signals "boredom." If a teacher yells at students, our mind registers "losing control." A judgment derives from an image or a description of events. We must be aware of splitting that almost simultaneous process of separating description from interpretation. When we lose the description of the event and retain only the interpretation, we create communication difficulties and obstacles to improvement.

Remember—if the goal of supervision is to enhance teachers' thought and commitment about improving classroom (and school) practice, observations should be used as a base of information to create an instructional dialogue between supervisor and teacher. Using description first when talking to a teacher about his or her classroom creates an instructional dialogue. Providing interpretations and evaluative statements first ushers in defensiveness, combativeness, or resentment in the teacher and stifles discussion (see Glickman and Jones, 1986).

Formative Observation Instruments Are Not Summative Evaluation Instruments

A *formative* observation instrument used to describe what is occurring in a classroom (consistent with what teacher and supervisor agreed to focus on and later discuss) is a means for professional growth and instructional improvement. Therefore, the use of a formative observation instrument is conditioned on prior agreement about what is most worthy of learning by that teacher in that classroom—whether the interest is derived from a desire to know more about himself or herself as a teacher, attempting a particular instructional model, experimenting with a new practice or strategy, or struggling with a problem or weakness. A *summative* evaluation instrument, however, is an externally imposed and uniformly applied measure, intended to judge all teachers on similar criteria to determine their worthiness, merit, and competence as employees. Distinctions between summative and formative evaluation are discussed in detail in Chapter 14, but in this chaper, we discuss formative observation systems.

Ways of Describing

We first look at quantitative observations, including categorical instruments, performance indicator instruments, visual diagramming, and space utilization. The second section deals with qualitative observations, including verbatim, detached open-ended narrative, participant open-ended observation, focused questionnaire observation, and educational criticism. Finally, we discuss tailored observations—quantitative or qualitative observations designed to gather data on specific teacher concerns.

Quantitative Observations

Quantitative observations are ways of measuring classroom events, behaviors, and objects. Definitions and categories must be precise. Eventually, the observations can be used for statistical operations.

Categorical Frequency Instrument

A *categorical frequency instrument* is a form that defines certain events or behaviors that can be checked off at frequency intervals and then counted. Figure 13.1 is a categorical instrument that measures the frequency of different types of questions asked by the teacher. The seven categories of teacher questions are based on a modified version of Bloom's taxonomy (Manson and Clegg, 1970). By dividing the number of questions in each category by the total number of questions asked by the teacher during the lesson, the observer can calculate the percentage of total questions each category represents.

Other classroom topics can be observed with categorical instruments. For example, one can focus on on-task and off-task behavior. To complete the instrument in Figure 13.2, the observer begins a sweep of the classroom every 5 minutes. During each sweep, the observer focuses on each student for approximately 20 seconds and then records that student's behavior. During a 40-minute lesson, 8 sweeps can be made. The instrument allows the observer to record specific on-task and off-task behaviors listed in the key at the bottom of the chart.

Question Category	Tally	Total	Percent
Evaluation		0	0
Synthesis	/	1	5
Analysis	/	1	5
Application	//	2	10
Interpretation	///	3	15
Translation	////	4	20
Memory	~~////~~ ////	9	45
Total of Questions Asked = 20			

figure 13.1 **Teacher Questions**

Student	Time When Sweep Began							
	9:00	9:05	9:10	9:15	9:20	9:25	9:30	9:35
Andrew	A	C	D	E	E	A	B	B
Shawn G.	A	A	D	E	E	A	C	B
Maria	A	A	D	E	E	C	B	B
Sam	I	F	F	E	F	A	B	C
Barbara	H	F	D	E	E	F	F	B
Angie	C	G	G	C	E	G	G	G
Jeff	A	A	C	E	E	A	B	B
Jessica	F	F	D	E	E	A	B	E
Shawn L.	A	A	D	E	H	H	B	B
Chris	F	F	D	E	E	A	B	C
Michele	A	A	D	E	H	H	B	B
Mark	A	I	I	F	I	I	I	F
Melissa	C	A	D	E	E	C	H	B
John	J	A	J	I	J	J	J	J
Rolanda	A	C	D	E	E	A	B	F

Key

A = on task, listening/watching
B = on task, writing
C = on task, speaking
D = on task, reading
E = on task, hands-on activity

F = off task, passive
G = off task, doing work for another class
H = off task, listening to others
I = off task, disturbing others
J = off task, playing

figure 13.2 **Student On-Task and Off-Task Behavior**

Performance Indicator Instruments

A performance indicator system records whether actions listed on the observation instrument have been observed. With some instruments, a third option—"not applicable" (N/A)—is included. Performance indicator instruments may also include space for the observer to add supplemental notes concerning the presence or absence of the action. Figure 13.3 is a performance indicator instrument used to record

Elements	*Response*	*Comments*
Anticipatory set	Yes ___ No ___ N/A ___	___
Statement of objective and purpose	Yes ___ No ___ N/A ___	___
Input	Yes ___ No ___ N/A ___	___
Modeling	Yes ___ No ___ N/A ___	___
Checking for understanding	Yes ___ No ___ N/A ___	___
Guided practice	Yes ___ No ___ N/A ___	___
Independent practice	Yes ___ No ___ N/A ___	___

figure 13.3 **Hunter Model Performance Indicators**

Source: Based on a model for lesson design described in M. Hunter (1984). "Knowing, Teaching, and Supervising." In P. L. Hosford (Ed.), *Using What We Know about Teaching.* Alexandria, VA: Association for Supervision and Curriculum Development.

the presence or absence of the elements in Madeline Hunter's lesson design model, a model well suited for direct instruction. Figure 13.4 is an instrument to assess whether each of the basic elements of a cooperative learning lesson is present.

The instrument in Figure 13.5 lists indicators of an authentic constructivist lesson, and that in Figure 13.6 lists indicators of culturally sensitive teaching. Because the indicators in Figures 13.5 and 13.6 are more open to interpretation than indicators in many instruments of this type, it is especially important for the observer to describe in the comments column specific classroom behaviors that are the basis for the observer's responses.

Elements	*Response*	*Comments*
Explanation of academic and social objectives	Yes ___ No ___ N/A ___	___
Teaching of necessary social skills	Yes ___ No ___ N/A ___	___
Face-to-face interaction	Yes ___ No ___ N/A ___	___
Positive interdependence	Yes ___ No ___ N/A ___	___
Individual accountability	Yes ___ No ___ N/A ___	___
Group processing	Yes ___ No ___ N/A ___	___

figure 13.4 **Cooperative Learning Performance Indicators**

Remember that performance indicators used for observation purposes should not imply an absolute standard. The fact that a teacher does not perform all of the activities listed on the observation instrument may or may not be a cause of concern. Only after the supervisor and teacher have discussed the circumstances surrounding the teacher's instructional procedures can they be properly interpreted.

Visual Diagramming

Visual diagramming is another way to portray what is occurring in a classroom. Video recording a classroom captures the closest representative picture of actual occurrences. Without video, however, there are other ways to portray observations, such as verbal interactions among teachers and students and how a teacher uses space. After diagramming the occurrence, the supervisor and the teacher can view the picture and then analyze the events.

Indicators	*Response*	*Comments*
Co-planned by teacher and students	Yes ___ No ___ N/A ___	___
In-depth explanation of big idea	Yes ___ No ___ N/A ___	___
Student initiated questions	Yes ___ No ___ N/A ___	___
Problem centered	Yes ___ No ___ N/A ___	___
Use of primary material	Yes ___ No ___ N/A ___	___
Students test own hypotheses	Yes ___ No ___ N/A ___	___
Dialogue fostered	Yes ___ No ___ N/A ___	___
Active learning	Yes ___ No ___ N/A ___	___
Collaborative learning	Yes ___ No ___ N/A ___	___
Students construct knowledge	Yes ___ No ___ N/A ___	___
Self- and group reflection on constructions	Yes ___ No ___ N/A ___	___
Learning assessed by teachers and students	Yes ___ No ___ N/A ___ Yes ___ No ___ N/A ___	___
Assessment of process and product	Yes ___ No ___ N/A ___	___

figure 13.5 **Indicators of a Constructivist Lesson**

Indicators	*Response*	*Comments*
The Teacher		
Displays understanding of diverse cultures	Yes ___ No ___	____________ ____________
Displays personal regard for all students	Yes ___ No ___	____________ ____________
Uses instructional materials free of cultural bias	Yes ___ No ___	____________ ____________
Uses examples and materials that represent different cultures	Yes ___ No ___	____________ ____________
Promotes examination of concepts and issues from different cultural perspectives	Yes ___ No ___	____________ ____________
Facilitates higher-level learning for all students	Yes ___ No ___	____________ ____________
Adopts materials and instruction to different student learning styles	Yes ___ No ___	____________ ____________
Provides equitable opportunities for student participation	Yes ___ No ___	____________ ____________
Provides individual assistance, when necessary, for all students	Yes ___ No ___ N/A ___	____________ ____________
Intervenes to address acts of student intolerance	Yes ___ No ___ N/A ___	____________ ____________
Uses "teachable moments" to address cultural issues	Yes ___ No ___ N/A ___	____________ ____________
Reinforces student acts of respect for diverse cultures	Yes ___ No ___ N/A ___	____________ ____________

figure 13.6 **Indicators of Culturally Sensitive Teaching**

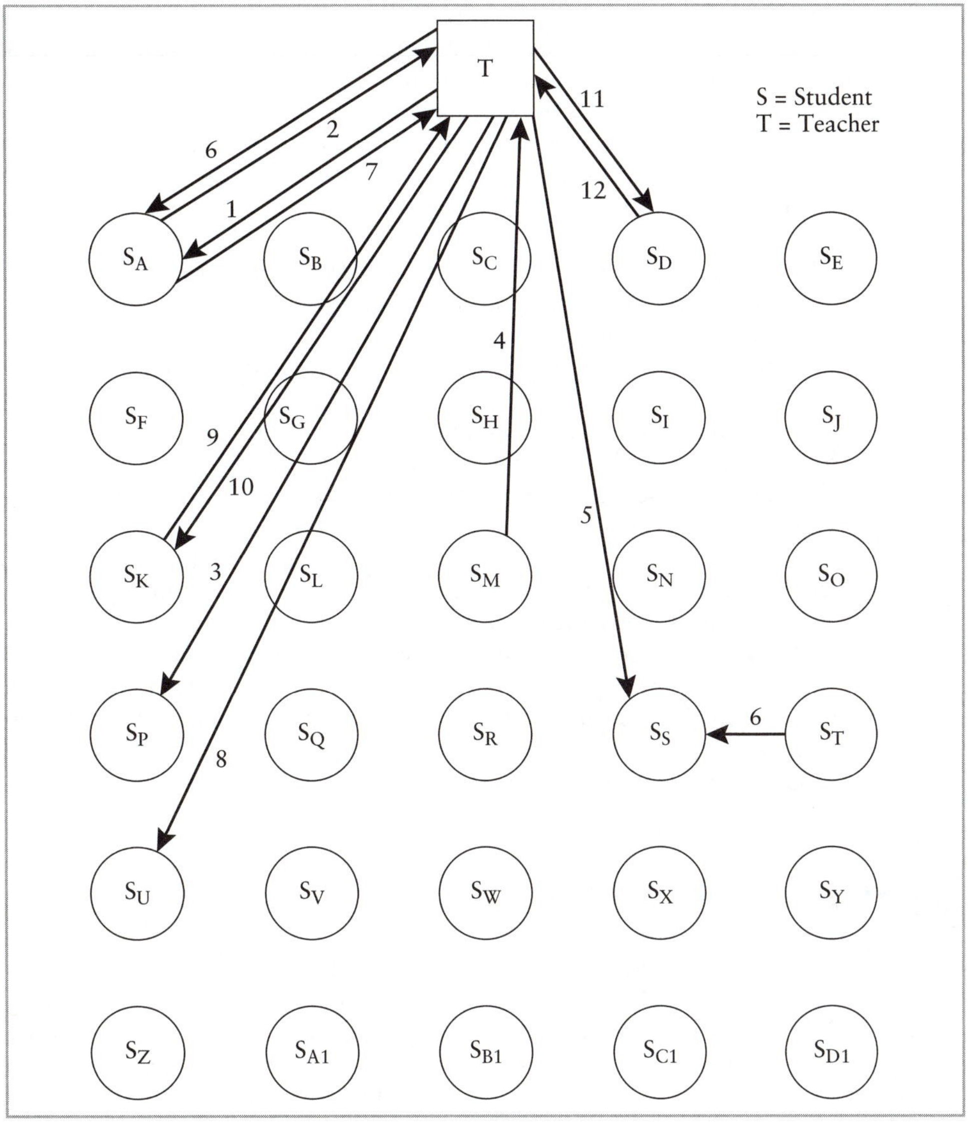

figure 13.7 **Diagram of Verbal Interaction, 9:10–9:15**

Classroom verbal interactions can be charted by drawing arrows symbolizing verbal statements between members in a classroom (see Figure 13.7). The observer can use six separate sheets of this diagram and fill out one sheet for each time sample of five minutes spaced throughout a thirty-minute discussion. Each arrow drawn on the diagram indicates a full statement directed to another person. The arrows are numbered in the sequence of statements. After diagramming, the observer then has information on the frequency of individual student interaction, the amount of interaction with different areas of the room, which students triggered interactions among others, and which students were excluded.

For illustration purposes, if the diagram was a sample consistent with the other five samples of the classroom period, the observer would be able to state some of the following conclusions:

1. Interaction is mainly directed toward the left aisle and front row.
2. There is almost no attention to the last two rows in the back of the room or the two rows on the right.
3. Of 14 interactions, 12 included the teacher and 2 were between students.

Another type of diagramming is flowcharting teacher space utilization, which follows the teacher's movement throughout the classroom. A sketch of the physical classroom is done first; then the observer follows the teacher by using arrows on the sketch (see Figure 13.8).

Figure 13.8 illustrates a period of reading instruction. The arrow follows the teacher with each movement and is labeled with the time on the clock. After a class period, the observer and the teacher can see where the teacher has been and for how long. Such information might help make a teacher aware of the relationship of his or her space utilization to concerns of classroom management and instruction. For example, in Figure 13.8, there is much physical presence in the front and on the left side of the classroom, with no presence at the rear learning centers or the middle work area.

Qualitative Observations

There are alternative means of observing based on not knowing exactly what is to be recorded. These are called *qualitative* or *descriptive* forms of observation. The observer goes into the classroom with a general focus or no focus at all and records events as they occur. The events are not made to fit into a specific category, nor are they measured. Only after the recording of events does the observer rearrange his or her observations into themes. Such recording of observations defies the use of an instrument. (An *instrument* is technically a measurement device.) Instead, qualitative observations record the complexity of classroom life.

There are several types of qualitative observations. We look at verbatim, detached open-ended narrative, participant open-ended observation, and focused questionnaire observation. These observations can be used by a supervisor to provide a broad and complex recording of classroom life.

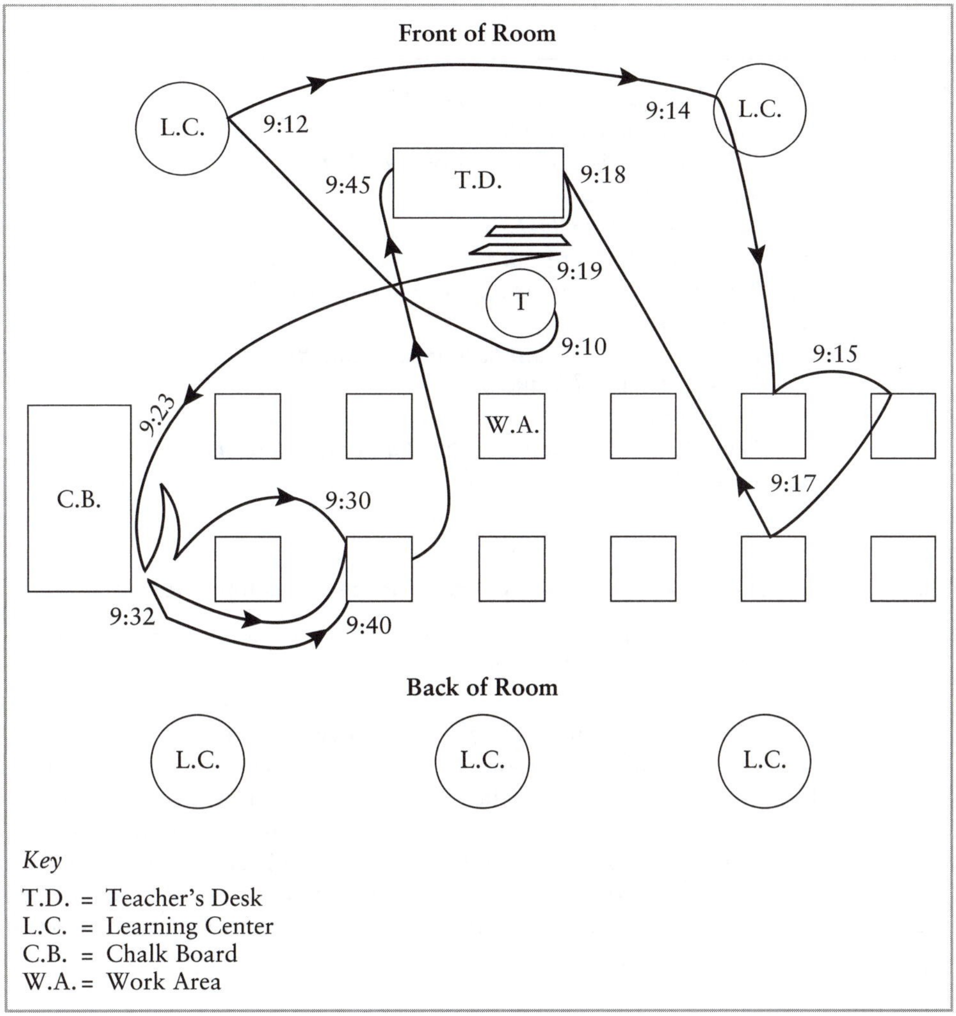

figure 13.8 **Teacher Space Utilization**

Verbatim and Selected Verbatim

The observer taking verbatim notes (sometimes called *scripts*) records all verbal interaction taking place in the classroom. Verbatim notes allow the observer and teacher to identify patterns of interpersonal behavior during a lesson. Verbatim also provides specific examples of teacher–student or student–teacher interactions. For more efficient recording, the observer may abbreviate words and leave out words that add no meaning to the transcript.

C = Chris D. 10:20
T = Teacher
T. C, What are 3 branches of Fed. Govt.?
C. President, House, Senate
T. What branch Fed. Govt. is pres. head of?
C. Ah, I don't know
T. The president is Chief ____________.
C. Executive! Executive branch!
T. The House and Senate are both part of what branch?
C. Legislative
T. Legislative branch, but both mean same thing. That's 2 branches, exec. and leg. What is the third branch?
C. The Courts.
T. What branch is made of Sup. Ct and other fed. cts.
C. Judicial
T. Right!

figure 13.9 **Excerpt from Selective Verbatim Notes**

Source: Stephen P. Gordon (1990). *Assisting the Entry-Year Teacher: A Leadership Resource.* Columbus, OH: Ohio Department of Education.

Despite these time-savers, verbatim can be an arduous process requiring the observer to spend every moment taking notes with no time for attention to anything else going on during the lesson. One alternative to verbatim is *selected verbatim,* in which the observer records only those interactions that relate to a particular focus agreed to by the observer and teacher prior to the observation. Figure 13.9 provides an excerpt from selective verbatim notes focused on teacher responses to students who initially gave incorrect or partially correct answers to teacher questions.

Detached Open-Ended Narrative

Detached open-ended narrative occurs when the supervisor steps into a classroom and records every person, event, or thing that attracts his or her attention. At the start, the pages are empty, without questions, indicators, or categories. The heading might simply say look like this:

Open-Ended Narrative

Observation Teacher:________________ Time: ____ Observer: ________________

The recorder then has the task of writing, writing, and more writing. A sample of such an observation might read as follows:

> Students begin arriving at 10:13; the teacher is at his desk correcting papers. The bell rings at 10:15 to begin third period. Students keep arriving. Mr. X gets up from his desk to begin class at 10:25. In the meantime, students have put away their school bags and are awaiting instruction, except three girls in the back corner who are talking, combing their hair, and spreading the contents of their pocketbooks on their desks. Five minutes after Mr. X begins, he talks to them and they put away combs and pocketbooks. Mr. X describes the activities for the day but then cannot find his prepared handouts. After two minutes of looking, he finds the papers in his desk drawer.

With practice, the observer can write in shorthand to keep up with the flow of events. It is impossible to record all that could possibly be seen and heard in a classroom. The observer must constantly scan the entire classroom and decide what is significant.

Participant Open-Ended Observation

Participant open-ended observation occurs when the supervisor becomes a functioning part of the classroom (Spradley, 1980). He or she assists in the instruction, helps students with questions, uses classroom materials, and talks with the teacher and students. Being involved in the classroom gives the supervisor an inside-out view of the classroom, different from that of the detached observer, who tries to be invisible and keep away from students and teachers. Obviously, events cannot be written down as they occur if the supervisor is engaged in talking, moving, and assisting. Instead, he or she must write between pauses in the action. The observation form can be carried on a clipboard so that notes can be taken on the run.

The participant observer takes sketchy notes (catch phrases and words) during classroom time so that afterward he or she can write in greater detail. These quick notes serve to remind the observer of the situation to be described more fully after the observation period is over. The following is an example of such short notes:

> Teacher X directs students into study groups.
>
> John B. does not understand the assignment. I work with him on organizing the theme of a play.
>
> Sally T. and Ramona B. are wandering around. I ask them if they need help; they say no and leave the room (ask teacher about this).
>
> Sondra and her group are ready to role play their theme. I listen as they read through their parts.
>
> Steven's group is stuck; he doesn't know how to find materials on historic buildings. I suggest calling the town historic society.

Susan is not participating at all—looking at *Teen Magazine*. The rest of the group just leaves her alone. (I wonder why?)

The filmstrip shown has everyone's attention.

Teacher B dismisses the class. I overhear a student say, "This class goes so quickly. I wish other classes were as much fun."

These are some notes from a 50-minute classroom period. Much more happened in the classroom than is noted, but the observer picks up insights from his or her involvement. The supervisor can later fill in details—the two girls leaving the classroom, the specifics of John's confusion about the theme, Susan's absorption in *Teen Magazine,* and so on.

Topic 1: Classroom
How is the classroom made attractive?

Topic 2: Teacher
What shows that the teacher has a warm, friendly relationship with the pupils?

Topic 3: Pupil
What indicates that pupils know what they are doing and why they are doing it?

Topic 4: Lesson
How do classroom and homework assignments indicate that consideration is given to, and use made of, resources of the community and real-life situations of pupils?

figure 13.10 **Focused Questionnaire**

Focused Questionnaire Observation

Qualitative observation can be done in a more focused manner by having general topics to use in recording events. An observer seeks information about specific questions. In order to answer the questions, the observer writes pertinent evidence. For example, Harris (1975, pp. 364–376) has developed a detached observation questionnaire that has as its topics (1) classroom, (2) teacher, (3) pupil, and (4) lesson. Figure 13.10 shows sample questions taken from each category. An observer enters the classroom with questions in hand and looks for the answers. It is the task of the observer to respond to these questions with descriptions of the evidence.

Tailored Observation Systems

Supervisors often observe lessons to collect data on unique instructional concerns or improvement efforts. If no observation system exists that is capable of gathering the desired data, the supervisor can design a *tailored observation system* that can be quantitative, qualitative, or a combination of both.

Figure 13.11 is a system designed to collect four specific types of data. The teacher in this example requested that the observer collect data on (1) how often the teacher called on each student; (2) whether each student's response was correct or incorrect; (3) whether the teacher drew out correct student responses through encouragement or prompting, especially after a student's initial response was incorrect; and

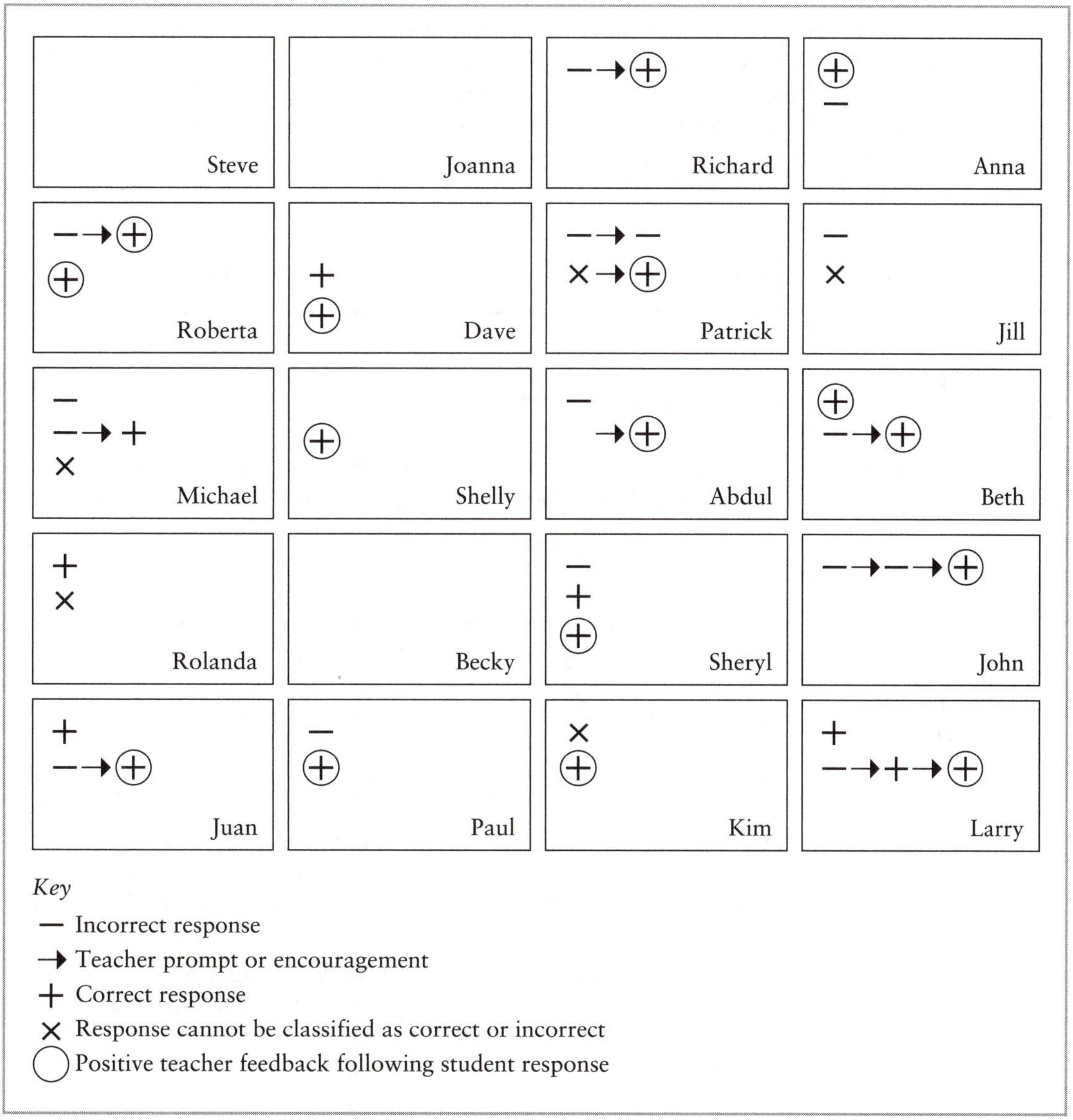

figure **13.11** **Tailored Question–Response Instrument**

(4) how often the teacher provided positive feedback to students making correct responses. In Figure 13.11, codes symbolize both student responses (−, +, ×) to teacher questions, and teacher reactions (→, ○) to student responses. Several codes on the same line indicate verbal behaviors that were part of the same series of interactions. Codes on different lines indicate separate series of interactions.

In another example, teacher Simmons was concerned about the conduct of one of his students and asked the supervisor to collect data on the student's behaviors, Simmons's responses, and the effects of those responses on the student. Figure 13.12 is the observation chart completed by the supervisor. Arrows point to immediate responses of the teacher to selected student behaviors and immediate responses of the student to relevant teacher behaviors. Some of the most meaningful and helpful classroom observation data we have viewed has been collected with observation systems designed by supervisors and teachers focused on specific teacher concerns.

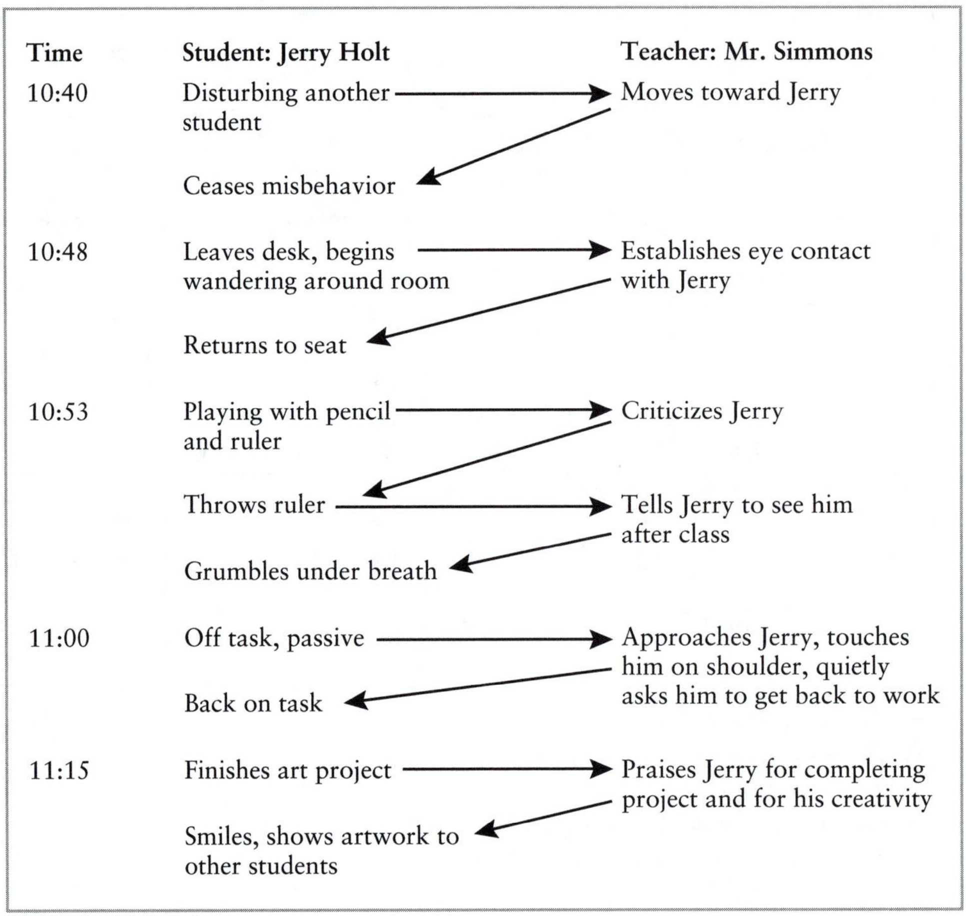

figure 13.12 **Tailored Behavior Response Observation**

Types and Purposes of Observation

Figure 13.13 illustrates the types of observation available to a supervisor. The purpose of the observation should determine the type, method, and role of observation:

	Method		*Role of Observer*		
Type	*Quantitive*	*Qualitative*	*Detached*	*Participant*	Purpose
Categorical frequency	x		x		Count behaviors
Performance indicator	x		x		Evident or not
Visual diagramming	x		x		Picture verbal interaction
Space utilization	x		x		Picture movement
Verbatim		x			Script of verbal interaction
Detached open-ended narrative		x	x		Attention to unfolding event
Participant open-ended observation		x	x		Inside-out view
Focused questionnaire		x	x or	x	Focus on particular events
Tailored	x or	x	x or	x	Address unique concerns

figure 13.13 **Observation Alternatives**

Cautions Concerning Observations

Quantum physics informs us that a phenomenon cannot be measured without the measurement process interacting with the phenomenon and thus affecting the measurement (Greene, 2004). Closer to home for those of us who are educators, the constructivist epistemology holds that rather than identifying a fixed reality through objective observation, we construct knowledge by interacting with our environment and with others.

One implication for classroom observation is our need to realize that our observations are affected by our personal experiences and values, our presence in the classroom during the observation, the observation instrument we use, our skill at recording data, and so on. Another implication is that the interpretation of what the observation data means is a construction and in most cases is best co-constructed with the teacher. Observation data, thus, should be an entry point for teacher–supervisor dialogue and co-interpretation during a post observation conference. Clinical supervision, discussed in Chapter 15, provides a structure for teacher–supervisor dialogue on classroom observation.

MyEdLeadershipLab™

Go to Topic 4, Supervisory Skills, in the MyEdLeadershipLab™ site at www.myedleadershiplab.com for *The Basic Guide to SuperVision and Instructional Leadership*, Third Edition, where you can:

- Find learning outcomes for Supervisory Skills along with the national standards that connect to these outcomes.
- Complete Assignments and Activities that can help you more deeply understand the chapter content.
- Apply and practice your understanding of the core skills identified in the chapter with the Building Leadership Skills unit.
- Prepare yourself for professional certification with a Practice for Certification quiz.

REFERENCES

Glickman, C. D., and Jones, J. W. 1986. Research in supervision: Creating the dialogue. *Educational Leadership, 44*(3), 83.

Gordon, S. P. 1990. *Assisting the entry-year teacher: A leadership resource.* Columbus: Ohio Department of Education.

Greene, B. 2004. *The fabric of the cosmos: Space, time and the texture of reality.* New York: Vintage Books.

Harris, B. M. 1975. *Supervisory behavior in education* (2nd ed.). Englewood Cliffs, NJ: Prentice Hall.

Manson, G., and Clegg, A. A., Jr. 1970. Classroom questions: Keys to children's thinking? *Peabody Journal of Education*, *47*(5), 304–305.

Spradley, J. P. 1980. *Participant observation.* New York: Holt, Rinehart and Winston.

chapter 14

Evaluation Skills

outline

- Judgments
- Key Decisions in the Program Evaluation Process
- Overall Instructional Program Evaluation
- Program Evaluation and Teacher Empowerment
- Teacher Evaluation

Visit the **MyEdLeadershipLab™** site for *The Basic Guide to SuperVision and Instructional Leadership*, Third Edition to enhance your understanding of chapter concepts. You'll have the opportunity to practice your skills through video and case based Assignments and Activities as well as Building Leadership Skills units, and prepare for your certification exam with Practice for Certification quizzes.

Perhaps no area in education has gone through such a dramatic expansion in knowledge, techniques, and attention than the field of educational evaluation. What once seemed the province of experts, consultants, and "university types" doing laboratory experiments has now become a part of day-to-day operations in schools. The national accountability and testing movement has certainly been a contributing cause. More important has been the role of the literature on successful schools, which has made clear that decisions about instructional changes should be made from a base of comprehensive and credible data about students and that those affected most directly by instructional change (i.e., teachers) should be involved in defining, implementing, and interpreting the evaluation agenda.

Judgments

How do we know our instructional programs are successful? Should we continue with the same curriculum, instructional methods, scheduling, and grouping practices, or should changes be made? *Evaluating* is the act of making such a judgment. How do we decide whether something is good or bad? Frequently, we make judgments with statements such as: "What a great reading program," "What a lousy classroom," and "What wonderful students." How do we really know if something is great, lousy, or wonderful? Wolfe (1969) offers a tongue-in-cheek classification of five typical methods by which we make such judgments:

> *Cosmetic method:* You examine the program, and if it looks good, it is good. Does everybody look busy? The key is attractive and full bulletin boards covered with projects emanating from the project.
>
> *Cardiac method:* No matter what the data say, you know in your heart that the program was a success. This is similar to the use in medical research of subclinical findings.
>
> *Colloquial method:* After a brief meeting, preferably at a local watering hole, a group of project staff members conclude that success was achieved. No one can refute a group decision.
>
> *Curricular method:* A successful program is one that can be installed with the least disruption of the ongoing school program. Programs that are truly different are to be eschewed at all costs.
>
> *Computational method:* If you have to have data, analyze it to death. Whatever the nature of the statistics, use the most sophisticated multivariate regression discontinuity procedures known to humans.

Wolfe's humor aside, let's look at reasonable and valid ways of evaluating. In the turbulence of instructional change, it is useful to know whether the new practice is going to be any better than the old. If not, then we may be investing large amounts of energy without a justifiable increase in instructional benefits to students. As discussed in Chapter 12 (assessing and planning), if we are to make a commitment to instructional change, we must also make a commitment to evaluating that instructional change. If not, then we truly do not know what we are doing.

Key Decisions in the Program Evaluation Process

A number of key decisions must be made in any systematic program evaluation. We examine each of these decisions.

What Is the Purpose of the Evaluation?

There are two broad purposes of educational evaluation. *Formative evaluation* is intended to improve a program. It is carried out while the program is in progress and can be ongoing throughout the life of the program. *Summative evaluation* results in a definitive judgment about the value of a program. It is carried out after a program has been in existence for a period of time. A summative evaluation is usually the basis for a decision about whether the program will continue, undergo major revisions, or be terminated. Formative and summative program evaluations are not always mutually exclusive. For instance, data gathered for formative evaluations might be reanalyzed later as part of a summative evaluation.

Who Performs the Evaluation?

Whether the supervisor, a team of faculty members, central office personnel, or private consultants should have major control over evaluation depends on the particular school's resources and the purpose of the evaluation. However, it is critical that teachers be involved in evaluation of instructional programs and the overall instructional effectiveness of their schools and district. All stakeholders (those affected by the decisions from the evaluation) should be not only subjects of study but co-investigators of the study as well. As Greene (1986) notes, there is a "consensus on the need for stakeholder participation" (p. 1), and such participation is defined as "shared decision making, rather than just advising or providing input" (p. 9).

What Questions Must Be Answered?

Evaluation questions depend on the nature of the program and what members of the evaluation's audience wish to learn about the program. Let's say that a new social studies curriculum is to be evaluated. An *implementation* question might be: To what extent has the new curriculum been implemented at the classroom level? An *outcomes* question might be: What changes in students' knowledge, skills, and attitudes have resulted from the new curriculum? Once the evaluation questions have been formulated, they become the basis for the remainder of the evaluation.

What Data Is Gathered and How?

Data sources are persons, places, things, events, or processes from which data needed to answer evaluation questions can be gathered. Examples of data sources are students, teachers, principals, parents, teaching episodes, student products, and school records. *Data-gathering methods* are ways to collect data from sources. Examples include testing, observations, content analysis, case studies, review of records, administration of rating scales and surveys, and interviewing. Our bias is toward using multiple sources of data and multiple data-collection methods for each evaluation question. Multiple sources and methods increase the likelihood that the evaluation results will be valid.

How Are the Data Analyzed?

Data analysis is largely determined by the evaluation questions and types of data. Decisions to be made include how to organize, summarize, and display data, and how to reach conclusions based on the data. Central office, university, or private experts may be necessary to assist with complex quantitative or qualitative analysis. Stakeholders, however, can make valuable contributions to data analysis, especially by reviewing results and suggesting explanations, implications, and conclusions.

How Is the Evaluation Reported?

After collecting and analyzing the results of tests, observations, surveys, interviews, and testimonials, how should the evaluation be reported? The answer is largely determined by the audience. Most school board members and superintendents will not read a 200-page technical report on the raw data, statistical treatments, and evaluation methodologies. They are interested in the results and conclusions. The technical report should be available to decision makers as a reference to the summarized paper. Any reader of the condensed paper who is confused or desires more information about certain parts of the paper can check the complete technical report.

However, if the audience for the evaluation report consists of people with sophisticated evaluation skills, a complete technical report would be in order. In a study of violations of evaluation standards (Newman and Brown, 1987, p. 9), among the most frequent violations were "those concerning the evaluator's lack of knowledge of the audience."

Regardless of the audience, certain types of information are included in most evaluation reports. (Again, these components will vary in length and technical sophistication depending on the audience.) Typical evaluation reports include discussions of the following:

1. The purpose of the evaluation
2. A description of the program being evaluated
3. Evaluation questions or objectives
4. Methodology, including data sources, data-gathering methods, and data analysis methods
5. Results and conclusions, including strengths and weaknesses of the program
6. Recommendations for the future

Overall Instructional Program Evaluation

Evaluating a school's overall instructional program is different from evaluating specific programs. In this section, we outline an evaluation model that we have used when serving as consultants to schools wishing to evaluate the quality of their instruction with an eye toward comprehensive and schoolwide instructional improvement. We always recommend extensive participation by the school community in planning the evaluation, developing data-collection methods, analyzing data, and drawing conclusions about current quality and needed change.

Phase One: Selecting Areas to Be Examined

The evaluation process begins with a meeting with the school's administration and an evaluation steering committee representing key stakeholders from the school community. At that meeting, we recommend the following broad areas for evaluation, based on the rationale that each of these areas is significantly related to the success of the school's overall instructional program:

1. Community characteristics
2. School culture and climate
3. School governance
4. Student characteristics
5. Teacher characteristics
6. Parent characteristics
7. Instructional supervision
8. Curriculum and curriculum development process
9. Classroom teaching practices
10. Student assessment methods
11. Student achievement
12. Professional development programs
13. Parent and community involvement programs
14. Relationships with other schools, central office, and external organizations

Of course, it's up to the school district or school to decide which areas to evaluate, and the steering committee may wish to delete or add evaluation areas. However, most steering committees agree that a comprehensive evaluation must examine all of the preceding areas. At this initial meeting, we also propose the remainder of the evaluation process outlined here, with the understanding that the actual evaluation plan results from a collaborative effort of the consultants and steering committee with input from all of those affected by the evaluation.

Phase Two: Identifying Specific Evaluation Questions

The second phase of the process begins with a large-group session attended by administrators, teachers, other staff members, parents, and other community members. After a general session to review the areas to be examined in the evaluation, the group splits up into small planning teams. The number of planning teams is equal to the number of areas to be examined. To the extent possible, each of the stakeholder groups listed earlier is represented within each planning team. Each team is assigned one of the areas for evaluation decided on in phase one and the task of recommending specific evaluation questions for their area. For example, the *community characteristics* planning team agrees on a set of evaluation questions about the community that it believes should be answered by the evaluation, the *school culture and climate* team proposes a set of evaluation questions concerning their assigned area, and so on. A *community characteristics* evaluation question might be, "To what extent are community resources used to enhance teaching and learning in our school?" A *school culture and climate* question might be, "Is our school culture consistent with the research on successful schools?"

After all planning teams agree on proposed evaluation questions for their broad area, each team presents and explains its recommendations to a general session. Suggestions for deleting, adding, or revising questions are made by general session participants and then considered by the appropriate teams. After each planning team has had the opportunity to revise proposed questions, each team presents its final recommendations to another general session. At this final general session, the entire body of participants votes on whether to include each proposed evaluation question in the evaluation. After the large-group session is completed, the consultants and steering committee rewrite the evaluation questions for each area, so that the questions can be presented in a common format. Although the language of a question may be revised, the basic content of the question must remain as it was approved at the general session.

Phase Three: Designing the Evaluation

Phase three consists of consultants, the steering committee, and planning teams collaborating to design the evaluation proper. Teams propose sources (persons, places, things, events, processes) from which data necessary to answer each of their evaluation questions can be gathered, as well as data-gathering methods (testing, observations, content analysis, case studies, record review, rating scales, surveys, interviews, and so on). For reasons of coordination and efficiency, however, it is the evaluation steering committee that makes the final decisions on data sources and data-gathering methods.

After identifying sources and methods, it is time to select or design data-gathering instruments such as tests, classroom observation systems, written surveys, interview guides, and so on. Planning teams make suggestions for specific test items, survey and interview questions, classroom behaviors to be observed, and so on, and then the consultants and steering committee construct the instruments. With the wide variety of areas to be assessed, efficiency becomes critical. For example, let's assume that six planning teams each propose several teacher survey questions aimed at gathering data for their assigned areas and research questions. Rather than construct six different surveys, the consultants and evaluation committee might design a single survey divided into six sections, with the questions within each section designed to gather data sought by a different evaluation team.

Figure 14.1 provides a matrix for planning an evaluation of a school's overall instructional program. The grid is used to develop an overview of data sources and data-gathering methods relative to each area to be assessed.

Phase Four: Gathering and Analyzing Data

Teachers, supervisors, and consultants can all assist in gathering data needed to answer evaluation questions. For example, teachers can interview or survey students, gather representative student work, or videotape sample lessons. Supervisors can conduct classroom observations, interview or survey parents, or gather schoolwide student achievement data. Consultants can provide technical assistance, interview or survey teachers, or conduct qualitative case studies. The best matches of personnel with data-gathering assignments depend on the nature of the data to be collected and the skills and interests of participants, and thus vary from school to school. In any evaluation, however, it is essential to clearly define (1) who is responsible for collecting each type of data and (2) the data-gathering procedures they will follow. Teachers and other staff who collect data may need staff development to acquire necessary data-gathering skills.

Teachers can also work with supervisors and consultants to analyze evaluation data. Although it may be necessary for consultants to perform more complex statistical or qualitative analysis, teachers can engage in a variety of data analysis activities. They can assist in organizing, reviewing, comparing, and interpreting most types of data, and can participate in data-based decisions concerning needed improvements in the school's instructional program.

Data gathering and data analysis need not be treated as discrete activities. Analysis of data gathered early in the evaluation process may indicate the need to collect additional data in order to answer an evaluation question adequately. Data gathering and analysis thus can be viewed as an interactive cycle rather than a linear process. The data-gathering and analysis process is coordinated by the consultants and steering committee. Figure 14.2 contains an example of a chart that can be used to coordinate gathering and analysis of data for each evaluation question.

Areas to Be Assessed	Data Sources and Data-Gathering Methods																															
	Students				*Teachers*				*School Leadership*				*Parents*				*Community*				*Central Office*				*Written Curriculum*				*School Records*			
	R	*O*	*S*	*I*	*R*	*O*	*S*	*I*	*R*	*O*	*S*	*I*	*R*	*O*	*S*	*I*	*R*	*O*	*S*	*I*	*R*	*O*	*S*	*I*	*R*	*O*	*S*	*I*	*R*	*O*	*S*	*I*
Community Characteristics																																
School Culture & Climate																																
School Governance																																
Student Characteristics																																
Teacher Characteristics																																
Parent Characteristics																																
Instructional Supervision																																
Curriculum																																
Classroom Teaching																																
Student Assessment																																
Student Achievement																																
Professional Development																																
Parent–Community Involvement																																
External Relations																																

Key: R = Review of existing data (demographic data, student achievement data, etc.)
O = Observation or videotaping
S = Written survey, rating scale, etc.
I = Interview

Checks (✓) are placed in appropriate cells to indicate the relationship of areas to be assessed, data sources, and data-gathering methods.

figure **14.1** **Planning Grid for Evaluating Overall Instructional Program**

Evaluation Question	Coordinator	Evaluation Team Members	Data Sources	Data-Gathering Methods	Data Analysis Methods	Evaluation Timeline	Resources Needed
1)							
2)							
3)							
4)							
5)							
6)							

figure **14.2** **Chart for Planning Data Gathering and Analysis**

Phase Five: Preparing and Presenting the Evaluation Report

Because of the variety of areas addressed in an evaluation of the overall instructional program, this type of evaluation report is more extensive than an evaluation report on a specific program. The report should address not only each area that was assessed but also *relationships* between those areas. For example, if most teachers report that the school culture (one area assessed) affects their classroom teaching (another area), observed effects should be discussed in the report. Conclusions made in the report should be based on data gathered during the study and collaborative interpretation of that data.

Recommendations for improving the school's overall instructional program should be related directly to the study's results and conclusions. Some recommendations for improvement will be for specific areas (school governance, curriculum, classroom teaching, and so on), but others will be comprehensive, involving suggested changes that have an impact on several or all of the areas that have been assessed. Because implementation of all recommendations may not be feasible, they should be prioritized. Like reports on specific programs discussed earlier, the depth and length of the report on an evaluation of the overall instructional program should be tailored to the intended audience, with different audiences receiving different types of reports. Finally, just as we have argued that teachers and other stakeholders should be involved in planning and carrying out the evaluation, we also recommend that representatives of these various groups participate in scheduled presentations of results to the central office, school board, and community groups.

Program Evaluation and Teacher Empowerment

Fetterman (1996) uses the term *empowerment evaluation* to describe program participants evaluating their own program. Empowerment evaluation has two purposes: improving the program and fostering self-determination. Fetterman describes five stages of empowerment evaluation that can be applied to supervisors working with teachers to evaluate instructional programs:

- *Training.* The supervisor teaches teachers how to conduct the program evaluation.
- *Facilitation.* The supervisor coaches teachers as they plan and implement the program evaluation.
- *Advocacy.* The supervisor seeks support for the self-evaluation from the administration, parents, and community. If the evaluation results show the need for program changes, the supervisor advocates that teachers be allowed to change the program accordingly.
- *Illumination.* As a result of the evaluation, teachers tend to develop new understanding of the program, their roles, and their relationships with others.
- *Liberation.* Empowerment evaluation often serves to free teachers from previous constraints and roles and enables teachers to become more self-directed.

Empowerment evaluation does not replace program evaluation by external evaluators, but it can complement traditional evaluation by providing rich data to outside evaluators. Because most external evaluations are one-time snapshots of instructional programs, self-evaluations have benefits not typically provided by external evaluations, such as ongoing program improvement and teacher development.

Teacher Evaluation

Although teacher evaluation involves some of the same skills as program evaluation (e.g., data gathering, data analysis), it is essentially a separate process requiring different strategies and techniques. In this section, we compare summative and formative teacher evaluation, propose that these two types of evaluation be carried out separately, and discuss self-evaluation.

Comparing Summative and Formative Teacher Evaluation

Summative and formative are two broad categories of teacher evaluation. *Summative teacher evaluation* is an administrative function intended to meet the organizational need for teacher accountability. It involves decisions about the level of a teacher's performance. Summative evaluation always seeks to determine if the teacher has met minimum expectations. If the teacher has not met his or her professional responsibilities, the summative process documents inadequate performance for the purpose of remediation and, if necessary, termination. Sometimes summative evaluation also gathers data to determine if a teacher is eligible for rewards provided by the district for outstanding performance.

Summative evaluation is based on policies that mandate its purpose, frequency, and procedures. Teacher performance is usually documented on an evaluation form. On the form, an administrator completes checklists, rating scales, or narratives indicating the extent to which the teacher has met performance criteria. Evaluation forms usually are standard (same criteria for all teachers) and global (general enough to apply to teachers with different responsibilities). Evaluation forms judge teachers on the quality of their instruction, including such areas as classroom climate, planning, the teaching act, and classroom management (Danielson and McGreal, 2000). However, evaluation criteria usually include noninstructional areas as well, such as compliance with school regulations, cooperation with colleagues, and completion of extracurricular assignments.

Evaluation instruments must be valid (accurate) and reliable (consistent). *Valid instruments* are those that include all criteria considered essential for effective performance, exclude criteria considered extraneous to effective performance, and weight-relevant criteria in proportion to their importance (Haefele, 1993; Danielson and McGreal, 2000). *Reliable instruments* include low-inference (as nearly objective as possible) rather than high-inference (requiring a high level of evaluator subjectivity) indicators. For example, "teacher clarity" is an example of a high-inference indicator, and "uses examples when explaining" is an example of a low-inference indicator (Haefele, 1993, p. 25). Reliability also requires that administrators be trained properly in the use of the evaluation instrument, so that they become aware of rating errors to avoid and develop a high level of interevaluator reliability (agreement with experts and other administrators in their ratings of the same teacher).

In addition to concerns with and reliability of individual evaluations, experts suggest that evaluations be done several different times during the evaluation period rather than rely on a one-shot visit to a teacher's classroom. Finally, legal and ethical considerations require that when a teacher's performance has been judged to be inadequate, the teacher be notified of deficiencies, given an opportunity to respond, provided a remediation plan and support for implementing the plan, and be reevaluated (Sutton, 1989).

Formative teacher evaluation is a supervisory function intended to assist and support teachers in professional growth and the improvement of teaching. It is focused on the needs of teachers rather than on the organization's need for accountability. Unlike summative evaluation, which usually considers teacher behavior inside and outside the classroom, formative evaluation is focused only on teaching and learning. Summative evaluation is concerned with a summary of performance over a specific time period, whereas formative evaluation is ongoing and concerned with continuous improvement. Rather than rely on standardized evaluation instruments that gather data on all essential performance criteria, formative evaluation is usually based on *systematic observation,* which is limited to a single aspect of classroom process (e.g., questioning techniques, student participation, classroom movement). Thus, the observation systems described in Chapter 13 are well suited for formative evaluation.

Because it is not concerned with standardized, global criteria, formative evaluation can concentrate on particular contexts and needs of individual teachers. Because its purpose is helping teachers, not judging them, formative evaluation is not concerned with legal issues like due process. Rather, it is concerned with building trust and rapport, developing a collegial relationship between evaluator and teacher, and addressing teacher needs and concerns. Table 14.1 summarizes our comparison of summative and formative teacher evaluation.

Why Summative and Formative Teacher Evaluation Should Be Separate

Most school districts have a single evaluation system and maintain that their system meets both summative and formative needs. However, when schools attempt to carry out summative and formative evaluation simultaneously, they tend to place primary emphasis on summative goals, and formative evaluation is reduced to secondary status. "Too often school districts espouse a strong growth-oriented position but the evaluation system constructed does not reflect that stance" (McGreal, 1989, p. 38).

table 14.1 Comparison of Summative and Formative Teacher Evaluation

	Summative	Formative
Function	Administrative	Supervisory
Purpose	Accountability; Judgment on teacher performance; Employment decisions	Assistance; Professional development; Improvement of teaching
Scope	Instruction; Compliance with regulations; Extracurricular responsibilities; Personal qualities	Instruction
Focus	Evaluation form	Any classroom data (observation, artifacts, etc.) relevant to the teacher's instructional concerns and needs
Duration	Set period (usually one academic year)	Ongoing (aimed at continuous improvement)
Concerns	Standardization, validity, reliability, due process	Building trust, rapport, collegiality; Understanding context; Understanding and addressing teacher concerns and needs
Evaluator	Usually an administrator; Final decision by administrator	Administrator, supervisor, self, peers, students, sometimes parents

Evaluation systems that purport to combine summative and formative evaluation while relying on rating scales alone are particularly suspect. "A school system that relies solely on periodic evaluations of teacher performance through rating scales *may* capture data suited for in-system summative purposes but will be handicapped in pursuing formative/developmental objectives" (Allison, 1981, p. 15; emphasis in original). One reason for this is that summative rating scales are designed to be standardized, global, legally defensible, efficiently completed and processed, and include many noninstructional criteria. This means not only that the ratings have little value for formative evaluation but also that the richest, most meaningful data for formative assessment is precluded (Allison, 1981; Stiggins and Bridgeford, 1984).

It is widely recognized that summative evaluation, although necessary to make employment decisions, does not lead to instructional improvement for most teachers (Stiggins and Bridgeford, 1984). In fact, summative evaluation can actually discourage improvement by promoting "negative feelings about evaluation which, in turn, lead to a lack of participation and a lower likelihood of teachers being willing to alter classroom behavior" (McGreal, 1983, p. 303). Successful formative evaluation depends on trust and open communication between the teacher and evaluator. Yet summative evaluation is potentially punitive (Sutton, 1989). The possibility of a bad performance rating is always lurking in the background. It's no wonder that the two types of evaluation don't mix!

We're not arguing that summative evaluation should be eliminated in favor of formative evaluation. Both types of evaluation are necessary. Like Popham (1988), we maintain that because they have entirely different purposes, they must be kept separate. With McGreal (1983), we argue that the likelihood that either type of evaluation system will succeed is greater if both systems are internally consistent, which can be accomplished only by the two systems being kept separate. If separated, can the two systems coexist? Yes, but only if the purpose of each is clearly defined, they are perceived by teachers as distinct, and the integrity of each is protected (Allison, 1981).

How to Separate Summative and Formative Evaluation

One way to separate the two types of evaluation is to use different evaluators. Teachers could receive summative evaluation from the principal and formative evaluation from an assistant principal for instruction, lead teacher, peer coach, or mentor. There are many different combinations of summative and formative evaluators. The important thing is to make clear to everyone who is responsible for each type of evaluation and to have each evaluator carry out their assessment separately from the others.

Another way to separate summative and formative evaluation relates to the time period when each is carried out. For example, all summative evaluations could be carried out in the fall of each schoolyear, leaving the remainder of the year for formative assessment. When this strategy is used, the same person or persons can perform both types of evaluation. This strategy does not work as well if formative evaluation is carried out in the fall and summative evaluation takes place throughout the rest of the year, because the teacher involved in formative evaluation during the fall realizes that summative evaluation is looming on the horizon. That knowledge may affect the willingness of the teacher to engage in open and honest communication about his or her need for instructional improvement. It's better to get the summative evaluation out of the way early in the year, give the teacher his or her "seal of approval," and then allow the teacher and supervisor to engage in nonjudgmental assessment for the remainder of the schoolyear. A long-term variation of the "separate time periods" strategy is to conduct summative evaluation throughout the first year of a multiyear cycle and then focus on formative evaluation for the next two to three years, returning to a summative year at the beginning of the next three- to four-year cycle. Should serious problems with a teacher's performance develop during a formative assessment year, that teacher could be shifted back to a summative evaluation–remediation track until the problem is resolved.

A third way of separating summative and formative evaluation was suggested by Thomas McGreal (1983). Under McGreal's model, a clear and visible set of minimum performance expectations is developed, including administrative, personal, and instructional expectations. Teacher performance regarding these minimal expectations is continuously and informally monitored, but no special procedures or evaluation instruments are established. If a problem occurs with a teacher's performance, the administrator reminds the teacher of minimum expectations. If the problem continues to occur, the administrator issues to the teacher a written notice of the teacher's deficiency, with a copy placed in the teacher's file. If serious violations continue even after the formal notice, the administrator recommends more serious administrative action. Beyond these contingencies, there is no standard summative evaluation process or annual write-up. This takes care of summative evaluation. Most of the time and energy spent on evaluation is for formative assessment, including goal setting, a focus on teaching, systematic classroom observation, and collecting and analyzing additional classroom data. This additional data could include peer, parent, student, and self-evaluation, as well as student performance and classroom artifacts (McGreal, 1983).

Which strategy for separating summative and formative evaluation is the best for a district or school depends on the level of administrative and supervisory expertise, the size of the staff, teacher preference, and available resources. The important thing is that they be kept separate. Doing so means that both summative and formative evaluation are carried out more effectively.

Self-Evaluation

Self-evaluation can be an important part of the formative evaluation process for teachers functioning at moderate or high levels of development, expertise, and commitment. Self-assessment can take a variety of forms, including any of the following:

- Visits to the classrooms of several expert teachers for the purpose of comparing expert teaching to one's own teaching and identifying self-improvement goals based on such comparison
- Video recording one's own teaching across several lessons and then analyzing teaching performance while reviewing the video
- Designing or selecting and analyzing results of surveys or questionnaires administered to students or parents
- Interviewing supervisors, peers, students, or parents about effective teaching and learning or about one's own instructional performance
- Keeping a journal of teaching experiences, problems, and successes, accompanied by critical reflection for the purpose of instructional improvement
- Conducting a comprehensive review of student achievement on traditional tests as well as student projects, presentations, portfolios, social behavior, and so on
- Developing a teaching portfolio for the purpose of self-reflection and analysis

Danielson (1996) recommends a variety of items for possible inclusion in a portfolio, including unit and lesson plans, knowledge of students and resources, videos of teaching, examples of student work, written reflections on lessons taught, and logs on professional service, growth, and research. Langer (Teaching for Performance, 1996) argues for a more focused approach, in which the teacher's portfolio documents a process in which the teacher defines a problem, sets an improvement goal, designs a plan to reach the goal, implements the plan, collects data on professional growth, and reflects on results. Both Danielson's broad approach and Langer's focused approach go beyond the documentation of teaching accomplishments (the purpose of portfolios used in summative teacher evaluation) by providing teachers with opportunities for self-assessment as the basis for instructional improvement.

It's important to note that self-evaluation of teaching need not be done in isolation. Videos, survey or interview results, journals, student achievement data, and teacher portfolios can be analyzed and discussed collaboratively with a supervisor or peers, and in some cases with students or parents. The process is called *self-evaluation* because the teacher assumes full responsibility for decision making regarding planning and implementing the evaluation as well as the instructional improvement plan that results (Keller and Duffy, 2005).

MyEdLeadershipLab™

Go to Topic 5, Research and Evaluation, in the MyEdLeadershipLab™ site at www.myedleadershiplab.com for *The Basic Guide to SuperVision and Instructional Leadership*, Third Edition, where you can:

- Find learning outcomes for Research and Evaluation along with the national standards that connect to these outcomes.
- Complete Assignments and Activities that can help you more deeply understand the chapter content.
- Apply and practice your understanding of the core skills identified in the chapter with the Building Leadership Skills unit.
- Prepare yourself for professional certification with a Practice for Certification quiz.

REFERENCES

Allison, D. J. 1981. *Process evaluation: Some summarizing and integrating notes on the organizational implications of this form of teacher evaluation.* (ERIC ED 235 580)

Danielson, C. 1996. *Enhancing professional practice: A framework for teaching.* Alexandria, VA: Association for Supervision and Curriculum Development.

Danielson, C., and McGreal, T. L. 2000. *Teacher evaluation: To enhance teacher professional practice.* Alexandria, VA: Association for Supervision and Curriculum Development.

Fetterman, D.M. (1996). Empowerment Evaluation: An Introduction to Theory and Practice. In Fetterman, D.M., Kaftarian, S.J., Wandersman, A. (1996). *Empowerment Evaluation: Knowledge and Tools for Self-assessment and Accountability*. Thousand Oaks, CA: Sage.

Greene, J. C. 1986. *Participatory evaluation and the evaluation of social programs: Lessons learned from the field.* Paper presented to the annual meeting of the American Educational Research Association, San Francisco, April.

Haefele, D. L. 1993. Evaluating teachers: A call for change. *Journal of Personnel Evaluation in Education, 7*(1), 21–31.

Keller, C. L., and Duffy, M. L. 2005. "I said that?" How to improve your instructional behavior in just 5 minutes per day through data-based self-evaluation. *Teaching Exceptional Children, 37*(4), 36–39.

McGreal, T. L. 1983. *Successful teacher evaluation.* Alexandria, VA: Association for Supervision and Curriculum Development.

Newman, D. C., and Brown, R. D. 1987. *Violations of evaluation standards: Frequency and seriousness of occurrence.* Paper presented at the annual meeting of the American Educational Research Association, Washington, DC, April.

Popham, J. 1988. The dysfunctional marriage of formative and summative evaluation. *Journal of Personnel Evaluation in Education, 1,* 269–273.

Stiggins, R. J., and Bridgeford, N. J. 1984. *Performance assessment for teacher development.* Portland, OR: Northwest Regional Educational Lab Center for Performance Assessment.

Sutton, J. H. 1989. *Evaluation: A primer for teachers.* (ERIC ED 310 146)

Teaching for performance: New assessments help reshape classroom practice (1996, December). *Education Update, 38*(8), 1, 6.

Wolfe, R. 1969. A model for curriculum evaluation. *Psychology in the Schools, 6,* 107–108.

part 5

Technical Tasks of SuperVision

If one has responsibility for the improvement of instruction, what does one do? We've accounted for what the supervisor must possess in terms of knowledge, interpersonal skills, and technical skills. What are the technical tasks of supervision that can bring about improved instruction? They are direct assistance to teachers, group development, professional development, curriculum development, and action research.

- *Direct assistance.* The supervisor can provide or facilitate one-to-one feedback with teachers to improve instruction.
- *Group development.* The supervisor can provide for instructional problem-solving meetings among teachers to improve instruction.
- *Professional development.* The supervisor can provide learning opportunities with teachers to improve instruction.
- *Curriculum development.* The supervisor can provide for changes in teaching content and instructional materials to improve instruction.
- *Action research.* The supervisor can provide teachers with ways to evaluate their own teaching to improve instruction.

Each of these tasks is directly related to improved instruction. A supervisor must take responsibility for these tasks if a school is to become increasingly effective. Part 5 details how these tasks can be performed so that teachers take individual and collective responsibility for instructional improvement.

chapter 15

Direct Assistance to Teachers

outline

- Clinical Supervision
- Comparing Clinical Supervision with Teacher Evaluation
- Integrating Clinical Supervision and Developmental Supervision
- Peer Coaching
- Other Forms of Direct Assistance
- Improving Classroom Culture

Visit the **MyEdLeadershipLab™** site for *The Basic Guide to SuperVision and Instructional Leadership*, Third Edition to enhance your understanding of chapter concepts. You'll have the opportunity to practice your skills through video and case based Assignments and Activities as well as Building Leadership Skills units, and prepare for your certification exam with Practice for Certification quizzes.

Direct assistance to help teachers improve instruction can come from different sources. The authors of this book contend that someone must take responsibility for the supervisory function of direct assistance to ensure that teachers receive feedback, are not left alone, and are involved as part of a collective staff.

In this chapter, we look at clinical supervision, an established structure for assisting teachers, and then at some alternative ways of providing direct assistance.

Clinical Supervision

Although there are multiple ways of observing, the model for conducting observations with teachers is relatively standard and accepted and has a respectable research base (Sullivan, 1980; Adams and Glickman, 1984; Pavan, 1985; Nolan, Hawkes, and Francis, 1993; Glickman, 2002). In fact, more than 90 percent of school administrators in a southern state and a midwestern state have cited their knowledge of the use of this structure with teachers (Bruce and Hoehn, 1980). The model, commonly referred to as *clinical supervision,* is derived from the pioneering work of Morris Cogan with supervisors of intern teachers at Harvard University. Cogan's *Clinical Supervision* (1973) and Robert Goldhammer's book, also entitled *Clinical Supervision* (1969), are publications resulting from this pioneer work. Since then, numerous refinements and alterations of clinical supervision have been made (Costa and Garmston, 1985; Acheson and Gall, 1992; Anderson and Snyder, 1993; Goldhammer, Anderson, and Krajewski, 1993; Pajak, 1993, 2002). Those desiring an in-depth study of the research and development of clinical supervision can find references at the end of this chapter.

Clinical supervision is both a concept and a structure. Goldhammer, Anderson, and Krajewski (1993) reviewed nine characteristics of clinical supervision as a concept:

1. It is a technology for improving instruction.
2. It is a deliberate intervention into the instructional process.
3. It is goal oriented, combining the school needs with the personal growth needs of those who work within the school.
4. It assumes a professional working relationship between the teacher(s) and the supervisor(s).
5. It requires a high degree of mutual trust, as reflected in understanding, support, and commitment to growth.
6. It is systematic, although it requires a flexible and continuously changing methodology.
7. It creates a productive (i.e., healthy) tension for bridging the gap between the real and the ideal.
8. It assumes that the supervisor knows a great deal about the analysis of instruction and learning and also about productive human interaction.

9. It requires both preservice training (for supervisors), especially in observation techniques, and continuous in-service reflection on effective approaches. (pp. 52–53) (parenthetical explanations added)

The structure of clinical supervision can be simplified into five steps:

1. Preconference with teacher
2. Observation of classroom
3. Analyzing and interpreting observation and determining conference approach
4. Postconference with teacher
5. Critique of previous four steps

Step 1: Preconference

At the *preconference,* the supervisor sits with the teacher and determines (1) the reason and purpose for the observation, (2) the focus of the observation, (3) the method and form of observation to be used, (4) the time of observation, and (5) the time for postconference. These determinations are made before the actual observation, so that both supervisor and teacher are clear about what will transpire. The purpose of the observation, as mentioned in Chapter 13, should provide the criteria for making the remaining decisions on focus, method, and time of observation.

Step 2: Observation

The next step, *observation,* is the time to follow through with the understandings of the preconference. The observer might use any one observation or combinations of observations. Methods include categorical frequencies, performance indicators, visual diagramming, space utilization, verbatim, detached open-ended narratives, participant observation, focused questionnaire, and tailored observation systems.

Step 3: Analysis and Interpretation

The *analysis* and *interpretations* of the observation and determination of approach are now possible. The supervisor leaves the classroom with his or her observations and seeks solitude in an office or corner. He or she lays out the recorded pages of observations and studies the information. The task might be counting up frequencies, looking for recurring patterns, isolating a major occurrence, or discovering which performance indicators were present and which were not. Regardless of the instrument, questionnaire, or open-ended form used, the supervisor must make sense out of a large mass of information. Then the supervisor can make interpretations based on the analysis of the description.

A case study might help clarify this worksheet. Supervisor A has completed a verbal interaction instrument for students and teacher. She reviews the 10 sheets, tallies the columns, and writes in the worksheet under analysis:

1. The teacher asked 27 questions and received 42 answers.
2. Out of 276 total verbal moves, 6 were student to student; the other 270 were teacher to student or student to teacher.
3. . . .

The supervisor, knowing that the purpose of the lesson was to encourage student involvement, now makes interpretations on the worksheet *corresponding* to the analysis:

1. The teacher encouraged students to answer questions.
2. There was little interaction among students.
3. . . .

Note the relationship between analysis 1 and interpretation 1. There is clear documentation of evidence leading to the supervisor's judgment. Although one could argue with the supervisor's interpretation, it is readily apparent how it was logically derived from the recorded descriptions.

The last determination for the supervisor to make in step 3 of the clinical structure is to choose what interpersonal approach to use with the teacher in the postconference. The directive informational, collaborative, and nondirective approaches to supervision were explained in Chapters 8, 9, and 10, respectively. Should the supervisor use a directive informational approach by presenting his or her observations and interpretations, asking for teacher input, setting a goal, and providing teachers with alternative actions to choose from? Should the supervisor be collaborative by sharing the observation, allowing the teacher to present his or her own interpretations, and negotiating a mutual contract for future improvement? Should the supervisor be nondirective by explaining his or her observations and encouraging the teacher to analyze, interpret, and make his or her own plan?

The supervisor must consider the individual teacher's level of development, expertise, and commitment, as explained in Chapter 11. When working with a teacher who is best matched with a collaborative or nondirective approach and who has experience with clinical supervision, some supervisors provide the teacher with the observation data prior to the postconference. This allows the teacher to review the data in advance and bring his or her preliminary interpretations to the postconference.

Step 4: Postconference

With the completed observation form, completed analysis, and interpretation form and with the chosen interpersonal approach, the supervisor is ready to meet with the teacher in a *postconference*. The postconference is held to discuss the analysis of the observation and finally to produce a plan for instructional improvement.

Postconference Date ______________	Observed Teacher ______________
Time ______________	Peer Supervisor ______________
Objective to be worked on:	
Activities to be undertaken to achieve objectives:	
Resources needed:	
Time and date for next preconference:	

figure 15.1 **Plan for Instructional Improvement**

The first order of business is to let the teacher in on the observation—to reflect back to the teacher what was seen. Then the supervisor can follow the chosen approach—directive informational, collaborative, or nondirective. The responsibility for developing a future plan may reside with the supervisor, be equally shared, or belong to the teacher. The conference ends with a plan for further improvement. Figure 15.1 can be used to develop such a plan.

The *objective* is a statement of what the teacher will attain for the next observation: "I will improve student-to-student interaction by 50 percent in group discussions." *Activities* are the listed preparation points to accomplish the objective: (1) Practice pausing at least three seconds before answering a student response. (2) Practice using open-ended questions. (3) Set up ongoing mini-debates. *Resources* are the materials or people needed to do the activities: (1) Read a book on leading discussion groups. (2) Attend a workshop on "Involving Students." (3) Observe Mr. Filler when he holds a science discussion. *Date* and *time* specify when the teacher will be ready to display his or her improvement. Such a plan—whether designed by the teacher, the supervisor, or both—should be clearly understood by both parties before they leave the postconference.

Step 5: Critique

The *critique* of the previous four steps is a time for reviewing whether the format and procedures from preconference through postconference were satisfactory and whether revisions might be needed before repeating the sequence. The critique can be held at the end of the postconference. It need not be a formal session but can be a brief discussion, consisting of questions such as: What was valuable in what we have been doing? What was of little value? What changes could be suggested?

The critique has both symbolic and functional value. It indicates that the supervisor is involved in an improvement effort in the same way as the supervisee. Furthermore, the feedback from the teacher gives the supervisor a chance to decide on what practices to continue, revise, or change when working with the teacher in the future.

The five steps are now complete, and a tangible plan of future action is in the hands of the teacher. The supervisor is prepared to review the plan in the next preconference and reestablish focus and method of observation.

Comparing Clinical Supervision with Teacher Evaluation

In Chapter 14, we discovered the differences between summative and formative evaluation. Clinical supervision is consistent with formative evaluation; it provides nonjudgmental assistance aimed at improving the teacher's instruction. Indeed, it has been equated by some with formative evaluation. Clinical supervision actually includes but goes beyond formative evaluation by helping the teacher design and implement an action plan to meet instructional improvement goals.

Clinical supervision is *not* consistent with summative evaluation; it is not intended to gather data to make judgments about whether teachers are meeting performance criteria for continued employment. Some school districts have confused the two processes by calling their summative evaluation cycle *clinical supervision.* At one level, this is understandable. Both clinical supervision and summative evaluation can take place within similar structures, including a preconference, classroom visit, and postconference. To understand the difference between the two concepts, we must look beyond the structure to the purpose and principles of clinical supervision, which clearly are not consistent with those of summative evaluation. The two processes need to be separate, for the same reasons that summative and formative evaluation should be separate (see Chapter 14).

Integrating Clinical Supervision and Developmental Supervision

As discovered in Part 3, developmental supervision calls for the supervisor to match one of four interpersonal approaches—directive control, directive informational, collaborative, or nondirective—with teachers' developmental levels, expertise, and commitment. Are all four of these interpersonal approaches consistent with clinical supervision? The answer to this question depends to some extent on the model of clinical supervision being considered. Goldhammer's (1969) text on clinical supervision emphasizes a nondirective interpersonal approach. Cogan's (1973) clinical cycle reflects a collaborative orientation. Hunter's (1980, 1983, 1984, 1986) clinical model supports a directive approach. Our own view is that directive informational, collaborative, and nondirective supervisory approaches are all consistent with the clinical model.

Using a directive informational approach, the supervisor can suggest and explain two or three alternative observation foci and data-collection methods in the preconference and ask the teacher to select from the options provided. In the post-conference, the supervisor can help the teacher to interpret observation data and ask the teacher to choose from a limited range of possible improvement objectives, activities, and follow-ups. The supervisor and teacher engaged in a collaborative preconference can consider observation alternatives and select a mutually agreeable observation focus and data-collection method. In the collaborative postconference, the supervisor and teacher can share decision-making responsibility as they build an action plan for instructional improvement. The supervisor using nondirective behaviors in a preconference can ask the teacher to choose the focus of the observation and facilitate the teacher as he or she chooses or creates an observation system that the supervisor feels comfortable using. In the postconference, the supervisor clarifies encourages, and reflects as the teacher designs his or her own improvement plan.

Although directive control behaviors are necessary in rare situations, over the long term, we do not consider those behaviors to be consistent with the purpose and principles of clinical supervision. Directive control should be used only in short-term, crisis situations, not as part of a normal clinical cycle.

Peer Coaching

Because teachers naturally turn to each other for help more often than to a supervisor, and because supervision is concerned primarily with improving instruction rather than with summative evaluation (renewal of contracts), teachers helping teachers has become a formalized and well-received way of ensuring direct assistance to every staff member.

If teachers become proficient in observation skills and the format of clinical supervision, the supervisor can take on the role of clarifier, trainer, scheduler, and troubleshooter—clarifier by determining the purpose; trainer by preparing the teachers for the task; scheduler by forming teams or trios of teachers who take responsibility for preconferencing, observing, and postconferencing with each other; and troubleshooter by consulting with teams of teachers who are experiencing difficulties and with individual teachers who need more specialized attention. The use of teachers helping teachers through clinical supervision is known as *peer coaching*.

Obviously, the way to begin such a program is not to call a staff meeting and announce, "Because I can't see each of you as much as I would like, why don't you start to visit each other? Go to it!" Without planning and resources, disaster is inevitable. To be successful, peer coaching needs components addressing purpose, preparation, scheduling, and troubleshooting. Let's take each in turn.

Purpose

Before beginning a peer-coaching program, clarifying purpose and goals is necessary (Garmston, 1987; Barbknecht and Kieffer, 2001). First, is it reciprocal assistance (interactions of equals) or is it a matter of expert, one-way assistance (a better trained or more experienced teacher helping less well-trained or less experienced teachers)? Second, in a peer program, who is to be the recipient of assistance? Should a teacher who is the observer take from the observation some ideas to use, or should the teacher who is the observed take from the observation some actions to use? Third, should the observations and feedback focus on common instructional skills that each teacher is attempting to learn and implement, or on the teacher's own idiosyncratic concern with his or her teaching? Fourth, should the observations and feedback focus on the teacher's teaching, or on individual students' behaviors? Fifth, is the goal of coaching to be greater awareness and more reflective decision making, or is it to implement particular teaching skills? Ultimately, how does the coaching goal fit into the larger school goal of improving instruction for students?

These are not idle questions. A peer-coaching program void of articulated definition and purpose has no rudder for steering and selecting the training, scheduling, and troubleshooting essential for success. If there is a lack of direction in peer-coaching programs, well-intentioned teachers have a vague sense of having done something pleasant but little sense of accomplishment (see Little, Galagaran, and O'Neal, 1984).

Therefore, the first step is to meet with teachers to discuss how a proposed peer-coaching program fits into a school's or district's instructional goals and then to decide on the specific purposes of the program.

Preparation

Before implementation, preparation of teachers includes training on (1) understanding the purpose and procedures of peer coaching, (2) conducting a preconference for determining the focus of observations, (3) conducting and analyzing an observation to distinguish between observing and interpreting classroom events, and (4) conducting two postconferences with different approaches for developing action plans—one using a nondirective approach, the other using a collaborative approach.

A standard form for writing instructional improvement plans in the postconference should be reviewed. The form should be simple and easy to fill out. Each peer member should understand that a completed plan is the object of the first four clinical steps and the basis for beginning the next round of supervision. For purposes of training, you may use the forms found in this chapter and in Chapter 13.

Training sessions of about six hours should provide the minimum knowledge and skills to begin peer coaching. After peers have gained some familiarity with the process through demonstrations, modeling, and practice in the workshop setting, they will be anxious but ready to begin a coaching cycle. For the initial attempts, perfection is not expected, of course.

After the first cycle of implementation, a follow-up meeting should be held to discuss what occurred and what revisions must be made before beginning the second cycle. It is often convenient to review the past cycle and conduct the preconference for the next cycle during the same meeting. This gives participants a sense of sharing and learning from each other, enables the trainer to answer questions, allows for observation schedules to be arranged, and eliminates the need to meet another time to hold the preconference. From this point on, follow-up meetings concluding and beginning further cycles can be held every two to three weeks until the agreed-on number of peer cycles have been finished. For the first year, it is recommended that at least four cycles be conducted—two times being the coach and two times being coached.

Toward the end of the year, a culminating meeting should be held to summarize the advantages and disadvantages of using peer coaching and to make a recommendation on whether to continue the program for the following year.

Let's emphasize that the program should be based on *agreement* and *volunteerism*. If an entire staff is willing to be involved, that's fine, but if, for example, only three teachers are willing, it is still a beginning and a previously unavailable source of help for those three teachers.

Scheduling

A teacher will have a more difficult time becoming enthusiastic about a project if it means increasing the amount of personal time and energy expended beyond an already full day. Because peer coaching requires additional time, the program should be voluntary, at least in the beginning. Greater participation of teachers is likely if the supervisor can schedule time for peer coaching during the schoolday.

For example, placing teachers together in teams that share the same planning or lunch periods would allow for pre- and postconferences during the schoolday. Hiring a few substitutes for two days, twice a year, allows teachers to be relieved of class duties so that they can observe their peers. One substitute could relieve six classroom teachers for one period at a time. Relief could also be found by having the supervisor (we mean you!) occasionally substitute for a teacher for one class period. This enables the teacher to observe and also gives the supervisor a glimpse into the operating world of the classroom. Another way of freeing time for peer observations is for teachers to release each other by periodically scheduling a video, lecture, or some other large-group instruction so that two classes can be taught by one teacher. Whatever the actual schedule used to release teachers for peer coaching, preplanning by supervisor and teachers is needed to ensure that teachers can participate without extreme personal sacrifice. Research on lasting classroom change has shown that scheduling released time for teachers during the schoolday is critical (Humphries, 1981; Ballinger, 2000).

Troubleshooting

The fourth component of establishing a peer-coaching program is the close monitoring of peer progress. The supervisor should be available to peer teams as a resource person. For example, what happens when the preconference concludes with an agreement to observe a teacher's verbal interaction in the classroom and the peer coach is at a loss about where to find such an observation instrument? The training program should answer such questions, but orientation meetings cannot cover all possible needs. The supervisor must, therefore, monitor the needs of peer teams and be able to step in to help.

An elaborate monitoring device is not necessary. The supervisor might simply wander around the halls and check with peer coaches every few weeks. At periodic faculty meetings, he or she might ask peer coaches to write a note on their team progress. The supervisor should be sure that books, videos, and methods/instruments for observations are catalogued and available to teachers in the professional library.

Now that the supervisor can attend to *purpose, training, scheduling,* and *troubleshooting,* a peer-coaching supervision program can be implemented. The initial implementation of such a program undoubtedly will create more work for the supervisor. However, the initial work is less than that necessary for providing clinical supervision to every teacher two or three times a year. If it is important enough to supervisor and staff, the time spent at the start in preparing for the program will pay off with ongoing instructional improvement of teachers.

Other Forms of Direct Assistance

Clinical supervision and peer coaching are currently two of the most popular forms of direct assistance in schools, but a variety of other forms are available. A few additional examples of direct assistance include the following:

- *Demonstration teaching.* The supervisor or expert peer can be a guest teacher, demonstrating a new teaching model or method for the teacher requesting assistance. Alternatively, the teacher seeking to learn new skills can visit an expert peer's classroom for a demonstration lesson.
- *Co-teaching.* The supervisor or expert peer and the teacher seeking assistance together can plan, teach, and evaluate a lesson. Co-teaching establishes trust and rapport, and fosters the collegiality, dialogue, and mutual reflection that foster teacher growth.
- *Assistance with resources and materials.* An unglamorous but vital supervisory activity is providing, explaining, and demonstrating instructional resources and materials. All of us in education are aware of teachers who make little or no use of particular instructional resources and materials (from manipulatives to technology) because of a lack of awareness or expertise. Many teachers would benefit greatly from the effective use of such resources and

materials, but they need individualized assistance for technical mastery and adaptation to teaching content and students.

- *Assistance with student assessment.* There is a clear trend within the educational reform movement toward alternative forms of student assessment, such as student portfolios, real-world performances, and integrative projects. Adapting new assessment techniques to particular content areas, grade levels, and individual students requires individualized assistance.
- *Problem solving.* Teachers experience a variety of professional problems that can be solved in one-to-one conferences and without classroom observation. Once a relationship of openness, trust, and rapport has been established, a supervisor can assist a teacher through a problem-solving process involving (1) identification of the problem, (2) generation and weighing of alternative actions, (3) selection of the most appropriate actions, and (4) planning follow-up to assess the results of chosen actions.
- *Mentoring.* In schools, mentoring typically is direct assistance provided by an experienced teacher to a beginning teacher. The mentor might provide any of the forms of direct assistance discussed previously—expert coaching, demonstration teaching, co-teaching, and so on. The heart of mentoring, however, goes beyond any specific form of direct assistance to the ongoing relationship of mentor and beginner. This trusting and helping relationship can make the difference between a successful and a failed entrance to the profession. The supervisor has a significant role to play in mentoring programs, helping to select and prepare mentors, assisting with the matching of mentors with beginners, and providing ongoing support for mentors.

Improving Classroom Culture

A great deal of direct assistance is for the purpose of improving teachers' instructional skills or solving immediate instructional problems. As important as these goals are, direct assistance can help teachers reach deeper goals based on democratic and moral purposes. By modeling and encouraging adherence to democratic and moral values in the classroom, the teacher fosters a democratic and moral society.

The teacher and supervisor can begin the process of improving classroom culture by asking such questions as the following:

1. Are students treated equitably by the teacher and by each other?
2. Do the teacher and students follow democratic principles appropriate to the students' ages and maturity levels?
3. Do the teacher and students demonstrate compassion to those in need?
4. Do students feel physically and emotionally safe?
5. Are all cultures respected, valued, and celebrated?

Processes such as clinical supervision and peer coaching can be used to answer questions such as these. Quantitative observation data can be gathered in this arena (for example, data can be gathered on whether the teacher gives students response opportunities, assistance, or praise in an equitable manner), but often rich narrative is needed to describe classroom culture adequately. The teacher and supervisor can work together to interpret the meaning of data on classroom culture, and to develop action plans for cultural improvement. Because classroom culture is so complex, teacher–supervisor conferral and action planning for cultural improvement is more complicated than conferral and planning for technical improvement, and cultural improvement takes much longer than implementing a new teaching skill. However, if a critical goal of education is a more democratic society, then the increased complexity and longer duration of cultural improvement efforts are well justified.

MyEdLeadershipLab™

Go to Topic 3, Types of Supervision, in the MyEdLeadershipLab™ site at www.myedleadershiplab.com for *The Basic Guide to SuperVision and Instructional Leadership*, Third Edition, where you can:

- Find learning outcomes for Types of Supervision along with the national standards that connect to these outcomes.
- Complete Assignments and Activities that can help you more deeply understand the chapter content.
- Apply and practice your understanding of the core skills identified in the chapter with the Building Leadership Skills unit.
- Prepare yourself for professional certification with a Practice for Certification quiz.

REFERENCES

Acheson, A. A., and Gall, M. D. 1992. *Techniques in the clinical supervision of teachers* (3rd ed.). New York: Longman.

Adams, A., and Glickman, C. D. 1984. Does clinical supervision work? A review of research. *Tennessee Educational Leadership, 11*(11), 38–40.

Anderson, R. H., and Snyder, K. J. (Eds.). 1993. *Clinical supervision: Coaching for higher performance*. Lancaster, PA: Technomic Publishing.

Ballinger, J. 2000. Programs aim to stop teacher washout. *Journal of Staff Development, 21*(2), 28–33.

Barbknecht, A. and Kieffer, C. (2001). *Peer coaching*. Andover, MA: Skylight Publishing.

Bruce, R. E., and Hoehn, L. 1980. *Supervisory practice in Georgia and Ohio*. Paper presented at the annual meeting of the Council of Professors of Instructional Supervision, Hollywood, FL, December.

Cogan, M. 1973. *Clinical supervision*. Boston: Houghton Mifflin.

Costa, A. L., and Garmston, R. 1985. Supervision for intelligent teaching. *Educational Leadership, 42*(5), 70–80.

Garmston, R. J. 1987. How administrators support peer coaching. *Educational Leadership, 44*, 18–26.

Glickman, C. D. 2002. *Leadership for learning: How to help teachers succeed.* Alexandria, VA: Association for Supervision and Curriculum development.

Goldhammer, R. 1969. *Clinical supervision: Special methods for the supervision of teachers.* New York: Holt, Rinehart and Winston.

Goldhammer, R., Anderson, R. H., and Krajewski, R. J. 1993. *Clinical supervision: Special methods for the supervision of teachers* (3rd ed.). Fort Worth, TX: Harcourt Brace Jovanovich.

Humphries, J. D. 1981. *Factors affecting the impact of curriculum innovations on classroom practice: Project complexity, characteristics of local leadership and supervisory strategies.* Unpublished Ed.D. dissertation, University of Georgia.

Hunter, M. 1980. Six types of supervisory conferences. *Educational Leadership, 37,* 408–412.

Hunter, M. 1983. Script-taping: An essential supervisory tool. *Educational Leadership, 41*(3), 3.

Hunter, M. 1984. Knowing, teaching, and supervising. In P. L. Hosford (Ed.), *Using what we know about teaching.* Alexandria, VA: Association for Supervision and Curriculum Development.

Hunter, M. 1986. Let's eliminate the preobservation conference. *Educational Leadership, 43*(6), 69–70.

Little, J. W., Galagaran, P., and O'Neal, R. 1984. *Professional development roles and relationships: Principles and skills of "advising."* (Contract 400–83–003.) San Francisco: Far West Laboratory for Educational Research and Development.

Nolan, J., Hawkes, B., and Francis, P. 1993. Case studies: Windows into clinical supervision. *Educational Leadership, 51*(2), 52–56.

Pajak, E. 1993. *Approaches to clinical supervision: Alternatives for improving instruction.* Norwood, MA: Christopher-Gordon.

Pajak, E. 2002. Clinical supervision and psychological functions: A new direction for theory and practice. *Journal of Curriculum and Supervision, 17*(3), 189–205.

Pavan, B. N. 1985. *Clinical supervision: Research in schools utilizing comparative measures.* Paper presented at the annual meeting of the American Educational Research Association, Chicago, April.

Sullivan, C. G. 1980. *Clinical supervision: A state of the art review.* Alexandria, VA: Association for Supervision and Curriculum Development.

chapter 16

Group Development

outline

- Dimensions of an Effective Group
- Group Member Roles
- Dealing with Dysfunctional Members
- Resolving Conflict
- Preparing for Group Meetings

Visit the **MyEdLeadershipLab™** site for *The Basic Guide to SuperVision and Instructional Leadership,* Third Edition to enhance your understanding of chapter concepts. You'll have the opportunity to practice your skills through video and case based Assignments and Activities as well as Building Leadership Skills units, and prepare for your certification exam with Practice for Certification quizzes.

A vertical team at Highlands Elementary School is using action research to improve student literacy. The Level Six team at M. L. King Middle School is developing a new interdisciplinary curriculum. A teacher task force at Edwards High School is examining strategies for assisting students with special needs.

The teams described above are different in terms of school level and purpose, but they also have much in common. Each of the groups is expected to complete a task that involves making a number of decisions along the way. Each group must be concerned about maintaining positive interpersonal relationships. And each group is almost certain to face some level of conflict and some types of dysfunctional behavior along the way.

There are myriad teams with myriad purposes operating at schools across the nation, but they all possess some common roles, developmental phases, and challenges. This chapter discusses task and personal roles needed by all groups, dysfunctional roles that can impede any group, and general approaches to conflict management and decision making. This chapter also discusses a developmental approach to working with groups, matching supervisory approach to the group's level of development, expertise, and commitment.

Groups that work productively, efficiently, and harmoniously generally have a skillful leader. Unfortunately, because being part of a group is such an everyday occurrence in professional, personal, and social life, we seldom stop to think about what makes some groups work well and others fail. It is unrealistic for the leader of a new group to expect the group to proceed naturally in a professional manner. A leader must be conscious of the elements of a successful group, select clear procedures for group decision making, be able to deal with dysfunctional behavior, use conflict to generate helpful information, and determine appropriate leadership style.

Dimensions of an Effective Group

There are two dimensions of an effective professional group (Bales, 1953): the task dimension and the person dimension. The *task* dimension represents the content and purpose of the group meeting. The task is what is to be accomplished by the end of the meetings. Typical tasks of professional groups might be deciding on a new textbook, writing a new instructional schedule, coordinating a particular curriculum, or preparing a professional development plan. An effective group, obviously, accomplishes what it sets out to do. The *person* dimension of an effective group is composed of the interpersonal process and the satisfaction participants derive from working with each other. Concern and sensitivity to participants' feelings create a climate of desiring to meet with each other from week to week to accomplish and implement the group task.

Let's explain these two dimensions in a different way. Specific task behaviors are clarifying the group's purpose, keeping discussions focused, setting time limits, and appraising group progress toward the goal. A leader who says, "We're getting off the track; let's get back to discussing textbooks," is exhibiting a task behavior.

Specific person behaviors seen in a group include recognizing people for their contributions, smiling, injecting humor, and listening attentively. A leader who says, "Fred, I'm following what you've been saying; it's a point worth considering," demonstrating a person behavior.

Imagine a group that exhibits only task behaviors. The meeting would be formal, cold, and tense. People would not receive feedback, would not be encouraged, and probably would swallow hard before addressing the unsmiling, staring faces. Such a group would accomplish its task quickly, with little mutual support. The decision would be quick because participants would wish to remove themselves from the tense environment as soon as possible. The formality of the sessions would prevent in-depth discussions of feelings, attitudes, and differences of opinion. Decisions would be made on the basis of incomplete information and commitment from group members. The implementation of the decision would be problematic at best.

Next, imagine a group that exhibits only person behaviors. There would be much personal chatter, humorous storytelling, and frequent back slapping and touching. People would be smiling and laughing. The image of a raucous cocktail party might characterize a group with all person behaviors and no task behaviors, and the morning-after hangover is also analogous to the sense of accomplishment after a meeting devoid of task behaviors. People would enjoy each other's company for its own sake; everyone would have a wonderful time, but little would be done.

Group Member Roles

First, the leader must determine what behaviors are indicative of roles already in existence. Are some members displaying task roles or person roles? What roles are ongoing? Are certain roles lacking? Remember that both task and person roles are functional to group performance. Another set of roles and behaviors, called *dysfunctional,* distract a group from task and person relations. Dysfunctional roles, unlike functional roles, are a concern when present. After listing and briefly describing the most common functional member roles, we examine dysfunctional roles.

Task Roles

The following descriptions are adapted from those listed by Benne and Sheats (1948):

Initiator–contributor. Proposes original ideas or changed ways of regarding group problem, goal, or procedure. Launches discussion, moves group into new areas of discussion.

Information seeker. Asks for clarification in terms of factual adequacy. Seeks expert information and relevant facts.

Opinion seeker. Asks for clarification of values pertinent to the group undertaking or to proposed suggestions. Checks on others' attitudes and feelings toward particular issues.

Information giver. Provides factual, authoritative information or gives own experience relevant to the issue.

Opinion giver. Verbalizes his or her own values and opinions on the group problem; emphasizes what the group should do.

Elaborator. Picks up on others' suggestions and amplifies with examples, pertinent facts, and probable consequences.

Coordinator. Shows the link between ideas and suggestions; attempts to pull diverse proposals together.

Orienter. Clarifies the group's position; gives a state-of-the-scene review. Summarizes what has been discussed, points out where discussion has departed from the goal, and reminds the group of their ultimate goal.

Evaluator–critic. Evaluates the proposals of the group against a criteria of effectiveness. Assesses whether proposals are "reasonable," "manageable," "based on facts," and derived through fair procedures.

Energizer. Focuses the group to move toward decisions. Challenges and prods group into further action.

Procedural technician. Facilitates group discussion by taking care of logistics. Sees that the group has the necessary materials for the task (paper, pencils, chalk, and so on).

Recorder. Writes down the group's suggestions and decisions. Keeps an ongoing record of what transpires in the group.

A group needs these member roles to keep moving toward accomplishing its task. A leader can use these descriptions to figure out what roles are missing. Additional roles might need to be assigned to group members or incorporated by the leader. For example, a group might contain most of the task roles except for a procedural technician or recorder. Such a group probably would converse easily but bog down on recalling what has been said. The leader who knows what roles are needed can ask for a volunteer to be a recorder and summarizer. Knowledge of task roles and behaviors enables a leader to assess what roles are evident and what further roles must be assigned. The leader might take on some of the missing roles, assign them to others, or add particular persons to a group.

Person Roles

The knowledge of person roles and behaviors provides a guide to the group leader. Consider the following descriptions:

Encourager. Affirms, supports, and accepts the contribution of other members. Shows warmth and a positive attitude toward others.

Harmonizer. Conciliates differences between individuals. Looks for ways to reduce tension between members through nonthreatening explanations and humor.

Compromiser. Offers to change his or her proposals for the good of the group. Willing to yield position or to acknowledge own errors by meeting other opposing ideas halfway.

Gatekeeper or expediter. Regulates flow of communication by seeing that all members have a chance to talk. Encourages quiet persons to speak and puts limits on those who dominate the conversation. Proposes new regulations for discussions when participation becomes unbalanced.

Standard setter: Ego ideal. Appeals to group's pride by not letting group members give up when trouble occurs. Exudes confidence that the group is a good one and can make sound decisions.

Observer and commentator. Monitors the working of the group. Records who speaks to whom, where and when most roadblocks occur, and the frequency and length of individual members' participation. Provides feedback when the group wishes to evaluate its procedures and processes.

Follower. Is willing to accept the decisions of the group and follow them even though he or she has not been active or influential in those decisions. Serves as a listener to group discussion.

The seven person roles provide human satisfaction and group cohesiveness. People feel positive about meeting and talking with each other and comfortable enough to express their ideas. As a result, meetings are seen as pleasant times to continue the group's work. When person roles are missing, a group may face severe difficulties in making acceptable and committed decisions. Without person behaviors and roles, only the strongest, most assured, and vocal members will speak. Decisions might be made that more timid persons strongly reject but the group may not know that such strong disapproval exists.

Again, it is the group leader's responsibility to see if people roles are evident. If roles are missing, then he or she can confront the group with their absence, pick up the role(s) himself or herself, quietly suggest particular roles to existing members, or add to the group other individuals who more naturally play such roles. *Both task and person roles, when not already in existence, must be added.*

Dysfunctional Roles

Dysfunctional roles and behaviors are those that are conspicuous in their presence. Such roles and behaviors disrupt the progress toward a group goal and weaken group cohesiveness. Consider the following:

Aggressor. Personally attacks the worth of other members. Belittles and deflates the status, wisdom, and motivation of others. Examples of such verbal attacks are: "That's the most ridiculous thing I've ever heard," "You must be crazy to suggest . . ."

Blocker. Sees all opinions and suggestions by group members as negative. Opposes any decision being made and stubbornly refuses to propose alternatives. Examples of such blocking statements are: "That's a terrible idea," "I don't want to do that," "It's futile to do anything."

Recognition seeker. Uses the group setting to receive personal attention. Examples of such behaviors are dropping books, scattering papers, coughing incessantly, pretending to be asleep, raising hand and then forgetting what one was going to say.

Self-confessor. Uses the group to ventilate personal feelings not related to the group's tasks. Talks about personal problems or feelings of inadequacy whenever he or she can see ways to slip such confessions into the group discussion. Examples of self-confessing statements are: "This discussion reminds me of when I was a little child and the weight problem I had," or when the group is talking about differences of opinion, "You should hear my son and me fight; I don't know what to do about him."

Playboy or playgirl. Lacks interest and involvement by using the group setting to have a merry time. Distracts other members from the group's purpose. Tells private jokes, passes notes, makes faces at others, plays cards, and so on.

Dominator. Asserts superiority in controlling group discussion and dictates what certain members should do. Claims to know more about the issue under discussion and have better solutions than anyone else. Has elaborate answers to almost every question and monopolizes the discussion.

Help seeker. Tries to gain group's sympathy by expressing feelings of inadequacy or personal confusion. Uses such self-derogation as reason for not contributing: "This is all too confusing for me," "I can't make a decision on my own," "Why ask me? I can't help."

Special-interest pleader. Has no opinion or suggestions of his or her own but instead speaks for what others would say or do. Cloaks own bias by using an outside group: "We couldn't do that. Do you know what the school board would think?" "If those parents down in the local restaurant ever heard that we were going to change . . ."

Dysfunctional roles are fairly self-evident in a group. The leader's responsibility is to reduce or eliminate such dysfunctional roles before they severely harm the morale and efficiency of the group. He or she might try to understand the dysfunctional member's reason for acting as an aggressor, playboy, special interest pleader, and so on and then either confront the person privately or provide changes within the group to satisfy the unmet needs that are leading to the dysfunctional behavior. In the following section, we discuss in detail how to deal with dysfunctional group members.

Dealing with Dysfunctional Members

The fact that a group is made up of individuals with varying temperaments and motivations is important when thinking about ways to work with groups. Dealing with individuals, particularly those who display dysfunctional behaviors, is an additional responsibility of a group leader.

If the leader has observed the group at work and has determined that his or her own leader behaviors are appropriate for most members of the group, yet there continue to be a few dysfunctional members, then individual treatment might be in order. The procedure for treating a dysfunctional member is (1) observe the member, (2) try to understand why the member is acting unproductively, (3) communicate with the member about the behavior, (4) establish some rules for future behavior, and (5) redirect the unfavorable behavior (Kemp, 1970; Corey and Corey, 1982). Let's look at each step in more detail:

1. *Observe the member.* When and with whom does the dysfunctional behavior occur? What does the group member do, and how do others respond? For example, a dominator might start monopolizing the conversation as soon as he or she walks into the meeting. Other people might be interested in the dominator's talk for the first few minutes of the meeting but become increasingly annoyed as the dominator continues. They might roll their eyes, yawn, fidget, or make comments to each other.
2. *Try to understand the member.* Why does the member persist with dysfunctional behavior? Does he or she know the behavior is unproductive? Is the behavior being used to mask some underlying emotion? For example, a playboy might be insecure about his own worth and pretend not to care rather than exposing inner thoughts to the scrutiny of the group.
3. *Communicate with the member.* What can you communicate about the group member's behavior and the situation? Describe the situation and the behavior to the member without denigration. Instead of saying "You're being an aggressive son of a gun," say, "I've noticed that you speak loudly and angrily to Sara. At the last meeting, you told her to keep her mouth shut." Tell the dysfunctional member the effect of the behavior on you as group leader: "When you tell Sara to shut up and tell Bob that he's stupid, it starts an argument that takes time away from the meeting. I can't complete the agenda on time when those arguments take place" (see Gordon, 1980).
4. *Establish some rules for future behaviors.* Either ask the member to suggest some rules that he or she can abide by in the future, or tell the member your future rules, or establish them jointly. Regardless of which tactic is chosen, the leader should think of rules that would minimize further disruptions to the group. For example, the leader might say to a self-confessor, "The next time you have a personal problem, come speak to me privately about it," or to a domina-

tor, "I'm going to enforce a two-minute limit on every member's participation," or to a blocker, "If you don't think we're on the right course, tell us your objection once and only once."

5. *Redirect the unfavorable behavior.* Pick up on the group member's dysfunctional behavior, and try to make it functional. A dominator can be assigned the role of recorder, summarizer, or time keeper. A playboy can be given an opening time for sharing a funny story to relax the group before starting official business. An aggressor can be asked to play devil's advocate and argue the position of an adversary.

The five steps outlined here help the meeting leader understand and deal with individual dysfunctional behavior. The steps are predicated on the leader confronting the dysfunctional member in private. Dysfunctional behaviors that occur infrequently and in isolated situations might simply be ignored. The leader can respond to infrequent misbehaviors or make light of them: "Sara, I guess you really got wound up today; perhaps we might hear from someone else now." Only incessant behaviors that distract the entire group must be dealt with via direct confrontation. Confrontation is not easy but is necessary at times for the sake of the group. Role Play 16.1 provides a demonstration of how to deal with a dysfunctional group member.

Resolving Conflict

The key to a productive group is the way ongoing conflict is resolved. *Conflicts* are particular disagreements that occur between two or more members at a particular time. *Conflict is not necessarily dysfunctional.* In fact, research has shown that successful groups exhibit much conflict (Johnson and Johnson, 1987; Fullan, 2000). As Roger Johnson states: "A critical moment of truth in a . . . group is when two teachers disagree strongly with each other and argue" (Brandt, 1987, p. 18). A group can make wise decisions only when there is a wealth of information and ideas to consider. Information and ideas are generated through conflict. To suppress conflict is to limit the group's decision-making capacity. Therefore, the leader should encourage conflict, not stifle it. Of course, conflict, if not handled correctly, can degenerate into adversarial and harmful relations. It is not conflict that is bad; it is the way the leader deals with it that determines its value.

Conflict occurs when there is a disagreement over ideas. The leader should keep the disagreement focused on the ideas rather than on the personalities of the members. The following procedure for handling conflict serves as a ready reference for the group leader:

1. Ask each member to state his or her conflicting position.
2. Ask each member to restate the other's position.

role play 16.1

Dealing with a Dysfunctional Group Member

Context. The purpose of this role play is for a subgroup of four to provide a demonstration to the remainder of the group on how to effectively deal with a dysfunctional group member. Participants need approximately 20 minutes of preparation time away from the rest of the group. In the role play, a "supervisor" and three "teachers" are members of a committee meeting to discuss a schoolwide instructional issue. In their preparation for the role play, the role players may choose the school level (elementary, middle, or high school), the issue to be discussed, and any other details of the fictional situation that they must agree on to perform an effective role play. The group is assigned or chooses a dysfunctional role that one member of the group assumes during the role play. The role play is presented in three scenes.

Scene 1 (10 minutes). The supervisor and three teachers begin the meeting. Throughout the scene, one of the teachers assumes a dysfunctional role that is clearly impeding the rest of the group's efforts to resolve the issue. The supervisor observes the teacher's dysfunctional behaviors. This scene ends with a break in the meeting, with the issue unresolved. During the break the other two teachers leave to get a cup of coffee, and the supervisor and the dysfunctional teacher are left alone.

Scene 2 (10 minutes). In a private discussion with the dysfunctional teacher during the break, the supervisor uses techniques suggested under this chapter's heading "Dealing with Dysfunctional Members" to address the teacher's behaviors. The specific discussion depends on the dysfunctional role that the teacher has been playing. The discussion culminates with an agreed-on plan for minimizing future disruptions.

Scene 3 (10 minutes). The other teachers return and the meeting resumes. Because of the agreements worked out during the break and the supervisor's support during the second part of the group meeting, the teacher's dysfunctional behaviors are greatly reduced. The group is able to resolve the issue under discussion.

Whole-Group Processing (10 minutes). The entire group discusses what the dysfunctional role was, specific behaviors that indicated the dysfunctional role, and effects of the dysfunctional role on the group in Scene 1. Next, the group discusses the techniques used by the supervisor in Scenes 2 and 3 to deal with the dysfunctional role and the effects of those techniques on the teacher and group.

3. Ask each member if conflict still exists.
4. Ask for underlying value positions: Why do they still stick to their positions?
5. Ask other members of the group if there is a third position that synthesizes, compromises, or transcends the conflict. If not, reclarify the various positions. Acknowledge that there seems to be no apparent reconciliation, and move the discussion to other matters.

Conflict cannot and should not be avoided. Conflict, if encouraged and supported, enables a group to make better decisions. It is the group leader's handling of

role play 16.2

Resolving Conflict

Context. The purpose of this role play is for a subgroup of five to provide a demonstration to the remainder of the group on how to resolve conflict effectively within a group. Participants need approximately 20 minutes of preparation time away from the rest of the group. In the role play, a "supervisor" and four "teachers" are members of a committee meeting to discuss a schoolwide instructional issue. In their preparation for the role play, the role players may choose the school level, the issue to be discussed, and any other details of the fictional situation that they must agree on to perform an effective role play. The group is assigned or chooses a conflict to be played out between two members of the group during the meeting. The role play is presented in two scenes.

Scene 1: Wrong Way (10 minutes). Soon after the beginning of the meeting, a conflict breaks out between two of the teachers. The supervisor and the other teachers in the group deal with the conflict poorly, and the meeting deteriorates rapidly. The meeting breaks up with neither the interpersonal conflict nor the original issue resolved.

Scene 2: Right Way (10 minutes). This scene involves the same group, the same setting, and the same issue. The same conflict breaks out between the same two teachers. This time, however, the supervisor and teachers in the group use procedures discussed under this chapter's topic "Resolving Conflict" to facilitate a resolution of the conflict and the original issue by the end of the meeting.

Whole-Group Processing (10 minutes). The entire group discusses the nature of the conflict, the failed efforts to resolve it, and effects of the conflict on the group in Scene 1. Also discussed are the techniques used to resolve the conflict and the effects of the conflict resolution process in Scene 2.

conflict that makes the difference. The group should have the feeling that it is all right to disagree and that anyone who does disagree will be able to make his or her full position known. Role Play 16.2 provides for demonstrations of the right way and the wrong way to deal with conflict within a group.

Preparing for Group Meetings

A group can proceed more easily with its task if the leader has made certain preparations. Shelton and Bauer (1994) suggest that premeeting planning should involve decisions about whether a meeting is necessary, who should attend the meeting, setting, agenda, and preparation. Figure 16.1 includes specific questions that Shelton and Bauer recommend planners consider when preparing for a meeting. Some especially important aspects of preparing for a meeting include planning an agenda, establishing ground rules, and writing guided discussion questions.

Should We Meet?

1. Can a memo be used instead of holding a meeting?
2. Is there a goal for the meeting?

Who Should Attend the Meeting?

3. Who must come to the meeting?
4. Will there be fewer than 15 participants?

The Setting

5. Where will the meeting be held?
6. Is the site convenient to participants?
7. Will a circular table arrangement be used?
8. Is the room temperature comfortable?
9. Have refreshments been arranged?

The Agenda

10. Have all participants been asked for agenda input?
11. Are the "For Information" items stated in sentence format?
12. Are the "For Discussion" items stated in question format?
13. Has the draft agenda been proofed?
14. Has the agenda been distributed, with at least two days lead time?

The Preparation

15. Have possible "troublesome items" been thought through?
16. If problem solving is a goal of the meeting, has the problem been adequately explained to meeting participants?
17. Has someone been asked to take minutes?
18. Has a follow-up on the previous evaluations been done?
19. Have evaluation forms (Blips) been distributed?

figure 16.1 **Shelton and Bauer's Premeeting Planner**

Source: Maria M. Shelton and Laurie K. Bauer (1994). *Secrets of Highly Effective Meetings,* p. 43. Copyright © 1994 by Sage Publications, Inc., Books. Reproduced with permission of Sage Publications, Inc., Books via Copyright Clearance Center.

Agendas

A group has to be clear on its task and purpose. Why are they meeting? What are they to accomplish? Is there to be a product? An agenda distributed several days before the actual meeting will inform members of the reasons for the meeting and what will be accomplished. The agenda need not be elaborate. See Figure 16.2 as a sample agenda. Notice how the agenda includes a brief explanation and a break-

To: All physical education teachers
From: Morris Bailey, athletic director
Subject: Agenda for the meeting of February 23 in Room 253, 3:30–5:00

Next Thursday will be the last meeting before voting on the revisions of our student progress forms. Remember, bring any progress forms you have collected from other school systems. Sally and Bruce are to report on the forms provided by the State Department. At the conclusion of the meeting, we are to make specific recommendations of changes.

Agenda

I. Review purpose of meeting	3:30–3:40
II. Report from Sally and Bruce on State Department forms	3:40–4:00
III. Report on other school system forms	4:00–4:20
IV. Discussion of possible revisions	4:20–4:40
V. Recommendations	4:40–5:00

See you Thursday. Please be on time!

figure **16.2** **Sample Agenda**

down of items. Time limits for each item provide members with a sense of priorities as well as the assurance that the leader plans to end on time. Keeping to starting and ending times displays respect for group members' personal schedules.

Establishing Ground Rules

Participants should know not only agenda items like the meeting's purpose, place, time, and topics but also behaviors that are expected of them at the meeting. Ground rules can be established in advance concerning any of the following:

- Type of participation expected (sharing of information, professional dialogue, choosing from established alternatives, brainstorming, problem solving, conflict resolution, and so on)
- Roles to be assigned (coordinator, time keeper, information giver, recorder, etc.)
- Interpersonal expectations (everyone contributes, use active listening, criticize ideas but not people, consider each person's views, use agreed-on conflict management strategies, and so on)
- Decision-making method (decision by averaging individuals' opinions, majority vote, consensus, etc.)
- Type of follow-up expected (assigned tasks, continued dialogue, classroom implementation, follow-up meeting, and so on)

Guided Discussion

When meeting with a group to discuss an issue, it is helpful to have in mind the type of questions to ask. Typically, questions to be asked will shift during a meeting. At the beginning of the meeting, the leader usually spends time clarifying the topic for discussion. During the meeting, the leader uses open-ended questions that allow for seeking, elaborating, and coordinating of ideas, opinions, and information. At the conclusion of the meeting, the leader asks questions that summarize what has been accomplished and what remains to be done.

Some discussion questions that might help as a reference are presented in Figure 16.3. Prior to a meeting, the leader might review the questions in Figure 16.3 and write down specific questions concerning the topic to have in front of him or her. When the discussion stalls, the leader can look at his or her notes and ask one of the preselected questions. A discussion guide helps the leader ensure that the topic is examined thoroughly.

figure **16.3** **Questions for Use in Leadership Discussion**

Questions Designed to Open Up Discussion
1. What do you think about the problem as stated?
2. What has been your experience in dealing with this problem?
3. Would anyone care to offer suggestions on facts we need to better our understanding of the problem?

Questions Designed to Broaden Participation
1. Now that we have heard from a number of our members, would others who have not spoken like to add their ideas?
2. How do the ideas presented so far sound to those of you who have been thinking about them?
3. What other phases of the problem should be explored?

Questions Designed to Limit Participation
1. *To the overactive participant:* We appreciate your contributions. However, it might be well to hear from some of the others. Would some of you who have not spoken care to add your ideas to those already expressed?
2. You have made several good statements, and I am wondering if someone else might like to make some remarks?
3. Because all our group members have not yet had an opportunity to speak, I wonder if you would hold your comments until a little later?

Questions Designed to Focus Discussion
1. Where are we now in relation to our goal for this discussion?
2. Would you like to have me review my understanding of the things we have said and the progress we have made in this direction?
3. Your comment is interesting, but I wonder if it is germane to the chief problem that is before us.

Questions Designed to Help the Group Move Along
1. I wonder if we have spent enough time on this phase of the problem. Should we move to another aspect of it?
2. Have we gone into this part of the problem far enough so that we might now shift our attention and consider this additional area?
3. In view of the time we have set for ourselves, would it be appropriate to look at the next question before us?

(*Continued*)

figure 16.3 Continued

Questions Designed to Help the Group Evaluate Itself

1. I wonder if any of you have a feeling that we are blocked on this particular question? Why are we tending to slow down?
2. Should we take a look at our original objective for this discussion and see where we are in relation to it?
3. Now that we are nearing the conclusion of our meeting, would anyone like to offer suggestions on how we might improve our next meeting?

Questions Designed to Help the Group Reach a Decision

1. Am I right in sensing agreement at these points? (Leader then gives brief summary.)
2. Because we seem to be tending to move in the direction of a decision, should we consider what it will mean for our group if we decide the matter this way?
3. What have we accomplished in our discussion up to this point?

Questions Designed to Lend Continuity to the Discussion

1. Because we had time for partial consideration of the problem at the last meeting, would someone care to review what we covered then?
2. Because we cannot reach a decision at this meeting, what are some of the points we should take up at the next one?
3. Would someone care to suggest points on which we need further preparation before we convene again?

Source: Produced in group development course at the University of Georgia.

MyEdLeadershipLab™

Go to Topic 7, Group Development, in the MyEdLeadershipLab™ site at www.myedleadershiplab.com for *The Basic Guide to SuperVision and Instructional Leadership*, Third Edition, where you can:

- Find learning outcomes for Group Development along with the national standards that connect to these outcomes.
- Complete Assignments and Activities that can help you more deeply understand the chapter content.
- Apply and practice your understanding of the core skills identified in the chapter with the Building Leadership Skills unit.
- Prepare yourself for professional certification with a Practice for Certification quiz.

REFERENCES

Bales, R. F. 1953. The equilibrium problem in small groups. In T. Parsons, R. F. Bales, and E. A. Shils (Eds.), *Working papers in the theory of action* (pp. 111–161). Glencoe, IL: Free Press.

Benne, D. D., and Sheats, P. 1948. Functional roles of group members. *Journal of Social Issues, 4*(2), 41–49.

Brandt, R. 1987. On cooperation in schools: A conversation with David and Roger Johnson. *Educational Leadership, 45*(3), 14–19.

Corey, G., and Corey, M. 1982. *Groups: Process and practice.* Monterey, CA: Brooks/Cole.

Fullan, M. 2000. *Change forces: The sequel.* Philadelphia, PA: George H. Buchanan.

Gordon, T. 1980. *Leadership effectiveness training—L. E. T.* New York: Bantam Books.

Johnson, D. W., and Johnson, R. T. 1987. *Joining together: Group theory and group skills* (3rd ed.). Englewood Cliffs, NJ: Prentice Hall.

Kemp, C. G. 1970. *Perspectives on the group process: A foundation for counseling with groups* (2nd ed.). Boston: Houghton Mifflin.

Shelton, M. M., and Bauer, L. K. 1994. *Secrets of highly effective meetings.* Thousand Oaks, CA: Corwin Press.

chapter 17

Professional Development

outline

- Characteristics of Successful Professional Development Programs
- Integrating Schoolwide, Group, and Individual Professional Development
- Alternative Professional Development Formats
- Examples of Effective Professional Development Programs
- Stages of Professional Development
- The "Nuts and Bolts"
- Extending the Concept of Professional Development
- Evaluating Professional Development Programs
- Teachers as Objects or Agents in Professional Development

Visit the **MyEdLeadershipLab™** site for *The Basic Guide to SuperVision and Instructional Leadership,* Third Edition to enhance your understanding of chapter concepts. You'll have the opportunity to practice your skills through video and case based Assignments and Activities as well as Building Leadership Skills units, and prepare for your certification exam with Practice for Certification quizzes.

Education is a human enterprise. The essence of successful instruction and good schools comes from the thoughts and actions of the professionals in the schools. So, if one is to look for a place to improve the quality of education in a school, a sensible place to look is the continuous education of educators—that is, professional development. Virtually any experience that enlarges a teacher's knowledge, appreciation, skills, and understandings of his or her work falls under the domain of professional development.

Because professional development should be a responsibility of those who supervise, the research and application discussed here focus on the use of successful professional development to improve instruction.

Characteristics of Successful Professional Development Programs

There is a considerable knowledge base concerning successful professional development, including original research and reviews of research and best practice (Loucks-Horsley et al., 1987; Orlich, 1989; Wood and Thompson, 1993; Guskey, 1994, 1997, 2003; Corcoran, 1995; Hawley and Valli, 1996; U.S. Department of Education, 1996; Kennedy, 1998; Joyce, Calhoun, and Hopkins, 1999; Birman, Desimone, Porter, and Garet, 2000; Fullan, 2000; Gordon, 2000; Zech, Gause-Vega, and Bray, 2000; Bernauer, 2002; Harris, 2002; Wenglinsky, 2002). Although these reports do not agree on all factors, they identify a number of the same characteristics of successful programs:

1. Involvement of participants in planning, implementing, and evaluating programs
2. A foundation of schoolwide goals but integration of individual and group goals with school goals
3. Long-range planning and development
4. Coherence, marked by the coordination and integration of different professional development activities
5. The incorporation of research on school and instructional improvement
6. Administrative support, including provision of time and other resources during program planning, delivery, and evaluation
7. Adherence to the principles of adult learning (see Chapter 4)
8. Relevant, job-embedded professional development focused on student learning (Examples of relevant topics include how students learn particular content, teaching diverse student populations, and teaching for higher-level thinking.)
9. Collegiality and collaboration among teachers as well as between teachers and administrators
10. Active learning

11. Attention to the research on change (see Chapter 20)
12. Follow-up and support for transfer of learning to the classroom
13. Ongoing assessment and feedback
14. Continuous professional development that becomes part of the school culture

As you review these characteristics, think of a professional development program with which you are familiar. How many of the 14 characteristics are present in that program?

Integrating Schoolwide, Group, and Individual Professional Development

One characteristic of effective professional development is the integration of schoolwide, group, and individual goals. How does a school go about doing this? To begin, it is critical that all members of the school community provide input into schoolwide professional development goals. The schoolwide goals should be broad enough to allow groups and individuals to set their own goals, consistent with school goals.

For an example of integrating schoolwide and group professional development, let us assume that a middle school has identified improved student discipline as a schoolwide professional development goal. Different grade-level or instructional teams, all committed to improved discipline, might identify different group goals relative to the school goal. One group might decide that they should focus their professional development on improving students' respect for others. Another group might determine that their primary need is to improve students' on-task behavior during class. A third group may wish to focus on finding ways to encourage self-discipline so that students take more responsibility for completing their homework, studying for tests, and asking for assistance.

Different groups also may decide that they prefer different professional development formats. One group may decide that they prefer to form a study group that shares readings, visits other schools to see how they address student discipline, and discusses how exemplary practices can be adapted to their students. The second group may decide that they wish to attend a training program on effective discipline, followed up by peer coaching at the classroom level. The third group might prefer to follow an action research format, gathering classroom data to find out more about the problem, designing an action plan, implementing the plan, and gathering evaluation data to determine effects. Although it is important that various groups within the school be allowed to adapt schoolwide goals to group needs, it also is important that each group show how its particular goals relate to and support the schoolwide goals.

A faculty is made up of individuals, and schoolwide professional development cannot take place without individual development. Thus, it is important to integrate individual professional development goals with group and schoolwide goals. Let us return to our example of the schoolwide goal of improved student discipline. You will recall that one possible group goal was improving students' respect for others. Even this more focused goal would have different meanings to different teachers within the group that chose the goal. For one teacher, it might mean helping students work together in cooperative groups. For another teacher, it could mean students respecting other students from different cultures. For a third teacher, it might mean working with students who are disrespectful to authority figures. Thus, even within the group goal of increased respect for others, there should be opportunities for teachers to identify individual goals consistent with group and school goals.

Because adults, like students, have different experiences and learning styles, teachers within the study group might pursue different learning activities and make different contributions to the group. One teacher might bring to the group reports from visits to other schools, another teacher might share journal articles related to the topic of student respect for others, and so forth. The individual teacher can connect individual goals to group and schoolwide goals in a manner that allows the same professional development activities to serve all three types of goals.

Alternative Professional Development Formats

We are rapidly moving away from the era when professional development usually means either a 60-minute speech by an outside consultant or a "one-shot" workshop. More recently, a variety of new formats for professional development have emerged, including the following:

- *Beginning teacher assistance programs.* The new teacher is provided ongoing and intensive assistance throughout at least the first year of teaching, including such things as an assigned mentor; an orientation to the school and community; assistance from a support team including the mentor, other teachers, and a supervisor; training in classroom management and effective teaching; and support seminars focused on beginning teachers' concerns.
- *Skill development programs.* The skill development programs consist of several workshops over a period of months, and classroom coaching between workshops to assist teachers to transfer new skills to their daily teaching.
- *Teacher centers.* Teachers can meet at a central location to engage in professional dialogue, develop skills, plan innovations, and gather or create instructional materials.
- *Teacher institutes.* Teachers participate in intensive learning experiences on single, complex topics over a period of consecutive days or weeks.
- *Collegial support groups.* Teachers within the same school engage in group inquiry, address common problems, jointly implement instructional innovations, and provide mutual support.

- *Networks.* Teachers from different schools share information, concerns, and accomplishments and engage in common learning through computer links, newsletters, and occasional seminars and conferences.
- *Teacher leadership.* Teachers participate in leadership preparation programs and assist other teachers by assuming one or more leadership roles (workshop presenter, cooperating teacher, mentor, expert coach, instructional team leader, curriculum developer). The teacher–leader not only assists other teachers but also experiences professional growth as a result of being involved in leadership activities.
- *Teacher as writer.* This increasingly popular format has teachers reflect on and write about their students, teaching, and professional growth. Such writing can be in the form of private journals, essays, or reaction papers to share with colleagues, or formal articles for publication in educational journals.
- *Individually planned professional development.* Teachers set individual goals and objectives, plan and carry out activities, and assess results.
- *Partnerships.* Partnerships between schools and universities or businesses, in which both partners are considered equal, have mutual rights and responsibilities, make contributions, and receive benefits. Such partnerships could involve one or more of the previously described formats (Moore and Seeger, 2004).

There can be considerable overlap between various professional development formats (not to mention between professional development and the other four tasks of supervision). Our own experience as staff developers and researchers has led us to conclude that many of the most successful professional development programs combine multiple formats. Next, we describe several professional development programs, each including a combination of formats.

Examples of Effective Professional Development Programs

We describe three model professional development programs, including a districtwide program, a school-based program, and an individualized program. Each of the examples is either an actual program or a composite based on several actual programs.

Districtwide Professional Development

Buckeye School District's efforts to support beginning teachers began with the design of a beginning teacher assistance program by a planning committee made up of administrators, supervisors, and teachers. A key component of the program is a pool of experienced mentor–teachers. Volunteer mentors are selected by a screening committee. Selection criteria include years of experience in the school system, effective teaching performance, interpersonal skills, past commitment to the profession, flexibility, and willingness to spend time helping beginning teachers.

The selected teachers take part in an intensive mentor preparation program, including the following elements:

- Introduction to the knowledge base on problems of beginning teachers, beginning teacher assistance programs, and mentoring
- Overview of the district's beginning teacher assistance program
- Research on effective classroom management
- Research on effective teaching
- Principles of adult learning
- Adult and teacher development
- Goal setting and action planning
- The coaching of teaching, including conferencing skills and observation skills
- Action research

A number of variables are considered when assigning mentors to beginning teachers, including grade level and content area, classroom location, and philosophical and personal compatibility of mentor and beginner. An attempt is made to make an overall best match of mentor and beginner.

Prior to the beginning of the schoolyear, a special orientation for beginners is attended by novices and their mentors. During this orientation, new teachers are walked through key information about the community, district policies and procedures, and the curriculum they will be responsible for teaching. Later in the orientation, they are given tours of their schools and meet with building administrators and instructional leaders. Their mentors review building policies and procedures and provide them with a profile of the school, its staff, students, and parents.

The orientation is only the beginning of assistance for the beginning teacher in Buckeye School District. Ongoing support is provided throughout the schoolyear. For each beginner, a support team is formed, consisting of a building administrator, department chairperson or team leader, and mentor. The team meets on a regular basis. Continuous assistance is based on written needs assessments and discussions with support teams. Workshops are provided for beginners on such topics as classroom management, effective teaching, and working with parents. Mentors visit beginners' classrooms on a regular basis to provide nonevaluative assistance, including expert coaching following the five-step model presented in Chapter 15. Beginners visit the classrooms of mentors and other effective teachers to observe best practice. Mentors are available on a daily basis to provide beginners with psychological support, information, and instructional assistance.

Mentors, too, are given support by the district in the form of follow-up workshops, support seminars, tuition reimbursement for relevant university coursework, released time, and stipends. Their contributions to beginners and the district are recognized during faculty meetings, in district publications, and at an annual recognition dinner.

Buckeye School District's support program includes a partnership with a nearby university. Professors from the university collaborated with Buckeye School District in the design of its support program. The same professors assist with mentor preparation and offer course credit for mentors willing to do outside work beyond the mentor workshops. Finally, the professors assist in the delivery of several of the workshops for beginning teachers. To summarize, although mentoring is the heart and soul of Buckeye School District's beginning teacher assistance program, other formats—such as skill-development programs, collegial support groups, and partnerships—are part of the overall program.

School-Based Professional Development

Ponticell (1995) provided a description of a site-based professional development program in an inner-city Chicago high school. The aim of the program was instructional improvement based on collegial learning and support. The program was supported by a grant from a nearby university and facilitated by a professor from the university. The program began with a professional retreat where teachers engaged in reflective dialogue about teaching and began to build collaborative relationships.

Following the retreat, the teachers began to read and discuss research on effective teaching and professional development alternatives. Next, the teachers developed a cycle of monthly professional development activities, including the following phases:

1. Teachers identified an instructional concern, read current research addressing that concern, selected ideas that made sense, developed a strategy for classroom implementation, and created a checklist of planned teacher behaviors.
2. Teachers video recorded themselves implementing improvement strategies, analyzed their own videos, and compared their actual behaviors to the checklist of anticipated behaviors.
3. Teachers used peer coaching, focused on the month's strategy, with a coaching cycle consisting of a preconference, observation, and postconference.
4. Teachers held end-of-month group meetings in which they met to share video clips, discussed what aspects of the month's strategy had worked and not worked, reflected on what they had learned, and determined the topic of study for the following month.

Based on pre- and postinventories, direct observation, analysis of audio recordings of group discussions, and interviews with participants, Ponticell (1995) found that the site-based program had increased collegiality, improved self-analysis of teaching, enabled teachers to learn new ways of collaboratively observing and discussing each other's teaching, and fostered learning and experimenting with new teaching strategies.

Individualized Professional Development

At Leander (Texas) Middle School, individual improvement plans are tied to the school's annual improvement plan. Individual projects follow the PDSA cycle (Plan, Do, Study, Act) and are documented in teacher portfolios. In the *planning phase,* teachers gather a variety of self-assessment data (videos of lessons, student achievement data, peer observations, and so on), analyze the data, and design individualized professional development plans. The individual plans include objectives, learning activities, needed resources, and plans for self-evaluation.

The teacher implements the improvement plan during the *doing* phase. Professional development activities might include attending workshops or conferences, observing other teachers, peer coaching, participation in study groups, and so on. The teacher's portfolio documents learning activities, support received from colleagues, and changes in practice.

The *studying* phase involves gathering data to evaluate the plan's effectiveness. Data is gathered on the teacher's professional growth as well as changes in student learning. Evaluation data might include the teacher's reflective writing, classroom observation data, student achievement data, or artifacts of student work.

The *acting* phase consists of a portfolio conference with the teacher's supervisor. During the conference, the teacher reflects on activities completed, learning that has taken place, and future directions for professional growth. In Leander, all adults—teachers, supervisors, and staff—implement individual development plans and construct portfolios. Each spring, all members of the school community share their individual projects at a portfolio fair.

In this section, we presented examples of various levels (district, school, individual) and formats for professional development. In the next section, we discuss stages of professional development that apply to any long-term professional development program.

Stages of Professional Development

Professional development typically involves three stages of learning: (1) orientation, (2) integration, and (3) refinement. To illustrate these three stages, we relate them to staff development on the cooperative learning instructional model.

In the ***orientation stage,*** benefits, responsibilities, and personal concerns about involvement in staff development are addressed. Next, participants engage in learning necessary for initial real-world application. In our cooperative learning example, orientation topics might include the following*:

- Differences among cooperative, competitive, and individual learning
- Differences between cooperative learning and traditional group work

*Outlining a complete professional development program on cooperative learning is beyond the scope of this text. Some critical topics are listed to provide examples of the types of learning in each stage of professional development. Sources of cooperative learning professional development topics are Johnson, Johnson, and Holubec (1991) and Kagan (1992).

- Research on cooperative learning
- Basic elements of cooperative learning (teaching social skills, positive interdependence, face-to-face interaction, individual accountability, group processing)
- Forming cooperative groups
- Standard cooperative learning structures (think-pair-share, jigsaw, student teams achievement divisions [STAD], teams-games-tournaments [TGT], group investigation, and so on)
- Planning cooperative lessons

Failure to take teachers beyond the orientation stage is one reason why many staff-development programs are ineffective: Teachers are given rudimentary knowledge or skills and then are left to fend for themselves.

In the ***integration stage,*** teachers are assisted as they apply previous learning in their classrooms and schools. One aspect of integration is learning to adapt general learning to specific situations. In the cooperative learning example, this means learning to alter cooperative teaching strategies to make them appropriate for different learning content and students. A related aspect of integration is regular and effective use of the new learning. This means, for example, the teacher develops enough competence and confidence in cooperative learning methods to make them part of his or her standard repertoire of instructional strategies.

In the ***refinement stage,*** teachers move from basic competence to expertness through continuous experimentation and reflection. In the refinement stage of staff development on cooperative learning, teachers become expert at a wide range of cooperative learning strategies and at mixing and matching those strategies for optimal student learning. Teachers in the refinement stage synthesize different types of previous learning in order to create new learning. In our cooperative learning example, a teacher at this stage might combine aspects of two or more standard cooperative learning structures to create a more complex structure. For another example, a teacher at the refinement stage might synthesize whole language and cooperative learning strategies to create an entirely new teaching strategy. Perhaps the best thing that a supervisor can do when teachers reach this stage is to sign them up as teacher–staff developers!

The "Nuts and Bolts"

Professional development need not always take place in group sessions, but groups remain a major component of the majority of staff development formats and programs. The best planning for a group session is useless if the supervisor forgets the nuts and bolts. What value is an excellent speaker who lectures in a room where the acoustics garble every word? What good is a fast-paced microteaching demonstration if it conflicts with other teacher meetings so that few can attend? What good is an exciting role-playing activity whose participants have had no chance to eat, unwind, or use the restroom during the previous two hours?

If one is going to the trouble to plan professional development, then one should go the extra step to ensure an environment that enables participants to be responsive and comfortable. Here are six important considerations:

1. *Prepare speakers by telling them exactly what they are expected to do.* If a speaker is invited to conduct an activity, make sure he or she understands the assignment. Speakers will do whatever they usually do unless someone tells them otherwise. Most speakers have their own topics, their own rehearsed presentations, and their own formats. If a speaker is expected to demonstrate a particular skill (for example, asking higher-order questions) or to include role-playing (scripts of classroom discussions), *tell him or her so.* The speaker and participants are both in an embarrassing situation when the speaker, through no fault of either party, is not doing what the participants have been led to expect.
2. *Check the facility beforehand for seating arrangements, media, and acoustics.* Make sure the facility is appropriate to the activity. For example, small-group discussions in an auditorium give teachers stiff necks and a stiffer attitude toward the next in-service. See that all equipment is operating correctly. Check microphones, computers, and projectors. Move around the room to see if displays on a screen or walls can be viewed clearly by everyone. Have at hand spare bulbs and replacement equipment in case of an equipment failure.
3. *Provide refreshments and transition time at the beginning.* Tell participants where the restrooms are. Provide drinks and snacks. Informally greet the participants at the door and tell them when the session will begin. When formally beginning, inform participants when other breaks are scheduled.
4. *Check the comfort of the room.* Beforehand, check whether the room will maintain a comfortable temperature. Find out if the heating or cooling system is turned off at the time of the meeting and, if so, arrange to have the system operating. Estimate the temperature of the room when it is full. A room that feels comfortable when only a few people are present can become oppressively hot when full to capacity.
5. *Have materials run off and a plan for easy dissemination to participants.* Prior to the session, check with the leader of the activity to make sure all desired materials will be prepared. Also before the session, figure out a distribution system for materials. Often it is sufficient to place a table next to the entrance with collected materials and make one person responsible for telling entrants to pick up the materials.
6. *Have evaluation forms for participants to fill out after the session.* Asking participants to evaluate the session allows existing problems to be corrected before the next session.

Extending the Concept of Professional Development

For much of its history, professional development focused primarily on the development of pedagogical skills. Pedagogical development remains a critical purpose of professional development, but in recent years the field has expanded to include a variety of other purposes:

- *Personal development* entails helping teachers to move toward better understanding of their own adult life cycle, transition events, and roles, as well as improving teachers' self-concepts and self-efficacies.
- *Career development* supports teachers as they move through phases of the teaching career from induction to retirement, helping teachers to address concerns as well as providing new professional opportunities and rewards during each career phase. Career development includes assisting teachers to assume various types of leadership roles as their careers progress.
- *Moral development* enables teachers to model the principles of compassion, equality, and justice that they hope to instill in their students. Every word a teacher speaks and every action a teacher takes during the schoolday has moral implications, and professional development can enhance teachers' moral insight and decision making in ways that foster students' overall well-being.
- *School improvement* is largely dependent on professional development. Almost any significant change in the school organization, curriculum, or instructional program is dependent on professional development to provide teachers with the capacity to implement the change. It is difficult to imagine *any* school improvement effort succeeding without professional development.
- *Improvement of the teaching profession* has become a national goal in recent years, and professional development is the engine driving this movement. Although much of the impetus for improving the profession has come from national certification boards, associations, and networks, professional development for meeting and applying new standards often takes place at the local level.

Evaluating Professional Development Programs

The information on program evaluation in Chapter 14 can be used to design a comprehensive evaluation of a professional development program. Guskey (2002) proposes a system designed specifically to evaluate professional development that is consistent with our general discussion of program evaluation in Chapter 14.

table 17.1 **Five Levels of Professional Development**

Evaluation Level	What Questions Are Addressed?
1. Participants' Reactions	Did they like it? Was their time well spent? Did the material make sense? Will it be useful? Was the leader knowledgeable and helpful? Were the refreshments fresh and tasty? Was the room the right temperature? Were the chairs comfortable?
2. Participants' Learning	Did participants acquire the intended knowledge and skills?
3. Organization Support & Change	Was implementation advocated, facilitated, and supported? Was the support public and overt? Were problems addressed quickly and efficiently? Were sufficient resources made available? Were successes recognized and shared? What was the impact on the organization? Did it affect the organization's climate and procedures?
4. Participants' Use of New Knowledge and Skills	Did participants effectively apply the new knowledge and skills?
5. Student Learning Outcomes	What was the impact on students? Did it affect student performance or achievement? Did it influence students' physical or emotional well-being? Are students more confident as learners? Is student attendance improving? Are dropouts decreasing?

Source: Thomas R. Guskey. (2002). "Does It Make a Difference? Evaluating Professional Development." *Educational Leadership, 59*(6), pp. 48 and 49. Copyright 2002 Thomas R. Guskey. Permission granted by author.

Guskey's system includes gathering data on five different levels: participants' reactions, participants' learning, organization support and change, participants' use of new knowledge and skills, and student learning outcomes. For each level, Guskey proposes questions to be addressed, methods of data gathering, what should be measured, and how information gathered at that level should be used. Table 17.1 summarizes Guskey's system.

How Will Information Be Gathered?	What Is Measured or Assessed?	How Will Information Be Used?
Questionnaires administered at the end of the session	Initial satisfaction with the experience	To improve program design and delivery
Paper-and-pencil instruments Simulations Demonstrations Participants' reflections (oral and/or written) Participant portfolios	New knowledge and skills of participants	To improve program content, format, and organization
District and school records Minutes from follow-up meetings Questionnaires Structured interviews with participants and district or school administrators Participant portfolios	The organization's advocacy, support, accommodation, facilitation, and recognition	To document and improve organization support To inform future change efforts
Questionnaires Structured interviews with participants and their supervisors Participant reflections (oral and/or written) Participant portfolios Direct observations Video or audio tapes	Degree and quality of implementation	To document and improve the implementation of program content
Student records School records Questionnaires Structured interviews with students, parents, teachers, and/or administrators Participant portfolios	Student learning outcomes: Cognitive (Performance & Achievement) Affective (Attitudes & Dispositions) Psychomotor (Skills & Behaviors)	To focus and improve all aspects of program design, implementation, and follow-up To demonstrate the overall impact of professional development

Teachers as Objects or Agents in Professional Development

A superintendent remarked that he had been at a national conference and attended a presentation on "Elements of Effective Instruction." He decided that this was exactly what the teachers needed. As a result, the district was off and running with a three-year commitment to training all principals and teachers in "elements." Highly paid national consultants were brought in; personnel were identified for advanced training and traveled during the summer to faraway sites; and virtually all contracted in-service time and school supervision was devoted to "elements."

It was not long before a new evaluation instrument was established to check that every teacher was using the training in effective instruction in the same prescribed manner. Over the three years, expenditures by the school district exceeded $300,000, not including the cost of human time. What have been the results? No appreciable gain in student achievement, considerable grumbling by a core of "malcontent" teachers, enthusiasm by the chosen core of teachers who received special training and compensation, and a firm claim by the superintendent that "We now have focused long-term professional development on scientifically derived principles, and our teaching is more effective."

In recent years, education has been bombarded by packaged programs on "effective teaching," "effective schools," "effective supervision," and "effective discipline." All claim to be derived from research and to have documented success, and all use the components and sequence of transfer of training that have been sorely lacking in traditional professional development programs. The programs provide for explanation, demonstration, modeling, role playing, practice, and coaching. They are not one-shot programs—they are focused and they are classroom based.

The only problem is that the people who think these programs are worth the cost and effort are the same people who have a personal investment and commitment to use them (see DiBernardo and Stiles, 1988; Garman and Hazley, 1988). If the programs are not as successful as predicted, the decision makers do not blame the program but rather the lack of enough training to ensure that teachers "do it right" (Lambert, 1988). Schools, districts, and states that have committed themselves to such programs come to the ludicrous conclusion that they need more training, more money, and greater enforcement to see that all teachers finally learn to teach as prescribed more frequently and correctly. This is an incredible rationalization by policy makers that their initial decision was right, regardless of the effect that the program is having on teachers.

This rationale underscores the point that was made about adult development earlier in the book. Commitment is premised on two dimensions: choice and responsibility to make knowledgeable decisions about one's work. That's why the superintendent wants so badly to see this program on "effective elements" work. The superintendent had the choice and took responsibility for making the decision. The selected core of teachers also want to see this program work, because they were given choice and responsibility in making decisions on how to train others. Yet most teachers and principals were not given any choice or responsibility in these decisions about the needs of their students and themselves. Instead, they were treated as objects rather than as agents of professional development, without due regard for their capacity to make wise decisions in the interest of students and teaching. Without choice or responsibility to make knowledgeable decisions about their work, they have little motivation or commitment to somebody else's program.

To use knowledge about characteristics, formats, and stages of professional development, without an awareness of the need truly to involve teachers as decision makers in professional development, will leave us where we currently are. We will be more sophisticated in teaching teachers how to follow someone else's program, but we will find little commitment on the part of teachers or little stimulation to increase teachers' own collective and critical capacities to make lasting changes.

MyEdLeadershipLab™

Go to Topic 8, Professional Development, in the MyEdLeadershipLab™ site at www.myedleadershiplab.com for *The Basic Guide to SuperVision and Instructional Leadership*, Third Edition, where you can:

- Find learning outcomes for Professional Development along with the national standards that connect to these outcomes.
- Complete Assignments and Activities that can help you more deeply understand the chapter content.
- Apply and practice your understanding of the core skills identified in the chapter with the Building Leadership Skills unit.
- Prepare yourself for professional certification with a Practice for Certification quiz.

REFERENCES

Bernauer, F. 2002. Five keys to unlock continuous school improvement. *Kappa Delta Pi Record, 38*(2), 89–92.

Birman, B. F., Desimone, L., Porter, A. C., and Garet, M. S. 2000. Designing professional development that works. *Educational Leadership, 57*(8), 28–33.

Corcoran, T. B. 1995. *Helping teachers teach well: Transforming professional development.* CPRE Policy Briefs, RB-16-June. New Brunswick, NJ: Rutgers University, Consortium for Policy Research in Education.

DiBernardo, G., and Stiles, D. 1988. The Madeline Hunter and Lee Canter teacher improvement packages: What every school needs? *Democratic Schools, 3*(2), 1–9.

Fullan, M. 2000. *Change forces: The sequel.* Philadelphia: George H. Buchanan.

Garman, N. B., and Hazley, H. M. 1988. Teachers ask: Is there life after Madeline Hunter? *Kappan, 69*(9), 669–672.

Gordon, S. P. 2000. *Professional development for teacher and school renewal: Alternative pathways, common characteristics.* Paper presented at the University Council for Educational Administration Annual Convention, Albuquerque, NM, November.

Guskey, T. R. 1994. *Professional development in education: In search of the optimal mix.* Paper presented at the annual meeting of the American Educational Research Association, New Orleans, April. (ERIC ED 369 181)

Guskey, T. R. 1997. Research needs to link professional development and student learning. *Journal of Staff Development, 18*(2), 36–40.

Guskey, T. R. 2002. Does it make a difference? Evaluating professional development. *Educational Leadership, 59*(6), 45–51.

Guskey, T. R. 2003. Analyzing lists of the characteristics of effective professional development to promote visionary leadership. *NASSP Bulletin, 87*(637), 4–20.

Harris, A. 2002. *School improvement: What's in it for schools?* New York: Routledge Falmer.

Hawley, W. D., and Valli, L. 1996. *The essentials of effective professional development: A new consensus.* Paper presented at the AERA Invitational Conference on Teacher Development and School Reform, Washington, DC.

Johnson, D. W., Johnson, R. T., and Holubec, E. J. 1991. *Cooperation in the classroom.* Edina, MN: Interaction Book Company.

Joyce, B., Calhoun, E., and Hopkins, D. 1999. *The new structure of school improvement: Inquiring schools and achieving students.* Philadelphia: Open University Press.

Kagan, S. 1992. *Cooperative learning.* San Juan Capistrano: Kagan Cooperative Learning.

Kennedy, M. 1998. *Form and substance in service teacher education.* Madison: National Center for Improving Science Education, University of Wisconsin.

Lambert, L. 1988. Staff development redesigned. *Kappa, 69*(9), 665–668.

Loucks-Horsley, S., Harding, C. K., Arbuckle, M. A., Murray, L. B., Dubea, C., and Williams, M. K. 1987. *Continuing to learn: A guidebook for teacher development.* Andover, ME: The Regional Laboratory for Educational Improvement of the Northeast and Islands.

Moore, R., and Seeger, V. 2004. Validating teaching and learning communities for teacher education reform. *The Teacher Educator, 40*(2), 116–132.

Orlich, D. C. 1989. *Staff development: Enhancing human potential.* Boston: Allyn & Bacon.

Ponticell, J. A. 1995. Promoting teacher professionalism through collegiality. *Journal of Staff Development, 16*(3), 13–18.

U.S. Department of Education. 1996. National Center for Education Statistics. *Measures of inservice professional development: Suggested items for the 1998–1999 Schools and Staffing Survey.* Working Paper No. 96–25, Washington, DC: Author.

Wenglinsky, H. 2002. How schools matter: The link between teacher classroom practices and student academic performance. *Education Policy Analysis Archives, 10*(12). Retrieved June 10, 2008, from http://epaa.asu.edu/epaa/v/0n12

Wood, F. W., and Thompson, S. R. 1993. Assumptions about staff development based on research and best practice. *Journal of Staff Development, 14*(4), 52–57.

Zech, L. K., Gause-Vega, C. L., and Bray, M. H. 2000. Content-based collaborative inquiry: A professional development model for sustaining educational reform. *Educational Psychologist, 35*(3), 207–217.

chapter 18

Curriculum Development

outline

- Sources of Curriculum Development
- Legislated Learning
- Curriculum Development as a Vehicle for Enhancing Collective Thinking about Instruction
- What Should Be the Purpose of the Curriculum?
- What Should Be the Content of the Curriculum?
- How Should the Curriculum Be Organized?
- In What Format Should the Curriculum Be Written?
- Curriculum Format as Reflective of Choice Given to Teachers
- Relationship of Curriculum Purpose, Content, Organization, and Format
- Levels of Teacher Involvement in Curriculum Development
- Integrating Curriculum Format with Developers and Levels of Development
- Matching Curriculum Development with Teacher Development
- The Curriculum and Cultural Diversity

Visit the **MyEdLeadershipLab™** site for *The Basic Guide to SuperVision and Instructional Leadership*, Third Edition to enhance your understanding of chapter concepts. You'll have the opportunity to practice your skills through video and case based Assignments and Activities as well as Building Leadership Skills units, and prepare for your certification exam with Practice for Certification quizzes.

"Teaching is a moral activity that implies thoughts about ends, means, and their consequences" (Zeuli and Buchmann, 1987, p.13). Moral activity is explicitly expressed in a school's curriculum. To be an effective school is of little matter unless the personnel within an organization first have defined what is meant by a *good school*—what should students learn in order to be well educated? The institutional job then becomes one of effectively achieving that definition of goodness. As Sergiovanni (1987) remarked, "It's not important to do things right, unless we are doing the right things!" Curriculum is the moral deliberation on what is "right" for students to be taught.

Ultimately, decisions about a good school, appropriate curriculum, and needs of students should be made by those closest to students. After considering the available experts, research, readings, and articulated conflicts, people in the schools, districts, and local communities should ultimately decide what is worthy to teach. However, by default, pressure, and abdication, curriculum decisions have generally been made by those farthest from the classroom action.

Sources of Curriculum Development

Curricula can be developed at many levels—by outside specialists, school district specialists, school curriculum teams, and teachers alone. At the national level, commercial materials such as textbooks, learning kits, and audiovisual materials are developed mainly by outside specialists. The No Child Left Behind Act of 2001 (Public Law 107–110) introduced unprecedented federal controls over K–12 school curriculum in the 50 states. At the state level, departments of education have become increasingly active in curriculum development. States have legislated statewide competency tests for student promotion and graduation and have developed curriculum guides for local schools to ensure the teaching of those competencies. At the local level, many school systems have written their own curriculum guides for coordinating instruction across grade levels. This is done either by having curriculum specialists at the district level write the guides themselves or by having such specialists work with representative teams of teachers (perhaps with community and student representation). Rarely do local schools turn curriculum development entirely over to teachers.

We can think about sources of curriculum development according to Figure 18.1 (see Oliva, 1992). Much curriculum is developed at the state, federal, and commercial levels. In other words, most curricula are produced far away from the local teacher and the local schools.

Legislated Learning

It is a shame that most educators experience curriculum as something given that they must follow. Why is it that curriculum is no longer a province for school inquiry and action but rather a matter of complying with external mandates? The

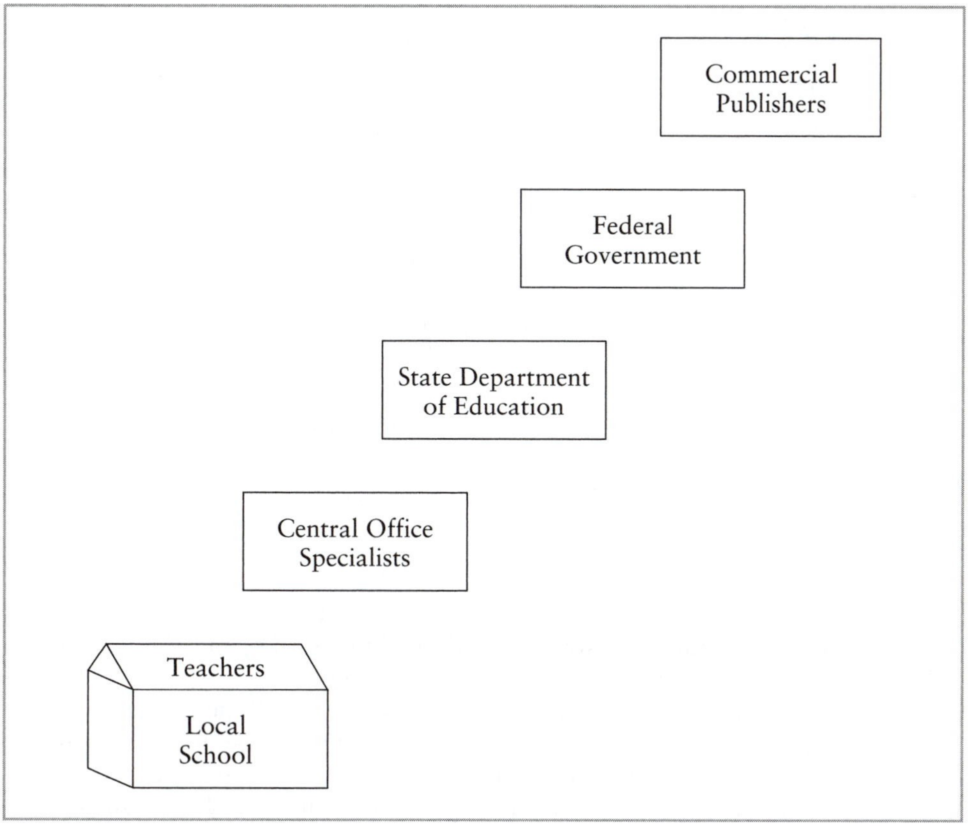

figure 18.1 **illustration of Sources of Curriculum Development**

reason is that in the era of legislated learning, teachers and school leaders are seen as incapable of knowing what their students should be taught (Fitzharris, 2005).

State-Mandated Curriculum

In many states, legislatures are now mandating the curriculum to be taught in all public PK–12 schools. The purpose of the mandated curriculum is to transmit knowledge and skills deemed essential by the state legislature or educational bureaucracy. The required curriculum is often presented as a laundry list of required objectives in each subject area (or at least each basic subject area) at each grade level. Objectives tend to be within the lower categories of Bloom's (1956) taxonomy, at the knowledge or comprehension level (Table 18.1). There are seldom any connections made between the objectives in different content areas. Even the objectives within a given content area are usually discrete from one another. In short, in terms of purpose, content, organization, and format, state-mandated curriculum tends to be at

table 18.1 Bloom's Taxonomy

Level of Thinking	Description
1. Knowledge	Student recalls or recognizes information.
2. Comprehension	Student demonstrates understanding of information.
3. Application	Student uses the learned information to solve a problem.
4. Analysis	Student classifies or breaks down the learned information to draw conclusions or make generalizations.
5. Synthesis	Student applies the learned information to create a new and original product.
6. Evaluation	Student judges the value of the learned information based on his or her values and beliefs.

Source: Based on Benjamin Bloom (1956). *Taxonomy of Educational Objectives. Handbook I: The Cognitive Domain.* New York: David McKay.

the lowest level of curriculum development. It is therefore very difficult for teachers in states with mandated curricula to function beyond the imitative maintenance level of involvement in curriculum development.

One argument often made by state officials discussing this reality is that teachers don't need to have a say in the curriculum because they can use their professional expertise and creativity when they plan how to teach the curriculum in their classrooms. These policymakers fail to understand that *the curriculum, if rigidly enforced, has a significant impact on how teachers teach.* For example, teachers working under a highly prescribed curriculum with long lists of required objectives approach instruction quite differently than teachers with a webbed curriculum that they have designed themselves. In short, *what* gets taught (curriculum) has a strong impact on *how* it gets taught (instruction).

High-Stakes Tests and the Curriculum

One way the federal government and states attempt to control curriculum in schools is through the use of high-stakes tests. When aligned with the state-mandated curriculum, state test scores are used as a measure of whether teachers are implementing the curriculum effectively. In states without a mandated curriculum but with high-stakes tests, the test itself becomes the curriculum. In these states, the original notion of alignment (start with the curriculum and align instruction and assessment with the curriculum) is turned on its head, with local schools aligning their curricula with the state test:

> A standardized test would set the educational objectives for the teacher. Curriculum alignment would insure that the teacher would cover the material to be tested. The teacher would prepare plans and write reports to inform supervisors in the

bureaucracy that the material was being covered. Evaluators would observe and inspect to make sure that teachers were using the proper methods. And, finally, the external test would demonstrate whether the teacher had properly executed his or her duties. (Wise, 1988, p. 330)

We don't want to imply that learning standards and assessment are, by their very nature, bad. Standards and assessment that have been constructed with wide participation and are thoughtful and reasonable for students to achieve can be a way to address class, race/ethnicity, and gender inequities of expectations, resources, and targeted assistance. The issue here is one of who should define such standards, what should be multiple ways of assessing such learning, what should be the consequences for students, teachers, and schools, and just as important, what flexibility, freedom, and authority should be given to classrooms and schools to be accountable? After all, it is hard to be accountable for what one has no control over (Darling-Hammond, 1997; Elmore and Rothman, 1999; Glickman, 1999, 2000/2001).

Curriculum Development as a Vehicle for Enhancing Collective Thinking about Instruction

The tragedy of curriculum being simply a response to state tests is the loss of a powerful vehicle for creating a broader instructional dialogue in a school or district, which could enhance teachers' individual and collective thinking about the following questions: What is worth teaching, how shall we teach, and how shall we assess? Most teachers—when trusted, when given time and money, and when given the assistance, choice, and responsibility to develop curricula—make extraordinarily sound decisions about what students should be taught. Often, their decisions are far superior to those made in central offices, state departments, or commercial publishing firms (McEvoy, 1986; McNeil, 1988).

Teachers who are involved in making decisions about school curriculum go through changes in their own thinking about teaching. To discuss, debate, and finally come to an agreement with peers about what is important for students to know is an intellectually challenging experience.

It is clear that in order for schools to be successful, teachers must be involved in curriculum development. The issues that remain are as follows:

1. What should be the purpose of the curriculum?
2. What should be the content of the curriculum?
3. How should the curriculum be organized?
4. In what format should the curriculum be written?
5. At what level of curriculum development should teachers be involved?

The following sections discuss each of these issues.

What Should Be the Purpose of the Curriculum?

Alternative beliefs about the purpose of the curriculum are described by Miller and Seller (1985) as orientations to curriculum. They describe three *metaorientations,* or positions:

- In the *transmission position* the function of education is to transmit facts, skills, and values to students. Specifically, this orientation stresses mastery of traditional school subjects through traditional teaching methodologies. (pp. 5 and 6) (emphasis supplied)
- In the *transaction position* the individual is seen as rational and capable of intelligent problem solving. Education is viewed as a dialogue between the student and the curriculum in which the student reconstructs knowledge through the dialogue process. The central elements in the transaction position are an emphasis on curriculum strategies that promote problem solving, . . . application of problem solving skills within social contexts in general and within the context of the democratic process, . . . and development of cognitive skills within the academic disciplines. (pp. 6 and 7) (emphasis supplied)
- The *transformation position* focuses on personal and social change. It encompasses . . . teaching students skills that promote personal and social transformation . . . [and] a vision of social change as movement toward harmony with the environment rather than an effort to exert control over it. (p. 8) (emphasis supplied)

If Miller and Seller's three orientations to curriculum sound vaguely familiar, it may be because of your review of educational philosophies in Chapter 5. The transmission curriculum orientation is related to the educational philosophy of essentialism. The transactional curriculum orientation is based largely on the philosophy of experimentalism. Finally, aspects of the transformation orientation are related to the philosophy of existentialism. In Chapter 5, we found that our educational beliefs help to shape our definition of effective teaching and instructional improvement. Similarly, curriculum orientations drive the curriculum development process and affect curriculum purpose, content, organization, and format.

Therefore, it is important that early in the curriculum design process the curriculum development team examines alternative curriculum orientations and clarifies its own orientation. The most basic decision the team must make (with input from all stakeholders) is whether the purpose of the curriculum is to transmit, transact, transform, or accomplish some combination thereof.

What Should Be the Content of the Curriculum?

Curriculum, for purposes of this book, is the *what* of instruction—what is intentionally taught to students in a district, school, or classroom. The elements of curriculum are sequence and continuity, scope, and balance (Doll, 1989). *Sequence* is the ordering of learning experiences, and *continuity* is the length or duration of such experiences. *Scope* is the range of learning experiences to be offered. *Balance* is the degree and amount of topics, subjects, and learning experiences that adequately prepare students. A curriculum is developed by deciding (1) What should students learn? (2) What is the order of content for the student to follow? (3) How is the learning to be evaluated? (see Firth and Newfield, 1984; Glatthorn, 1987; Brandt, 1988; Clark and Clark, 2000; Gandal and Vranek, 2001).

Decisions about curriculum content are influenced by priorities of state and federal governments, values of professional educators and the local community, knowledge of student development, current economics, and future societal conditions. Underlying all decisions about curriculum content are curriculum orientations (transmission, transaction, or transformation), which ultimately are derived from educational philosophies (essentialism, experimentalism, or existentialism).

Benjamin Bloom's (1956) taxonomy of learning might serve as a guide for determining types of learning within or across content areas (see Table 18.1). His lower-level learnings—(1) knowledge and (2) comprehension—are based on students recalling and demonstrating known answers. Curriculum objectives calling for knowledge and comprehension tend to dominate a curriculum with the purpose of transmission. Bloom's intermediate levels of learning—(3) application and (4) analysis—are based on students using logic to solve problems and reflect on their own thought process. Curriculum objectives at the application and analysis levels are emphasized in a curriculum with the purpose of transaction. Finally, Bloom's higher levels of learning—(5) synthesis and (6) evaluation—are based on combining various knowledge, facts, skills, and logic to make unique personal judgments. Curriculum objectives at the synthesis and evaluation levels are prevalent in a curriculum with the purpose of transformation. By examining a written curriculum, then, we can ascertain whether its purpose (and the curriculum developers' underlying orientation) is transmission, transaction, or transformation.

How Should the Curriculum Be Organized?

Three broad approaches to organizing curriculum content are discipline based, interdisciplinary, and transdisciplinary. A *discipline-based curriculum* is described by Jacobs (1989):

> The discipline-based content design option focuses on a strict interpretation of the disciplines with separate subjects in separate time blocks during the school day. No attempt for integration is made, in fact, it is avoided. Traditional approaches to subjects such as language arts, mathematics, science, social studies, music, art, and physical education are the usual fare. In secondary programs, these general academic and arts areas break down into more specific fields, such as algebra under mathematics or American history under social studies. There are some variations of block scheduling and the way the week or cycle is programmed. Nevertheless, knowledge is presented in separate fields without a deliberate attempt to show the relationships among them. (p. 14)

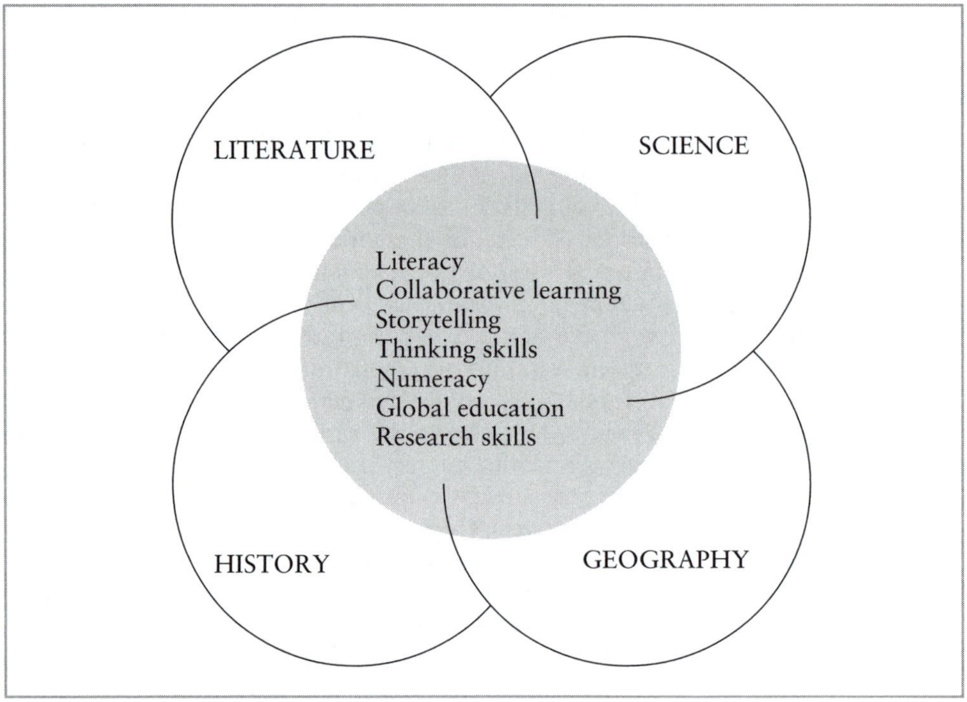

figure 18.2 **Illustration of an Interdisciplinary Curriculum**

Source: S. M. Drake, J. Bebbington, S. Laksman, P. Mackie, N. Maynes, & L. Wayne (1992). *Developing an Integrated Curriculum Using the Story Model,* p. 4. Ontario: The Ontario Institute for Studies in Education Press. Reprinted with permission of University of Toronto Press.

Because of its emphasis on breaking learning down into discrete segments of traditional content to be learned in specified blocks of time, the discipline-based approach is best suited to a curriculum with the purpose of transmission. This approach clearly has been the dominant curriculum organization pattern in the United States.

In an *interdisciplinary curriculum,* common themes connect traditional content areas. For instance, different aspects of an instructional unit on transportation might be taught in science, math, social studies, language arts, art, music, and physical education, or a set of common concepts or skills (for example, technology or problem-solving skills) might connect different subject areas throughout the year. Figure 18.2 illustrates an interdisciplinary curriculum. A curriculum organization of this type requires extensive team planning. Because the interdisciplinary approach encourages students to discover relationships and make applications across existing content areas, it is most appropriate for a curriculum with the purpose of transactional learning (Jenkins, 2005).

In a *transdisciplinary curriculum,* traditional disciplines do not exist. The entire curriculum is organized around common themes, skills, or problems. Daily learning activities are built around the topic being studied rather than conforming to academic disciplines or class schedules. For example, while studying the concept of commerce, students could spend all of their school time developing, managing, and analyzing their own in-school "marketplace." Students might study selected content from economics, math, sociology, communication, politics, ethics, history, and other academic disciplines, but only as such content became relevant to the commercial community they were developing.

Transdisciplinary curricula usually begin with very broad intended learning outcomes. The integration into the curriculum of contemporary problems from the real world and students' interests and concerns become part of an ongoing curriculum development process. This type of curriculum organization can be successful only if teachers are willing to completely reconceptualize their concept of the school curriculum. A transdisciplinary curriculum organization requires students to synthesize knowledge and skills from various content areas and encourages student creativity and self-direction. Such an organizational pattern is most consistent with a curriculum with the purpose of transforming teaching and learning.

In What Format Should the Curriculum Be Written?

This section discusses various formats used in writing curriculum. Behavioral-objective, webbing, and results-only formats are described. Like the content and organization of curriculum, the format it is written in reflects a curriculum orientation. Behavioral–objective formats reflect a transmission orientation. Webbing formats reflect a transaction orientation. Results-only formats reflect a transformation orientation.

Behavioral–Objective Format

Predetermined knowledge, facts, and skills are written in curriculum guides in a linear cause-and-effect format. The curriculum developers determine what is to be learned, state the learning as a behavioral objective, specify the teaching/learning activities, and conclude with a posttest to see if the objective has been achieved. The progression is as follows:

Objective → Activity → Evaluation

Figure 18.3 is an example of a behavioral–objective guide written for a fifth-grade social studies class. Curriculum developers break their unit into the most important facts or skills that cover the subject. They write behavioral objectives for each fact or skill. Each behavioral objective is the basis for a sequence of activities and evaluation. The teacher who uses such a curriculum guide is expected to follow the sequence of activities and administer the evaluation. Recycling activities might

Behavioral objective: At the end of the week, students will recall and spell the original 13 colonies at a 100 percent level of mastery.

Activities:
1. Lecture on 13 colonies.
2. Students fill in map of 13 colonies.
3. Students read pp. 113–118 of text and do assignments on p. 119 as homework.
4. Call on students at random to spell the various colonies.

Evaluation: Ask students to recall the names and spell correctly each of the 13 original colonies on a sheet of paper.

figure **18.3** **Behavioral—Objective Format**

be included in the guide for those students who do not pass the evaluation. Each behavioral–objective plan is tightly sequenced so that one objective is mastered before a student moves to the next. (For example, after identifying and spelling the original 13 American colonies, the next objective might be identifying and spelling those states that came into the Union from 1776 to 1810.)

Most school curricula that have been written since the early 1990s follow a behavioral–objective format. It is particularly easy to use in subjects such as mathematics and physical sciences, where skills are obvious and facts are clear (2 plus 2 is always 4, for example, but is war always justifiable?). So prevalent has been the behavioral–objective format in curriculum writing in the last few years that many educators know of no other way to write curricula.

Webbing

Curriculum can be written in a format that shows relationships of activities around a central theme. William Kilpatrick popularized this type of curriculum in writing about the work unit (Kilpatrick, 1925). Instead of predetermining the knowledge or skills, the curriculum developer determines the major theme, related themes, and then possible student activities.

The webbing format can be conceived of in this way:

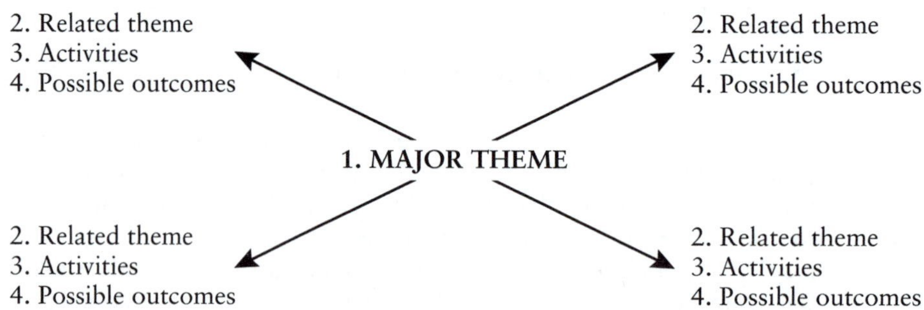

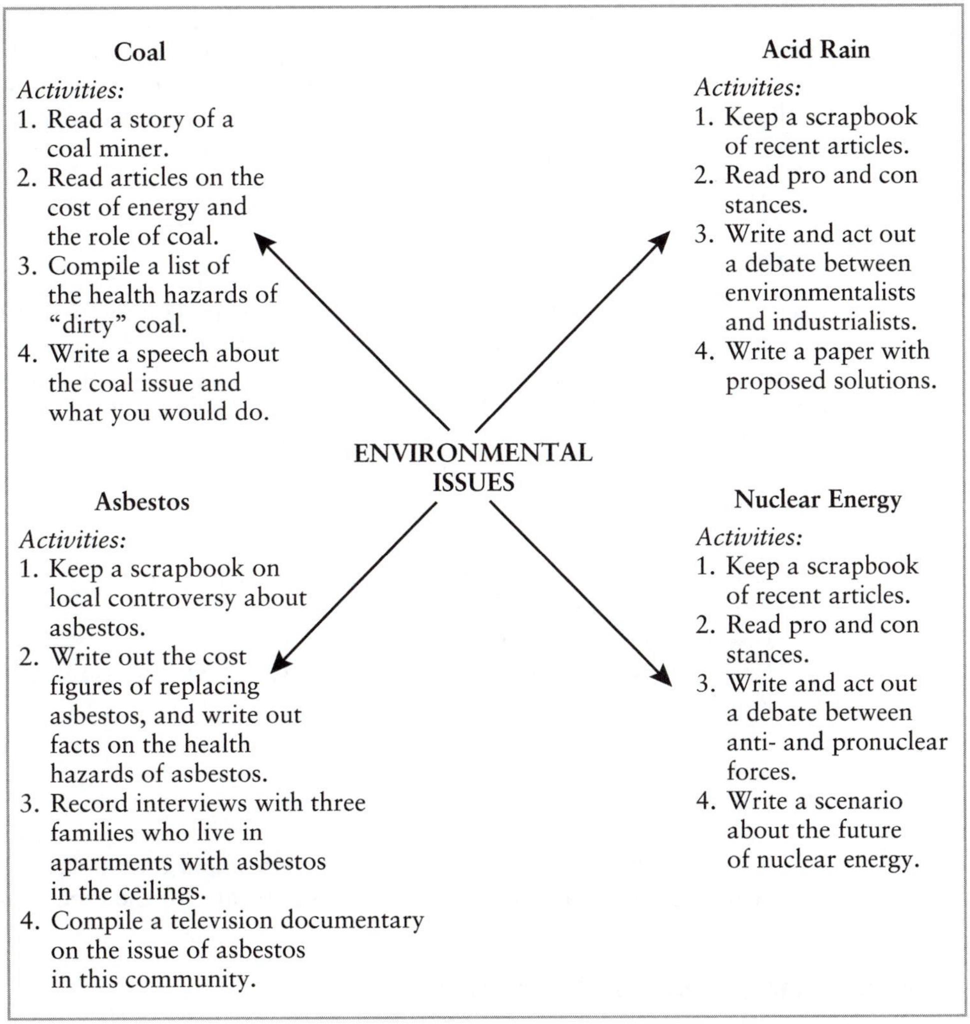

figure 18.4 **Webbing Format**

After the activities have been written, the curriculum developers write possible learning outcomes: "Students will be able to identify four major environmental issues," "Students will be able to argue and give evidence for both the pro and con sides of each issue," "Students will take a personal stance on each issue." In planning activities, developers consider multimodes of learning via reading, writing, listening, and constructing and then integrate many fields of knowledge around a central theme. In Figure 18.4, notice how the theme of environmental issues integrates activities in sociology, mathematics, economics, history, journalism, physics, and biology.

A webbing curriculum guide would contain a blueprint of the web followed by sections for each related theme with activities, possible outcomes, and resources needed. Notice that the webbed curriculum includes possible outcomes and allows for the possibility of others. In a behavioral–objective curriculum, activities are controlled toward predetermined ends. In a webbed curriculum, activities lead to possible and unanticipated learning.

Results-Only Format

A results-only format for curriculum provides teachers with the widest latitude for using materials, activities, and methods. Such a curriculum specifies the goals and general learning about a subject, theme unit, or course. The guide might include ways to evaluate the learning. For example, a results-only guide in elementary reading might specify the following skills to be learned:

Comprehension

1. Develops powers of observation
2. Classifies by name, color, shape, size, positions, use
3. Anticipates endings to stories
4. Discriminates between fact and fantasy
5. Understands who, what, when, where, how, and why phrases
6. Recalls a story sequence
7. Reads to find the main ideas of a story
8. Reads to draw a conclusion
9. Compares and contrasts stories

It is then left to the teacher to determine when and how to teach these skills. The teacher is held accountable only for the results, not for the procedures used.

Curriculum Format as Reflective of Choice Given to Teachers

The less specificity and detail a curriculum has, the greater the choice given to teachers to vary instruction according to the situation. Figure 18.5 illustrates the enlargement of teacher choice by curriculum.

Picture being in a curriculum cone where, at the behavioral–objective bottom, a teacher can barely budge. As the teacher moves toward the webbing area, he or she finds room to move hands, feet, elbows, and knees. At the results-only end of the cone, the teacher can extend fully. If the teacher is allowed to step out of the curriculum cone, there are no limits on where and how he or she can move. Behavioral–objective formats predetermine the *what* and *how* of teaching as much as possible in a loosely coupled organization. A webbing format focuses on themes and relation-

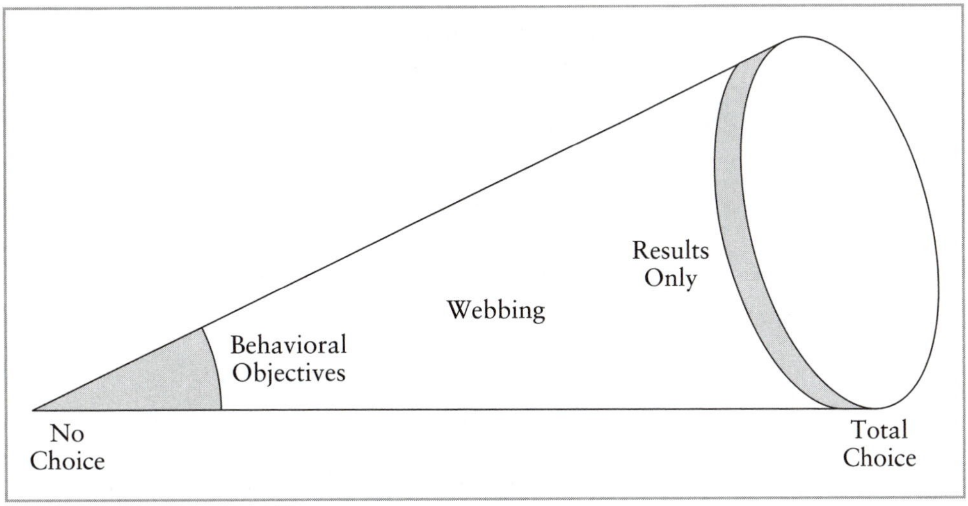

figure **18.5** **Curriculum Format as a Reflection of Teacher Choice: The Curriculum Cone**

ships of possible activities for teachers but gives them a choice of actual activities, duration of activities, and evaluation methods. A results-only format focuses on generalized learning and gives teachers the latitude to proceed as they wish.

It appears relatively easy to match teacher stages of development to curriculum formats. It is not so easy, however; further examination of type and degree of involvement in curriculum development is necessary.

If a school has decided to use a behavioral–objective format, that does not necessarily mean that classroom teachers have little choice about how to teach. Perhaps the teachers have chosen to use that format; perhaps they wrote the curriculum themselves. Also, an elaborately detailed behavioral–objective curriculum could be presented to teachers as a reference guide to use as they wish. Simply knowing the format of the curriculum does not tell us how much choice was given to teachers. Although behavioral curricula usually are used as prescriptive teaching and can be equated with limiting choice, this is not always so. Therefore, before completing the picture of curriculum and teacher choice, it is necessary to consider how curricula are developed, interpreted, and implemented.

Relationship of Curriculum Purpose, Content, Organization, and Format

In previous sections we have proposed logical links among curriculum purpose, content, organization, and format. To review, a curriculum with the purpose of transmission is logically matched with knowledge and comprehension learning content, discipline-

table 18.2 **Logical Relationships of Curriculum Purpose, Content, Organization, and Format**

Curriculum Purpose	Transmission	Transaction	Transformation
Curriculum Content	Knowledge Comprehension	Application Analysis	Synthesis Evaluation
Curriculum Organization	Discipline Based	Interdisciplinary	Transdisciplinary
Curriculum Format	Behavioral Objective	Webbing	Results-Only

based curriculum organization, and behavioral–objective format. A curriculum with the purpose of transaction is well matched with application and analysis learning content, interdisciplinary curriculum organization, and webbing format. A curriculum with the purpose of transformation is consistent with synthesis and evaluation learning content, a transdisciplinary curriculum organization, and a results-only format. Table 18.2 illustrates logical relationships of curriculum purpose, content, organization, and format.

The natural matches we've outlined, of course, don't occur in all curricula. For instance, not all webbing formats are found within interdisciplinary curricula. The webbing format in Figure 18.4, for example, could be part of a science course within a discipline-based curriculum. For another instance, a results-only curriculum format could focus on learning content at the lower and intermediate as well as the higher levels of Bloom's taxonomy, or it could be part of a discipline-based or interdisciplinary rather than a transdisciplinary curriculum. In general, however, our own review of K–12 curricula indicate that the logical matches in Table 18.2 tend to hold true in most schools.

Levels of Teacher Involvement in Curriculum Development

Tanner and Tanner (1980) write of teachers and local schools functioning in curriculum development at one of three levels: (1) imitative maintenance, (2) mediative, or (3) generative. Teachers at level 1 are concerned with maintaining and following the existing curriculum. Teachers at level 2 look at development as refining the existing curriculum. Teachers at level 3 are concerned with improving and changing the curriculum according to the most current knowledge about learning and societal conditions. Tanner and Tanner explained these three levels as follows:

> ***Level I: Imitative Maintenance***
>
> Teachers operating at Level I rely on textbooks, workbooks, and routine activities, subject by subject. Skills are treated as dead ends rather than as means of generating further learning. Readymade materials are used without critical

evaluation, resulting in a multiplicity of isolated skill-development activities. (The already segmental curriculum is further fragmented.) The imagination of the teacher does not go beyond maintaining the status quo. This teacher would like to think that he or she has less freedom than he or she may actually have for curriculum improvement. In the secondary school, concern for curriculum development is largely confined to each departmental domain.

When change is made, it is made on the adoption level, without adaptation to local needs. Curriculum development at this level is plugging in the package to the existing situation without attention to the resulting interactions. Teachers at this level tend to be left alone to struggle with innovations that are handed to them from above. Schools are turned inward, with the principal as the sole resource for classroom assistance.

Level II: Mediative

Teachers at Level II are aware of the need to integrate curriculum content and deal with emergent conditions. (Societal problems such as the energy crisis and children's questions about things that interest and concern them are examples of emergent conditions.) Although teachers at this level may have an aggregate conception of curriculum, implementation does not go beyond the occasional correlation of certain subjects. The focus of curriculum remains segmental; theory remains divorced from practice; curriculum improvement remains at the level of refining existing practice.

Yet teachers at the second level of curriculum development do not blindly plug in an innovation or curriculum package to the existing situation. The necessary adaptations, accommodations, and adjustments are made and teachers capitalize on a range of resources for curriculum improvement, including pupils, parents, and peers; and they utilize resources beyond the local school. Teachers are consumers of professional literature on approved practices and tap the resources of the university through in-service courses. The mediative level is a level of awareness and accommodation. Teachers are attracted to, and can articulate, new ideas but their efforts to improve the curriculum fall short of the necessary reconstruction for substantive problem solving.

Level III: Creative–Generative

Teachers at Level III take an aggregate approach to curriculum development. Ideally, the curriculum is examined in its entirety by the teacher and the whole school staff, and questions of priority and relationship are asked. While individual teachers can and should be at the generative–creative level, a macrocurricular approach requires cooperative planning for vertical and horizontal articulation.

Granted that teachers as individuals usually cannot create new schoolwide curricula, an individual teacher can establish continuities and relationships in his or her own teaching and with other teachers. Teachers at Level III use generalizations and problems as centers of curriculum organization. They stress the broad concepts that specialized subjects share in common, and they use and develop courses of study that cross subject fields. These are aggregate treatments.

Teachers at the third level of curriculum development think about what they are doing and try to find more effective ways of working. They are able to diagnose their problems and formulate hypotheses for solutions. They experiment in their classrooms and communicate their insights to other teachers.

Teachers at this level are consumers of research and seek greater responsibility for curriculum decisions at the school and classroom levels. They exercise independent judgment in selecting curriculum materials and adapt them to local needs. They regard themselves as professionals and, as such, are continually involved in the problems of making decisions regarding learning experiences. To this end, their antennae are turned outward to a wide range of resources.*

Integrating Curriculum Format with Developers and Levels of Development

To integrate what has been said about curriculum format, developers, and development, refer to Figure 18.6. When the developers are either outside the school system or from the district level and the curriculum is in a tightly prescribed format, development is primarily *imitative,* characterized by teachers following the course of study. When the developers are intermediate teams of teachers led by district specialists and the curriculum is written with objectives and suggested activities, development is primarily *mediative,* characterized by teachers revising and adapting the course of study to their immediate situation. When curriculum developers are teams of teachers using specialists as resource persons or individual teachers with a results-only curriculum format that identifies what students should learn and leaves activities to the teacher, then development is *generative,* characterized by ongoing creativity.

Matching Curriculum Development with Teacher Development

A progression of curriculum development matched with teacher development might look like Table 18.3. The supervisor might think of his or her staff in terms of the commitment, thinking, and expertise they currently bring to curriculum and then

*Excerpt from Daniel Tanner and Laurel N. Tanner, *Curriculum Development: Theory into Practice,* 2nd ed., pp. 636, 638–639. Copyright © 1980 by Macmillan Publishing Co., Inc., New York. Reprinted by permission.

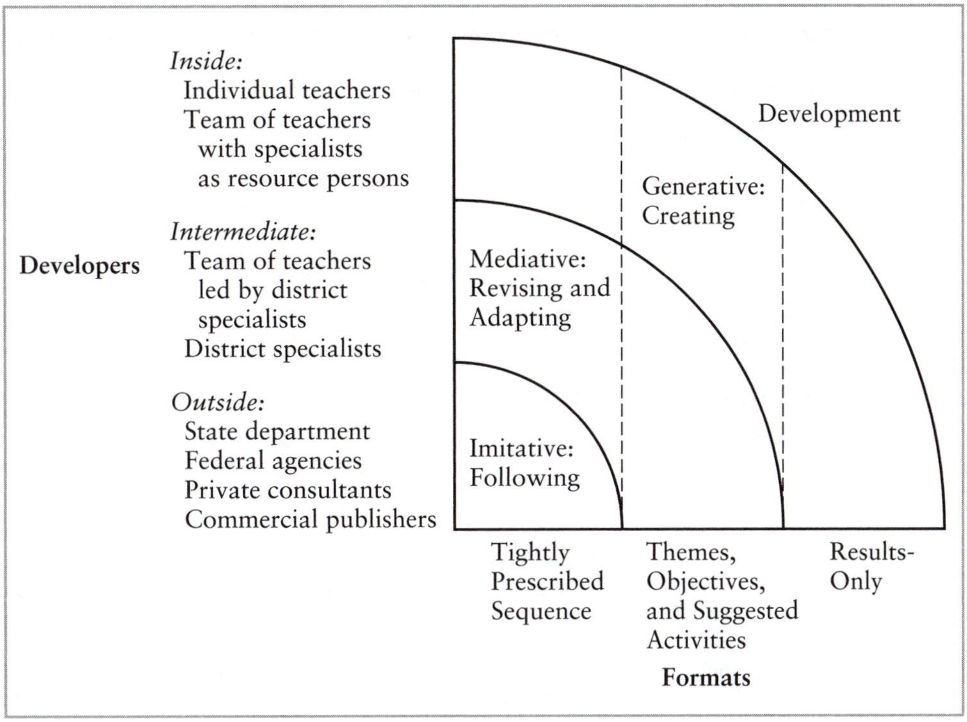

figure 18.6 **Integrating Curriculum Format with Developers and Levels of Development**

determine whether the current curriculum is appropriately matched with the teachers' level of curriculum functioning. If the present curriculum is inappropriate to teachers' development, readjustments to the curriculum are in order.

A staff that has a low level of curriculum functioning—as displayed by little commitment to change, little ability to suggest possible changes, and little curriculum expertise—initially would be matched with an outside-developed, behavioral–objective, and imitative curriculum. They should be allowed to make minor revisions in adapting the curriculum to their classrooms. However, a staff that has a moderate level of curriculum functioning (as displayed by a desire to change, ability to think of possible changes, but a lack of expertise in writing curriculum) would be appropriately matched with a curriculum originally developed by outside experts but substantially revised by an internal team of teachers led by a curriculum specialist. The format of the curriculum might be eclectic in its use of behavioral objectives and webbing. Throughout the development and implementation, teachers should have problem–solving meetings for purposes of curriculum adaptation. Finally, a staff at a high level of curriculum functioning (as displayed by initiating and suggesting ways to change and knowing how to proceed in creating curriculum) would be appropriately matched

table 18.3 **Progression of Curriculum Matched with Characteristics of Staff**

Characteristics	Low ——→	Moderate ——→	High
Staff Characteristics			
Commitment to curriculum change	Low commitment to change	Would like to make change	Eager to make change
Level of thinking about curriculum	Low ability to think about possible changes	Can think of some possible changes	Has many suggestions
Expertise in curriculum procedures	Low expertise in how to proceed	Does not know how to write curriculum	Knows how to proceed
Curriculum Characteristics			
Developers	Outside developers	Outside developed but substantially revised by team of teachers led by specialists	Internally developed by team of teachers with specialists as resource
Format	Behavioral–objective, highly structured	Eclectic format using behavior objectives, webbing	Results-only, with suggested activities
Development	Imitative, with allow–ance for minor revisions	To be adapted mutually	To be discussed and changed continually

with an internally developed curriculum. The format should emphasize results only with *suggested* activities and should be continuously open to revision.

The supervisor should keep in mind the question: How does one increase teacher control over curriculum making? If a staff has been matched appropriately—for example, low-functioning staff with an imitative curriculum—and successful implementation is occurring, then the supervisor should plan for the next cycle of curriculum development to give teachers additional responsibilities by serving on decision-making teams under the leadership of a curriculum specialist. This leads to more mutually adaptive curriculum and at the same time continues to stimulate and increase teacher commitment, development, and expertise.

The supervisor wishing to facilitate changes in curriculum purpose, content, organization, and format must remember that successful change is based on teachers changing their conceptions of curriculum and their level of involvement in curriculum development. Change in teachers *and* curriculum is more likely to be successful if done in an incremental manner. For example, rather than announcing that the school is moving from a discipline-based to interdisciplinary curriculum organization, the supervisor could initially encourage small teams of teachers functioning at moderate to high levels of development, expertise, and commitment to plan and teach a few interdisciplinary units of instruction throughout the school year.

In another school already operating at an interdisciplinary level, movement toward a transdisciplinary curriculum could begin with a group of teachers operating at high levels of development, expertise, and commitment forming a "broad field." A *broad field* results from the fusion of two or more separate disciplines. Courses or subjects (rather than departments) with titles like "Humanities," "Social Science," and "Natural Science" usually reflect a broad-field approach. The formation of one or more broad fields involving a subset of faculty and curricula would not represent a fully transdisciplinary curriculum, but it would be a major step in that direction.

Large-scale teacher-driven changes in curriculum content, organization, and format will not take place unless teachers change their curriculum orientations or beliefs about the purpose of curriculum. Yet, teachers are not likely to change their orientations unless their levels of understanding of and involvement in curriculum development gradually increase. Supervisor openness and trust building, staff development in curriculum design, and time, support, and rewards for teacher involvement can all foster teacher *and* curriculum development. Throughout the curriculum development process, the supervisor must remember that if he or she has a curriculum orientation or favors a curriculum content, organization, or format different from teachers, he or she is not necessarily right and the teachers wrong. Government mandates, the community, the school's mission and culture, parents, teachers, and students must all be considered when deciding which direction curriculum development should take and at what rate it should proceed.

The Curriculum and Cultural Diversity

There are a variety of reasons why the curriculum should be culturally diverse. First, students from nondominant cultures are not likely to reach their learning potential if the curriculum ignores their culture. Second, a society cannot offer democracy, equal opportunity, and justice for all unless it experiences, understands, and respects the variety of cultures that make up the society. Third, communities and societies that recognize the value of diversity and invite citizens from different cultures to participate in their development experience more educational, economic, and social success: The quality of life for all citizens improves. A culturally diverse curriculum, then, benefits all students, as well as the community and society.

How do schools integrate multicultural and ethnic content into their curriculum? James Banks (2005) describes four approaches to integration. Banks presents the approaches as four levels of integration, with Level 1 the least effective and Level 4 the most effective.

Level 1, the *contributions approach,* calls for inserting minority culture heroes, holidays, and elements (food, dances, music, art) into the curriculum alongside mainstream content. This is the easiest approach to implement, but it leaves the curriculum virtually unchanged.

Level 2, the *additive approach,* adds concepts and perspectives from other cultures to the mainstream curriculum without changing the curriculum's basic structure.

This approach might include adding books by minority authors, a few units of instruction, or a single course to the curriculum.

Level 3, the *transformation approach,* changes the fundamental structure of the curriculum by enabling students to consider concepts, issues, and problems from several different cultural perspectives rather than from only the dominant culture's perspective.

Level 4, the *social action approach,* includes all aspects of the transformation approach but also requires students to engage in critical inquiry about cultural issues and problems and to take action for social change.

Figure 18.7 summarizes the four approaches.

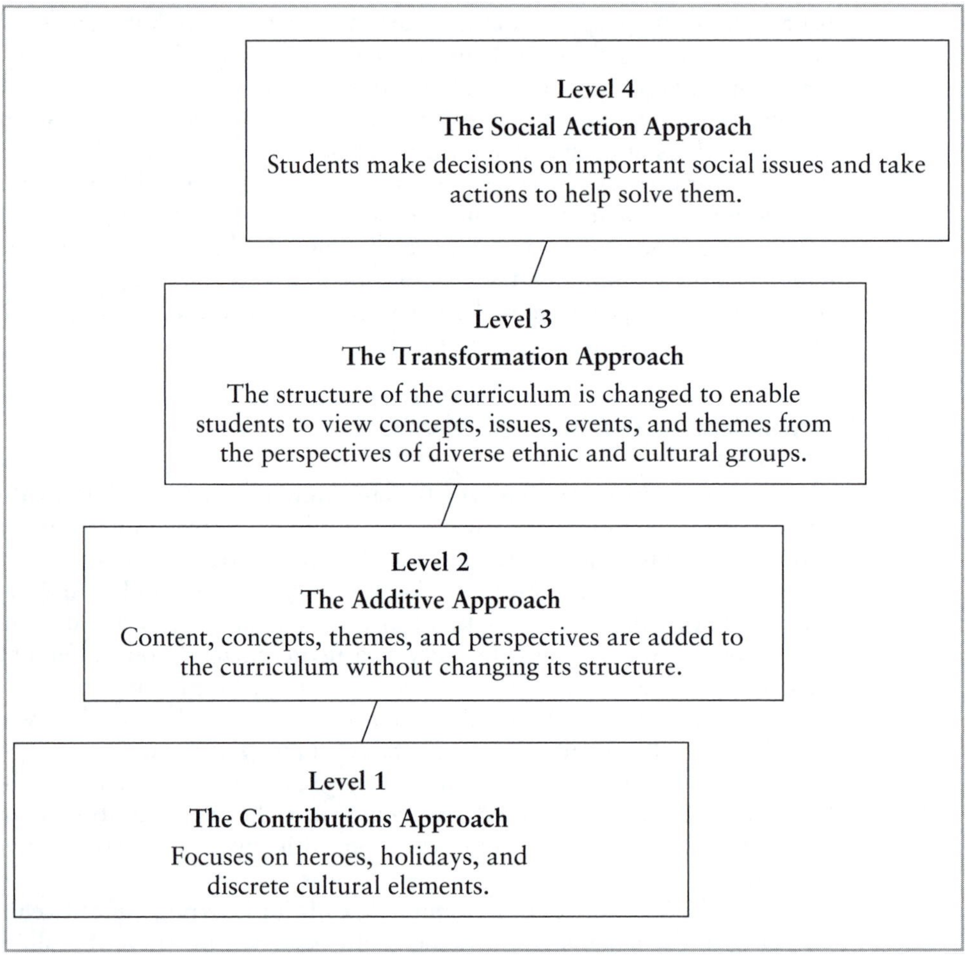

figure 18.7 **Banks's Approaches to Multicultural Curriculum Reform**

Source: Reprinted with permission from James A. Banks (1988). "Approaches to Multicultural Curriculum Reform." *Multicultural Leader, 1*(2), 1–3. Copyright © 1988 by James A. Banks.

Other scholars support Banks's assertion that transformative and social action approaches are more effective at integrating multicultural content into the curriculum than the contributions or additive approaches (Gay, 1995; Nieto, 2000; Bennett, 2003). Unfortunately, many school curricula have not gone beyond the contributions approach. Why the gap between scholarship on multicultural curriculum and practice? Geneva Gay (2005) offers an explanation:

> Most school teachers and administrators have good intentions about implementing the ideas and proposals suggested in the scholarship on multicultural education. Unfortunately, many do not have the knowledge base and pedagogical skills needed. Others are still struggling with how to resolve what they see as inherent tensions between the national ideals of the United States embedded in the motto *E Pluribus Unum* and recognizing, accepting, and promoting diversity in schools and society. Confusion is still rampant over calls for diversity, equity, and excellence in education. Too many educators continue to believe that to treat students differently based on their cultural heritages, ethnic identities, and background experiences is synonymous to discrimination, and to promote diversity is to compromise high-quality performance and standards of excellence. This confusion drives some educators to question the merits of education for diversity, to judge it divisive and counterproductive, and to redefine it in ways that reaffirm their comfort levels and serve their own purposes. These reactions have different consequences on efforts to implement multicultural education, but in general they produce distortions, inaccuracies, and misconceptions that are not consistent with the thinking, research, and writing of multicultural education scholars. (pp. 109–110)

Gay (2005) proposes that we begin to close the gap between scholarship and practice by developing well-articulated guidelines for translating theoretical principles into practice, establishing performance standards for educators, and providing professional development to help educators meet those standards. The professional development Gay proposes is long-term, assisting educators in developing self-understanding, cultural knowledge, and multicultural education skills.

MyEdLeadershipLab™

Go to Topic 6, Curriculum Planning and Assessment, in the MyEdLeadershipLab™ site at www.myedleadershiplab.com for *The Basic Guide to SuperVision and Instructional Leadership*, Third Edition, where you can:

- Find learning outcomes for Curriculum Planning and Assessment along with the national standards that connect to these outcomes.
- Complete Assignments and Activities that can help you more deeply understand the chapter content.
- Apply and practice your understanding of the core skills identified in the chapter with the Building Leadership Skills unit.
- Prepare yourself for professional certification with a Practice for Certification quiz.

REFERENCES

Banks, J. A. 2005. Approaches to multicultural curriculum reform. In J. A. Banks and C. A. McGhee Banks (Eds.), *Multicultural education: Issues and perspectives* (5th ed., pp. 242–264). Hoboken, NJ: John Wiley & Sons.

Bennett, C. I. 2003. *Comprehensive multicultural education: Theory and Practice* (5th ed.). Boston: Allyn & Bacon.

Bloom, B. (1956). *Taxonomy of educational objectives. Handbook I: The cognitive domain.* New York: David McKay.

Brandt, R. S. (Ed.). 1988. Content of the curriculum, 1988. In *ASCD Yearbook*. Alexandria, VA: Association for Supervision and Curriculum Development.

Clark, D. C., and Clark, S. N. 2000. Appropriate assessment strategies for young adolescents in an era of standards-based reform. *The Clearing House, 73*(4), 201–204.

Darling-Hammond, L. 1997. *The right to learn: A blueprint for creating schools that work.* San Francisco: Jossey-Bass.

Doll, R. C. 1989. *Curriculum improvement: Decision making and process* (6th ed.). Boston: Allyn & Bacon.

Elmore, R. F., and Rothman, R. (Eds.). 1999. *Testing, teaching, and learning; A guide for states and school districts.* Washington, DC: National Academy Press.

Firth, G. R., and Newfield, J. W. 1984. Curriculum development and selection. In J. M. Cooper (Ed.), *Developing skills for instructional supervision.* New York: Longman.

Fitzharris, L. H. 2005. Making all the right connections. *Journal of Staff Development, 26*(1), 24–28.

Gandal, M., and Vranek, J. 2001. Standards: Here today, here tomorrow. *Educational Leadership, 59*(1), 6–13.

Gay, G. (1995). Bridging multicultural theory and practice. *Multicultural Education, 3,* 4–9.

Gay, G. (2005). Standards for diversity. In S. P. Gordon (Ed.), *Standards for instructional supervision: Enhancing teaching and learning.* Larchmont, NY: Eye on Education.

Glatthorn, A. A. 1987. *Curriculum renewal.* Alexandria, VA: Association for Supervision and Curriculum Development.

Glickman, C. D. 1999. *School based authority and responsibility.* Unpublished invited report to the Georgia Governor's Education Reform Study Commission. Atlanta, GA: The Office of the Governor of Georgia.

Glickman, C. D. 2000/2001. Holding sacred ground: The impact of standardization. *Educational Leadership, 58*(4), 46–51.

Jacobs, H. H. 1989. *Interdisciplinary curriculum: Design and implementation.* Alexandria, VA: Association for Supervision and Curriculum Development.

Jenkins, R. A. 2005. Interdisciplinary instruction in the inclusion classroom. *Teaching Exceptional Children, 37*(5), 42–48.

Kilpatrick, W. H. 1925. *Foundations of method.* New York: Macmillan.

McEvoy, B. 1986. *"Against our better judgements." Three teachers' enactment of mandated curriculum.* Paper presented at the annual meeting of the American Educational Research Association, San Francisco.

McNeil, L. N. 1988. Contradictions of control, Part 2. Teachers, students and curriculum. *Kappan, 69*(6), 432–438.

Miller, J. P., and Seller, W. 1985. *Curriculum: Perspectives and practice.* New York: Longman.

Nieto, S. (2000). *Affirming diversity: The sociopolitical context of multicultural education.* New York: Longman.

Oliva, P. F. 1992. *Developing the curriculum* (3rd ed.). New York: HarperCollins.

Sergiovanni, T. 1987. *Introduction to the Breckinridge Conference on restructuring schools.* San Antonio, August.

Tanner, D., and Tanner, L. W. 1980. *Curriculum development: Theory into practice* (2nd ed.). New York: Macmillan.

Wise, A. 1988. Legislated learning revisited. *Kappan, 69*(5), 328–333.

Zeuli, J. S., and Buchmann, M. 1987. *Implementation of teacher thinking research as curriculum deliberation.* Presentation to the annual meeting of the American Educational Research Association, Washington, DC, April.

chapter 19

Action Research

THE SCHOOL AS THE CENTER OF INQUIRY

outline

- How Is Action Research Conducted?
- A Developmental Approach to Action Research
- Action Research: Vehicle for a Cause beyond Oneself
- Example of Action Research
- Expanding Boundaries: Alternative Approaches to Action Research
- Shared Governance for Action Research
- Suggestions for Assisting Action Research
- Conclusion: Focus, Structure, and Time for Development

Visit the **MyEdLeadershipLab™** site for *The Basic Guide to SuperVision and Instructional Leadership*, Third Edition to enhance your understanding of chapter concepts. You'll have the opportunity to practice your skills through video and case based Assignments and Activities as well as Building Leadership Skills units, and prepare for your certification exam with Practice for Certification quizzes.

Why should our schools not be staffed, gradually if you will, by scholar–teachers in command of the conceptual tools and methods of inquiry requisite to investigating the learning process as it operates in their own classrooms? Why should our schools not nurture the continuing wisdom and power of such scholar–teachers?

(Schaefer, 1967, p. 5)

The famous social scientist Kurt Lewin devoted his career to studying democracy and the relationships of individuals within groups. His contributions ushered in the school of gestalt psychology, group dynamics, and the concept of action research. He argued that social research should be based on the actions groups take to improve their conditions. Social research should not focus on controlled experiments, removed from real conditions. As people plan changes and engage in real activities, fact finding should determine whether success is being achieved and whether further planning and action are necessary (Lewin, 1948, p. 206).

Stephen Corey (1953) applied Lewin's concept of action research to education. He argues that traditional research is done mainly by researchers outside the public school and has little influence on school practice. Corey writes:

> Learning that changes behavior substantially is most likely to result when a person himself tries to improve a situation that makes a difference to him. . . . When he defines the problem, hypothesizes actions that may help him cope with it, engages in these actions, studies the consequences, and generalizes from them, he will more frequently internalize the experience than when all this is done for him by somebody else, and he reads about it. . . . The value of action research . . . is determined primarily by the extent to which findings lead to improvement in the practices of the people engaged in the research. (p. 9)

Thus, action research in education is study conducted by colleagues in a school setting of the results of their activities to improve instruction. Although an individual teacher can conduct action research, in most cases it is best done as a cooperative endeavor by faculty attempting to improve on a common instructional concern (see Calhoun, 2002).

As Richard Sagor (1993) writes: "By turning to *collaborative* action research . . . we can renew our commitment to thoughtful teaching and also begin developing an active community of professionals" (p. 10). Action research implies that the practitioners are the researchers. The objectivity and rigor of research methodology can be questioned by classical researchers, but the benefits of the process for students and teachers seem to outweigh the loss of experimental purity.

In addressing the power of teacher-led research, Hubbard and Power (1993, p. xiii) write: "Teachers throughout the world are developing professionally by becoming teacher–researchers, a wonderful new breed of artists-in-residence.

table 19.1 **Comparison of Traditional Research and Action Research**

	Traditional Research	Action Research
Usually led by	Outside expert	Practitioners
Purpose	Develop new knowledge	Solve practical problem; improve practice
Types of data gathered	Quantitative or qualitative	Quantitative or qualitative
Purpose of gathering and analyzing data	Gain better understanding of phenomenon; develop or test hypotheses	Explore practical problem; guide action planning; evaluate results
Standard for quality research	Peer review of methods and results	Research results in desired change
Primary audience(s)	Other researchers, the profession, government or private agencies	Members of the school community

Using our own classrooms as laboratories and our students as collaborators, we are changing the way we work with students as we look at our classrooms systematically through research." Table 19.1 compares traditional research with action research.

How Is Action Research Conducted?

In the first phase of action research, a focus area is selected—an area of teaching and learning in need of improvement. Second, a needs assessment gathers data on the focus area. The purposes of data gathering at this stage are to understand the problem and how it might be solved and to gather baseline data to help with the evaluation of improvement efforts. The third phase of action research is to design an action plan for solving the problem. The plan includes activities for evaluating the success of improvement efforts. The fourth phase is the implementation of the plan. The fifth phase of action research is the evaluation: data on the action plan's effects are gathered and analyzed. Based on the evaluation, action plan objectives and activities may be continued, expanded, revised, or discontinued.

If these five phases sound suspiciously similar to the development of action plans with individual teachers in Chapter 15 (direct assistance), you have won the first round of the supervision concentration game. The aim of direct assistance to teachers is to promote increased thought, choice, and responsibility in individual teachers, and this can be done through cycles of classroom action research. The supervisor's role is to determine what type of assistance the individual teacher needs (directive informational, collaborative, or nondirective), depending on the developmental levels of the teacher with respect to the particular topic. Figure 19.1 depicts the five phases of action research.

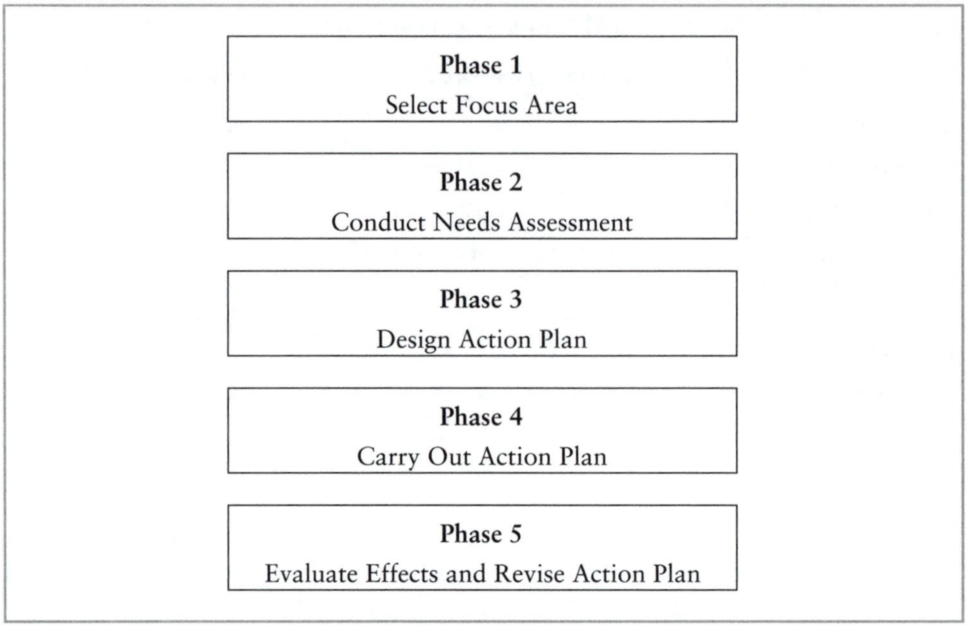

figure 19.1 **Five Phases of Action Research**

A Developmental Approach to Action Research

The developmental model we discuss throughout this text can be applied to action research. Of the four supervisory approaches discussed in Part 3, the directive informational, collaborative, and nondirective approaches are appropriate for supervising action research. Because teacher action research involves teachers making their own decisions about inquiry and instructional improvement, controlling directive supervision is inappropriate for such research.

Teachers of *very* low levels of development, expertise, and commitment are probably not ready to engage in action research. They must receive intensive direct assistance and staff development to help them develop the minimal decision-making capacity and motivation necessary for successful action research. They might be asked to read and discuss articles about action research, shadow a teacher or group engaged in research, or attend a workshop to develop action research skills. For teachers of *fairly* low levels of development, expertise, and commitment, the supervisor can use directive informational supervision while suggesting alternative goals, data-collection and analysis methods, and action plans and then asking teachers to choose from the alternatives. Because this type of action research involves limited teacher decision making, the supervisor may wish to move toward collaborative action research as soon as teachers are ready to assume more decision-making responsibility (McBee, 2004).

The supervisor can engage in collaborative action research with teachers of moderate or mixed levels of development, expertise, and commitment. In this approach, the supervisor engages in joint decision making with teachers during the goal identification, action planning, implementation, evaluation, and revision phases of action research.

The ultimate goal is for teachers to reach levels of development, expertise, and commitment that allow teacher-driven research, in which the supervisor uses nondirective supervision to facilitate teacher decision making during each of the five phases of action research. Houser (1990) describes full-fledged *teacher–researchers*: "They initiate every aspect of the research project. They are responsible for formulating the questions, selecting the (research) tools, and collecting, analyzing, and interpreting the data" (p. 58).

Action Research: Vehicle for a Cause beyond Oneself

Previously, each technical task of supervision (direct assistance, group development, professional development, and curriculum development) was discussed separately. In reality, any effort to improve instruction must relate each task to the others. It is time to soften the boundaries between the tasks and show how action research can be the vehicle for their integration.

Action research is focused on the need to improve instruction, as perceived by the faculty. As instructional improvements are identified, faculty and supervisor plan related activities to be implemented in each of the technical tasks of supervision (Figure 19.2).

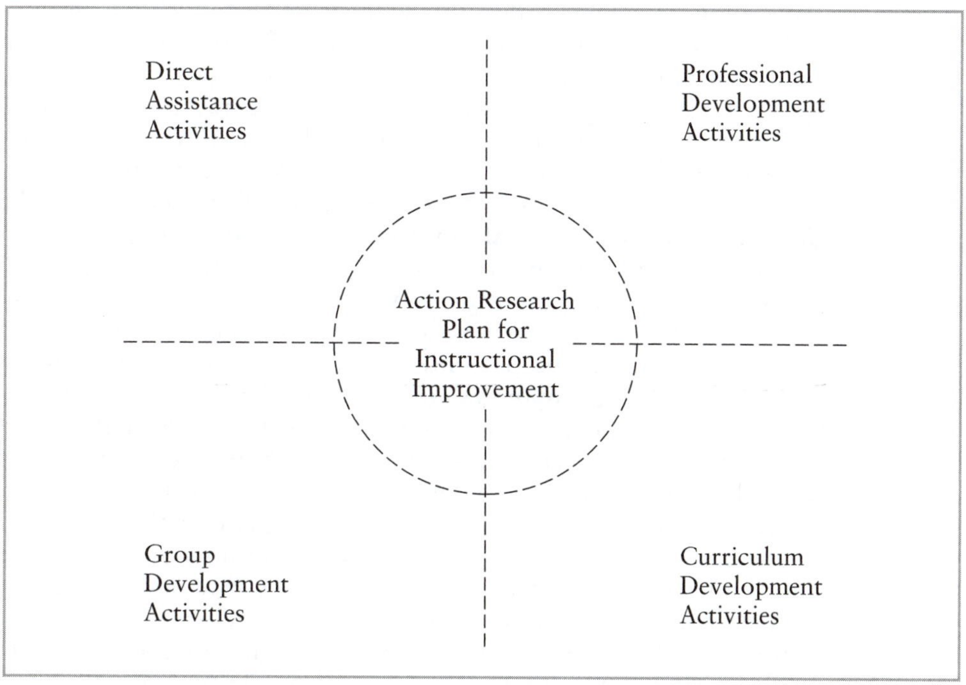

figure **19.2** **Action Research as the Core of Related Supervisory Activities**

Think of action research as a huge meteor falling into the middle of the supervision ocean. As it hits, it causes a rippling of water that activates the four seas of direct assistance, professional development, curriculum development, and group development. The rippling of water continues to increase in force until a giant wave gathers and crashes onto all instructional shores, sweeping away the old sand of past instructional failures and replacing it with the new sand of instructional improvement. Stepping away from the beach, let's look at example of action research related to supervisory activities.

Example of Action Research

Matthews Elementary School is located in the heart of Austin, Texas, and serves students from 32 different cultures. The student population includes children from the local Salvation Army shelter and city children's center. Matthews also serves the children of an international community of professors and graduate students from a nearby university. Approximately 50 percent of the students are classified as "at risk." The goal of action research at Matthews was to improve the school's balanced reading program. Needs assessment data included student results on two reading tests, indicating that a large number of students were reading below grade level. Data on teacher perceptions of the reading program were gathered through surveys and interviews. Based on the needs assessment, the action plan called for acquisition of additional resources for the reading program, professional development for teachers, and more effective monitoring of the program.

In the first component of the action plan teachers participated in discussion groups to identify needed resources. In response to these meetings, new nonfiction and fiction books, electronic books, and a variety of new instructional materials were added to the program. The professional development component included monthly meetings of support groups in which teachers learned new strategies, discussed concerns, and shared ideas. Balanced reading also was discussed at general faculty and vertical team meetings. A supervisor served as a mentor for new teachers, providing them assistance as they implemented balanced reading. Two literacy specialists served as support persons to all teachers, leading support groups, teaching demonstration lessons, and visiting classrooms. Teachers visited other schools to observe balanced reading lessons, participated in district workshops on balanced reading, and attended national reading conferences. The last component of the action plan was improved monitoring of the reading program. This included supervisors and reading specialists observing classrooms to determine if balanced reading was being implemented effectively and also to make sure that teachers were receiving the resources and support they needed. Teachers played a major role in monitoring. They assessed student progress daily by analyzing student work samples, keeping anecdotal records, and listening to students' oral reading. In addition, teachers used a standardized reading assessment to measure students' reading levels in September, January, and May.

Year-end evaluation of the action research included teacher surveys and interviews as well as pre–post comparisons of student reading levels. Teachers reported a high commitment to balanced reading, understanding of the reading program, and confidence in their ability to implement the program. The teachers stated that they now had adequate materials to implement balanced reading and that strategies they learned through professional development enabled them to understand strengths and needs of students and to individualize student learning. Analysis of student achievement data supported teacher perceptions. Over the schoolyear, there were increases in the percentage of students—including the percentage of economically disadvantaged students—reading on or above grade level. By the end of the school year, 85 percent of all students were reading on or above grade level.

Expanding Boundaries: Alternative Approaches to Action Research

The approach to action research emphasized in this book, as well as in most schools that use action research, is a problem-solving approach. A problem is identified, needs assessment data are gathered to find out more about the problem, an action plan is designed to solve the problem, the plan is implemented, and evaluation data are gathered to determine what progress was made and what revisions in the action plan might be needed. However, there are alternative approaches to action research that schools may wish to consider. These alternatives include interpretive and critical action research.

Interpretive Action Research

Teachers doing interpretive research are attempting to understand phenomena in schools and the meaning that participants make of those phenomena. Examples of phenomena that might be studied include a school's culture, classroom implementation of a new curriculum, and interactions between teachers and students during classroom discussions of controversial issues.

For a more detailed example, let us say a group of teachers decided to carry out an interpretive study on the use of a new inquiry-based science program. Research questions might include the following:

1. What does the teacher experience during inquiry learning?
2. What does the student experience during inquiry learning?
3. How does the teacher describe learning that results from inquiry learning?
4. How does the student describe learning that results from inquiry learning?

To gather data on these questions, interpretive researchers might observe inquiry lessons and take extensive field notes on class activities, interactions between teachers and students and among students, and so on. In addition, the teacher–researchers might conduct interviews with teachers and students on their experiences with inquiry learning and their interpretation of learning resulting from inquiry lessons. The researchers probably would find that different participants experience the same learning activities differently and construct different interpretations of inquiry learning. Through dialogue on alternative perspectives and interpretations identified in the action research, teachers can gain a more holistic understanding of the phenomena being studied. The dialogue and increased understanding that results can be the foundation for improved practice. For instance, based on the results of their interpretive research, teachers in our inquiry-learning example might modify the way they present science problems to students.

Critical Action Research

Critical research examines and challenges established, taken-for-granted ways of doing things that support inequity, with an eye toward changing practice to increase equity. In particular, critical research examines power relations that lead to inequity. External social, economic, and political forces that cause inequity also are examined, and ways to overcome those forces' negative effects are considered. An important process used by critical researchers is *praxis,* which denotes an interactive cycle of practice and theory building. In critical action research, praxis takes the form of an ongoing cycle of action and reflection aimed at emancipating groups and individuals from inequitable treatment.

Teachers engaged in critical action research on a high school's tracking system could begin the research by formulating a set of critical questions such as the following:

- Whose interests are served by the existence of the tracking system?
- What cultural values are reinforced by the tracking system? What cultural values are delegitimized?
- What power relations are present in the current tracking system?
- How does the tracking system reflect socioeconomic realities in the community that the school serves?
- How does the tracking system reflect ethnic and racial issues present in society?
- Who decides which students are placed in the various tracks?
- Who is placed at an advantage by the tracking system? Who is placed at a disadvantage?

Teachers who are engaged in critical action research find answers to these questions through repeated cycles of data gathering and dialogue on the meaning of the data. Eventually, the researchers begin to focus on a series of questions about changing the system to increase equity:

- How can we include parents and students in decisions about how best to meet student learning needs?
- How can the diverse learning needs of students be met in an emancipatory way?
- What ways of grouping students will benefit the least advantaged students?
- How can student grouping promote democracy and social justice?
- How can the growth and development of all students be placed in the center of the decision-making process at this school?

Again, teachers would go about finding answers to these questions through repeated cycles of data gathering and dialogue. In time, teachers and other members of the school community would use research results as the basis for changes in decision making, student grouping, curriculum, and instruction. The test for the effectiveness of critical action research is whether equity has been increased in a meaningful way.

Shared Governance for Action Research

A shortcoming of earlier studies of school improvement and action research has been the lack of descriptions of how individual schools or districts went about the process of change (Fullan, 1985, p. 398). Achieving "a cause beyond oneself" in pursuing collaborative and collective instructional goals for students sounds admirable, but how does a supervisor initiate and sustain such efforts?

What follows is one explanation using case studies from the public schools that are part of the League of Professional Schools (Glickman, 1992). The model of shared governance and schoolwide instructional change has been adapted and used in elementary, middle, and secondary schools in Georgia, South Carolina, Vermont, Michigan, and the United States Department of Defense Dependent Schools in Europe.

Premises

Three declarative premises underlie shared governance:

1. Every professional in the school who so desires can be involved in making decisions about schoolwide instructional improvements.
2. Any professional in the school who does not desire to is not obligated to be involved in making decisions about schoolwide instructional improvements.
3. Once a decision is made about schoolwide instructional improvements, all staff must implement the decision.

Thus, an individual can choose to be or not to be part of the decision-making process. However, once decisions are made, all individuals must implement the agreed-on actions.

Principles

The principles in operating shared governance for instructional improvement are as follow:

1. *One person, one vote.* Each representative has the same rights, responsibilities, and equal vote as any other representative. Each teacher who sits on the representative schoolwide council has the same vote as the school principal or any other administrator or formal supervisor.
2. *Limit decisions to schoolwide instruction within the control and sphere of responsibility of the school.* Action research and shared governance involves the core of a school's existence: curriculum and instruction, or teaching and learning. Areas for decision making should be schoolwide and instructional. Issues of day-to-day administration, contracts, school board policies, other schools, and personnel are not the concerns of shared governance for schoolwide action research. The scope of concerns for deliberations, decisions, and actions is always grounded in the question: What should *we* be doing *here* with *our* school to improve learning for *our* students?
3. *Authentic feedback necessitates small groups.* Large meetings result in input from the most confident, the loudest, and the most powerful persons—who are not necessarily the wisest, most insightful, or most interested persons. A true forum for intellectual discourse is a small group (ideally, 7 to 11 members); so, shared governance in large schools must operate in small groups.

Operational Model

The work of Schmuck, Runkel, Arends, and Arends (1977) provides the basis for an operational model for shared governance, action research, and school improvement that uses the premises of individual choice of involvement and implementation by all and the principles of one-person, one-vote; focus on teaching; and small groups. The model discussed here is a compilation of various models used by schools in the League of Professional Schools (see Glickman, 1992; Allen and Glickman, 1992). Many schools use comparable models of operation and have their own specific versions. The goal is not to advocate a particular model of shared governance, but rather to achieve the premises and principles of shared governance and action research, leading to a purposeful, collective, and thoughtful school—a school that is the center of inquiry.

The Formal Groups. Shared governance in this model involves three groups (Figure 19.3). The *executive council* is a 7- to 11-member body, consisting of a majority of

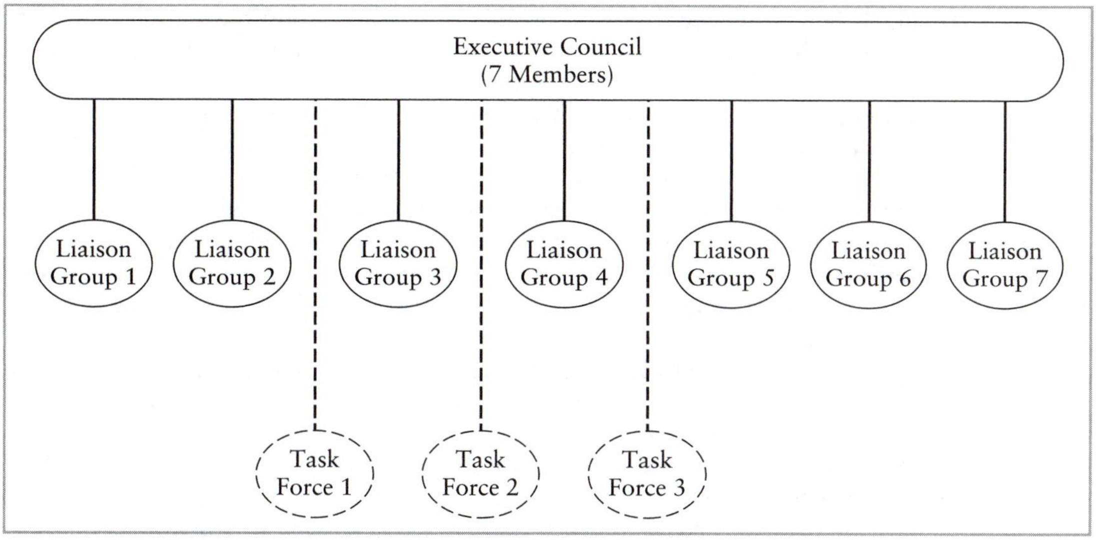

figure 19.3 **Action Research as the Core of Related Supervisory Activities**

teachers with administrators. Parent and student representatives can serve as well. Teachers could be democratically chosen from liaison groups (described in the following paragraph) or from among grade-level heads, team leaders, department heads, and union representatives. They could be elected at large from the faculty, or some combination of election and appointment could be used. They hold a term of at least three years and move off the council at staggered times. Teachers serve as chairperson and co-chairperson of the executive council. The principal is a member of the committee with the same rights and responsibilities as any other member. The executive council's responsibility is solely for acting on and monitoring schoolwide instructional improvement recommendations. *The council does not make recommendations;* it is an approving board. Recommendations must come from task force groups within the school. The executive council does not involve itself in administrative matters, school board policies, personnel matters, or issues that are departmental in nature. It acts on instructional improvement recommendations that the faculty has the legal power to carry out. This differentiation between instructional and administrative responsibilities helps avoid problems that can arise from delving into matters beyond the school's own control.

Liaison groups are formal groups set up as communication links between the faculty and executive council concerning needs, reactions, opinions, and ideas about schoolwide instruction. For example, in the case of a school with 50 teachers, there could be 7 liaison groups consisting of approximately 7 faculty members each. An alphabetized list of all faculty names is gathered and each person is assigned a number from 1 to 7. All 1s go to liaison group 1, all 2s go to liaison group 2, and so forth. This assignment procedure ensures that members in each liaison group come from various departments and grade levels. Each liaison group is a microcosm of the entire school. Each group elects a representative to the council. The executive council member can (1) call the liaison group together from time to time for a brief meeting to review a specific recommendation under executive council consideration, (2) gather written opinions about a particular proposal, or (3) simply drop by and talk to the various liaison group members.

Task forces are the last type of group shown in Figure 19.3. These ad hoc task groups of volunteers are formed after the executive council has solicited feedback from all the liaison groups about perceived schoolwide instructional needs and reviewed any existing data on schoolwide instruction. The executive council then targets priority instructional areas for the next one to three years. Schoolwide priorities might be such matters as increasing instructional time, coordinating curriculum, improving student attitudes, teaching higher-order thinking, increasing student success rates, improving school discipline, improving school and classroom climate, improving the quality of feedback to students, or improving test scores.

Once the needs for improvement have been selected by the executive council, ad hoc task force groups are formed by recruiting volunteers who have an interest in and a commitment to the particular topic. At least one executive council member serves on each task force, but this person usually does not serve as chair of the task force. The task force volunteers meet, review their task, select their own chairperson, schedule meetings, and set a time line for making a final recommendation for schoolwide action to the executive council. Depending on the topic, one task force might meet three times over three weeks to make a recommendation, whereas another task force might meet every other week for five months before making a recommendation.

Decision-Making Procedures. When the task force is ready to make a recommendation, it makes its report in three parts: (1) goals and objectives, (2) action plan (What will be done, by whoms, and when?), and (3) evaluation (How will the success of actions be known?). The executive council discusses the recommendations and either makes an immediate decision to approve (most councils use a consensus vote to approve a first-time recommendation) or, without the required vote, tables the recommendation until the next meeting. During the interim, the executive council members can discuss the recommendation and check with their respective liaison groups to gather input from the entire faculty. At the next meeting, a second vote can be taken. (Most councils use a two-thirds vote to approve a tabled recommendation.) By the second vote, the council will have a good sense of total faculty receptivity and the chances of successful implementation. Some issues are deemed so important by the council that the final decision is made by going back to the entire faculty, parents, and students.

Implementation. After a decision has been made, the executive council (with the task force) announces the approved plan to the school. The task force then disbands, and the executive council implements the plan. It becomes the responsibility of the executive council (including the principal) to enforce the schoolwide decisions and to oversee action research that monitors and evaluates the results.

Suggestions for Assisting Action Research

Our work with schools using action research leads to additional suggestions for increasing the quality of teacher research. First, it is important that teachers receive basic preparation in gathering and analyzing data. Here we are not talking about making every teacher an expert in research design and statistical analysis. Rather, teachers should be introduced to a variety of simple data-gathering methods, both quantitative and qualitative. Also, teachers must learn simple methods for reviewing and summarizing data and drawing data-based conclusions.

Second, to ensure that no teachers or students are placed at academic, social, or emotional risk, the school governance body should establish a set of ethical guidelines for action research, along with a process for reviewing research proposals to make sure they comply with the guidelines.

Third, resources must be provided for action research teams. The most important resource needed by teacher-researchers is *time* to plan action research, gather and analyze data, and implement action plans.

Finally, teachers should be provided opportunities to share action research with the school community, and even with teachers from other schools. Sharing action research gives recognition to the teacher–researchers, serves as a basis for reflective dialogue among teachers, and provides other teachers with ideas for improving instruction in their own classrooms and schools.

Conclusion: Focus, Structure, and Time for Development

Supervision provides a focus, structure, and time for teachers to be engaged in dialogue, debate, research, decisions, and actions about instruction. Without focus, teachers will not discuss teaching, because it has not been an accepted norm for discussion in most schools. Without structure, there are no clear apparatuses, procedures, and rules for how decisions are made and implemented. Without time, there is no functional or symbolic expression that teachers have the capacity to make collective and wise instructional decisions on behalf of students.

MyEdLeadershipLab™

Go to Topic 9, Action Research/Database Decision making, in the MyEdLeadershipLab™ site at www.myedleadershiplab.com for *The Basic Guide to SuperVision and Instructional Leadership*, Third Edition, where you can:

- Find learning outcomes for Action Research/Database Decision making along with the national standards that connect to these outcomes.
- Complete Assignments and Activities that can help you more deeply understand the chapter content.
- Apply and practice your understanding of the core skills identified in the chapter with the Building Leadership Skills unit.
- Prepare yourself for professional certification with a Practice for Certification quiz.

REFERENCES

Allen, L., and Glickman, C. D. 1992. School improvement: The elusive faces of shared governance. *NASSP Bulletin, 76*(542), 80–87.

Calhoun, E. F. 2002. Action research for school improvement. *Educational Leadership, 59*(6), 18–24.

Corey, S. M. 1953. *Action research to improve school practices.* New York: Teachers College, Columbia University.

Fullan, M. 1985. Change processes and strategies at the local level. *Elementary School Journal, 85*(3), 391–421.

Glickman, C. D. 1992. The essence of school renewal: The prose has begun. *Educational Leadership, 50*(1), 24–27.

Houser, N. O. 1990. Teacher–researcher: The synthesis of roles for teacher empowerment. *Action in Teacher Education, 12*(2), 55–60.

Hubbard, R. S., and Power, B. M. 1993. *The art of classroom inquiry: A handbook for teacher–researchers.* Portsmouth, NH: Heinemann.

Lewin, K. 1948. *Resolving social conflicts.* New York: Harper and Brothers.

McBee, M. T. 2004. The classroom as laboratory: An exploration of teacher research. *Roeper Review, 27*(1), 52–58.

Sagor, R. 1993. *How to conduct collaborative action research.* Alexandria, VA: Association for Supervision and Curriculum Development.

Schaefer, R. 1967. *The school as the center of inquiry.* New York: Harper and Row.

Schmuck, R. A., Runkel, P., Arends, J. H., and Arends, R. I. 1977. *The second handbook of organizational development in schools.* Palo Alto, CA: Mayfield.

part 6

Cultural Tasks of SuperVision

The chapters in Part 6 address cultural tasks of supervision that both transcend and utilize the technical tasks. Chapter 20 explores Education Change Theory, describes school cultures of continuous improvement, examines change at the individual level, and argues that we must change the conditions of teaching. Chapter 21 discusses achievement gaps among diverse groups, societal problems and cultural clashes that cause inequity, and how culturally responsive schools and teaching can increase equity for diverse socioeconomic, racial, and ethnic groups; females; and sexual minorities. Finally, Chapter 22 compares schools as organizations to schools as communities, describes attributes of authentic school communities, and urges schools to engage with the communities they serve.

chapter 20

Facilitating Change

outline

- Education Change Theory
- Change at the Individual Level
- Changing the Conditions of Teaching

Visit the **MyEdLeadershipLab™** site for *The Basic Guide to SuperVision and Instructional Leadership*, Third Edition to enhance your understanding of chapter concepts. You'll have the opportunity to practice your skills through video and case based Assignments and Activities as well as Building Leadership Skills units, and prepare for your certification exam with Practice for Certification quizzes.

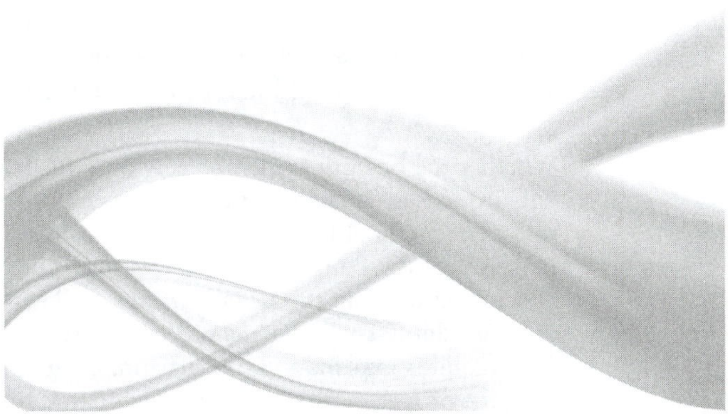

> *The imagery of educational reform says more about hope and good intentions than it does about anything else. That the road to hell is indeed paved with good intentions is an adage quite appropriate to the history of educational reform.*
>
> (Sarason, 1990, p. 129)

The need for educational change is as apparent as the fact that our world is continuously changing—changing at an ever-increasing rate. Changes in U.S. demographics, culture, environment, science, technology, and economy mean that our schools must change if they are to prepare students to be successful and contributing members of society and if society is going to offer all of its citizens life, liberty, and the pursuit of happiness.

Unfortunately, most efforts at school change fail to improve schools or student learning, and many make things worse. Why do we continue to experience what Sarason (1990) calls "the predictable failure of educational reform"? Sarason argues that one reason is that those attempting to bring about change (including those inside and outside schools) have only a superficial understanding of school culture, including the power relationships within that culture. Fullan (1997) believes that the complexity of educational change is a big part of its difficulty:

> Take any educational policy or problem and start listing all of the forces that could figure in the solution and that would need to be influenced to make for productive change. Then, take the idea that unplanned factors are inevitable—government policy changes or gets constantly redefined. Key leaders leave, important contact people are shifted to another role, new technology is invented, immigration increases, recession reduces available resources, and a bitter conflict erupts, and so on. Finally, realize that every new variable that enters the equation—those unpredictable but inevitable noise factors—produce ten other ramifications, which in turn produce tens of other reactions and on and on. (p. 33)

Evans (1996) proposes that the traditional model used for most change efforts in schools, the *rational–structural model,* is the reason that most change efforts fail. This model assumes that the organization and surrounding environment are stable and predictable and that planning for change is a rational, objective, and linear process that leads to a detailed blueprint for change. As described by Evans:

> Whether the blueprint calls for new outputs or for greater efficiency in current outputs it focuses on changes in the organization's structure and in its tasks, roles, and rules. The methodology for innovation is almost entirely top-down in nature, a combination of dissemination and pressure. There may be much lip service paid to "participation," but this usually means getting people to "go along," to have a "sense of ownership." The implementation goal is to have staff adopt the expert plan as is. This requires explanation, persuasion, training, and incentives; if these fail to produce the proper results, it requires mandates, requirements, and policies. (p. 8)

Evans argues that change efforts based on the rational–structural model have a high failure rate. Typically, Evans notes, teachers are blamed for the failure, when in fact the designers and the change model they use are responsible. Repeated failures at change can severely reduce a school's capacity for change in the future. Again, according to Evans:

> Most attempts at collective change in education seem to fail, and failure means frustration, wasted time, feelings of incompetence and lack of support, and disillusionment. . . . The more that teachers or others have had negative experiences with previous implementation attempts in the district or elsewhere, the more cynical or apathetic they will be about the next change presented regardless of the merit of the new idea or proposal. (pp. 73–74)

Repeated failures can create a reflexive resistance to change, with teachers and others sabotaging new change efforts in their early stages.

Given the facts that (1) schools must change if they are going to meet the needs of today's students and society and (2) most change efforts fail, what are we to do? Change experts have been urging us for years to consider alternative theories on change that go beyond the rational–structural approach. Sarason (1990) warns, "If you start by accepting the present structure, if you insist that those who seek to change it must guarantee ahead of time that it will work, you guarantee one thing: nothing will change" (p. 173). Fullan (1997) argues, "There are fundamental reasons why controlling strategies don't work. . . . The solution lies in better ways of thinking about, and dealing with, inherently unpredictable processes" (p. 33).

Education Change Theory

Over the last several years, a growing body of new theory on school change has emerged in the educational literature (examples include Evans, 1996; Fullan, 1997, 2002, 2003, 2005, 2007; Hargreaves, Lieberman, Fullan, and Hopkins, 1998; Senge et al., 2000; Zmuda, Kuklis, and Kline, 2004; Hall and Hord, 2006; Bain, 2007; Gordon, 2008). Much of this recent theory is based on the study of actual efforts at school change. As one might expect, the experts who present theories on school change do not agree completely, but they do agree in large part on key concepts. We present several of those concepts in the following sections. As you review them, note how different this emergent change theory is from traditional theories on how to change schools.

Capacity

Many schools lack the capacity to initiate significant improvement efforts with a reasonable chance of success. Poor communication, low trust levels, and the absence of collaboration are all typical reasons cited for low readiness. All of these problems are part of the school's *culture,* which is a complex system of relationships, norms, practices, beliefs, and assumptions.

A good first step toward improving a school's capacity for change is for members of the school community to study and critique their own school culture. What are the school's common instructional practices? What beliefs, values, and assumptions underlie these practices? How do these practices affect teachers and students?

Another focus for self-study is how past or current change efforts have interacted with various aspects of the school's culture. Determining this helps educators understand just how complex school change is. As Stiegelbauer (2008) notes, "Change in practice requires change in behaviors, skills, attitudes, beliefs, and, frequently, ways that people work with one another. Each of these is a kind of innovation in itself and a reason that change is always complex" (p. 122). Boyd (1992) argues that any significant change affects the entire school:

> A school is a complex organism. It is not just a building with people inside. To change schools it is necessary to consider the effects of change on all parts of the organism. Each part is dependent upon the other parts and all parts react to changes in any other part. (p. 1)

The complexity of change described by Stiegelbauer and Boyd can be best understood by teachers when they engage in reflective inquiry and dialogue on the interactive effects of change and culture in their own school.

Beyond developing a better understanding of the complexities of school culture and change efforts, a school can increase its capacity for change in a number of ways. One critical process is trust building. Allen and Glickman (1998) remind us that "trust is built by actions, not words" (p. 514). Teachers trust supervisors when they are allowed to share in decision making about change, when their opinions are respected, when the commitments made to them are consistently kept, and when they are supported during the change process. Supervisors trust teachers "when they observe that, given adequate information and opportunities to interact with each other, teachers are capable of making decisions that reflect a school wide perspective and concern for all children" (Allen and Glickman, 1998, p. 514).

Another way to develop readiness is to create opportunities for regular dialogue across the school community. Gordon, Stiegelbauer, and Diehl (2008) found that schools with a high capacity for change provided for cycles of small-group and whole-school dialogue. At the small-group level, dialogue took place in a variety of groups: leadership, grade level, content area, task force, and so on. At the whole-school level, dialogue involved small groups reporting to the large group and the large group holding general discussions of how information and ideas shared by small groups could be integrated within the schoolwide change effort. Bain (2007) recommends that schools establish communication networks:

> Networks make collaboration possible. They disperse control in self-organizing schools because they permit the ready flow of feedback to all levels in the school. . . .

> [In different areas of the network,] teachers work together in teaching and learning teams, instead of working alone. Teams are employed to capture the potential of small-world relationships by making it possible for individual teachers to engage in constant formal and informal professional communication." (p. 55)

Traditional change models call for the organization to develop a vision before proceeding with change. However, Fullan (1997) argues that, although a shared vision is necessary for success, the vision should not be established prior to initiating change. "Vision emerges from, more than it precedes, action" (p. 42). Fullan's rationale for this statement is that a truly *shared vision* must emerge from the joint work of leaders and teachers over time as they engage in the change process. Fullan also argues that, because of the complexity of schools and change, even after a school vision has emerged, it must be redefined over time to evolve with changing conditions.

An alternative to creating a vision prior to initiating change is for the school community to develop a broad set of principles that direct the change process. Some examples of agreed-on principles include the following:

- Change is the result of collaborative efforts among leaders, teachers, and representatives of the community that the school serves.
- Change is informed by both external research and by data gathered within the school and community.
- Change takes place within a framework of democratic governance.
- Change efforts consider the diversity among students and adults in the school community.
- Change efforts consider the need to reduce the achievement gap between different student groups.

Of course, each school must develop its own set of change principles, and consensus even on broad principles like those just listed require considerable study, reflection, and dialogue. Once principles are agreed on, however, they should be embedded deeply in future change efforts.

Studying the school's culture and the change process, building trust, engaging in dialogue, and establishing change principles all can help the school develop a capacity for *initiating* change. Developing that capacity, however, is only the beginning of the change process.

Commitment

How do teachers develop a commitment to change? On the one hand, merely mandating change does not work. On the other hand, one cannot expect teachers to take ownership of change at the beginning of the change process—before they have worked with the change over time, before they understand all of the implications of the change, and before the change has shown positive effects (Fullan, 2007). Nolan

(2007) suggests that one way to build commitment for change is to ask teachers to "interrogate the status quo":

> Questioning concerning why we do things the way we do and how effective those strategies are should be the starting point. Action research and data-driven decision-making can be powerful tools for raising questions about the status quo and examining the efficiency of current policies and procedures. (p. 6)

Evans (1996) agrees with Nolan, noting that "to even begin to be open to change, people must first be unhappy with the status quo in some way and must then find the change relevant to their concerns" (p. 80).

Fullan (2005) believes that engaging teachers' moral purpose is a pathway to commitment: "In education, moral purpose involves committing to raise the bar and close the gap in student achievement—for example, increasing literacy for all, with special attention to those most disadvantaged" (p. 54). Nolan (2007) advises, "Do not ask teachers to commit themselves to innovations per se; rather focus on the potential impact that the initiative will have on their students" (p. 5).

Although teachers cannot know in advance how an innovation will play out or whether it will be successful, they can be helped to know as much about the innovation as possible, including the theory underlying it, the responsibilities they will assume if they commit to it, and the potential advantages it offers to students. Finally, if teachers are going to commit to change, they must be shown that the change is *feasible*. According to Evans (1996):

> Teachers must not only want to implement a change, they must feel that they can achieve it. They need to see change not only as appropriate for students and as promising better learning but also as something practical that they and their school can manage. (p. 85)

The path to commitment includes many of the same processes as capacity building: inquiry, reflection, and dialogue. On the path to commitment, those processes are used to better understand the proposed change and to decide whether it is in the best interest of the school community.

Leadership

In matters of school change, traditional top-down leadership is a recipe for failure. "Leadership, to be effective, must spread throughout the organization" (Fullan, 2005, p. 57). One way to begin the distribution of leadership for change is to appoint a core leadership team with a majority of team members being teachers. This team can coordinate the change effort, and members can serve as liaisons to other teachers (Gordon, Stiegelbauer, and Diehl, 2008). Over time, other teachers throughout the school can assume various leadership roles in the change effort. Teachers can be leaders of action research teams, study groups, curriculum development teams, instructional support teams, community relations teams, and so on, with all of these leadership roles related to the change effort.

Successful change leaders continuously search for teachers who are ready to provide leadership in order to assign those teachers leadership roles (Gordon, Stiegelbauer, and Diehl, 2008). Allen and Glickman (1998) report that the school leaders they worked with in change efforts "came to realize that the heart of the decision-making process was not the leadership team, but the quality of involvement of everyone in the decision-making process" (p. 519). In the successful schools that Allen and Glickman studied,

> Leadership team members stopped defining themselves as decision makers and became coordinators of the involvement of all. . . . Small groups, formal and ad hoc, gave anyone who wanted the opportunity to participate in defining the issues, structuring courses of actions, and monitoring the effects of actions. (p. 520)

Evolutionary Planning

Fullan's (1997) admonition that change is a journey, not a blueprint, applies here. Significant change is a *long* journey along a winding, uneven path, with inevitable but unpredictable barriers along the way. The complexity of schools and nonlinear nature of change calls for planning that is continuously evolving. The essential component of evolutionary planning is *feedback*—feedback on how well the innovation is understood, how many are participating in the change process, the level of implementation, its effects on students, and so on. Ongoing data gathering, reflection, and dialogue all are critical here, as supervisors and teachers collaborate to make informed decisions during each phase of the change journey.

Although evolutionary planning requires a great deal of collaboration, it also requires individual teachers to make a steady stream of decisions on how to apply the innovation at the classroom level. Individual teachers must work out what schoolwide change means to them and their students (Fullan, 2007); they must integrate innovations with their own practices, beliefs, and teaching styles. Teachers must also gather data on the effects of the innovation on their students, reflect on that data, and make appropriate modifications to the innovation. Supervisors, in turn, must be flexible and supportive as teachers engage in evolutionary planning at the classroom level. Later in this chapter, we discuss change from the individual teacher's view in more detail.

Problem Solving

Given the complexity and unpredictability of change at the school level, problems will arise. Fullan (1997) tells us that "problems are our friends":

> It seems perverse to say that problems are our friends, but we cannot develop effective responses to complex situations unless we actively seek and confront the

> real problems which are in fact difficult to solve. Problems are our friends because it is only through immersing ourselves in problems that we can come up with creative solutions. Problems are the route to deeper change and deeper satisfaction. In this sense effective organizations "embrace problems" rather than avoid them. (p. 40)

Like problems, conflicts are also necessary to the success of the change process. In fact, supervisors should worry about an absence of conflict, which could signal either apathy about the innovation or opponents working behind the scenes to sabotage the innovation. As we said in Chapter 16, conflict generates information, ideas, and alternatives, all of which lead to better decision making.

Resistance to change typically is viewed as a problem to be overcome; however, Fullan (2002) urges change leaders to "redefine resistance." Resisters sometimes raise important issues, and addressing such issues can improve the innovation.

> The wise change leader will encourage resisters to make their objections public and attend carefully to the potential negatives that are identified. Once deficiencies or unintended negatives have been identified, it is possible to rethink the initiative or to find ways to minimize the potential problems. Using the work of resisters to your advantage can lead to imaginative solutions for overcoming potential problems. (Nolan, 2007, p. 7)

Support

Educational change theory suggests the need for both external and internal support. Networks of schools involved in change efforts, often sponsored by universities, can provide multiple types of external support (Allen and Glickman, 1998; Gordon, 2008). Such support might include the following:

- Regional professional development and planning meetings
- Critical friends from outside the school who provide on-site assistance
- Material resources to which individual schools may not have access
- Assistance with data gathering and data analysis
- Opportunities for schools to share ideas, data, successes, problems, and solutions with each other
- Opportunities for educators with experience and expertise in the change process to mentor less-experienced educators from other schools
- Electronic informational retrieval and networking systems
- Regional conferences where network schools can share their change efforts and results with educators from outside the network

Internal support includes providing all members of the school community with adequate information about the innovation. Educators almost always need resources to bring about change, and in most cases, the most critical resource is time to work on the change. Change efforts go through different phases—initiation, implementation, and continuation—and different types of support are needed during each phase.

The most powerful type of support, according to Stiegelbauer (2008), comes from the learning relationships that develop during the change process: "An implementation process needs models, teachers, coaches, mentors, and evaluators to address all phases. Further, such personnel need to be able to work together positively according to their strengths" (p. 127).

Change theory tells us that support for change must be accompanied by a certain amount of pressure, even when educators are committed to the innovation (Fullan, 2007). Nelson (2008) found that pressure and support best stimulate change when they are applied simultaneously.

Coherence

Two enemies of coherent change are overload and fragmentation. *Overload* means that a school is involved in too many change initiatives. *Fragmentation* means that different change initiatives are disjointed or even at cross purposes (Fullan, 1996). Some obvious ways to move toward coherence are to be selective about the number of change efforts and to make sure that change efforts are consistent. Bain (2007) proposes several strategies for building coherence:

1. *School-level schema.* This is a commonly held body of knowledge, beliefs, and strategies concerning the innovation. It includes all members of the school community being familiar with the underlying theory and research on the innovation, along with development of a common language associated with it. For example, if the innovation was cooperative learning, all teachers would be able to discuss concepts like *positive interdependence, individual accountability,* and *group processing.*
2. *Embedded design.* The design features of the innovation are embedded within each major subsystem of the school organization: professional development, school support systems, curriculum, teaching, assessment, technology, and so on. In our cooperative learning example, professional development is about cooperative learning and uses cooperative learning strategies, the curriculum fosters cooperative learning, student evaluation includes assessment of cooperative skills, and so on.
3. *Similarity of scale.* The school-level schema for the innovation is applied at each level of the organization. For example, just as students use the principles of cooperative learning to solve a problem they were assigned, so teams of teachers use the same principles to solve problems at the grade level or department level, and school leadership teams use these same principles to solve schoolwide problems.

Bain's (2007) strategies, all of which are work intensive and long term, support the suggestion that schools should carefully select a limited number of innovations rather than embrace every interesting innovation that appears on the horizon.

School Cultures of Continuous Improvement

As Stiegelbauer (2008) reminds us, "The broader agenda of change is the development of an organizational capacity to adapt to changing needs and conditions. . . . The goal is not mastery of a single innovation but ongoing learning and the development of collaborative work cultures" (p. 125). Schools that reach the cultural stage that Stiegelbauer refers to have been called different things by different change theorists: "self-renewing schools," "schools that learn," "self-organizing schools," and so on. Whatever we call these schools, we should recognize that they all have developed the capacity to continuously assess themselves in light of changing external and internal conditions, to identify needed change, and to move toward that change. It is not that these schools have reached a state of perfection. To borrow from the language Abraham Maslow used to identify high-performing individuals, they are "self-actualizing" (but never "self-actualized") schools.

A number of change theorists have identified cultural norms held by continuously improving schools (see, for example, Saphier and King, 1985; Mitchell, 1995; Senge et al., 2000; Gordon, Stiegelbauer, and Diehl, 2008). Figure 20.1 provides a composite list of cultural norms for continuous improvement that have been agreed on by many change theorists.

Change at the Individual Level

The previous section focused on the relationship of school culture and change. Although school culture is critical, we must not forget that it is made up, first and foremost, of individuals. As Hall and Hord (2006) point out, "An entire organization does not change until each member has changed" (p. 7). Moreover, individuals do not all change over the same period of time. Again quoting Hall and Hord, "Even when the change is introduced to every member of the organization at the same time, the rate of making the change and of developing skill and competence in using it will vary individually" (p. 7). In short, teachers and others need individualized assistance with schoolwide change. Hall and Hord (2006) extended Fuller's (1969) work on stages of concern and identified seven stages (0–6) of concern about the innovation. Figure 20.2 describes the seven stages.

Individuals may have concerns at several stages at any given time, but their most intense concerns often are at a particular stage. The stages of concern are developmental, moving from stage 0 (lowest stage) to stage 6 (highest stage). Individuals must have their intense concerns at a particular stage met before they can concentrate on the next highest stage. Hall and Hord (2006) describe three

1. *Distributed, supportive leadership:* The leader involves the entire school community in decision making, promotes teacher leadership, provides direct support, and coordinates external and peer support. Different types of support are provided during different phases of the change process.
2. *Professional dialogue:* Communication is open and honest, information is shared, sensitive issues are raised when necessary, and attempts are made to understand others' points of view.
3. *Trust and confidence:* Individuals keep their commitments and trust others to do the same. Individuals show professional respect for each other. Trust building and mutual respect lead to confidence in oneself and others.
4. *Critique:* Current practices, beliefs, values, and assumptions are analyzed critically. Power relationships and imbalances are critiqued. Cultural bias is identified and addressed.
5. *Reflective inquiry:* The external knowledge base is explored. Internal data on the school culture and student learning are gathered, analyzed, and discussed. Cycles of action and reflection are used at the individual, team, and school levels.
6. *Productive conflict:* Conflict is expected, acknowledged, and used to improve the change process. Conflict is resolved through communication, inquiry, and problem-solving processes.
7. *Unity of purpose:* Members of the school community are concerned with all students in the school, not just those they work with. Educators agree on a common focus for change and on principles that will be followed during the change process. Change efforts are coordinated and coherent.
8. *Incremental approach:* The school community "thinks big and starts small." Incremental steps are taken toward long-term goals. Evolutionary planning is used to adapt the change effort to changing conditions. Change is viewed as an ongoing, never-ending process.
9. *Professional development:* A variety of coordinated professional development formats are used to assist the change effort—study groups, skill development, mentoring, peer coaching, institutes, and so on.
10. *Collegiality and collaboration:* Teaching is deprivatized; teachers share strategies, materials, problems, and possible solutions. Teachers observe each other to learn new ways of teaching, gather classroom data, and provide feedback. Collegial groups analyze common problems, plan common solutions, and assess results of improvement efforts. Professional relationships are powerful sources of support for change.
11. *Experimentation and risk taking:* Teachers are open to new ways of teaching, encouraged to experiment with new practices, and supported if experiments do not succeed. Risk taking is encouraged in the classroom and in group efforts to improve the school environment, curriculum, instructional program, and so forth. Teachers are encouraged to engage in new forms of professional development and new leadership roles.
12. *Recognition, sharing, and celebration:* Teachers and others are recognized for participation and success in change efforts. Teachers and groups share their work on change with each other. The school shares its change efforts and results with parents, the community, and outside educators. The school celebrates the change process with special events and ceremonies and establishes new traditions consistent with new practices.

figure 20.1 **Norms Present in School Cultures of Continuous Improvement**

Impact		
6	Refocusing	The focus is on exploration of more universal benefits from the innovation, including the possibility of major changes or replacement with a more powerful alternative. Individual has definite ideas about alternatives to the proposed or existing form of the innovation.
5	Collaboration	The focus is on coordination and cooperation with others regarding use of the innovation.
4	Consequence	Attention focuses on impact of the innovation on students in his or her immediate sphere of influence. The focus is on relevance of the innovation for students, evaluation of student outcomes, including performance and competencies, and changes needed to increase student outcomes.
Task		
3	Management	Attention is focused on the processes and tasks of using the innovation and the best use of information and resources. Issues related to efficiency, organizing, managing, scheduling, and time demands are utmost.
Self		
2	Personal	Individual is uncertain about the demands of the innovation, his or her inadequacy to meet those demands, and his or her role with the innovation. This includes analysis of his or her role in relation to the reward structure of the organization, decision making, and consideration of potential conflicts with existing structures or personal commitment. Financial or status implications of the program for self and colleagues may also be reflected.
1	Informational	A general awareness of the innovation and interest in learning more detail about it is indicated. The person seems to be unworried about himself or herself in relation to the innovation. She or he is interested in substantive aspects of the innovation in a selfless manner such as general characteristics, effects, and requirements for use.
Unrelated		
0	Awareness	Little concern about or involvement with the innovation is indicated.

figure **20.2** **Stages of Concern about the Innovation**

Source: Adapted from G. E. Hall and S. M. Hord (2006). *Implementing Change: Patterns, Principles and Potholes,* p. 140. Boston: Allyn & Bacon.

Stages of Concern		Expressions of Concern
Impact		
6	Refocusing	I have some ideas about something that would work even better.
5	Collaboration	I am concerned about relating what I am doing with what other instructors are doing.
4	Consequence	How is my use affecting kids?
Task		
3	Management	I seem to be spending all my time getting material ready.
Self		
2	Personal	How will using it affect me?
1	Informational	I would like to know more about it.
Unrelated		
0	Awareness	I am not concerned about it (the innovation).

figure 20.3 **Stages of Concern: Typical Expressions of Concern about the Innovation**

Source: Adapted from G. E. Hall and S. M. Hord (2006). *Implementing Change: Patterns, Principles and Potholes*, p. 139. Boston: Allyn & Bacon.

ways supervisors and other change leaders can assess educators' stages of concern about an innovation: (1) informal conversations, (2) an open-ended question asking educators to write about their concerns, and (3) the 35-item Stages of Concern Questionnaire. Figure 20.3 describes expressions voiced at each stage of concern.

Once teachers' stages of concern have been identified, supervisors and other change leaders can assist change by addressing those concerns and fostering teacher development toward higher stages of concern. The innovation has a much greater chance for success once a critical mass of teachers reach the *impact* stages of concern (*consequence*, *collaboration*, and *refocusing*). Teachers with these higher stages of concern are a worthwhile innovation's best friend!

Changing the Conditions of Teaching

Any discussion on change in education would be incomplete if it did not address the conditions of teaching across the nation over the past few years. To say the least, these conditions have not been optimal. All of the research on change now available is of little value if changing the conditions of teaching is not a central goal of both external and internal school improvement efforts:

- Change is needed *away from* treating teachers as technicians expected to transmit curriculum developed by bureaucrats, using canned methods published by commercial interests, and measuring student learning through one-size-fits-all tests mandated by policy makers and *toward* treating teachers as professionals invited to make professional decisions about curriculum, instruction, and student assessment.
- Change is needed *away from* overloading teachers to the extent that they are unable to develop the teacher–student relationships, engage in the reflective planning, and perform the critical self-assessment required for effective teaching and *toward* the manageable class and student load that are prerequisites for quality teaching.
- Change is needed *away from* the physical and psychological isolation caused by outmoded school structures and norms of individualism and *toward* structures and norms that provide opportunities for professional dialogue and collaborative work.
- Change is needed *away from* bureaucratic organizations in which teachers are overwhelmed by regulations and paperwork or—worse yet—mistreated by authoritarian organizations more representative of old-style dictatorships than modern democracies and *toward* democratic school communities in which supervisors promote shared decision making, collegiality, and teacher leadership.
- Change is needed *away from* policies that treat teachers as part of the problem and consider education a low priority in the allocation of resources and *toward* policies that value teachers as part of the solution and provide the human and material resources teachers need to improve schools and provide all students with a quality education.
- Change is needed *away from* teaching as an unstaged career with minimal extrinsic rewards and *toward* teaching as a career in which teachers are properly inducted into the profession and provided new responsibilities, appropriate support, increased recognition, and significantly increased salary at each career stage.
- Change is needed *away from* diversity as a combination of colors and symbols and *toward* a vision of practice that values and honors respect and dignity as well as shared power and decision making.

Early in the twenty-first century, many teachers are facing negative conditions, but there are also efforts to improve the conditions of teaching. Many members of the business community, concerned citizens' groups, and policymakers are working to improve external conditions, and many supervisors have worked from the inside to make schools centers of democracy, inquiry, and dialogue. The door for improving external and internal conditions will never close; it's simply a matter of whether we care to step in and make a difference.

MyEdLeadershipLab™

Go to Topic 10, Facilitating Change, in the MyEdLeadershipLab™ site at www.myedleadershiplab.com for *The Basic Guide to SuperVision and Instructional Leadership*, Third Edition, where you can:

- Find learning outcomes for Facilitating Change along with the national standards that connect to these outcomes.
- Complete Assignments and Activities that can help you more deeply understand the chapter content.
- Apply and practice your understanding of the core skills identified in the chapter with the Building Leadership Skills unit.
- Prepare yourself for professional certification with a Practice for Certification quiz.

REFERENCES

Allen, L., and Glickman, C. D. 1998. Restructuring and renewal. In A. Lieberman, M. Fullan, and D. Hopkins (Eds.), *International handbook of educational change* (pp. 505–528). Dordrecht, The Netherlands: Kluwer Academic.

Bain, A. 2007. *The self-organizing school: Next generation comprehensive school reforms.* Lanham, MD: Rowman and Littlefield Education.

Boyd, V. 1992. *School context: Bridge or barrier to change?* Austin, TX: Southwest Educational Development Lab.

Evans, R. 1996. *The human side of change: Reform, resistance, and the real-life problems of innovation.* San Francisco: Jossey-Bass.

Fullan, M. 1997. The complexity of the change process. In M. Fullan (Ed.), *The challenge of school change.* Arlington Heights, IL: Skylight Professional Development.

Fullan, M. 2002. The change leader. *Educational Leadership, 59*(8), 16–20.

Fullan, M. 2003. *Change forces with a vengeance.* London: Routledge-Falmer.

Fullan, M. 2005. Eight forces for change. *Journal of Staff Development, 26*(4), 54–58, 64.

Fullan, M. 2007. *The new meaning of educational change* (4th ed.). New York: Teachers College Press.

Gordon, S. P. (Ed.). 2008. *Collaborative action research: Developing professional learning communities.* New York: Teachers College Press.

Gordon, S. P., Stiegelbauer, S. M., and Diehl, J. 2008. Characteristics of more and less successful action research programs. In S. P. Gordon (Ed.), *Collaborative action research: Developing professional learning communities* (pp. 79–94). New York: Teachers College Press.

Hall, G. E., and Hord, S. M. 2006. *Implementing change: Patterns, principles, and potholes.* Boston: Allyn & Bacon.

Hargreaves, A., Lieberman, A., Fullan, M., and Hopkins, D. 1998. *International handbook of educational change.* Dordrecht, The Netherlands: Kluwer Academic.

Mitchell, C. E. 1995. *Teachers learning together: Organizational learning in an elementary school.* Unpublished doctoral dissertation, University of Saskatchewan, Saskatoon, Saskatchewan, Canada.

Nelson, S. 2008. Becoming a critical friend. In S. P. Gordon (Ed.), *Collaborative action research: Developing professional learning communities* (pp. 26–45). New York: Teachers College Press.

Nolan, J. F. 2007. Five basic principles to facilitate change in schools. *Catalyst for Change, 35*(1), 3–8.

Saphier, J., and King, M. 1985. Good seeds grow in strong cultures. *Educational Leadership, 42*(6), 67–74.

Sarason, S. B. 1990. *The predictable failure of educational reform.* San Francisco: Jossey-Bass.

Senge, P., Cambron-McCabe, N., Lucas, T., Smith, B., Dutton, J., and Kleiner, A. 2000. *Schools that learn: A fifth discipline field book for educators, parents, and everyone who cares about education.* New York: Doubleday.

Stiegelbauer, S. M. 2008. The dimensions of learning: From plans to action. In S. P. Gordon (Ed.), *Collaborative action research: Developing professional learning communities* (pp. 112–133). New York: Teachers College Press.

Zmuda, A., Kuklis, R., and Kline, E. 2004. *Transforming schools: Creating a culture of continuous improvement.* Alexandria, VA: Association for Supervision and Curriculum Development.

chapter 21

Addressing Diversity

outline

- Achievement Gaps among Economic, Racial, and Ethnic Groups
- A Societal or a School Problem?
- Cultural Clashes
- Culturally Responsive Teaching
- Culturally Responsive Schools
- Gender Equity
- Equity for Sexual Minorities
- Overarching Patterns
- Connecting the Technical Tasks of Supervision to Cultural Responsiveness

Visit the **MyEdLeadershipLab™** site for *The Basic Guide to SuperVision and Instructional Leadership*, Third Edition to enhance your understanding of chapter concepts. You'll have the opportunity to practice your skills through video and case based Assignments and Activities as well as Building Leadership Skills units, and prepare for your certification exam with Practice for Certification quizzes.

> *A major problem facing the nation-state is how to recognize and legitimize differences and yet construct an overarching national identity that incorporates the voices, experiences, and hopes of the diverse groups that compose it. What groups will participate in constructing a new national identity, and what factors will be used to motivate powerful groups to share power with marginalized groups, are also issues that have to be addressed. Power sharing is an essential characteristic of a nation-state that reflects the culture of its diverse population.*
>
> (Banks, 2000, p. 28)

Given the growing diversity in the United States, and the continuing achievement gap between different student groups, addressing diversity in our schools is an increasingly critical need. People are not born with the prejudice and bias that contribute to the achievement gap. These attitudes are taught, and schools can teach future citizens different attitudes about those who belong to different cultures. Also, students from diverse cultures do not underachieve because they are less intelligent or less interested in learning than students from the dominant culture, but because of the incompatibility between their culture and traditional schooling in U.S. society. If we must change schools and the way we teach to close the achievement gap, then addressing diversity should be a task of instructional supervision.

In this chapter, we examine teaching and learning in relation to economic, racial, and ethnic groups as well as gender and sexual minorities. We examine how the conventional school culture and conventional teaching practices impede the learning of students who are not members of the dominant culture, and we discuss strategies for making schools and teaching more responsive to diverse cultures.

Achievement Gaps among Economic, Racial, and Ethnic Groups

Despite the United States' espoused commitment to equal opportunity for all, there is a wide gap in educational outcomes among various economic, racial, and ethnic groups. Table 21.1 shows percentages of students in selected economic, racial, and ethnic groups that demonstrated at least basic skill levels in reading, writing, math, and science on the National Assessment of Educational Progress (NAEP). Compared to students below the poverty level, far more students above the poverty level demonstrated basic skills across the various grade levels and content areas. Much higher percentages of Whites than African Americans and Latinos scored at a basic level or higher (National Center for Education Statistics, n.d.)

table **21.1** **Percentages of Selected Student Groups at or Above Basic Skill Level**

Subject Area	Year of Test	Grade Level	All Students	Students above Poverty Level*	Students below Poverty Level*	Whites	African Americans	Latinos
Reading	2007	4th	67	79	50	78	46	50
	2007	8th	74	83	58	84	55	58
	2005	12th	73	NR	NR	79	54	60
Writing	2007	8th	88	93	90	93	81	80
	2007	12th	82	85	69	86	69	71
Math	2007	4th	82	91	70	91	64	70
	2007	8th	71	81	55	82	47	55
	2005	12th	61	NR	NR	70	30	40
Science	2005	4th	68	82	48	82	38	45
	2005	8th	59	71	37	74	28	35
	2005	12th	54	60	31	66	19	30

*Classification of students as above or below poverty level was based on eligibility for free or reduced lunch.

NR = Not reported

Source: National Center for Educational Statistics, NAEP Data Explorer, http://nces.ed.gov/nationsreportcard/NDE

Less than 60 percent of students starting high school in high-poverty districts are likely to graduate, compared to more than 75 percent of students in low-poverty districts (Swanson, 2004a, 2004b). Between 70 and 75 percent of Whites who start high school graduate in four years, compared to approximately 50 percent of African American and Latino students (Swanson, 2004a, 2004b; Hoff, 2008). The negative effects of not completing high school in the United States are serious. High school dropouts not only have less earning power than graduates, but they are also more likely to live in poverty and become involved in criminal behavior (Boisjoly, Harris, and Duncan, 1998; Neild, Balfanz, and Herzog, 2007).

We all should ponder the reality that it is our society, our institutions, and our schools that have let so many lower-socioeconomic and racial/ethnic minority students down—that have failed to address the learning needs of so many bright young people with so much potential—in large part because of their parents' incomes, their ethnicity or race, or their first language. National shame is in order here. Rather than dwell on that shame, we must transform it into an urgent moral imperative to change the way we educate poor and racial/ethnic minority students.

As the educational and economic gaps between the haves and have-nots in our society increase, the United States is becoming increasingly diverse. Demographers suggest that by the year 2050, non-Hispanic Whites will be a minority in the United States, making up about 47 percent of the population (Passel and Cohn, 2008). Kirsch and associates (2007) warn that our nation's increasing diversity, the widening gaps in skill levels among different groups, and changes in the economy due to technology and globalization are all combining to create what they call "the perfect storm":

> We are in the midst of a perfect storm in which these three powerful forces are combining to generate waves that already have had a considerable impact on our nation. Unlike the perfect storm chronicled in the novel written by Sebastian Junger, the forces behind this storm continue to gain strength, and calm seas are nowhere in sight. We can't hope to ride this one out. If we continue on our present heading and fail to take effective action, the storm will have a number of predictable and dire implications for future generations, with consequences that extend well beyond the economic realm to the ethos of our society. (Kirsch, Braun, Yamamoto, and Sum, 2007, p. 7)

The aforementioned moral imperative to correct the inequalities in education should be the primary reason that supervisors and teachers respond to diversity as they work to close achievement gaps between student groups. The storm on the horizon, a storm whose winds we already feel, provides additional impetus for addressing issues of diversity.

A Societal or a School Problem?

Classism and racism have negative effects on the quality of life for many of our nation's poor and racial/ethnic minorities, and these negative effects extend to the quality of education for these groups. Rothstein (2004) has shown how inadequate wages, substandard housing, and poor health care create living conditions that place many poor and racial/ethnic minority students at a disadvantage right from the beginning of their formal education. Moreover, many lower-socioeconomic children have fewer out-of-school educational opportunities than middle- and upper-class students. For example, middle- and upper-class students are more likely to have access to a variety of books, go to summer camps or on family vacations, visit museums and zoos, take dance or music lessons, and so on. Rothstein (2004) argues that half or more of the variation in student achievement between lower-socioeconomic students and other students is the result of nonschool factors such as family income, housing conditions, health care, and out-of-school educational opportunities.

Educational policy in the United States—at the federal, state, and local levels—tends to reinforce the inequities present in society at large. For instance, the federal courts have ended many of the nation's most successful desegregation plans. There are now, once again, many public schools in the United States that have virtually

100 percent racial/ethnic minority students (Frankenberg, Lee, and Orfield, 2003). On average across the nation, if local and state expenditures are combined, states spend less money on their highest-poverty districts than their lowest-poverty districts (Wiener and Pristoop, 2006). Funding inequities also exist at the federal level. Because the federal government's Title I formula factors in the state's average per-student expenditure, high-spending states get more Title I money per poor child than low-spending states. "The net effect is that Title I does not reduce, but rather reinforces, inequality among states" (Liu, 2006, p. 2). Additionally, schools with many students who are poor or racial/ethnic minorities have higher percentages of out-of-field teachers (teachers without a major or minor in the subject they teach), are more likely to be assigned novice teachers, and have teachers with lower salaries than schools that serve wealthier students and lower numbers of racial/ethnic minority students (Peske and Haycock, 2006).

How are educators to respond to the systemic problems in U.S. society, as reflected in educational policy, that place lower-socioeconomic and racial/ethnic minority children at such a disadvantage? Some analysts say that unless our society addresses problems such as inadequate housing, poor health care, segregation, and inequitable school funding, schools will never be able to bridge the achievement gap. These experts admit that schools can make some difference, but argue that many of the conditions that cause the gap are beyond the schools' control. Other analysts believe that schools *can* bridge the achievement gap. They point to the effective schools and school improvement research and say that if some schools serving low-socioeconomic and racial/ethnic minority students can do it, then all schools can. These experts tell educators to forget about social conditions they cannot control and focus on increasing the achievement of poor and racial/ethnic minority students and on preparing them to overcome the barriers of poverty, classism, and racism present in U.S. society.

Our own position is that PK–12 educators need to take a two-tiered approach to the issue of inequitable treatment of diverse groups. First, supervisors and teachers must examine their own cultural identities, develop competencies for working with cultures different from their own, and create culturally responsive classrooms and schools. Second, supervisors and teachers must become directly involved in efforts to change public policy that works against lower-socioeconomic and racial/ethnic minority children. Educators in PK–12 should become involved in local and national efforts to ensure that all families have access to living wages, adequate housing, and basic health care. Moreover, supervisors and teachers must work to end segregation, inequitable school funding, and state and national educational policies that hurt lower-socioeconomic and racial/ethnic minority children. Supervisors and teachers are unable to do it alone; rather, they must become part of a coalition of PK–12 educators, university educators, parents, businesspersons, and policymakers who recognize the critical need for change. Members of this coalition must help educate the general public, the corporate world, and politicians on the need for change and to push for new legislation at the state and federal levels.

Now that we have considered issues of equity through a wide lens, the rest of this chapter focuses more narrowly on the classroom and school, including the cultural clashes that lead to inequitable treatment of some students and how culturally responsive teachers and schools can address diversity.

Cultural Clashes

Lower-socioeconomic and racial/ethnic minority students often have low levels of academic achievement because of clashes between their culture and the dominant culture's values and interests. The organizational structures, norms, values, curricula, instructional strategies, and student assessment methods in most schools support the dominant culture. Moreover, despite the increase in the number of students from diverse cultures, the number of White teachers and principals remains disproportionately high (Chamberlain, 2005; Saifer and Barton, 2007).

Part of the problem is caused by blatant stereotypes of lower-socioeconomic and racial/ethnic minority students: this or that group is "less academic" or "less motivated" or has parents who are "less concerned" about their children's education. However, much of the damage done to lower-socioeconomic and racial/ethnic minority students is more subtle and is often done by well-meaning educators who are not even aware of what they are doing (Carlisle, Jackson, and George, 2006). Often, the real problem is educators not understanding a group's cultural norms. For example, Valenzuela (1999) points out that the concept of *educación* is an important part of Mexican American culture:

> *Educación* is a conceptually broader term than its English language cognate. It refers to the family's role of inculcating in children a sense of moral, social, and personal responsibility and serves as the foundation for all other learning. Though inclusive of formal academic training, *educación* additionally refers to competence in the social world, wherein one respects the dignity and individuality of others. (p. 23)

One implication of *educación* for teaching Mexican American students is the need for the teacher to develop caring, reciprocal relationships with students and to promote such relationships among students. A teacher who remains distant from Mexican American students, isolates them from each other, and emphasizes academic competition does a disservice to them. According to Valenzuela (1999):

> When teachers deny their students the opportunity to engage in reciprocal relationships, they simultaneously invalidate the definition of education that most of these young people embrace. And since that definition is thoroughly grounded in Mexican culture, its rejection constitutes a dismissal of their culture as well. (p. 23)

Delpit (2006) provides another example of teachers not understanding students' cultures in her story of a White teacher's reaction to a story written by an African American student:

> Second-grader Marti was reading a story she had written that began, "Once upon a time, there was an old lady, and this old lady ain't had no sense." The teacher interrupted her, "Marti, that sounds like the beginning of a wonderful story, but could you tell me how you would say it in Standard English?" Marti put her head down, thought for a minute, and said softly, "There was an old lady who didn't have any sense." Then Marti put her hand on her hip, raised her voice and said, "But this lady ain't had no sense!" Marti's teacher probably did not understand that the child was actually exhibiting a very sophisticated sense of language. Although she clearly knew the Standard English form, she chose a so-called nonstandard form for emphasis, just as world class writers Charles Chesnutt, Alice Walker, Paul Lawrence Dunbar, and Zora Neale Hurston have done for years. (p. 169)

Not understanding cultural norms can cause teachers to underestimate the ability of poor and racial/ethnic minority students and thus "teach down" to them, focusing on basic skills, conducting drill and practice, and depriving students of developing the higher-level skills they are perfectly capable of learning (Bae, Halloway, Li, and Bempechat, 2008).

Another type of cultural clash consists of misinterpretation by the dominant culture of lower-socioeconomic and racial/ethnic minority students' behaviors. Students from lower-socioeconomic and minority groups often are viewed as not caring about education. But as Valenzuela (1999) points out, the school is sending the message to these students that their culture has no value and is asking them to reject their culture in favor of the dominant culture. Valenzuela argues that it is not *education* that many minority students don't care for; it is the *type of schooling* they are receiving. Thus, lower-socioeconomic and racial/ethnic minority students' behaviors can be viewed as a way of coping with how they are treated (Garcia and Dominguez, 1997) or of resisting the destruction of their culture by the dominant culture (Valenzuela, 1999).

Different communication styles often cause cultural clashes. Students from *high-context cultures* tend to take time to describe the context of a situation, often in the form of a story. Teachers from the dominant culture, however, tend to be *low context;* they prefer direct, explicit messages and often consider messages from members of high-context cultures to be rambling and confused. Students from high-context cultures may be corrected by teachers, come to believe that their communication style is inferior, and withdraw from classroom interaction (Chamberlain, 2005). European Americans tend to value written communication more than other forms of literacy, whereas people from many other cultures place a greater value on oral language. Also, European Americans tend to favor topic-centered, linear narratives, whereas people from some minority cultures prefer episodic narratives that shift from setting to setting and are nonlinear (Chamberlain, 2005; Delpit, 2006). Problems occur when European American teachers perceive narratives written in episodic style to be inferior to their own topic-centered preference.

Cultural differences are also responsible for the misdiagnosis of many lower-socioeconomic and racial/ethnic minority students as special education students, resulting in their overreferral to special programs. Conversely, the failure to identify lower-socioeconomic and racial/ethnic minority students as gifted results in their underreferral to gifted programs (De Valenzuela, Copeland, Qi, and Park, 2006; Fiedler et al., 2008). Banks (2000) argues that concepts like *mental retardation* and *giftedness* are socially constructed by the dominant culture: "When establishing categories for race, mental retardation, and giftedness, individuals and groups with power construct categories and characteristics and distribute rewards and privileges that benefit the existing hierarchies" (p. 38). Banks maintains that individuals who are judged competent within their own cultures and communities often are labeled as "mentally retarded" in schools. And to reiterate, lower-socioeconomic and racial/ethnic minority students are severely underrepresented in gifted and talented programs.

Banks believes that middle-class White parents use their knowledge of the system and political power to help get their children admitted to gifted and talented programs, which usually have better teachers, smaller classes, and more intellectual content. At the same time, many lower-socioeconomic and racial/ethnic minority students are placed in lower-track programs that lack intellectual engagement. As described by Banks, "Classes for lower-track students tend to be characterized by low-level instruction, drill exercises, and a lack of higher-level content" (p. 37).

According to Chamberlain (2005), many teachers from the dominant culture are unable to distinguish between underachievement because of a disability and underachievement as a result of cultural clashes. Chamberlain also describes how educational diagnosticians misidentify diverse students for special education or lower-track programs because of biased tests, inadequate opportunities for students to learn tested material, students' poor test-taking skills, culturally inappropriate test norms, failure to gather adequate data, and incorrect interpretation of data.

The curriculum in many schools clashes with diverse cultures because it is primarily a Eurocentric, middle-class curriculum. If other cultures are not represented in the curriculum, then students from diverse cultures must ignore their own cultures and learn Eurocentric content to be successful. Delpit (2006) expands on this point:

> In part, the problems we see exhibited in school by African American children and children of other oppressed minorities can be traced to this lack of curriculum in which they can find who represented the intellectual achievements of people who look like themselves. Were that not the case, these children would not talk about doing well in school as "acting white." Our children of color need to see the brilliance of their legacy, too. (p. 177)

The cultural conflict inherent in being forced to learn a Eurocentric curriculum puts children from other cultures at a tremendous disadvantage. Lower-socioeconomic and racial/ethnic minority students come to school with extensive funds of knowledge from their own culture—knowledge that is accessed through interacting with individuals and drawing on resources from supportive networks within the culture (Moll, Amanti, Neff, and González, 1992; Stritikus, 2006). However, if the only curriculum to be learned is a Eurocentric one, then the funds of knowledge within the student's culture become irrelevant to his or her schooling. Quoting Valenzuela (1999), "The extant curriculum fails to build on students' skills, knowledge, and cultural background" (p. 175).

Everything that we have been discussing—stereotypes, misunderstanding of cultural norms, misinterpretation of student behaviors, different communication styles, overreferral and misdiagnosis, and the Eurocentric, middle-class curriculum—contribute to a deficit model for educating lower-socioeconomic and racial/ethnic minority students. The dominant culture views the cultures of lower-socioeconomic and racial/ethnic minority students as deficits to be overcome, rather than assets to build on. Many schools thus engage in what Valenzuela (1999) refers to as *subtractive schooling*; they take away lower-socioeconomic and racial/ethnic minority students' cultures as well as the social capital that is part of those cultures.

One example of subtractive schooling is the goal of many schools to transition English as a second language (ESL) students to English-speaking rather than bilingual students. These students are classified as *limited English proficient*. Their Spanish language is viewed as a deficit to be replaced by English (Stritikus, 2006). Another example of subtractive schooling is separating low-socioeconomic and racial/ethnic minority groups into separate tracks or ability groups. Higher-achieving low-socioeconomic and racial/ethnic minority students have cultural capital and learning strategies to share with lower-achieving students from the same cultures. However, if higher- and lower-achieving students are separated by tracking or grouping, peer relationships cannot be established and social capital cannot be shared.

Why have so many educators from the dominant culture failed to develop a better understanding of lower-socioeconomic and racial/ethnic minority cultures and not learned how to be more culturally responsive? One reason is that most teacher and leadership preparation programs, as well as most in-service professional development programs, do not address cultural understanding adequately (Batt, 2008). Another reason is the low level of interaction between educators from the dominant culture and the families and communities of students from low-socioeconomic and racial/ethnic minority groups. As Delpit (2006) notes:

> We have created in most schools institutions of isolation. We foster the notion that students are clients of "professional" educators who are met in the "office" of the classroom where their deficiencies are remediated and their intellectual "illnesses" healed. Nowhere do we foster inquiry into what our students really are or encourage teachers to develop links to the often rich home lives of students, yet teachers cannot hope to understand who sits before them unless they can connect with the families and communities from which their students come. (p. 179)

There is typically little collaboration with parents and community members about how to make the school's curriculum and instruction more culturally responsive. Although educators often criticize low-socioeconomic and racial/ethnic minority parents for not being involved in their children's education, in fact, schools often set up barriers to parent involvement by scheduling impractical times and places for meetings, assuming a remedial approach, and manipulating communication through power tactics and the use of technical jargon. Because of such barriers, low-socioeconomic and racial/ethnic minority parents who try to become involved with their children's schools can soon become disillusioned and inactive (Garcia and Dominguez, 1997).

Culturally Responsive Teaching

Successful teaching of diverse students is *culturally responsive.* Ladson-Billings (1994) notes that culturally responsive teaching begins with a set of beliefs:

> Teachers who practice culturally relevant methods can be identified by the way they see themselves and others. They see their teaching as an art rather than a technical skill. They believe that all of their students can succeed rather than that failure is inevitable for some. They see themselves as part of the community and they see teaching as giving back to the community. They help students make connections between their local, national, racial, cultural, and global identities. . . . They believe that knowledge is continuously re-created, and shared by teachers and students alike. They view the content of the curriculum critically and are passionate about it. (p. 25)

Culturally responsive teachers accept all students as they are, but they also accept responsibility for helping all students learn. Here, *learning* means developing basic knowledge and skills but also critical and creative thinking (Delpit, 2006). Responsive teachers help students *choose* academic success (Ladson-Billings, 1995a, 1995b). How does a teacher do this? The key is to build relationships that are based on genuine care for all students. Caring leads to concern, which leads to an effort to develop relationships (Howard, 2002). A big part of relationship building is personal attention, including attention to nonacademic matters beyond the classroom (Brown, 2004). Relationship building also includes treating diverse students as individuals *and* as members of a particular culture (Ladson-Billings, 1992b).

The classrooms of culturally responsive teachers are multicultural. Linguistic diversity is accepted and incorporated into lessons, but language codes used by the dominant culture also are taught (Bernhard, Diaz, and Allgood, 2005). In the case of students with a dominant language other than English, linguistic diversity means bilingual education, with students learning the curriculum in their dominant language as they develop English-speaking skills. The goal is to develop bilingual students, rather than to replace students' dominant languages with English. More broadly speaking, culturally responsive teachers validate knowledge that is not valued by the dominant culture while teaching standard knowledge as well; they strive to maintain the integrity of each student's culture while fostering academic excellence (Ladson-Billings and Henry, 1990; Ladson-Billings, 1995b).

Culturally responsive teachers learn as much as they can about their students and their students' families and communities and use what they learn in their teaching (Saifer and Barton, 2007). Part of this learning comes from engaging in dialogue with adult members of the school community. Again, according to Delpit (2006):

> Appropriate education for poor children and children of color can only be devised in consultation with adults who share their culture. Black parents, teachers of color, and members of poor communities must be allowed to participate fully in the discussion of what kind of instruction is in their children's best interest. (p. 45)

Responsive teachers also learn from their students as students' share knowledge about themselves, their families, and their communities. Teachers then use this knowledge to become part of the students' world (Ladson-Billings, 1992a; Michael and Young, 2005).

Culturally responsive teachers take an *assets-based* approach to teaching low-socioeconomic and racial/ethnic minority students—the polar opposite of the deficit approach described earlier. An assets-based approach bases teaching and learning on strengths students already possess, including knowledge that they bring with them to the classroom. Because many of a low-socioeconomic and racial/ethnic minority student's assets have been acquired from his or her culture, teaching and learning are intentionally integrated with that culture; the student's heritage and real-life experiences become part of the curriculum (Ladson-Billings, 1992a). Learning is connected to the student's culture at the classroom, school, home, and community levels (Saifer and Barton, 2007). Ladson-Billings (1995a) provides an example of making such connections in her description of one teacher's "artist or craftsperson-in-residence" program, designed to highlight parents as knowledgeable resources and to affirm African American culture. Parents visited the classroom to conduct seminars on areas in which they possessed expertise. Students followed up on these seminars by conducting research to extend their knowledge on the topic.

Another part of assets-based education is helping students to realize that they have the potential for academic success. If students are treated as if they have potential, then they will be more likely to realize that potential (Michael and Young, 2005). Culturally responsive teachers make it clear that they are working with smart, capable students. Ladson-Billings (1995b) shares techniques used by responsive teachers she has observed. In one example, each student was asked to identify an area of expertise, become a "classroom expert" on that area, and deliver a presentation about it or assist other students who were having difficulty in that area. In another example, teachers assisted students whose futures were most tenuous (as indicated by a history of "misbehavior") to become their classrooms' intellectual leaders. These students were invited to lead discussions, inquiry, and student critique of the status quo. The purpose of strategies like these is to disrupt the denigration of lower-socioeconomic and racial/ethnic minority students and thwart self-fulfilling prophesies of failure, thus giving students an opportunity to choose academic success (Ladson-Billings, 1992a, 1994).

Another characteristic of culturally responsive teaching is the creation of a classroom environment that is caring and collaborative and that reflects the beliefs and values of students' families and communities (Michael and Young, 2005). Students in the classrooms of responsive teachers are made to feel they are part of an extended caring family, where the teacher cares for students and students are taught to take care of each other (Brown, 2004). This caring environment includes a great deal of collaborative learning, as described by Ladson-Billings (1995b):

> To solidify the social relationships in their classes, the teachers encouraged the students to learn collaboratively, teach each other, and be responsible for the academic success of others. These collaborative arrangements were not necessarily structured like those of cooperative learning. Instead, the teachers used a combination of formal and informal peer collaborations. One teacher used a buddy system, where each student was paired with another. The buddies checked each other's homework and class assignments. Buddies quizzed each other for tests, and, if one buddy was absent, it was the responsibility of the other to call to see why and to help with makeup work. The teachers used this ethos of reciprocity and mutuality to insist that one person's success was the success of all and one person's failure was the failure of all. These feelings were exemplified by the teacher who insisted, "We're a family. We have to care for one another as if our very survival depended on it." (p. 481)

Culturally responsive teachers combine extensive support with assertiveness. Responsive teachers collaborate with their students to develop clear behavioral and academic guidelines and to firmly enforce those guidelines (Saifer and Barton, 2007). Students are held accountable for meeting expectations but are treated with respect and dignity (Howard, 2002). Responsive teachers avoid power struggles with students by refusing to engage in arguments and providing students with "escape routes" so they are not embarrassed in front of their peers (Brown, 2004). Responsive teachers use a variety of techniques to convince students to choose success, while never using deficit language.

Ladson-Billings (1995b) describes how culturally responsive teachers hold students accountable for success:

> Students were not permitted to choose failure in their classrooms. They cajoled, nagged, pestered, and bribed the students to work at high intellectual levels. Absent from their discourse about students was the "language of lacking." Students were never referred to as being from a single-parent household, being on AFDC [welfare], or needing psychological evaluation. Instead, teachers talked about their own shortcomings and limitations and ways they needed to change to ensure student success. (p. 479)

A final characteristic of culturally responsive teachers is the transformational nature of their teaching. Responsive teachers do not ignore issues of race and culture but rather engage students in critiquing the status quo, in learning how to cope with prejudice and discrimination, and in working to bring about change (Ladson-Billings, 1992b, 1994). The focus of this work could be inside or outside the classroom. At the classroom level, the students and teacher might collaboratively critique the school curriculum, the textbooks they use, or the way their learning is assessed and then work together for curriculum and instructional change. Outside the classroom, the teacher and students could work collectively to identify and solve problems in the community—or even the larger society—caused by prejudice or discrimination. Following a transformational approach does not mean that the teacher ignores the codes used by the dominant culture or the power realities present in society. Culturally responsive teachers realize that low-socioeconomic and racial/ethnic minority students must learn the codes of the dominant culture to be successful and must understand power relations so they can work to change those realities (Delpit, 2006).

Culturally Responsive Schools

Having a few culturally responsive teachers in a school that serves diverse groups is simply not enough. The aim should be to create a culturally responsive *school*. Here, we discuss three important processes needed to move toward creating a culturally responsive school: teacher development, school development, and collaboration with families and the community.

Teacher Development

One goal of a school that aims to become culturally responsive is to move more and more members of the school community toward intercultural sensitivity. Sensitivity is not something that teachers do or don't have; teachers actually move through developmental stages of sensitivity. Cushner, McClelland, and Safford (2003) describe six stages of intercultural sensitivity that were originally identified by Bennett (1993):

1. *Denial.* Individuals in the denial stage are unable to see authentic cultural differences, isolate themselves within their own cultures, and stereotype and discriminate against members of other cultures, sometimes considering others to be mentally and socially deficient.
2. *Defense.* At this stage, individuals recognize some cultural differences but consider them negative attributes of the other culture. These individuals are unable to deal with cultural differences and become defensive, adopting an "us versus them" attitude. Persons at this stage consider their culture to be superior and denigrate other cultures.
3. *Minimization.* This is the "colorblind" stage, the stage where most teachers are. Individuals at this stage recognize and accept surface cultural differences,

such as traditional foods, music, and recreational activities, but they continue to believe that everyone is basically alike. They believe that everyone has the same basic values, needs, and motivations—that "we all want the same things out of life."

4. *Acceptance.* Persons at this stage accept the fact that different cultures have different values and behaviors and do not consider values and behaviors different from their own as bad. Cultural differences are seen as viable alternatives to the dominant culture. Individuals at this stage accept other cultures but still have not developed the skills necessary to work effectively with them.
5. *Adaptation.* Persons at this stage are able to shift from their own culture's frame of reference to other frames; they can view persons and situations through the worldview of other cultures. This enables them to better empathize with people from other cultures and to better communicate across cultures. Teachers at this stage are able to modify their teaching so that their expectations, interactions, and responses to students from different cultures vary in appropriate ways.
6. *Integration.* Individuals at this stage have internalized multiple frames of reference. They are bicultural or multicultural; their identity is not tied to any one culture. They feel equally comfortable with any of the multiple cultures with which they identify, and they are able to mediate between different cultural groups. Teachers who have reached the integration stage should be enlisted to build bridges between cultures.

The lower three stages on intercultural sensitivity (denial, defense, and minimization) are classified as *ethnocentric* stages, and the higher three stages (acceptance, adaptation, and integration) are considered *ethnorelative* stages. As mentioned earlier, most teachers are at the minimization stage and thus are ethnocentric. Teacher development, therefore, must move teachers toward the ethnorelative stages of cultural sensitivity.

Guerra and Nelson (2008) have presented a four-phase model for developing culturally proficient teachers. In phase 1, teachers analyze a variety of student data disaggregated by race, ethnicity, and socioeconomic status. The data examined include test scores, discipline referrals, placement in special education and gifted programs, course grades, retention rates, parent involvement, and college acceptance. The teachers' data analysis typically reveals patterns of inequity, showing that low-socioeconomic and racial/ethnic minority students have been ill served by the status quo. The data are reviewed without the names of students or teachers so teachers do not become defensive. Guerra and Nelson warn that teachers react differently during discussion of the patterns found in the data. Some recognize inequity in schooling as the cause of achievement gaps, but some blame the students and parents. In phase 1, teachers also become aware of strategies to address inequities by reading about and discussing how culturally responsive teachers overcome such inequities. Some teachers are motivated by the success stories; others dismiss them (Guerra and Nelson, 2008).

In phase 2, teachers' readiness for change is assessed by having them engage in simulations intended to demonstrate culture's influences and cultural clashes. After the simulations, teachers discuss the experience in debriefing sessions. Facilitators observe the teachers' behaviors closely to see which teachers recognize and accept cultural differences. Based on the teachers' reactions to the student data and success stories in phase 1 and the simulations in phase 2, those who are ready for more advanced work on cultural proficiency are invited to participate in phases 3 and 4. Those who are not ready for advanced work are provided with additional phase 1 and phase 2 activities to help them develop readiness and participate in phases 3 and 4 at a later time (Guerra and Nelson, 2008).

In phase 3, teachers learn how the culture they belong to includes a set of values, beliefs, and expectations, which in turn influences the way they teach. Teachers also learn about the cultures of their students, that conventional schools attempt to transmit the dominant culture to all students, and that the resulting cultural clashes have negative effects on low-socioeconomic and racial/ethnic minority students. Learning activities in phase 3 include book studies, video analyses, simulations, and participation in community events. The focus at this stage is on the practices of teachers in general, rather than those of individual participants (Guerra and Nelson, 2008).

Phase 4 involves teachers analyzing the same student data examined in phase 1, but this time, in addition to remaining disaggregated by ethnicity and socioeconomic status, the data are broken down by individual teachers, grade levels, and departments. Teachers thus become aware of patterns of inequity in their own classrooms and instructional teams. Teachers may also survey or interview students and parents to shed light on inequitable practices. Along with data gathering and analysis, teachers continue book study and video analysis to learn more about the negative effects of cultural clashes and deficit teaching on low-socioeconomic and racial/ethnic minority students. The activities in phase 4 often cause teachers cognitive dissonance (see Chapter 6), which can lead teachers to reframe their views of diverse cultures and begin to shift from a deficit approach to an assets-based approach to teaching and learning (Guerra and Nelson, 2008).

School Development

Culturally responsive teachers are the heart and soul of a culturally responsive school, but the school as a community also has a vital role to play in addressing diversity. Some suggestions for school development include the following:

- A schoolwide commitment to cultural responsiveness should be made by creating what Madsen and Mabokela (2005) call an *organizational identity* that addresses the complexity of diversity and is inclusive of and responsive to diverse cultures. According to these authors, "Organizational identity is defined as the organization members' collective understanding of the features that are presumed to be central and permanent and that distinguish the organization from other organizations" (p. 120). A school with an organizational identity as a culturally responsive school has not necessarily achieved that status. However, it is suggesting to everyone inside and outside the organization that cultural responsiveness is its goal, and it is inviting all stakeholders to critique its progress toward that goal.

- Schools must hire more racial/ethnic minority teachers in general but specifically more African American teachers for schools with African American students, more Latino teachers for schools with Latino students, and more bilingual and multilingual teachers for schools with ELL students.
- Schools with large low-socioeconomic and racial/ethnic minority student populations should hire more teachers from teacher education programs that teach cultural responsiveness, more teachers with majors in the subjects they are going to teach, and more highly qualified teachers in general.
- In schools with lower-socioeconomic and racial/ethnic minority students, all members of the school community must become immersed in the school's diverse cultures, continuously learning about their students and the students' families and communities (Michael and Young, 2005). This learning process can be facilitated by a network of adults (supervisors, teachers, parents, other community members) who are members of or knowledgeable about cultures represented in the school.
- The school should develop an inclusive curriculum that incorporates diverse students' languages and cultural backgrounds (Chamberlain, 2005). The curriculum should reflect both transformation and social action approaches (Banks, 1998). In the *transformational approach,* students view curriculum content from the perspectives of diverse groups. In the *social action approach,* students examine and act on social issues related to diversity (see Chapter 18). Basic skills are integrated into the rich content provided in the transformation and social action curriculum.
- All members of the school community must work at developing a nurturing school environment, with relationships between adults and students and among students based on authentic caring. This nurturing environment should be accompanied by high expectations for all students (Valenzuela, 1999).
- Tracking and grouping should be eliminated. This enables access for *all* lower-socioeconomic and racial/ethnic minority students to higher-level learning that traditionally is not provided to students in lower-level tracks and groups. Also, eliminating tracking and grouping allows higher-achieving poor and racial/ethnic minority students to network and share their funds of knowledge and learning strategies with lower-achieving poor and racial/ethnic minority students.
- Schools must establish infrastructures that allow adults from different cultural groups (instructional leaders, teachers, parents) to communicate on a regular basis and to collaborate on how to make schools more culturally responsive. Various groups can collaborate on school policies, curriculum development, instructional practices, and student assessment methods.

- Methods for student assessment must become more culturally responsive. Educators who conduct assessment must learn to avoid culturally biased assessments, to distinguish between underachievement as a result of disability and underachievement because of cultural incongruence, and to use a variety of culturally sensitive assessment methods, rather than rely exclusively on norm-referenced tests. Student assessment must shift from a diagnostic-prescriptive focus to one of student advocacy (Chamberlain, 2005).
- The school's ultimate goal should be to integrate cultural knowledge throughout *all* school operations. Cultural responsiveness must become institutionalized as part of the school culture (Lindsey, Roberts, and CampbellJones, 2005). New members of the school community must be socialized into the school's commitment to diversity and culturally responsive practices.

Collaboration with Families and the Community

The third leg that supports a culturally responsive school is collaboration with students' families and the community. First and foremost, supervisors and teachers should accept parents as essential partners in their children's education. Parents should be welcome at school, not just as visitors but as part of the school community. Schools should be organized so that supervisors and teachers are available to meet with parents to discuss their concerns. For both individual and group meetings, strategies should be developed to help overcome barriers to parents meeting with educators, such as work schedules, transportation problems, and child-care issues. During meetings, parents should always be treated as equals who have much to contribute. Parents' communication styles, cultural values, and childrearing practices should be respected.

Parents should be part of the school leadership. They can be given roles on the school leadership council and on important committees and task forces. Parents in leadership roles can serve as liaisons to other parents. Parents can also be invited to assume a variety of other educational roles based on their experience, interest, and available time.

An interesting concept with much promise is the school-based parent center, which is managed by parents for the benefit of other parents, the school, and the community. A center usually is provided its own space on campus and an operating budget, with parent volunteers doing most of the work. The center might provide parent education classes, forums for school–parent dialogue, services to students, or cultural events for the community. Parent centers can serve as a bridge between the school, the parents, and the community.

Schools serving diverse students need to collaborate not just with students' families but also with other members of the community the school serves. Diverse community members can sit on school advisory groups, be guest teachers, and serve as role models for students. Through service learning and social action, students can become directly involved in community development. The school can become a center of community assistance, providing a variety of human services to community members. In addition, the school can enter into partnerships with community agencies and programs, becoming part of a larger network of education and human support (see Chapter 22).

In our earlier discussion of school development, we discussed Madsen and Mabokela's (2005) idea of the school establishing an organizational identity as a culturally responsive school. These authors argue that work on organizational identity should be an interactive process, with the school projecting what type of organization it wishes to be, the community providing feedback on the school's actual performance, and the school modifying its performance accordingly. Through this process, the school continuously responds to a diverse community.

Gender Equity

Conventional schools tend to foster *gender inequity*, in which female students are subject to considerable sexual harassment and discrimination. In many textbooks and other curriculum materials, females are depicted as needy, passive, and subordinate to males. In conventional classrooms, teachers interact more with boys than with girls, and boys tend to control the classroom discussion. Girls are made to believe they are unable to solve problems on their own, yet they are less likely to receive helpful feedback. Thus, girls often become "invisible students" in the classroom (Bauer, 2000). The vast majority of females experience some form of sexual harassment at school and often find it difficult to get assistance if they report the harassment (Fry, 2003; Ormerod, Collinsworth, and Perry, 2008).

The inequitable treatment of females in schools can have devastating effects. Girls' self-confidence often drops dramatically during early adolescence (Mullen and Tuten, 2004; Kommer, 2006). Mullen and Tuten (2004) note that "resiliency, optimism, curiosity, and risk-taking all seem to take a nosedive. . . . Those teenagers who live such disablement have been viewed as passive, self-conscious, low in self-esteem, preoccupied with looking attractive and appearing unintelligent, and non–goal oriented" (p. 294). To make matters worse, teachers in conventional schools who attempt to address gender inequities often encounter hostility from colleagues and parents (Fry, 2003).

Although girls suffer the most from gender inequity, boys are affected as well. For example, boys are more likely to need reading instruction, receive a discipline referral, be identified as a special education student, be suspended or expelled, and drop out of school (Taylor and Lorimer, 2003; Kommer, 2006). Moreover, we are beginning to realize that boys have many of the same problems with self-esteem that girls do, although they are socialized to hide their feelings of inadequacy (Kommer, 2006). Boys, too, then, have been mistreated by traditional schooling (Kommer, 2006).

The goal of efforts to address gender issues in schools "is not to treat boys and girls equally, but to create equity by purposely addressing the particular needs of each gender" (Kommer, 2006, p. 250). A good place for supervisors to start efforts toward gender equity is to open a dialogue on the effects of such inequity on students. Research and other readings on gender issues can inform that dialogue. Fry (2003) suggests that schools develop a gender equity plan that has goals, guidelines, and benchmarks. Although such a plan would vary from school to school, some nonnegotiables would be in order. For example, one goal for all schools should be eliminating from the school all forms of sexual harassment.

Sanders and Cotton Nelson (2004) describe a process that involves teachers in working for gender equity. During an all-day workshop at the beginning of the process, teachers are presented data on girls' underachievement and discuss gender-related problems they observe in their classrooms. After the initial workshop, participants meet periodically for half-day workshops focused on topics such as gender stereotypes and teacher expectations, interpersonal dynamics among different groups, gender bias in the curriculum, and so on. Between workshops, teachers engage in a variety of learning activities. They observe gender issues being played out in public places and popular media and search for gender bias in their own schools and classrooms. They also do gender experiments, such as having colleagues observe their teaching for bias and trying out new strategies to make their classrooms more equitable. At the next workshop, teachers bring data they have gathered and share their learning experiences. Sanders and Cotton Nelson have found that this process helps teachers to realize that gender bias does exist—in society, in schools, and even in their own classrooms. In the workshops, teachers also develop knowledge and skills to promote gender equity.

Kommer (2006) suggests additional strategies that teachers can use to create gender equity, including balancing competitive and cooperative activities, considering gender when forming student groups, providing equal response opportunities, inviting gender role models to the classroom, and providing a gender-neutral learning environment. Another important thing teachers can do to promote gender equity is to facilitate dialogue among girls and boys in which they talk about inequity, its effects on them and their peers, and how students can work together with teachers to develop equitable classrooms and schools.

Equity for Sexual Minorities

Consider the following statistics:

- An estimated 10 percent of students in U.S. schools are homosexual (Weiler, 2003).
- More than 80 percent of gay and lesbian students have been verbally abused. Ninety percent have heard antigay remarks, and one-fourth of those remarks have been voiced by school staff (Glimps, 2005; Whelan, 2006).
- Twenty percent of gay and lesbian youth have been physically assaulted at school (Whelan, 2006).

- In one-third of the incidents in which gay and lesbian students were harassed at school, adults witnessed the abuse and did nothing to help (Weiler, 2003).
- Nearly two out of three gays and lesbians have reported that they felt unsafe at school (Weiler, 2003; Goodenow, Szalacha, and Westheimer, 2006).
- The grade-point averages of students reporting frequent harassment are more than 10 percent lower than those of other students (Whelan, 2006).
- Gay and lesbian youth commit suicide at a rate two to three times that of other youth. Issues of sexual identity play a role in 30 percent of youth suicides (van Wormer and McKinney, 2003).

Payne (2007) reminds us that most schools are *heteronormative*, which means popularity and group membership are equated with heterosexuality. Youth who do not conform to the expectations of heterosexuality are subject to ridicule, gossip, and isolation. Moreover, Payne notes, "Current school practices are invested in preserving the heterosexist structure of schools and continuing to reinforce heterosexuality as the norm" (p. 77). Payne cites school rituals like electing cheerleaders, prom kings and queens, and "cutest couple" as examples of the institutional support for heterosexual popularity and power. Many educators support the heteronormative nature of schools by ignoring the harassment of lesbian, gay, bisexual, and transgender (LGBT) students or even by joining the ridicule of these minorities. Even sexual minority teachers often remain silent as LGBT students are abused (van Wormer and McKinney, 2003).

How sexual minority students are treated in schools creates a serious dilemma for these students:

> The instinct for many is to hide their identity, which deepens their sense of confusion, isolation, and self-doubt. On the other hand, LGBT youth who do come out face the very real risk of violence, harassment, prejudice, discrimination, and stigmatization. (Weiler, 2003, p. 11)

The stress and lack of support eventually take their toll on many LGBT students:

> The stressors related to either hiding or revealing one's sexual identity place sexual minority students at a higher risk for developing mental health, physical, and educational problems. Because survival at school is the priority, many LGBT students experience academic and learning problems. (Weiler, 2003, p. 11)

Such problems include more frequent absences, less involvement in school activities, worse grades, and a higher dropout rate than heterosexual students (Weiler, 2003; Glimps, 2005; Whelan, 2006).

Problems resulting from the abuse of sexual minority students go beyond academics. LGBT students are more likely to engage in high-risk behaviors such as drinking, drug abuse, and unsafe sex (van Wormer and McKinney, 2003; Glimps, 2005). It is not the fact that they are sexual minorities but the abuse they receive that leads LGBT students to engage in such risky behaviors (Glimps, 2005). Many sexual minority students are homeless, having been thrown out of their homes by their parents because of their sexual orientation (van Wormer and McKinney, 2003; Weiler, 2003). And as noted earlier, the suicide rate of lesbian and gay students is far higher than that of heterosexual students (van Wormer and McKinney, 2003; Goodenow, Szalacha, and Westheimer, 2006).

The fact that many schools do nothing about prejudice and discrimination against LGBT students—indeed, that they contribute to the prejudice and discrimination—means that they are miseducating both sexual minority *and* heterosexual students. Grayson (1987) discusses this reality:

> The failure of school officials to provide protection from peer harassment and violence reflects only a portion of the harm caused by the hatred of gay males and lesbians in schools. Homophobia hinders the development of all school children from growing into tolerant and compassionate members of a harmonious and cohesive pluralistic society. Acceptance of prejudice against lesbians and gay males contributes to the authority of privileged groups, validating prejudice and discrimination against others. It reinforces rigid sex role behavior and the imposed silence and misinformation keeps people ignorant of accurate information and facts. (p. 136)

Schools can begin to promote equity for LGBT students by establishing a school policy that protects and supports sexual minority students (Goodenow, Szalacha, and Westheimer, 2006). The policy should not only rule out harassment of LGBT students but also affirm their right to be respected members of the school community. The policy should be disseminated to students, teachers, parents, and the community. This can be accomplished through public meetings in which information on the need for such a policy is shared and misinformation about LGBT students is dispelled.

As with professional development to promote equity for other marginalized student groups, developing self-awareness is a critical part of helping teachers to work with sexual minority students. Supervisors can help teachers develop self-awareness by facilitating a process proposed by Van Den Bergh and Crisp (2004). The process includes five phases:

1. Self-reflect on one's own sexual orientation, in terms of its development, influences, and experiences.
2. Reflect on one's previous contact with GLBT individuals, both personally and professionally.
3. Evaluate one's reaction to GLBT individuals, both in terms of positive and negative experiences.
4. Self-evaluate the cognitive, affective, and behavioral components of one's responses to GLBT individuals in order to develop awareness of potential heterosexism or homophobia.
5. Participate in personal and professional activities that foster a greater understanding of GLBT individuals and culture. (p. 227)

In addition to engaging in personal development, supervisors and teachers must collaboratively examine different aspects of schooling that might contribute to inequity, including (1) school policies that might conflict with the school's nondiscrimination policy, (2) the school climate, (3) student discipline, (4) the curriculum, (5) teaching practices, (6) interactions in classrooms and common areas, and (7) student achievement. Teachers can gather and analyze data in any of these areas, identifying foci for improvement.

Once problem areas have been identified, a variety of strategies can be used to foster equity for GLBT students. Depending on the needs of the particular school, any of the following strategies can promote equity:

- School safety and antibullying programs are a trend in public education. If a school initiates one of these programs, protection of sexual minority students should be a key feature. Both teachers and parents should be involved in designing and carrying out the program. The program should address educating students on the need to treat GLBT students with respect and include monitoring of student and adult behaviors toward sexual minority students. When abuse of a GLBT student occurs, adults must intervene promptly to work with both the abused and the abuser.
- Reform the curriculum. A curriculum that promotes heterosexuals as superior and sexual minorities as inferior must be changed. One way to do so is to introduce literature that promotes GLBT persons in a positive light. The work and lives of sexual minority persons who have made significant contributions in various fields can also be integrated into appropriate subjects. Case studies of prejudice and discrimination can be used to critique the dominant culture's treatment of GLBT persons. Advanced courses could focus on gay studies or involve students in social action against the abuse of sexual minorities.
- Teachers can work together to change their teaching practices so their classrooms are more inclusive of GLBT students and they do a better job of preventing prejudice and discrimination against GLBT students. This collaboration can include joint planning of inclusive lessons, observations of each other's teaching, and collegial dialogue on how to better support sexual minority students.
- The school can appoint an adult advocate or team of advocates for sexual minorities. The advocate or team can work directly with GLBT students, refer sexual minority students to external resources and outside support groups, be the liaison between GLBT students and adults in the school community, and press for changes in policy and practice that will make life at school better for sexual minority students (Goodenow, Szalacha, and Westheimer, 2006).
- The school can create an in-school support group for GLBT students. Gay–straight alliance clubs, for example, not only provide group support for sexual minority students but also help improve intercultural understanding between GLBT students and those from the dominant culture (Goodenow, Szalacha, and Westheimer, 2006).

Overarching Patterns

Although our discussions of (1) economic, racial, and ethnic minorities; (2) gender inequity; and (3) sexual minorities in schools are based on different bodies of literature, overarching patterns can be identified. Many of the problems faced by students in diverse groups are the result of cultural clashes between their culture and the dominant culture. These cultural clashes, in turn, result from a lack of understanding or an inability to respond to cultural differences.

To move forward, it is necessary for members of the dominant culture to learn about their own culture, other cultures, cultural clashes, and the negative effects of cultural clashes on diverse groups. This learning, especially if it involves teachers, seems to happen as a result of being confronted with data that are incongruent with one's beliefs about other cultures, reflecting on the data, engaging in dialogue with colleagues on the meaning of the data, and making a commitment to change the way diverse groups are treated. New knowledge gained through experiential learning leads to forming new attitudes, which leads to taking action on behalf of diverse groups.

Connecting the Technical Tasks of Supervision to Cultural Responsiveness

Our discussion on responding to diversity provides a good opportunity to show how the technical tasks of supervision cannot really be separated from the cultural tasks. Rather, the technical tasks can be used as vehicles to complete the cultural tasks. All five technical tasks (direct assistance, group development, professional development, curriculum development, and action research) can be integrated in responding to diversity.

Action research can be a framework for integrating the other technical tasks of supervision into a comprehensive program to address diversity. Early in the action research process, teachers can gather data on the achievement gap between various student groups, cultural clashes, and the negative effects of cultural clashes on diverse student groups. The task of *group development* is carried out through each phase of the action research project but is especially vital in the early phases of action research for addressing diversity. Early in the process, teachers are involved in critical discussions of the negative effects of schooling on diverse students and confronting their own role in maintaining the status quo. These group discussions require balancing task and personal roles, dealing with some dysfunctional behaviors, managing conflict in constructive ways, and facilitating small- and large-group decision making.

Once teachers have made a commitment to addressing diversity and selected a focus within that broad area, it is time for action planning. The remaining technical tasks of supervision all can be included in the action plan. *Professional development* can provide teachers with the knowledge, skills, and strategies to address the needs of diverse students. *Curriculum development* can enable teachers to critique the status quo and to develop a curriculum that is culturally responsive and informs social action. *Direct assistance* can help teachers to apply culturally responsive teaching through clinical supervision, peer coaching, demonstration teaching, mentoring, and so on.

After implementing the action plan for a period of time, teachers can continue action research by gathering data to assess the effects of the action plan on the school and its diverse groups and to plan future actions to increase the school's cultural responsiveness. In summary, the technical tasks of supervision—powerful processes for improving instruction by themselves—can also contribute to broader cultural tasks such as addressing diversity.

MyEdLeadershipLab™

Go to Topic 10, Facilitating Change, in the MyEdLeadershipLab™ site at www.myedleadershiplab.com for *The Basic Guide to SuperVision and Instructional Leadership*, Third Edition, where you can:

- Find learning outcomes for Facilitating Change along with the national standards that connect to these outcomes.
- Complete Assignments and Activities that can help you more deeply understand the chapter content.
- Apply and practice your understanding of the core skills identified in the chapter with the Building Leadership Skills unit.
- Prepare yourself for professional certification with a Practice for Certification quiz.

REFERENCES

Bae, S., Halloway, S. D., Li, J., and Bempechat, J. 2008. Mexican-American students' perceptions of teachers' expectations: Do perceptions differ depending on student achievement levels? *The Urban Review, 40*(2), 210–225.

Banks, J. A. 1998. Approaches to multicultural curriculum reform. *Multicultural Leader, 1*(2), 1–3.

Banks, J. A. 2000. The social construction of differences and the quest for educational equality. In R. S. Brandt (Ed.), *Education in a new era* (pp. 21–45). Alexandria, VA: Association for Supervision and Curriculum Development.

Batt, E. G. 2008. Teachers' perceptions of ELL education: Potential solutions to overcome the greatest challenges. *Multicultural Education, 15*(3), 39–43.

Bauer, K. S. 2000. Promoting gender equity in schools. *Contemporary Education, 71*(2), 22–25.

Bennett, M. J. 1993. Towards ethnorelativism: A developmental model of intercultural sensitivity. In M. Paige (Ed.), *Cross-cultural orientation* (pp. 27–69). Lanham MD: University Press of America.

Bernhard, J. K., Diaz, C. F., and Allgood, I. 2005. Research-based teacher education for multicultural contexts. *Intercultural Education, 16*(3), 263–277.

Boisjoly, J., Harris, K., and Duncan, G. 1998. Initial welfare spells: Trends, events, and duration. *Social Service Review, 72*(4), 466–492.

Brown, D. F. (2004). Urban teachers' professed classroom management strategies: Reflections of culturally responsive teaching. *Urban Education, 39*(3), 266–289.

Carlisle, L. R., Jackson, B. W., and George, A. 2006. Principles of social justice education: The social justice education in schools project. *Equity and Excellence in Education, 39*(1), 55–64.

Chamberlain, S. P. 2005. Recognizing and responding to cultural differences in the education of culturally and linguistically diverse learners. *Intervention in School and Clinic, 40*(4), 195–211.

Cushner, K., McClelland, A., and Safford, P. 2003. *Human diversity in education: An integrative approach* (4th ed.). New York: McGraw-Hill.

De Valenzuela, J. S., Copeland, S. R., Qi, C. H., and Park, M. 2006. Examining educational equity: Revisiting the disproportionate representation of minority students in special education. *Exceptional Children, 72*(4), 425–441.

Delpit, L. 2006. *Other people's children: Cultural conflict in the classroom.* New York: New Press.

Fiedler, C. R., Chiang, B., Van Haren, B., Jorgensen, J., Halberg, S., and Boreson, L. 2008. Culturally responsive practices in schools: A checklist to address disproportionality in special education. *TEACHING Exceptional Children, 40*(5), 52–59.

Frankenberg, E., Lee, C., and Orfield, G. 2003. *A multicultural society with segregated schools: Are we losing the dream?* Cambridge, MA: Harvard University, The Civil Rights Project.

Fry, S. W. 2003. Bite like a flea and keep them scratching: Steps to gender equity in America's schools. *Multicultural Education, 11*(1), 11–16.

Garcia, S. B., and Dominguez, L. 1997. Cultural contexts that influence learning and academic performance. *Academic Difficulties, 6*(3), 621–655.

Glimps, B. J. 2005. Students who are gay, lesbian, bisexual, or transgender. *Current Issues in Education, 8*(16). Retrieved August 1, 2008, from http://cie.ed.asu.edu/volume8/number16

Goodenow, C., Szalacha, L., and Westheimer, K. 2006. School support groups, other school factors, and the safety of sexual minority adolescents. *Psychology in the Schools, 43*(5), 573–589.

Grayson, D. A. 1987. Emerging equity issues related to homosexuality in education. *Peabody Journal of Education, 64,* 132–145

Guerra, P. L., and Nelson, S. W. 2008. Cultural proficiency: Begin by developing awareness and assessing readiness. *Journal of Staff Development, 29*(1), 67–68.

Hoff, D. J. 2008. States to face uniform rules on grad data. *Education Week, 27*(32), 1, 21.

Howard, T. C. 2002. Hearing footsteps in the dark: African American students' description of effective teachers. *Journal of Education for Students Placed at Risk, 7*(4), 425–444.

Kirsch, L., Braun, H., Yamamoto, K., and Sum, A. 2007. *America's perfect storm: Three forces changing our nation's future.* Princeton, NJ: Educational Testing Service.

Kommer, D. 2006. Boys and girls together: A case for creating gender-friendly middle school classrooms. *The Clearing House, 79*(6), 247–251.

Ladson-Billings, G. 1992a. Liberatory consequences of literacy: A case of culturally relevant instruction for African American students. *The Journal of Negro Education, 61*(3), 378–391.

Ladson-Billings, G. 1992b. Reading between the lines and beyond the pages: A culturally relevant approach to literacy teaching. *Theory into Practice, 31*(4), 312–320.

Ladson-Billings, G. 1994. *The dreamkeepers: Successful teachers of African American children.* San Francisco: Jossey-Bass.

Ladson-Billings, G. 1995a. But that's just good teaching! The case for culturally relevant pedagogy. *Theory into Practice, 34*(3), 159–165.

Ladson-Billings, G. 1995b. Toward a theory of culturally relevant pedagogy. *American Educational Research Journal, 32*(3), 465–491.

Ladson-Billings, G., and Henry, A. 1990. Blurring the borders: Voices of African liberty pedagogy in the United States and Canada. *Journal of Education, 172*(2), 72–88.

Lindsey, R. B., Roberts, L. M., and CampbellJones, F. 2005. *The culturally proficient school: An implementation guide for school leaders.* Thousand Oaks, CA: Corwin Press.

Liu, G. 2006. How the federal government makes rich states richer. In *Funding gaps* (pp. 2–4). Washington, DC: Education Trust. Retrieved August 1, 2008, from www2.edtrust.org

Madsen, J. A., and Mabokela, R. O. 2005. *Culturally relevant schools: Creating positive workplace relationships and preventing intergroup differences.* New York: Routledge.

Michael, C. N., and Young, N. D. 2005. *Seeking meaningful school reform: Characteristics of inspired schools.* (ERIC ED 490 677)

Moll, L. C., Amanti, C., Neff, D., and González, N. 1992. Funds of knowledge for teaching: Using a qualitative approach to connect homes and classrooms. *Theory into Practice, 3*(2), 132–141.

Mullen, C. A., and Tuten, E. M. 2004. A case study of adolescent female leadership: Exploring the "light" of change. *Journal of Educational Thought, 38*(3), 287–313.

National Center for Education Statistics. n.d. *NAEP Data Explorer.* Retrieved August 1, 2008, from http://nces.ed.gov/nationsreportcard/NDE

Neild, R. C., Balfanz, R., and Herzog, L. 2007. An early warning system. *Educational Leadership, 65*(2), 28–33.

Ormerod, A. J., Collinsworth, L. L., and Perry, L. A. 2008. Critical climate: Relations among sexual harassment, climate, and outcomes for high school girls and boys. *Psychology of Women Quarterly, 32*(2), 113–125.

Passel, J. S., and Cohn, D. 2008. *U.S. population projections: 2005–2050.* Washington, DC: Pew Research Center. Retrieved August 1, 2008, from http://pewsocialtrends.org/pubs/703/population-projections-united-states

Payne, E. C. 2007. Heterosexism, perfection, and popularity: Young lesbians' experiences of the high school social scene. *Educational Studies, 41*(1), 60–79.

Peske, H. G., and Haycock, K. 2006. *Teacher inequality: How poor and minority students are shortchanged on teacher quality.* Washington DC: Education Trust. Retrieved August 1, 2008, from www2.edtrust.org

Rothstein, R. 2004. *Class and schools.* New York: Teachers College Press.

Saifer, S., and Barton, R. 2007. Promoting culturally responsive standards-based teaching. *Principal Leadership, 8*(1), 24–28.

Sanders, J., and Cotton Nelson, S. 2004. Closing gender gaps in science. *Educational Leadership, 62*(3), 74–77.

Stritikus, T. T. 2006. Making meaning matter: A look at instructional practice in additive and subtractive contexts. *Bilingual Research Journal, 30*(1), 219–227.

Swanson, C. B. 2004a. *Projections of 2003–04 high school graduates: Supplemental analyses based on findings from* Who Graduates? Who Doesn't? Washington, DC: Urban Institute.

Swanson, C. B. 2004b. *Who graduates? Who doesn't? A statistical portrait of public high school graduation, class of 2001.* Washington, DC: Urban Institute.

Taylor, D., and Lorimer, M. 2003. Helping gays succeed: Which research-based strategies curb negative trends now facing boys? *Educational Leadership, 60*(4), 68–70.

Valenzuela, A. 1999. *Subtractive schooling: U.S. Mexican youth and the politics of caring.* Albany: State University of New York Press.

Van Den Bergh, N., and Crisp, C. 2004. Defining culturally competent practice with sexual minorities: Implications for social work education and practice. *Journal of Social Work Education, 40*(2), 221–238.

van Wormer, K., and McKinney, R. 2003. What schools can do to help gay/lesbian/bisexual youth: A harm reduction approach. *Adolescence, 38,* 409–420.

Weiler, E. M. 2003. Making school safe for sexual minority students. *Principal Leadership (Middle School Ed.), 4*(4), 11–13.

Whelan, D. L. 2006. Out and ignored. *School Library Journal, 52*(1), 46–50.

Wiener, R., and Pristoop, E. 2006. How states shortchange the districts that need the most help. In *Funding gaps 2006.* Washington, DC: Education Trust. Retrieved August 1, 2008, from www2.edtrust.org

chapter 22

Building Community

outline

- Democratic Community
- Moral Community
- Professional Learning Community
- Community of Inquiry
- Engagement with the Larger Community
- Five Attributes, One Community
- Conclusion

Visit the **MyEdLeadershipLab™** site for *The Basic Guide to SuperVision and Instructional Leadership*, Third Edition to enhance your understanding of chapter concepts. You'll have the opportunity to practice your skills through video and case based Assignments and Activities as well as Building Leadership Skills units, and prepare for your certification exam with Practice for Certification quizzes.

Sergiovanni (1999) and others have proposed viewing schools as *communities* rather than *organizations*. Organizations are known for their "linear lines of communication, chain-of-command decision making, differentiation of tasks, hierarchical supervision, and formal rules and regulations" (Scribner, Cockrell, Cockrell, and Valentine, 1999, p. 135). In an organization, the leader decides what must be done and bargains with workers to gain their cooperation, offering them something they want in exchange for doing what the leader wants. Rewards are provided for compliance and punishments for noncompliance. Individuals thus are bound together by bartering and self-interest (Sergiovanni, 1999). Classical organization theory is tied to the factory model, with its emphasis on efficiency and productivity:

> The adoption of this bureaucratic theory using the Carnegie units of grades and specializations adopted by the modern school system has resulted in the modern factory schools where the product is the student prepared for the work force to fuel the economy. The problem with this organizational theory for schools is that students are not products and don't usually respond positively to a culture that adds to them as if they were a car on an assembly line. Many students fall by the wayside in this factory model as rejects or seconds off the assembly line. (Martin and MacNeil, 2007, par. 1)

In contrast to organizations, relationships in communities are based on shared identity, beliefs, values, and goals. Members of a community are mutually committed to each other and the community (Hord, 2008).

Sergiovanni (1999) makes this comparison of communities and organizations:

> Life in organizations and life in communities are different in both quality and kind. In communities we create our social lives with others who have intentions similar to ours. In organizations relationships are constructed for us by others and become confided into a system of hierarchies, roles, and role expectations. Communities too are confronted with issues of control. But instead of relying on external control measures communities rely more on norms, purposes, values, professional socialization, collegiality, and natural independence. (p. 119)

Merely agreeing to view schools as communities rather than organizations, of course, is not a magic elixir for all of our schools' problems. For one thing, not all communities are good communities. A community can be insular, myopic, or prejudiced. Over time, communities can develop internal conflicts, become dysfunctional, and deteriorate. Shields and Seltzer (1997) note that "many schools may be just as accurately described as microcosms of the conflicts and disparities in the wider community than as examples of Sergiovanni's emotional and normative relationships" (p. 415). These authors believe that this reality can be addressed by educators committing to community development as a moral endeavor in which they explore differences and commonalities; work to create democratic, inclusive communities; and achieve unity *within* diversity.

Another caution about the concept of the school as a community comes from Furman (1998), who warns that there are disparities between a community, as typically defined, and our postmodern society. First, Furman doubts that traditional unity is possible in the chaotic and fragmented postmodern world. Second, she argues that postmodernism rejects the notion of community membership based on sameness, because it leads to false boundaries and exclusion. Furman believes that community and postmodernism can be aligned if the concept of community includes awareness of multiple cultures, beliefs, and values:

> Postmodern community is community of difference. It is based on the ethics of acceptance of otherness with respect, justice, and appreciation and on peaceful cooperation within difference. It is inspired by the metaphor of an interconnected, interdependent web of persons engaged in global community. It is fostered by processes that promote among its members the feelings of belonging, trust of others, and safety. (p. 312)

One thing that modernists and postmodernists agree on is that if we are going to use community as the preferred metaphor for school, we must establish what we mean by community. Based on our work with many schools and our research on successful schools, we suggest five attributes of a fully functioning school community: (1) democracy, (2) moral principles, (3) professional learning, (4) inquiry, and (5) engagement with the wider community. We explore each of these attributes in this final chapter.

Democratic Community

There are at least three powerful reasons that schools should be democratic communities. First, the most important reason that U.S. public schools exist is to sustain democracy by preparing students to be informed and responsible citizens (Schultz, 2007). Second, with democratic governance, schools work better and are more likely to improve. Third, in a democratic community, students experience higher-level learning and higher levels of achievement than in conventional schools (Flanagan, Cumsille, Gill, and Gallay, 2007).

Goodlad (2004) argues that educating students in democracy is essential to sustaining a democratic society:

> In a democracy, schooling is vitally important and very different from schooling in other societies. No other institution in our society is as suited as the public schools for introducing the young to both the ideas inherent in a social and political democracy as well as the ideals from which democracy is derived. That is why thoughtful men and women dating back to the very origins of our country have consistently envisioned a prominent and essential role for public schooling in the creating and sustaining of a democratic republic. (p. 19)

John Dewey is one of those thoughtful men and women to whom Goodlad refers. Dewey (1916) wrote, "A democracy is more than a form of government; it is primarily a mode of associated living, of conjoint communicated experience" (p. 93). In other words, democracy is about the social relationships of community members. Citizens must understand how others' actions affect them and how their actions affect others. In an authentic democracy, citizens seek to understand the experiences, values, and needs of others and balance their interests with those of others (Rhoads, 1998). Dewey believed not only that schools must prepare students for democratic life but also that the way to do so is for students to *experience* democracy within the school community.

If schools are to promote democracy, then they should do the following:

- Value and respect each individual and promote the well-being of all members of the school community
- Work to understand, be responsive to, and assure equitable treatment of all minority groups
- Involve all members of the school community—including teachers, students, and parents—in decision making and expand the areas of decision making in which they are involved
- Encourage two-way communication, the free flow of ideas, and open discussion of controversial issues
- Foster critical reflection on and critique of power relations, school structures, the curriculum, and instructional practices and be open to change for the common good
- Engage in collaborative work and collective leadership
- Allow freedom of choice
- Embrace norms of civic participation and service to others

In addition to preserving our democratic society, democratic schools work better and improve more than conventional schools. Indeed, Mallory and Reavis (2007) conclude that "a school culture based on democracy-centered principles is essential to continuous school improvement" (p. 10). School improvement has been associated with a number of variables, including teacher empowerment, teacher leadership, collaboration, collegiality, reflective dialogue, and teacher choice (Gordon, Stiegelbauer, and Diehl, 2008). If you examine these variables, you find that they are all far more likely to occur in a democratic community than a school in which decisions are made by the principal or a small leadership team.

Our concepts of democracy and community are compatible with recent scholarship that indicates true leadership does not consist of a single person in a leadership role making decisions, but results from relationships and interactions among many individuals, including formal and informal leaders (Spillane, 2005; Scribner, Sawyer, Watson, and Myers, 2007). Scribner and colleagues (2007) suggest that "decisions emerge from collaborative dialogues between many individuals, engaged in mutually dependent activities" (p. 70). This description of leadership sounds a lot like leadership in the communities described by Sergiovanni (1999) as well as the relational democracy espoused by Dewey (1916).

Democracy is not only a way of governing and relating to one another but also a theory of how students learn. In schools practicing a democratic pedagogy, students do the following:

- Work actively with problems, ideas, materials and other people as they learn skills and content
- Have escalating degrees of choices, both as individuals and groups, within the parameters provided by the teacher
- Are responsible to their peers, teachers, parents, and school community, using educational time purposefully, intelligently, and productively
- Share their learning with one another, teachers, parents, and other community members
- Decide how to make their learning a contribution to their community
- Assume escalating responsibilities for securing resources (of people and materials outside of school) and finding places where they can apply and further their learning
- Demonstrate what they know and can do in public settings and receive public feedback
- Work together and learn from another, individually and in groups, at a pace that challenges all (Glickman, 1998, p. 18)

A long line of research shows that students taught in a democratic community using the pedagogy just described—regardless of their socioeconomic, racial, or ethnic status—perform at a higher level than other students on a variety of achievement measures (Joyce, Wolf, and Calhoun, 1993; Meier, 1995; Newmann, Marks, and Gamoran, 1995; Darling-Hammond, 1997; Flanagan, Cumsille, Gill, and Gallay, 2007).

Moral Community*

A moral school community is committed to the overall well-being, growth, and development of each community member. Moral communities are built around moral principles that, when taken together and taken seriously, foster the development of a school that enables students to develop as moral persons prepared to contribute to a better society. Several of those moral principles are suggested here.

Care

In *caring* schools, adults are open and receptive to students. They engage students in informal conversations, listen to students attentively, and are aware of what is going

*Portions of this section originally were published in Stephen P. Gordon (2001), "The good school." *Florida Educational Leadership, 1*(2), 13–15.

on in students' lives inside and outside school. Adults try to place themselves in students' shoes to understand their experiences, concerns, and actions and put forth time and energy to respond to students' needs, to bring out the best in students, and to promote students' success. Care is reciprocal; it is not complete unless the student receiving the care recognizes it, accepts it, and responds to it (Noddings, 2005). Schussler and Collins (2006) found that students felt cared for when they were provided opportunities to succeed, were treated with respect, and felt they belonged in school because of positive relationships with teachers and other students and when the school showed flexibility in accommodating them and provided a family atmosphere.

Noddings (2005) reminds us that teachers need not only care for students but also help them develop the capacity to care for others. This begins with *modeling*. Teachers can't just tell students to care for others; they must show them by developing caring relationships. Another component of teaching care is *dialogue*—open-ended, two-way conversation in which the outcome cannot be predicted. Engaging in dialogue develops students' capacity to communicate, to share decision making, and to support each other in problem solving. A third part of teaching students to care is providing opportunities to *practice* caregiving in order to develop skills and attitudes associated with care. Finally, teachers should use *confirmation* to teach care, identifying students' "better selves" and encouraging them to develop those better, caring selves (Noddings, 2005).

Although teachers caring for students and teaching students to care for others is at the heart of a caring school community, the principle of care applies to everyone associated with the school. In a community of care, school leaders, teachers, students, and parents are all caregivers and care receivers.

Wholeness

Authentic care for students leads to the realization that one cannot separate different aspects of student growth. The moral school is committed to students' cognitive, physical, emotional, creative, social, and moral development (Oser, Althof, and Higgins-D'Alessandro, 2008). Not only is growth in all of these areas necessary for the development of the whole person, but the different domains of learning are interactive and interdependent as well; growth in one domain is enhanced by growth in the others. The principle of *wholeness* applies to adult members of the school community as well. For example, the school must concern itself with teachers' pedagogical growth, their physical and emotional well-being, and their creative, social, and moral development.

Connectedness

Schools have an obligation to break down artificial barriers to natural relationships in students' lives and learning. For example, the education provided to students must be relevant to both their present and their future, not focused on one at the expense of the other. Connections between different content areas must be made, and the world of the classroom must be connected to life outside the school, including the local, national, and world communities (National Commission on Service Learning, 2002). The principle of *connectedness* also means that members of the school community should not be restricted to single roles. Administrators, teachers, and students should all engage in leadership, teaching, and learning, albeit at different levels and with different emphases.

Inclusion

Inclusion, as a moral principle, combines the beliefs in equality and equity. It begins with equality. All students are of equal worth as human beings and as members of the school community. A belief in equality leads to a commitment to equity. Those who have physical, cognitive, emotional, or social challenges should be provided the necessary assistance, including extraordinary measures if necessary, to enable them to remain members of the community and to lead fulfilling lives first as students and later as adults. The moral school responds to all cultures and all students—low-socioeconomic students, racial and ethnic minorities, immigrants, non-English-speaking students, gay and lesbian students, and so on (Flanagan, Cumsille, Gill, and Gallay, 2007).

Justice

Teaching about social justice is part of this principle, as is providing justice as a means of facilitating teaching and learning. *Justice* includes holding teachers accountable for effective instruction and holding students accountable for learning. In an educational context, however, *accountability* should mean providing feedback on one's performance and assistance for improving future performance, not issuing rewards and punishments.

At its core, *justice* means treating members of the school community in a fair and consistent manner. By being just with students, educators can to some extent counter the injustice that students may face in society. By modeling justice, educators can teach students to treat others justly (Schultz, 2008). Such justice, repeated daily, can facilitate student learning in all areas and eventually lead to a more just society. Justice must also be provided to all adults in the school community. Adults who are treated justly learn better how to treat students justly. A school will very likely provide its students no more justice than it provides its staff.

Peace

Student misbehavior is one of the major school problems reported by supervisors and teachers. Especially troublesome is misbehavior that interferes with the right of other students to learn. Worse yet, in recent years, there has been a frightening increase in student violence (Akiba, 2008). Perhaps one way to approach this problem is to change from a school characterized by effective student discipline to a school of *peace*. Moving toward this vision requires supervisors, teachers, and students to develop or enhance communication, collaboration, and conflict management skills. Doing so also requires supervisors, teachers, and students to develop a new self-concept, viewing themselves not just as leaders or teachers or students but as healers and peacemakers. For those who argue that we cannot afford to spend school time learning about healing and peacemaking, our response is that considering the growing incivility in our communities and schools, we can no longer afford *not* to engage in such learning.

Freedom

Learning and freedom—freedom to dream, to explore, to take risks, and to learn from failures—go hand in hand. Educators need freedom to grow professionally, and likewise, students need freedom to develop to their full potential. Granted, students and adults function at varying stages of development and thus possess varying capacities for responding to freedom. For some, it may be necessary to introduce freedom gradually, initially presented as restricted choice. Regardless, it is the *directionality* of the school's efforts that is important. All members of the school community should be moving toward increased freedom of choice in what they learn, how they learn, and how they demonstrate learning (Dooner, Mandzuk, and Clifton, 2008). Those who equate school reform with external control find this principle particularly difficult to accept.

Trust

Consistent efforts on behalf of care, wholeness, connectedness, inclusion, justice, peace, and freedom can lead to trusting relationships among members of the school community. *Trust* is both a product of adhering to the other principles and a requirement for those principles to flourish over the long run. Authentic learning is based not merely on the transmission of knowledge and skills but primarily on personal relationships, and trust is the ground on which those relationships are built (Hord, 2008). For all its importance, however, personal trust is not the only type of trust present in a good school. There is also trust in the moral principles to which the school is committed—trust that these principles, if adhered to, will result in a better education and more fulfilling lives for students and a better future for society.

Empowerment

As a moral principle, *empowerment* certainly includes involving members of the school community in making decisions about matters that affect them, but it also goes beyond this standard definition. *Empowerment* also means changing assumptions, norms, roles, and relationships that act as barriers to educators' and students' growth toward self-reliance and self-actualization. It includes not only an invitation to become involved in decisions concerning leadership, teaching, and learning but also to acquire the information and skills necessary to engage in effective decision making in each of these areas. Finally, *empowerment* means instilling in educators and students a commitment to facilitate the empowerment of *other* members of the school community.

Professional Learning Community

Hord and Sommers (2008) define *professional learning communities (PLCs)* as "communities of professionals working to improve student learning together, by engaging in continuous collective learning of their own" (p. ix). Descriptions of specific characteristics of PLCs vary (see Louis, Kruse, and Marks, 1996; DuFour, 2005; DuFour, Eaker, and DuFour, 2005; Hord and Sommers, 2008), but most descriptions include these six characteristics:

1. *Shared beliefs, values, and norms.* Educators reach consensus on a clear set of views about the purpose of school, about children and how they learn, and the roles of school leaders, teachers, students, and parents in the learning process. "Clear shared values and norms, collectively reinforced, increase the likelihood of teachers' success" (Louis, Kruse, and Marks, 1996, p. 181).
2. *Distributed, supportive leadership.* It is not surprising that the same type of leadership discussed in Chapter 20 as needed to facilitate change also fosters PLCs. Hord and Sommers (2008) describe two types of support provided to PLCs: (1) structural support (time to meet, a place to work, material resources) and (2) relational support (the fostering of openness, honesty, respect, and caring among educators). The supervisor shares decision making with teachers and other members of the school community and distributes leadership throughout the school with the goal of "developing the leadership potential of all staff members" (DuFour, Eaker, and DuFour, 2005, p. 23).
3. *Collective learning.* The rationale of collective learning is that individual teachers learning new knowledge and skills in isolation is not enough to improve student learning schoolwide (Hord, 2008). Collective learning is job embedded and involves educators in the same school learning together (DuFour, Eaker, and DuFour, 2005). The process begins with conversations among educators about students, teaching, and learning. The school community chooses an area for improvement, decides what it must learn to make the improvement, and plans collective learning experiences. Part of the learning process is trying out new skills and strategies, discussing the effects of the

new practice, and deciding how the new practice can be improved (Hord and Sommers, 2008).

4. *Deprivatization of teaching.* One of the traditional norms of teaching is that teaching is a private act; the teacher's classroom is not open to other teachers. This privatization of teaching has kept teachers from providing each other instructional assistance. In a deprivatized school, teachers visit each other's classrooms for various reasons: to observe, gather data, and provide feedback; to pick up new ideas from each other; to team teach; and so on. Another part of deprivatization is the open discussion among teachers of problems and concerns about teaching and the sharing of ideas about how to address those problems and concerns.

5. *Focus on student learning.* DuFour (2005) suggests that PLCs focus on three critical questions:
   - What do we want each student to learn?
   - How will we know when each student has learned it?
   - How will we respond when a student experiences difficulty in learning? (p. 33)

   In PLCs, the focus of attention is on students' intellectual development, not merely on techniques or activities that seem interesting and are likely to keep students engaged (Louis, Kruse, and Marks, 1996). The focus of student assessment in PLCs is ongoing formative assessment to identify student learning needs, to provide feedback to help teachers adjust their teaching, and to track student progress over time. Student assessments "are easily accessible and openly shared between teachers who then assist each other in addressing areas of concern" (DuFour, Eaker, and DuFour, 2005, p. 22).

6. *Collaboration.* In Chapter 2, we describe how the legacy of the one-room school and the "egg crate" structure of traditional schools kept teachers in their classrooms and out of contact with other adults for most of the school-day. PLCs free teachers from isolation and provide peer support as they share information and expertise; work together to develop curriculum, create instructional materials, and assess student learning; and engage in joint problem solving (Louis, Kruse, and Marks, 1996).

The research on the effects of PLCs is promising. In a review of that research, Vescio, Ross, and Adams (2008) found that PLCs make teachers more student centered, improve the teaching culture, and improve student achievement. Some researchers, however, advise caution regarding PLCs. Scribner, Hager, and Warne (2002), for example, conclude that, in addition to the shared identity of the PLC, teachers should be allowed to maintain an individual identity and some level of professional autonomy. According to the authors, "This autonomy does not preclude them from participating in and belonging to the professional community" (p. 70). The idea here is to create a balance, addressing both the school community's goals and the individual teacher's needs.

Community of Inquiry

Although some scholars equate a community of inquiry with reflective dialogue alone, we take a broader view, as illustrated in Figure 22.1. If you think that the process shown in this figure looks a lot like a generalized version of action research, as described in Chapter 19, you are correct! However, the cycle of inquiry can be used in many ways other than in action research. For instance, the inquiry cycle is used on a small scale in clinical supervision or peer coaching (see Chapter 15) when participants select a focus during the preconference and use data gathered during the classroom observation to inform reflective dialogue in the postconference, culminating in an action plan to improve teaching. The cycle of inquiry can be used in a broader scale in curriculum development (see Chapter 18) when teachers gather data on the effects of a curriculum on students, engage in reflective dialogue on the meaning of the data, and take action by designing new curriculum units. Examples of the cycle of inquiry integrated into a cultural task of supervision can be found in programs to increase equity (see Chapter 21), in which teachers analyze data on achievement gaps, participate in reflective dialogue on how the school's culture and their own teaching contribute to the gaps, and take action to become more culturally responsive. In short, the cycle of inquiry is not only applied in the supervision task of action research; it can be integrated with any technical or cultural task of supervision.

Data gathering and analysis are essential to systematic inquiry, but the word *data* evokes a negative response from many teachers. Earl and Katz (2006) encourage

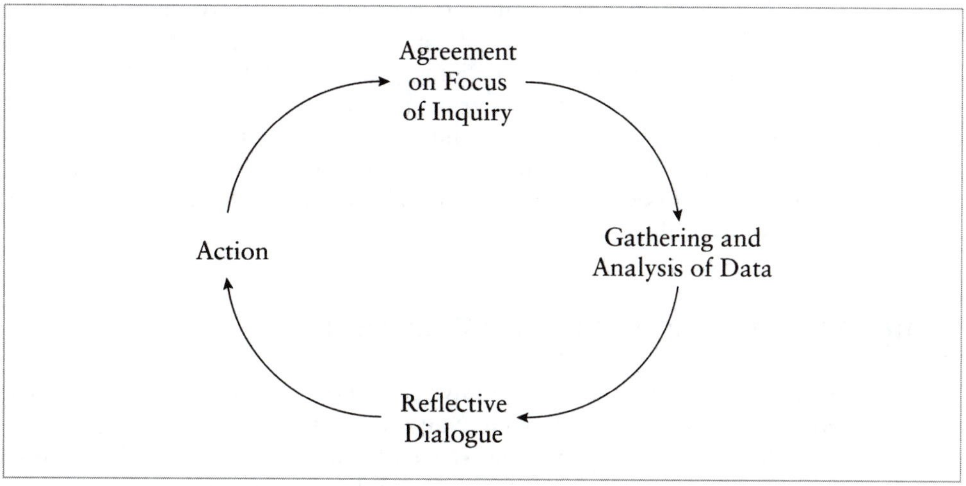

figure **22.1** **The Cycle of Inquiry**

educators to become more comfortable with using data as part of their everyday efforts to improve practice:

> Using data does not have to be a mechanical or technical process that denigrates educators' intuition, teaching philosophy, and personal experience. In fact using data wisely is a human thinking activity that draws on personal views but also on capturing and organizing ideas in some systematic way, turning the information into meaningful actions. . . . Data are a necessary part of an ongoing process of analysis, insight, new learning, and changes in practice. (pp. 14, 15)

Earl and Katz (2006) also suggest ways schools can promote the use of data, including structuring opportunities for teachers to engage with data, using data to foster a sense of moral urgency to work for change, providing time for inquiry, and enlisting the services of outside critical friends to critique and support data-based improvement of practice.

Data and data analysis provide a basis for *reflective dialogue* among teachers: dialogue about student learning, student assessment, equity, school–community relations, and so on. The dialogue can center on teachers helping teachers to examine their classroom practice or on a collective critique of the school as a learning community. Over time, reflective dialogue creates a network of knowledge and support for all members of the school community (Smith-Maddox, 1999; Hipp, Huffman, Pankake, and Oliver, 2008).

The final phase in the cycle of inquiry is *action* to improve teaching and learning. In a community of inquiry, this action is informed by data gathering and analysis and reflective dialogue, and the action itself becomes the subject of a new cycle of inquiry, using new data and continued dialogue to assess and modify improvement efforts.

In schools that are communities of inquiry, classrooms become their own centers of inquiry, as teachers introduce the cycle of inquiry to their students. Students are presented with problems or issues, gather and analyze data, present and defend alternatives, expand and integrate ideas, and take action to solve problems or address issues (Hord, 2008). Communities of inquiry foster students' cognitive and metacognitive skills (Brown and Campione, 1994) and motivate students to receive and provide assistance as they learn to be socially responsible members of a learning community (Elbers, 2003).

Engagement with the Larger Community

Children come to school with physical, emotional, and social needs that will affect their learning if not addressed. Many of these are *co-occurring needs*—needs that their families and communities share (Anderson-Butcher, Stetler, and Midle, 2006). It makes sense, then, for schools to work with families and communities to meet these needs. Also, communities are valuable sources of knowledge and rich learning environments that teachers can tap to make learning more relevant and meaningful. Historically, instructional supervision has paid little attention to the relationships among community development, school development, and student learning or to the enormous potential of community-based learning. In recent years, the scope of supervision has expanded beyond the classroom in recognition of the need for schoolwide, collaborative efforts to enhance teaching and learning. The scope of supervision must expand still further, to include school–community collaboration. Here, we discuss three aspects of engagement with the wider community: school-based and school-linked community service, community development, and the community as a learning environment.

School-Based and School-Linked Community Service

Dryfoos (1994) defines the *full-service school* as one that "integrates educational, medical, social and/or human services that are beneficial to meeting the needs of children and youth and their families on school grounds or in locations which are easily accessible" (p. 142). The services provided to students, families, and community members might include the following:

- Welcoming and orientation for new members of the community
- Providing basic needs such as food, clothing, and school supplies free or at reduced cost
- Providing meals on weekends and holidays and during vacations
- Health screening and basic health services
- Dental services
- Vision services
- Mental health services
- Substance abuse treatment
- Parental care
- Adult education
- Parent education
- Community empowerment programs
- Social services
- Early childhood/preschool education
- Child care
- Family support programs

Lawson (1999) advocates a wide range of services like those just listed, but believes that a variety of community organizations should work with schools to provide them: "Collaboration is required. It both reflects and promotes interdependent relationships. Schools, community agencies, neighborhood organizations, religious institutions depend on each other. When one succeeds, the others' results often improve. When one fails, others may follow" (p. 19). Lawson maintains that the various community organizations are motivated to collaborate in community service because of enlightened self-interest.

Community Development

The community development approach begins with the idea that the school is part of a much larger ecosystem that is responsible for the growth and development of all its members (Hiatt-Michael, 2006). Because the school is continuously affecting and affected by other parts of the larger educational environment (the community), it should integrate its educational efforts with other community efforts to assist all members of the ecosystem to grow and develop. As described by Timpane and Reich (1997):

> Community development changes the core identity of schools from isolated, independent agencies to institutions enmeshed with other community agencies in an interconnected landscape of support for the well-being of students and learners. It beckons schools to consider and respond to learning needs throughout the community, not just to those of children within the school building. (p. 466)

Because the community's overall health affects school development and student learning, it is appropriate for supervisors, teachers, and, in many cases, students to participate in *community development*, defined as a process to improve the "economic, social, cultural, and/or environmental situation" (Christenson, Fendley, and Robinson, 1989, p. 14). Two guidelines for schools to participate in community development are (1) to connect the community development process directly to school development and student learning, and (2) to coordinate participation in community development with other community agencies and organizations.

The Community as a Learning Environment

According to Arrington and Moore (2001), "When we purposefully involve students in learning experiences that stretch far beyond the school walls into the community and the world, we provide motivation and relevance that can make a difference in children achieving school success" (p. 56). Learning models that connect students to the community and larger society include service learning, place-based learning, and democratic learning.

Service Learning. The service learning model integrates the curriculum with community service and occurs only when service is accompanied by academic learning. In service learning, students analyze community issues, choose a service project, plan activities, perform the service, and engage in individual and group reflection on the project (Arrington and Moore, 2001; Flanagan, Cumsille, Gill, and Gallay, 2007).

Service learning can take place within any content area and often cuts across several content areas.

Place-Based Learning. The place-based learning model uses social, cultural, and natural aspects of the students' local environment as the context for learning. Smith (2002) provides a snapshot of place-based learning:

> When Environment Middle School students go to Brookside Wetlands, . . . their water samples and inventories of macro invertebrates, collected and compiled over the course of the year, become part of a report to Portland's Bureau of Environmental Services. The project allows for a direct rather than mediated experience of the world. The water is cold—the mud, slippery. And when the class spots two geese threatening with outstretched necks a third who tries to cross the invisible boundary that marks their territory, everyone watches in silence. (p. 31)

In place-based learning, students produce rather than consume knowledge, teachers are co-learners and guides rather than instructors, and students solve real-world problems rather than fictitious ones (Smith, 2002; Powers, 2004).

Democratic Learning. The democratic learning model asks students to integrate their personal concerns with concerns about the larger world and the common good. Students decide on a common theme, often dealing with race, ethnicity, class, gender, or another issue of diversity. Within the common theme, small groups and individuals develop their own questions and projects. The questions that students ask in democratic learning tend to focus on serious social issues, such as war and peace, the environment, and the family. As students explore issues, they engage in rigorous academic work, display high-level cognitive skills, show mutual respect, and build community (Beane, 2002; Marri, 2005).

Five Attributes, One Community

The relationship of the five attributes of a school community is shown in Figure 22.2. Although each attribute is different, there is considerable overlap and interaction among the five attributes. Let us consider for a moment one of the attributes, democracy, in relationship to the others. Historically, *democracy* has never been defined merely as majority rule; rather, it has been considered a way of life based on underlying moral principles (the second attribute). Also, professional learning (the third attribute) works best if supported by democratic leadership and conducted by teachers in a democratic manner. Inquiry (the fourth attribute) requires the openness and freedom of a democratic environment. Finally, school–community engagement (the fifth attribute) works best if school and community participants use a democratic process for making decisions about school and community development.

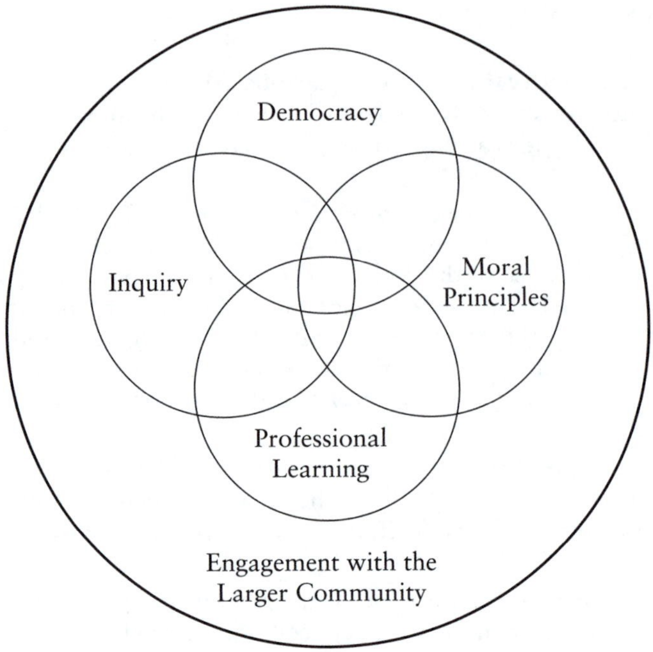

figure 22.2 **Relationship of Attributes of an Authentic School Community**

We could go through this same process with any of the attributes of community. Each attribute of an authentic community flows into and supports each of the other attributes.

Conclusion

This book, *The Basic Guide to SuperVision and Instructional Leadership*, is first and foremost about the ideas of purpose, hope, and growth and development for all of our students. Figure 22.3 reviews the knowledge, skills, technical tasks, and cultural tasks for achieving a purposeful school dedicated to the continuing enhancement of teaching and learning.

Please remember that competence without a clear purpose results in directionless change, and purpose without competence provides inefficiency and frustration. We hope that you, the reader, in whatever role of instructional leadership, add coherence and congruence to the education of all students in your own school and community. After all, this is the primary reason we chose to be educators—to practice what we believe.

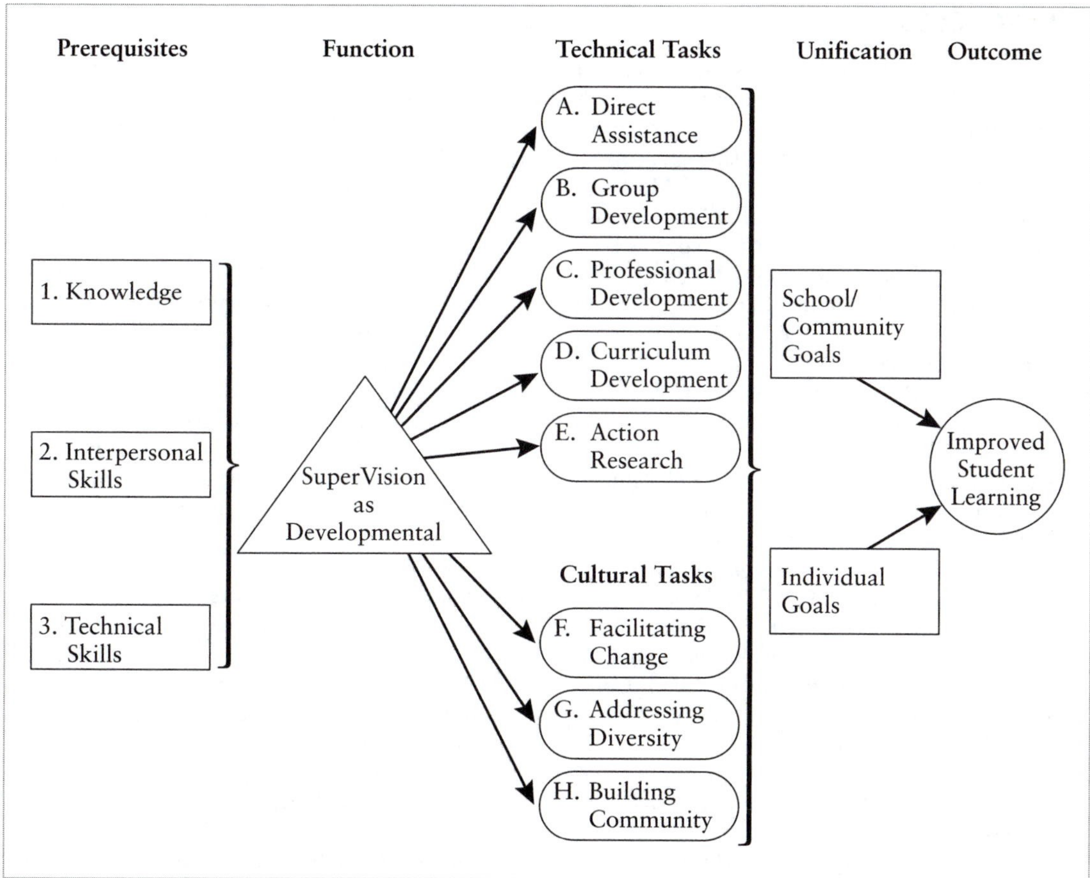

figure **22.3** **SuperVision and Successful Schools**

MyEdLeadershipLab™

Go to Topic 10, Facilitating Change, in the MyEdLeadershipLab™ site at www.myedleadershiplab.com for *The Basic Guide to SuperVision and Instructional Leadership*, Third Edition, where you can:

- Find learning outcomes for Facilitating Change along with the national standards that connect to these outcomes.
- Complete Assignments and Activities that can help you more deeply understand the chapter content.
- Apply and practice your understanding of the core skills identified in the chapter with the Building Leadership Skills unit.
- Prepare yourself for professional certification with a Practice for Certification quiz.

REFERENCES

Akiba, M. 2008. Predictors of student fear of school violence: A comparative study of eighth graders in 33 countries. *School Effectiveness and School Improvement, 19*(1), 51–72.

Anderson-Butcher, D., Stetler, G., and Midle, T. 2006. A case for expanded school-community partnerships in support of positive youth development. *Children and Schools, 23*(3), 155–163.

Arrington, H. J., and Moore, S. D. 2001. Infusing service learning into instruction. *Middle School Journal, 32*(4), 55–60.

Beane, J. A. 2002. Beyond self-interest: A democratic core curriculum. *Educational Leadership, 59*(7), 25–28.

Brown, A. L., and Campione, J. C. 1994. Guided discovery in a community of learners. In K. McGilly (Ed.), *Classroom lessons: Integrating cognitive theory and classroom practice* (pp. 229–270). Cambridge, MA: MIT Press.

Christenson, J. A., Fendley, K., and Robinson, J. W. 1989. Community development. In J.A. Christenson and J. W. Robinson (Eds.), *Community development in perspective* (pp. 3–25). Ames: Iowa State University Press.

Darling-Hammond, L. 1997. *The right to learn: A blueprint for creating schools that work.* San Francisco: Jossey-Bass.

Dewey, J. 1916. *Democracy and education.* New York: Macmillan.

Dooner, A., Mandzuk, D., and Clifton, R. A. 2008. Stages of collaboration and the realities of professional learning communities. *Teaching and Teacher Education, 24,* 564–574.

Dryfoos, J. G. 1994. *Full-service schools.* San Francisco: Jossey-Bass.

DuFour, R. 2005. What is a professional learning community? In R. DuFour, R. Eaker, and R. DuFour (Eds.), *On common ground: The power of professional learning communities.* Bloomington, IN: National Educational Service.

DuFour, R., Eaker, R., and DuFour, R. 2005. Recurring themes of professional learning communities and the assumptions they challenge. In R. DuFour, R. Eaker, and R. DuFour (Eds.), *On common ground: The power of professional learning communities.* Bloomington, IN: National Educational Service.

Earl, L. M., and Katz, S. 2006. *Leading schools in a data-rich world: Harnessing data for school improvement.* Thousand Oaks, CA: Corwin Press.

Elbers, E. 2003. Classroom interaction as reflection: Learning and teaching mathematics in a community of inquiry. *Educational Studies in Mathematics, 54,* 77–99.

Flanagan, C., Cumsille, P., Gill, S., and Gallay, L. 2007. School and community climates and civic commitments: Patterns for ethnic minority and majority students. *Journal of Educational Psychology, 99*(2), 421–431.

Furman, G. C. 1998. Postmodernism and community in schools: Unraveling the paradox. *Education Administration Quarterly, 34,* 298–328.

Glickman, C. D. 1998. Revolution, education, and the practice of democracy. *The Educational Forum, 63,* 16–22.

Goodlad, S. J. 2004. Democracy, schools, and the agenda. *Kappa Delta Pi Record, 41*(1), 17–20.

Gordon, S. P., Stiegelbauer, S. M., and Diehl, J. 2008. Characteristics of more and less successful action research programs. In S. P. Gordon (Ed.), *Collaborative action research: Developing professional learning communities* (pp. 79–94). New York: Teachers College Press.

Hiatt-Michael, D. 2006. Reflections and directions on research related to family community involvement in schooling. *The School Community Journal, 16*(1), 7–30.

Hipp, K. K., Huffman, J. B., Pankake, A. M., and Oliver, D. F. 2008. Sustaining professional learning communities: Case studies. *Journal of Educational Change, 9,* 173–195.

Hord, S. M. 2008. Evolution of the professional learning community. *Journal of Staff Development, 29*(3), 10–13.

Hord, S. M., and Sommers, W. A. 2008. *Leading professional learning communities.* Thousand Oaks, CA: Corwin Press.

Joyce, B. J., Wolf, J., and Calhoun, E. 1993. *The self-renewing school.* Alexandria, VA: Association for Supervision and Curriculum Development.

Lawson, H. A. 1999. Two new mental models for schools and their implications for principals' roles, responsibilities, and preparation. *NASSP Bulletin, 83*(8), 8–27.

Louis, K. S., Kruse, S. D., and Marks, H. M. 1996. Schoolwide professional community. In F. M. Newmann and Associates (Eds.), *Authentic achievement: Restructuring schools for intellectual quality* (pp. 179–203). San Francisco: Jossey-Bass.

Mallory, B. J., and Reavis, C. A. 2007. Planning for school improvement: Closing the gap of culture with democratic principles. *Educational Planning, 16*(2), 8–18.

Marri, A. R. 2005. Building a framework for classroom-based multicultural democratic education: Learning from three skilled teachers. *Teachers College Record, 107*(5), 1036–1059.

Martin, G., and MacNeil, A. 2007. *School as community versus school as factory.* Retrieved August 1, 2008, from http://cnx.org/content/m14666/1.3

Meier, D. 1995. *The power of their ideas: Lessons for America from a small school in Harlem.* Boston: Beacon Press.

National Commision on Service Learning. 2002. *Learning in deed.* Battle Creek, MI: W. K. Kellogg Foundation and the John Glenn Institute for Public Service. (Available from the W. K. Kellogg Foundation, (800) 819–9997, wkkford@iserv.net)

Newmann, F. M., Marks, H. M., and Gamoran, A. 1995. Authentic pedagogy: Standards that boost student performance. *Issues in Restructuring Schools, 8,* 1–11.

Noddings, N. 2005. *The challenge to care in schools: An alternative approach to education* (2nd ed.). New York: Teachers College Press.

Oser, F. K., Althof, W., and Higgins-D'Alessandro, A. 2008. The just community approach to moral education: System change or individual change? *Journal of Moral Education, 37*(3), 395–415.

Powers, A. L. 2004. An evaluation of four place-based education programs. *The Journal of Environmental Education, 35*(4), 17–32.

Rhoads, R. A. 1998. In the service of citizenship: A study of student improvement in community service. *The Journal of Higher Education, 69*(3), 277–297.

Schultz, B. 2007. Not satisfied with stupid Band-Aids: A portrait of a justice-oriented, democratic curriculum serving a disadvantaged neighborhood. *Equity and Excellence in Education, 40*(1), 166–176.

Schultz, B. 2008. Strategizing, sustaining, and supporting justice-oriented teaching. *Democracy and Education, 17*(3), 8–19.

Schussler, D. L., and Collins, A. 2006. An empirical exploration of the who, what, and how of school care. *Teachers College Record, 108,* 1460–1495.

Scribner, J. P., Cockrell, K. S., Cockrell, D. H., and Valentine, J. W. 1999. Creating professional communities in schools through organizational learning: An evaluation of a school improvement process. *Educational Administration Quarterly, 35*(1), 130–160.

Scribner, J. P., Hager, D. R., and Warne, T. R. 2002. The paradox of professional community: Tales from two high schools. *Educational Administration Quarterly, 38*(1), 45–76.

Scribner, J. P., Sawyer, R. K., Watson, S. T., and Myers, V. L. 2007. Teacher teams and distributed leadership: A study of group discourse and collaboration. *Educational Administration Quarterly, 43*(1), 67–100.

Sergiovanni, T. J. 1999. Changing our theory of schooling. In T. J. Sergiovanni (Ed.), *Rethinking leadership: A collection of articles.* Arlington Heights, IL: Skylight Training and Publishing.

Shields, C. M., and Seltzer, P. A. 1997. Complexities and paradoxes of community: Toward a more useful conceptualization of community. *Educational Administration Quarterly, 33,* 413–439.

Smith, G. A. 2002. Going local. *Educational Leadership, 60*(1), 30–33.

Smith-Maddox, R. 1999. An inquiry-based reform effort: Creating the conditions for reculturing and restructuring schools. *The Urban Review, 31,* 283–304.

Spillane, J. P. 2005. Distributed leadership. *The Educational Forum, 69*(2), 143–150.

Timpane, M., and Reich, B. 1997. Revitalizing the ecosystem for youth. *Phi Delta Kappan, 78,* 464–470.

Vescio, V., Ross, D., and Adams, A. 2008. A review of research on the impact of professional learning communities on teaching practice and student learning. *Teaching and Teacher Education, 24,* 80–91. Retrieved August 1, 2008, from www.sciencedirect.com

appendix A

Review of Interpersonal Behavior in the Four Supervisory Approaches

The four supervisory approaches used in developmental supervision are briefly summarized and compared on the next page. We suggest that graduate students and practitioners practicing the different approaches during role plays have the summaries at hand for use as a quick reference during practice sessions.

Directive Control

1. Present problem.
2. Ask teacher for input into problem.
3. Listen to understand teacher's perception of problem.
4. Mentally determine solution.
5. State solution to teacher.
6. Ask teacher for input into solution.
7. Modify and detail expected actions.
8. Summarize expected actions and describe follow-up.

Directive Informational

1. Identify problem.
2. Ask teacher for input into problem.
3. Listen to understand teacher's perception of problem.
4. Mentally determine two or three alternative solutions.
6. Ask teacher for views on each alternative solution.
7. Modify alternative solutions and frame final choices.
8. Ask teacher to choose one of alternative solutions.
9. State specific actions to be taken and follow-up.
10. Summarize expected actions and follow-up.

Collaborative

1. Ask for teacher's perception of problem.
2. Listen to understand teacher's perception of problem.
3. Verify teacher's perception of problem.
4. Present your perception of problem by building on teacher's perception when possible.
5. Check for teacher's understanding of your perception of problem.
6. Exchange possible solutions (allow teacher to first offer solutions; build on teacher solutions when possible) and jointly consider consequences of each alternative.
7. Accept conflict that may arise.
8. Negotiate a mutually acceptable solution.
9. Agree on specific actions to be taken, including follow-up.
10. Summarize final plan.

Nondirective

1. Listen while teacher identifies problem.
2. Verbalize teacher's initial description of problem.
3. Probe for additional information.
4. Encourage teacher to reflect on various aspects of problem.
5. Continuously paraphrase teacher's message.
6. Ask teacher to think of possible solutions.
7. For each possible solution, ask teacher to consider consequences.
8. Ask teacher to decide on solution and specific actions.
9. Ask teacher to set times for actions and criteria for plan.
10. Summarize teacher's plan.

Name Index

Y

Z

Subject Index

E

L

M

N